Hands-on iOS App Development Projects

Turn Your Ideas into Actionable, Real-World iOS Apps with Swift, Xcode, UI Kit, Core Data, AWS and OAuth

Aish Kodali

AF517163

www.orangeava.com

Copyright © 2024, Orange Education Pvt Ltd, AVA®

All rights reserved. No part of this book may be reproduced, stored in a retrieval system, or transmitted in any form or by any means, without the prior written permission of the publisher, except in the case of brief quotations embedded in critical articles or reviews.

Every effort has been made in the preparation of this book to ensure the accuracy of the information presented. However, the information contained in this book is sold without warranty, either express or implied. Neither the author nor **Orange Education Pvt Ltd** or its dealers and distributors, will be held liable for any damages caused or alleged to have been caused directly or indirectly by this book.

Orange Education Pvt Ltd has endeavored to provide trademark information about all of the companies and products mentioned in this book by the appropriate use of capital. However, **Orange Education Pvt Ltd** cannot guarantee the accuracy of this information. The use of general descriptive names, registered names, trademarks, service marks, etc. in this publication does not imply, even in the absence of a specific statement, that such names are exempt from the relevant protective laws and regulations and therefore free for general use.

First Published: December 2024

Published By: Orange Education Pvt Ltd, AVA®

Address: 9, Daryaganj, Delhi, 110002, India

275 New North Road Islington Suite 1314 London,
N1 7AA, United Kingdom

ISBN (PBK): 978-93-48107-47-3
ISBN (E-BOOK): 978-93-48107-98-5

Scan the QR code to explore our entire catalogue

www.orangeava.com

Dedicated To

My Beloved Parents

Kodali Venkata Subrahmanyeswara Rao
Kodali Sailaja

and

My Brother Kodali Lakshman

About the Author

Aish Kodali is a senior iOS developer with expertise in UIKit and Swift. Inspired by her father's dream, she embarked on a tech career, driven by a passion for improving lives through innovation. A fan of Steve Jobs, she believes in the transformative power of technology and its ability to advance humanity.

As a career ambassador for the ChooseMaths campaign, Kodali encourages young girls to pursue STEM careers, emphasizing the importance of math in app development. She has received several state-level awards for her work, including the Government as a Platform award and the Social Hack award. Her team's winning app at GovHack enabled users to report public property issues directly to the council.

Kodali has also shared her expertise through talks and workshops, discussing her projects and inspiring others to learn coding. Her passion for knowledge sharing led her to author this book on iOS App development with the aim of empowering others to create impactful technology.

With nine years of industry experience, Kodali's love for coding drives her belief in the potential of apps to simplify people's lives. This book reflects her motivations and knowledge, inspiring readers to build remarkable apps that could change the world.

About the Technical Reviewer

Dương Đình Bảo Thăng's journey in the tech world demonstrates the power of passion and persistence in mastering new skills. Despite having a background in Finance and Economics, Thăng was drawn to the transformative potential of mobile applications. Recognizing the integral role of smartphones in daily life, he dedicated himself to learning mobile app development. Through self-education and hard work, Thăng successfully transitioned into a professional mobile developer, accumulating over four years of experience.

Thăng's expertise encompasses the entire mobile development spectrum, from crafting intuitive user interfaces to architecting scalable and high-performance applications. He has conceptualized, developed, and launched eight diverse apps across industries such as Finance, Augmented Reality, Gaming, EdTech, and point-of-sale systems. These apps have reached thousands of users and effectively addressed real-world problems.

Acknowledgements

I would like to express my deepest gratitude to everyone who supported me throughout the writing of this book.

First and foremost, I would like to thank my parents for their unwavering encouragement. Without their constant support, this book would not have been possible. I also extend my thanks to my brother, my unwavering cheerleader, for his endless belief in me.

A special thanks goes to my grandmother, Chirumamilla Jhansi, for gifting me my first laptop, the very tool that ignited my coding journey.

I am incredibly grateful to Professor Caslon Chua from Swinburne University of Technology. His advice and guidance, particularly in encouraging me to take the iOS App development subject, played a pivotal role in shaping my career path.

My immense gratitude goes to Josh Rowe for giving me the incredible opportunity to develop my first official app, Realas.com. It was a truly formative experience. I am thankful to ANZ for the support and development opportunities they provided, which allowed me to flourish as a skilled app developer.

I am particularly grateful to Mr. Dương Đình Bảo Thăng (James) for his invaluable technical review and insightful feedback on this book. My sincere appreciation also goes to the AVA team for their incredible understanding.

Preface

This book covers many aspects of iOS App development using Swift, focusing on project-based learning. It covers essential components for building engaging and user-friendly apps.

The book takes a practical approach, using real-world industry examples to guide iOS App development learners. It not only covers UI elements but also delves into connecting with APIs, fetching data, and updating apps in response to data changes. Additionally, the book outlines the app development process and addresses secure authentication.

The book is divided into nine chapters, each covering crucial aspects of app development. These include UI elements, building sample apps, networking with APIs, utilizing location services, saving data, and implementing authentication.

Here is a breakdown of the chapter details:

Chapter 1 will cover the fundamentals of Xcode, including its usage and debugging features. It will also explore UIKit and its key elements, along with relevant coding examples.

Chapter 2 will delve into the app development process, which shows how an idea can turn into a fully-fledged app. It will also cover UITableViews, a ubiquitous component in modern apps.

Chapter 3 will discover the different UI elements like UIScrollView, UIButton and more, which are essential for creating a wonderful app.

Chapter 4 will explore navigation techniques, including the use of Navigation controllers and Navigation bars, to guide users between screens.

Chapter 5 will put theory into practice by developing a sample app from concept to completion, demonstrating the entire app development process.

Chapter 6 will cover networking which includes fetching the data from APIs and decoding it effectively.

Chapter 7 will explain about leveraging location services to incorporate features like weather information based on the user's location.

Chapter 8 will cover the concept of data modeling and explore techniques for saving data within your apps.

Chapter 9 will cover authentication, which will help in providing secure authentication for our apps.

Get a Free eBook

We hope you are enjoying your recently purchased book! Your feedback is incredibly valuable to us, and to all other readers looking for great books.

If you found this book helpful or enjoyable, we would truly appreciate it, if you could take a moment to leave a short review with a 5 star rating on Amazon. It helps us grow, and lets other readers discover our books.

As a thank you, we would love to send you a free digital copy of this book, and a **30%** discount code on your next cart value on our official websites:

www.orangeava.com

www.orangeava.in (For Indian Subcontinent)

☑ **Here's how:**

Leave a review for the book on Amazon.

Take a screenshot of your review, and send an email to **info@orangeava.com** (it can be just the confirmation screen).

Once, we receive your screenshot, we will send you the digital file, within 24 hours.

Thank you so much for your support – it means a lot to us!

Downloading the code bundles and colored images

Please follow the links or scan the QR codes to download the **_Code Bundles and Images_** of the book:

https://github.com/ava-orange-education/Hands-on-iOS-App-Development-Projects

The code bundles and images of the book are also hosted on **_https://rebrand.ly/8469d7_**

In case there's an update to the code, it will be updated on the existing GitHub repository.

Errata

We take immense pride in our work at **Orange Education Pvt Ltd,** and follow best practices to ensure the accuracy of our content to provide an indulging reading experience to our subscribers. Our readers are our mirrors, and we use their inputs to reflect and improve upon human errors, if any, that may have occurred during the publishing processes involved. To let us maintain the quality and help us reach out to any readers who might be having difficulties due to any unforeseen errors, please write to us at :

errata@orangeava.com

Your support, suggestions, and feedback are highly appreciated.

DID YOU KNOW

Did you know that Orange Education Pvt Ltd offers eBook versions of every book published, with PDF and ePub files available? You can upgrade to the eBook version at **www.orangeava.com** and as a print book customer, you are entitled to a discount on the eBook copy. Get in touch with us at: **info@orangeava.com** for more details.

At **www.orangeava.com**, you can also read a collection of free technical articles, sign up for a range of free newsletters, and receive exclusive discounts and offers on AVA® Books and eBooks.

PIRACY

If you come across any illegal copies of our works in any form on the internet, we would be grateful if you would provide us with the location address or website name. Please contact us at **info@orangeava.com** with a link to the material.

ARE YOU INTERESTED IN AUTHORING WITH US?

If there is a topic that you have expertise in, and you are interested in either writing or contributing to a book, please write to us at **business@orangeava.com**. We are on a journey to help developers and tech professionals to gain insights on the present technological advancements and innovations happening across the globe and build a community that believes Knowledge is best acquired by sharing and learning with others. Please reach out to us to learn what our audience demands and how you can be part of this educational reform. We also welcome ideas from tech experts and help them build learning and development content for their domains.

REVIEWS

Please leave a review. Once you have read and used this book, why not leave a review on the site that you purchased it from? Potential readers can then see and use your unbiased opinion to make purchase decisions. We at Orange Education would love to know what you think about our products, and our authors can learn from your feedback. Thank you!

For more information about Orange Education, please visit **www.orangeava.com**.

Table of Contents

1. Getting Started **1**

Introduction 1

Structure 1

Xcode 2

Building Screens 5

UIKit 6

UIViewController 6

Constraints 10

Auto Layout 10

View Hierarchy 10

Safe Area 11

UIImageView 13

Adding Image to the `ImageView` 20

The Story Behind the Scales 22

Adding Code References 26

ViewDidLoad 28

Debugging 29

Conclusion 32

Points to Remember 33

2. App Process and TableViews **34**

Introduction 34

Structure 34

App Development Process 35

Idea 35

Design 35

Development 36

Test 36

Release 36

TableViews 37

- *UITableView* 37
- *Function* 43
- *Protocol* 43
- *Delegate* 43
- *UITableViewDataSource* 43
- *UITableViewDelegate* 43
- *Sections* 45
- *UITableViewCell* 46
- *IndexPath* 46
- *Deprecation* 47
- *Array* 49
- *Adding Header to the `TableView`* 52
- *CGRect* 53
- *Footer* 56
- *Footer for Section* 57
- *didSelectRowAt:* 59
- *UIAlertController* 60
- *Dictionary* 61
- *UIAlertAction* 64
- Conclusion 66
- Points to Remember 66

3. The Other UI Elements 67

- Introduction 67
- Structure 67
- UIScrollView 67
- UIButton 75
- UITextField 80
- *UITextView* 90
- UIStackView 94
- UIPageControl 106
- UIPickerView 112
- Conclusion 119

Points to Remember 119

4. Navigation 121

Introduction 121

Structure 121

Navigation 121

NavigationController 121

Navigation Bar 132

Navigating Programmatically 134

Conclusion 145

Points to Remember 145

5. Sample App 146

Introduction 146

Structure 146

Sample App 146

Idea 147

Design 147

Development 148

Structs 164

DispatchQueue 166

beginUpdates() 169

endUpdates() 170

UIBarButtonItem 182

UIDatePicker 184

IF Let 186

Guard Let 187

Conclusion 195

Points to Remember 195

6. Networking 197

Introduction 197

Structure 197

Introduction to `URLSession` 198

`URLSession`.shared 198

Closures 198

Closures with Parameters and Return Type 199

Implicit Returns 199

Shorthand Arguments 200

Closure Types 200

Trailing Closures 200

Escaping Closures 200

Non-Escaping Closures 201

URL 201

URLRequest 201

URLSessionDataTask 201

URLSessionUploadTask 202

URLSessionDownloadTask 202

Codables 204

Encodable 204

Decodable 205

JSONDecoder 209

JSONEncoder 212

Conclusion 213

Points to Remember 214

7. Leveraging Location Services 215

Introduction 215

Structure 215

Weather App 215

Core Location 216

Extensions 219

WeatherKit 223

ObservableObject 228

@Published 228

Task.detached 230

CLGeocoder 233

UITapGestureRecognizer 255

`viewWillAppear(_:)` 257

Conclusion 264

Points to Remember 265

8. Saving Data for iOS Applications 266

Introduction 266

Structure 266

Data Modeling 267

SQLite 268

Opaque Pointers 270

`sqlite3_prepare_v2` 272

`sqlite3_step` 272

`sqlite3_finalize` 272

`sqlite3_bind_text` 273

`sqlite3_bind_int` 273

AWS 280

AWS S3 281

Swift Package Manager 281

Layer 287

`masksToBounds` 287

`putObject` 298

`putObjectInput` 298

`clipsToBounds` 303

Conclusion 305

Points to Remember 305

9. Authentication 306

Introduction 306

Structure 306

Creating `UITableViewCell` in a Different Way 306

XIB 307

Auth0 311

The Big Why 311

OAuth 2.0 311

Working of Auth0 311
Working Flow of Auth0 312
`plist` 316
Adding Associated Domains 318
JWT 325
Conclusion 332
Points to Remember 332
Index 334

CHAPTER 1
Getting Started

Introduction

Steve Jobs revolutionized the world with the evolution of personal computers. Apple, the company he co-founded, didn't just build computers for basic tasks such as sending emails but also prioritized empowering developers to build applications. Jobs emphasized the importance of learning how to program, seeing it as a way to teach critical thinking and viewing computer science as a liberal art. His focus on developer innovation ultimately benefited both developers and Apple.

One of the most iconic moments in tech history was Jobs introducing the first iPhone in 2007. Watching that keynote event can inspire developers to build clean, efficient, and user-friendly apps that have the potential to change the world.

It's essential not only to build apps but to prioritize user-friendly designs. Developers often face challenges with designers who prioritize aesthetics over functionality. For example, a designer once provided a design with a small, unclear button for changing locations in an app. Post-launch, users struggled to find the functionality, leading to negative feedback in app reviews. To avoid such issues, always ensure user experience takes precedence.

This chapter will cover the basics of app development, focusing on Xcode. It will guide you through building screens, arranging elements using constraints, modifying them with code, and using debugging tools.

Structure

In this chapter, we shall cover the following topics:

- Xcode
- `UIKit`
    - `UIViewController`
    - Constraints
    - `Autolayout`

- View hierarchy
- Safe area
- `UIImageView`
- Adding code references
- Debugging

Xcode

Apple introduced Xcode in October 2007, providing developers with an invaluable platform for innovation. Xcode has since become one of the premier integrated development environments (IDEs), offering a powerful pathway for development, creation, and innovation. Using Xcode we can build wonderful apps for all Apple devices, including iPhones, iPads, and MacBooks. Xcode provides a wonderful code editor, an excellent UI interface builder, best debugging tools and simulators to simulate the app. This means that you don't need to buy multiple iPhones to test your App in different screen sizes. We can even simulate matching face IDs.

Let's explore Xcode now.

Step 1: Download the recent version of Xcode from the App Store or via this link: https://xcodereleases.com/. The one we are using is version Xcode 14.2.

Step 2: After downloading, open the file and the following screen will appear:

Figure 1.1: *Creating a new project*

Step 3: Click **"Create on new Xcode project"** -> Select App -> click **'Next'** and enter the project details:

a. **Product Name**: **Basics** (or any name you prefer for the App).

b. **Team**: Select **"None"** for now.

c. **Organization Identifier**: If you are developing apps for your organization then this is the unique identifier of your organization. It follows a reverse DNS format, such as **com.orangeAva.** If you are not working for an organization, you can use **com.'yourName'** or **com.example** . You can change it to a more meaningful identifier when you release your app.

d. **Bundle Identifier**: This is the unique identifier for your App, which combines the Organization Identifier and Product name by default. However, we don't have to stick to what is given by default, we can always change the Bundle Identifier, as long as it is unique.

e. **Interface**: Choose **"Storyboard"** (SwiftUI in future).

f. **Language**: Select **"Swift."**

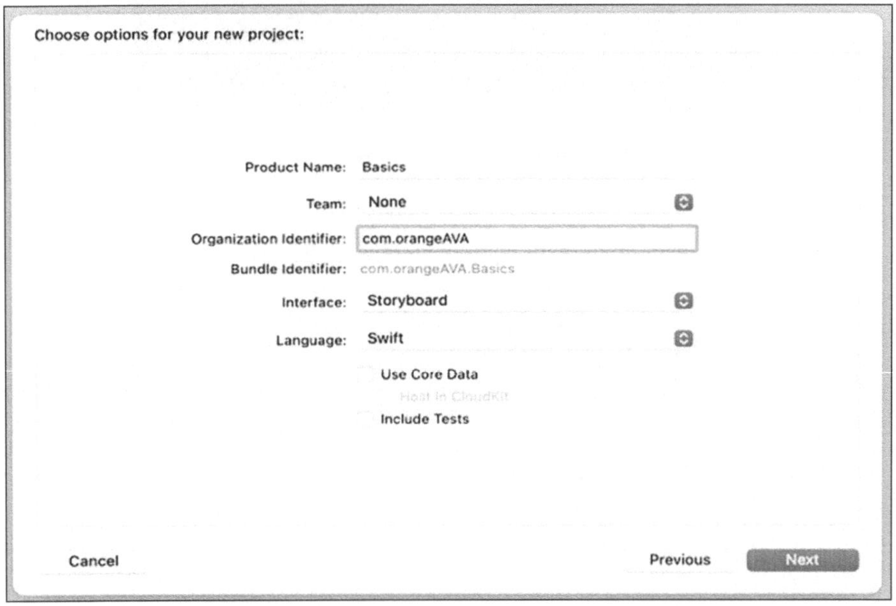

Figure 1.2: *Project details for a new project*

g. **Core Data and Tests:** We don't need to select Core Data or Tests for now, so leave those options and click **"Next."**

h. **Save Location**: Select the folder where you want to save your project and click **"Create."**

And Voila! We have our first iOS project.

Now, let us explore the project to understand how and what tools to use for creating apps efficiently.

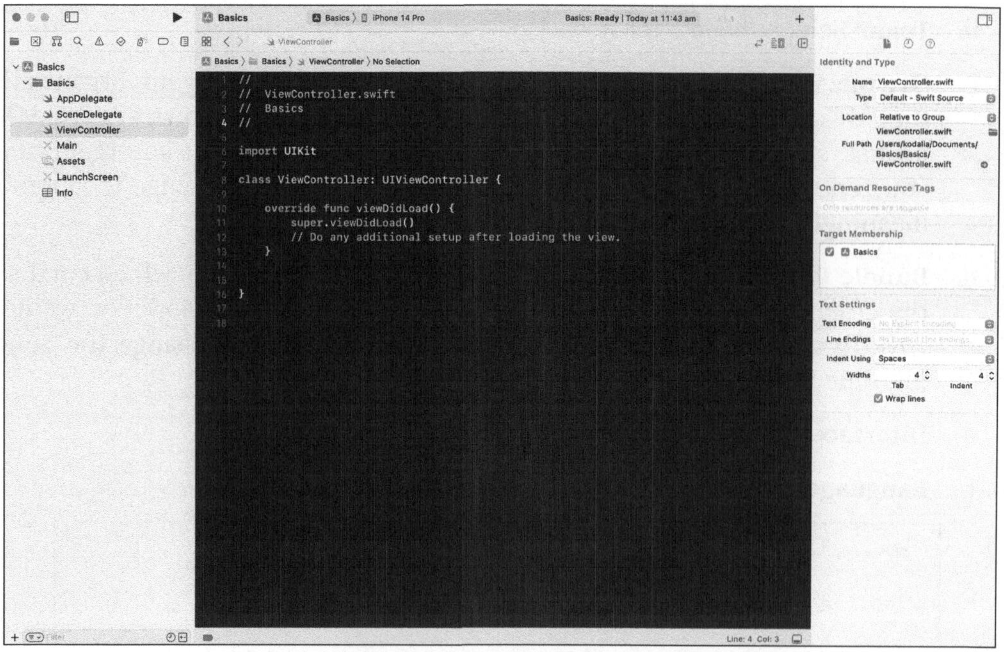

Figure 1.3: *Exploring Xcode with a new project*

- On the left side of Xcode, we have a Navigation Pane, where you can see your project files, assets, audio files (if any), and storyboards.
- We have an editor at the center where you can edit the files.
- To the right, we have the Utilities pane.
- When you select the Storyboard, the Attribute Inspector will appear on the right.

  You will learn more about this when we start building our first screen.

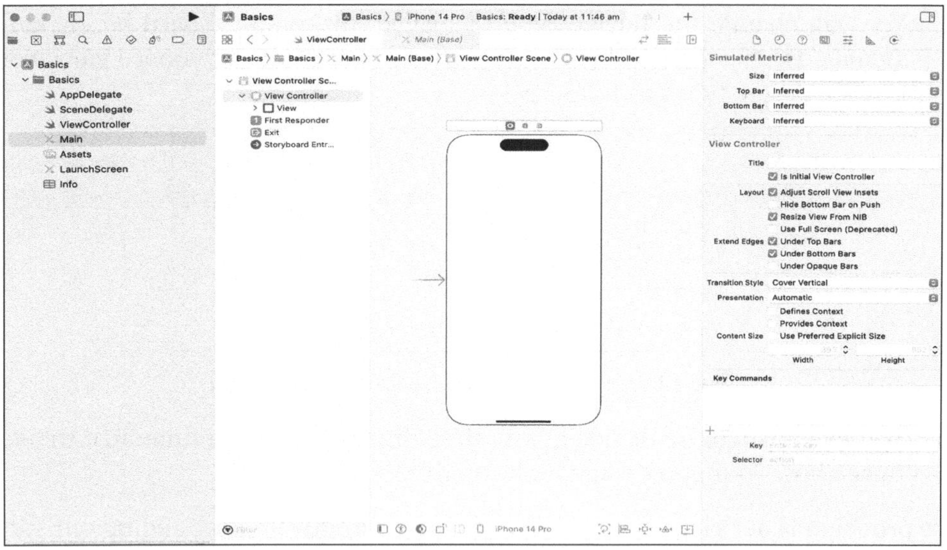

Figure 1.4: *Storyboard with attribute inspector*

Now that we explored a bit of Xcode, let's start implementing.

Building Screens

Let's get started to build our very first screen using storyboards.

1. Go to the **`Navigator`** pane and select **`Main.storyboard`**.

   When you select the storyboard, this is what you should see:

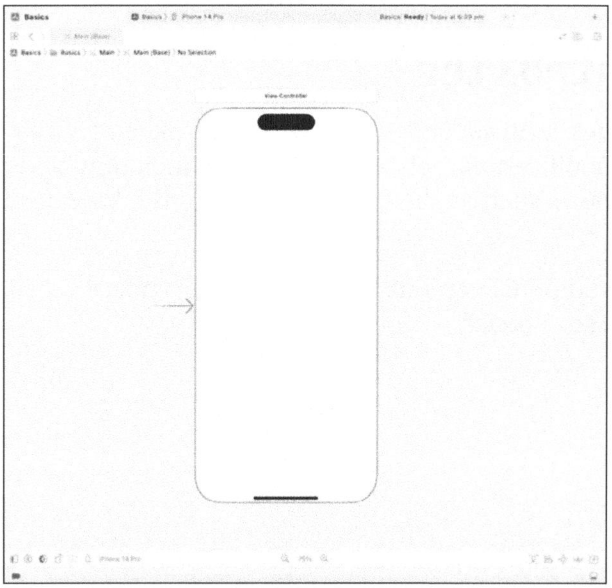

Figure 1.5: *Storyboard*

2. You can change the device type displayed in the storyboard by clicking the **`iPhone 14 Pro`** icon at the bottom-left corner of the storyboard view. You will see the device types as follows:

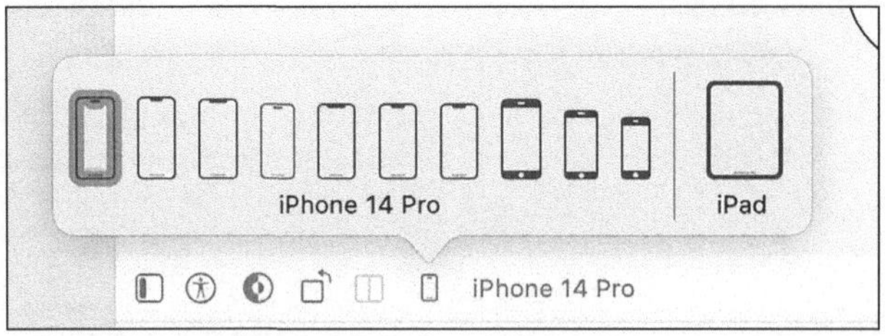

Figure 1.6: *Selecting the device for the storyboard*

You can change the device at any time during the development of the screen to see how your app design looks on different devices.

Before proceeding, let's learn about `UIKit` as it is prerequisite for building our screens.

`UIKit`

`UIKit` is a framework provided by Apple that helps us to build beautiful and creative apps. It includes all the essential elements needed while building screens such as `UIView`, `UIButton`, and `UILabel` among many others. Every element provided by UIKit is prefixed with "UI", which indicates its association with the framework.

When you create a project with a storyboard, it includes a storyboard with an initial `UIviewController`. In simpler terms, `UIViewController` is a screen.

`UIViewController`

As the name implies, a `ViewController` is a controller of view. It controls all the interactions and modifications related to the view, including actions and updates. It also manages subviews such as the buttons added to the View (or parent view) of the `ViewController`.

You can also add additional screens to the same storyboard by clicking **'+'** on top-right corner of the storyboard.

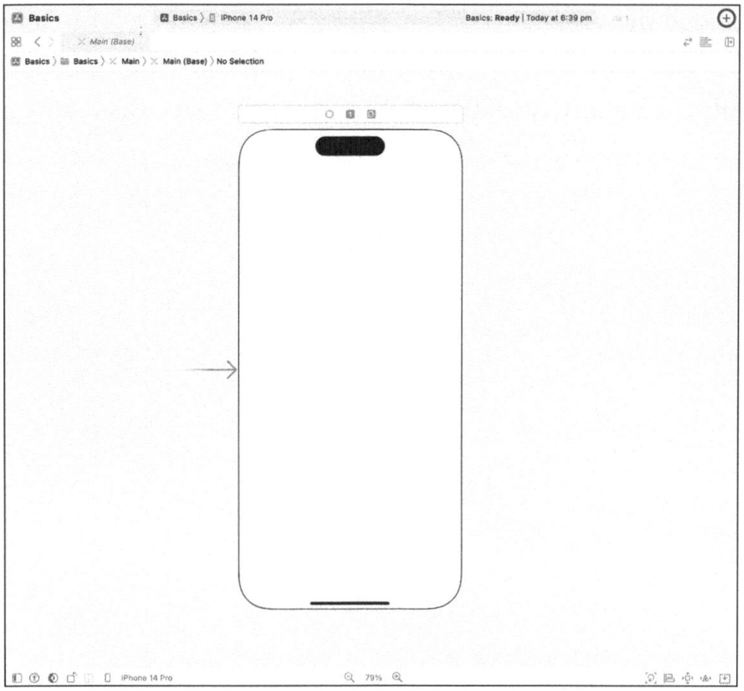

Figure 1.7: *Adding new elements to the storyboard*

Search for the `viewController` and drag the yellow icon of the **`View Controller`** into a storyboard. This will add your second screen to the storyboard.

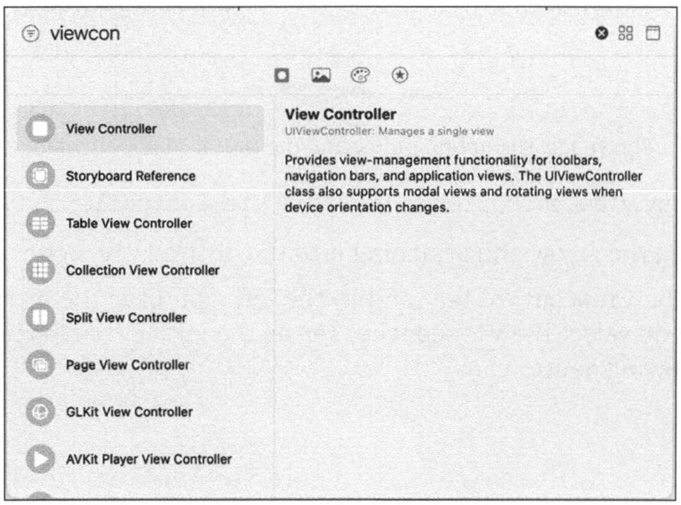

Figure 1.8: *Adding ViewController*

We will cover how to connect two screens or navigate from one screen to another in further projects. For now, let us focus on adding elements such as Labels and images to our first `viewController`.

Just like you added the `viewController`, click **'+'** again, search for **`label`**, and add it to the initial `viewController` (not the new screen you added).

You can identify the initial `UIViewController` by looking for the arrow pointing to it.

Figure 1.9: *The arrow indicating the initial ViewController*

You can make any `viewController` as the initial `ViewController` in two ways:

- Dragging the arrow and attaching it to the desired `ViewController`
- Select the `ViewController` and to the left, you have the attribute Inspector where you select the `viewController` as the initial `ViewController`. Refer to the following figure:

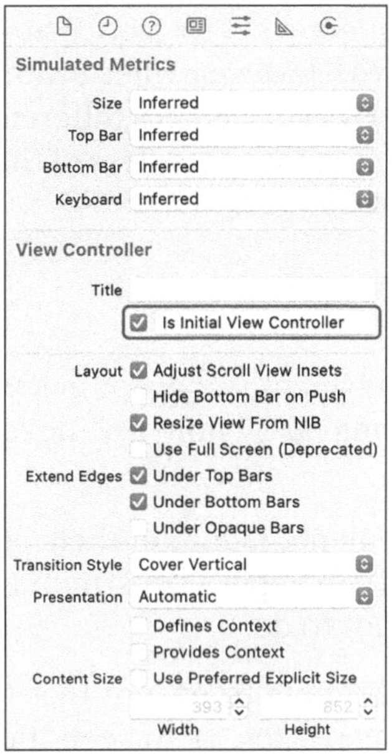

Figure 1.10: *Making an initial ViewController in the attribute inspector*

Now, let's add the label to our initial `Viewcontroller` at the center of the screen by following the preceding steps and run it in the iPhone 14 simulator.

To run the app in the simulator, click the  button shown in the following figure or use Xcode shortcut "*Command + R*". Before running the app, we need to select the device type in which you want to simulate such as iPhone 14, iPhone 8, iPhone X, or any other device. For that, click the device list as shown in the following figure and you will see the list as follows:

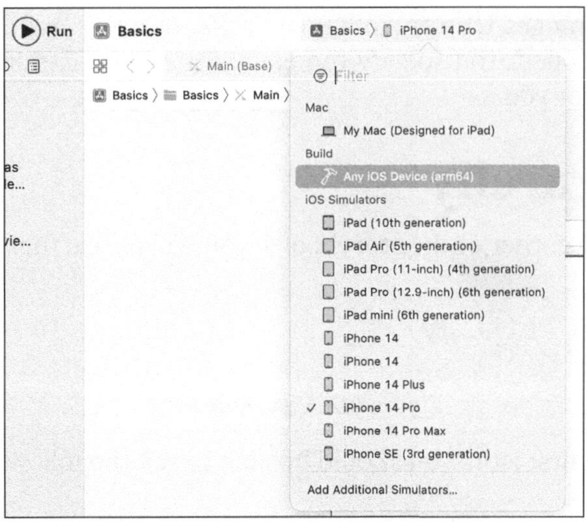

Figure 1.11: *Choosing simulator type*

First, let us run the app on the iPhone 14 Pro. Notice how the label appears in the same place as it does in the storyboard. However, when switching to the iPhone 8 simulator, it can be observed that the label was placed in a different place. We don't want that, we want the label to stay in the same place regardless of the screen size or device type. To fix that we use a concept called **Constraints**.

Constraints

Constraints is a crucial and fundamental concept in iOS development. In fact, the skill of a UI developer can be determined by how well he/she can manage and utilize the constraints.

Constraints ensure that UI elements maintain their positions and sizes consistently across different devices. When you apply a constraint to an element, it's like telling an element what to do and what not to do.

For example, you can use constraints to ensure that the label maintains a height of 30 and a width of 30 on all screen sizes, or to keep the label centered both vertically and horizontally across all screen sizes. This facility is provided by Apple through the concept called Auto Layout. By defining the constraints, Auto Layout automatically adjusts the layout for all the screen sizes according to the constraints given.

Auto Layout

Auto Layout automatically calculates the position and the size of the views placed in the view hierarchy based on the constraints applied to them. For better understanding, think of Auto layout as the interior decorator of our screen. Just as an interior decorator arranges furniture according to the rules the interior designer gave him/her, Auto layout arranges UI elements (like views, buttons, and labels) according to the constraints provided. You specify the elements and constraints, and Auto layout adjusts the screen for you.

View Hierarchy

In the bottom-right corner of the storyboard, you will notice this little menu:

Figure 1.12: *View hierarchy*

When you click the first icon, you should be able to see the following options:

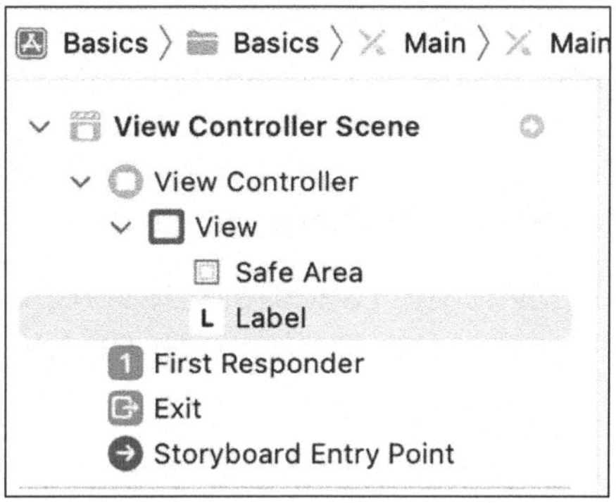

Figure 1.13: *Label in the View hierarchy*

Whenever you add the `viewController`, it comes with the parent view that has a **`Safe Area`** (only the view that comes with `viewController` comes with the safe area).

Safe Area

We don't want your screen views or elements to be overlapped with a status bar or navigation bar, isn't it? Imagine you designed a button at the very top of the screen, which will be overlapped by the status bar. The interaction could be interrupted by the user, which could be the worst user experience. This is where the Safe Area comes to our rescue. The Safe Area ensures that UI elements are placed within the visible and non-obstructed part of the screen, avoiding areas that might be covered by navigation bars, toolbars, or other interface elements.

Figure 1.14: *Safe area*

In the preceding figure, the selected blue area is the Safe Area. It is important to note that Safe Area will be different across devices such as various iphone and ipad models). We can confidently use it and guarantee things look good across devices. You can confidently place your UI elements, and the element's interaction and visibility will not be disturbed by the status bar, rounded corners, navigation bar or toolbar.

Now we want our label to stay in the center of our screen, specifically at the center of the safe area across all screen sizes, we need to apply constraints that position it accordingly.

Remember, when adding constraints, you are linking the label to the safe area. Click and hold the *ctrl* key, then drag that blue line to a safe area like this:

Figure 1.15: *Adding constraints to the label*

Release the drag, and you will see something as follows:

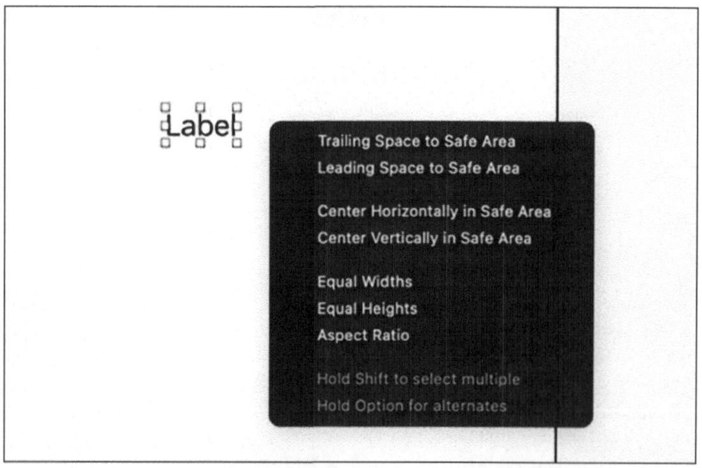

Figure 1.16: *Constraints to the label*

Click the **`'Center Horizontally in Safe Area'`** and **`'Center Vertically in Safe Area'`**.

If the label we placed is above or below the center after applying the constraints, it shows something like this:

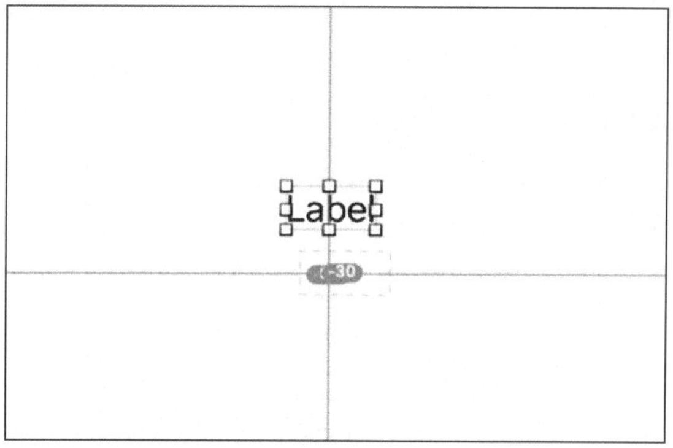

Figure 1.17: *Label after adding constraints*

To fix it, we have a little menu to the bottom-right corner of the storyboard.

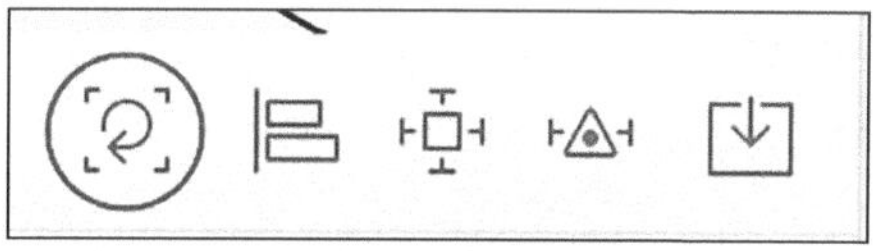

Figure 1.18: *Update frames*

When you click the first icon – **`'update frames'`**, the label gets updated according to the constraints. Now, run in a simulator of any type, and our label stays at the center of the screen.

Try running it in different simulators to experience the Auto layout magic.

Since you learnt about Auto layout and adding constraints, let's make our Basic sample app more interesting. Let us add an image to our screen. It could be anything from a fun image of yourself to flowers or a beautiful sunrise image. So, the idea here is we will have an image at the center of the screen and underneath it we have our label. For example, we will have a beautiful image of the sunrise and the label underneath says, 'Good Morning!!!'

UIImageView

`UIImageView` is a type of view specifically designed to display images. It functions as a view that shows an image. If you want to display a single image or series of animated images, then `UIImageView` is an appropriate choice.

Now that you know what is `UIImageView`, let us put it to the implementation. This whole book is designed in the same way. You learn about something, and you will put it into implementation just like science experiments, what is the better way to learn rather than implement?

Now, click the **'+'** button on the top-right of the storyboard and search for the `imageView`. Drag it to the inital `Viewcontroller`. Before adding the constraints to the `imageView/UIImageView`, let's remove the existing constraints on the label because we don't want our label to be the center of the screen.

You can do that in two ways:

1. The first way to do this is to go to the bottom-left of the storyboard, where you will find the following menu.

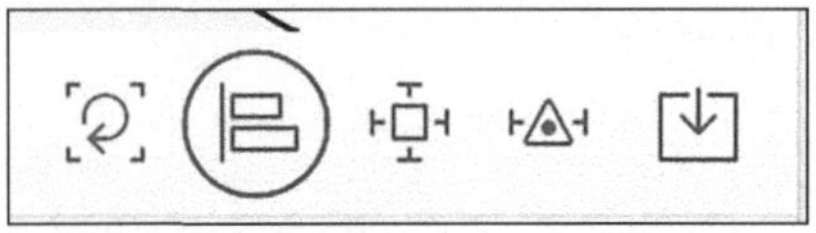

Figure 1.19: *To update constraints*

   a. Click the second icon from the right and you will see the following:

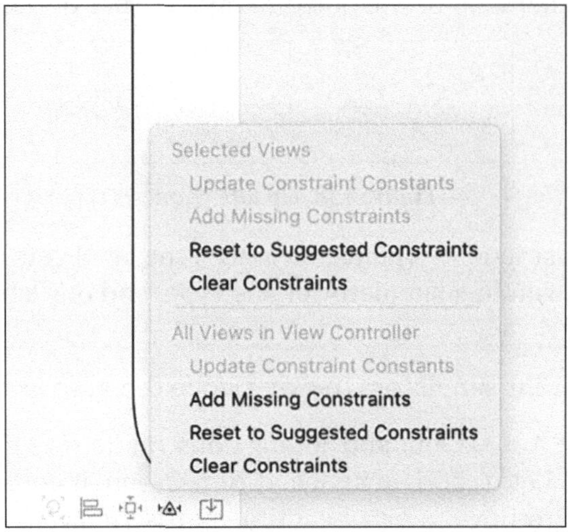

Figure 1.20: *Clearing the constraints*

   b. Click the **`'Clear constraints'`** in the **`'All Views in View Controller'`** section as we don't want any other old constraints on the screen.

2. The second way to delete the constraints is to click the label on the left. You have a size inspector, where you will have the constraints displayed. Check the following figure:

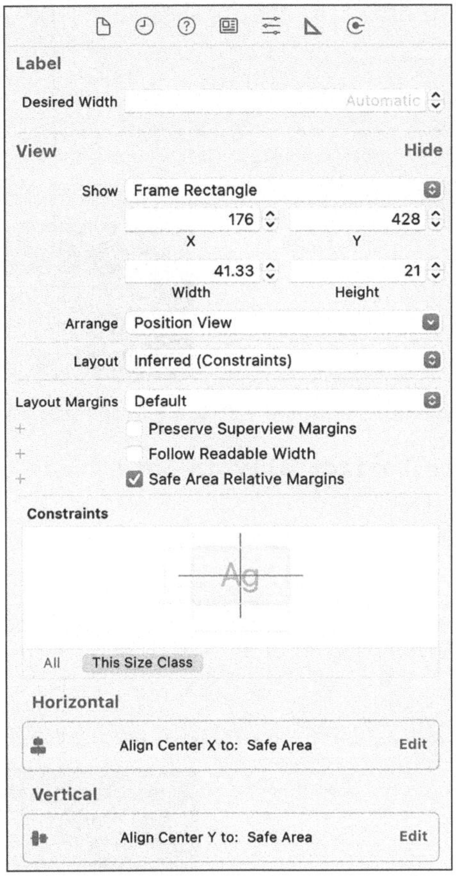

Figure 1.21: *Deleting the constraints in the size inspector. The third way is to delete the Constraints from the View Hierarchy.*

a. Select both the constraints **"`Align Center X to: Safe Area`"** and **"`Align Center y to: Safe Area`"**, and delete them.

b. Add constraints for the `ImageView` to make it stay at the center of the screen.

   We have seen previously how to add these constraints to the label, now the exercise for you is to add for image and try doing it by yourself without looking at the next steps that are mentioned as follows:

Adding center constraints to the `ImageView`:

1. *Control* + drag from `UIImageView` to Safe Area and release, you should be able to see the following:

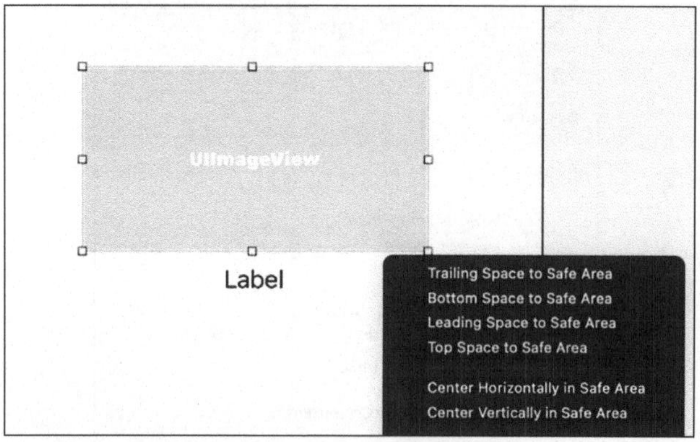

Figure 1.22: *Adding constraints to the imageView*

2. Select the **`'Center Horizontally in Safe Area'`** and **`'Center Vertically in Safe Area'`**.

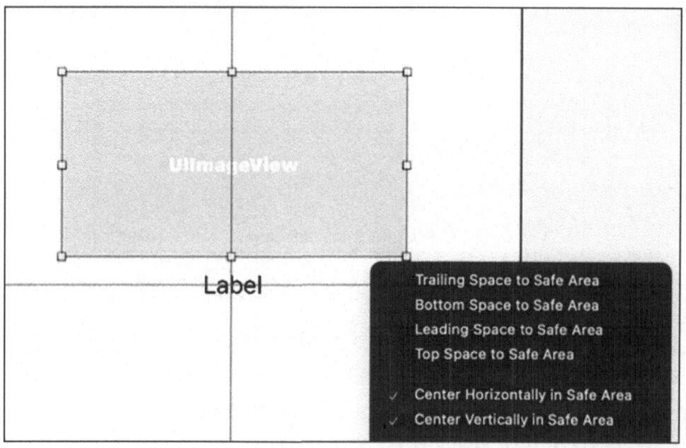

Figure 1.23: *After adding the center constraints to imageView*

Don't worry if you see the red lines, they are just telling you about the missing constraints that help you build a beautiful screen.

So, you now have the center constraints, just use your imagination you have an image on your screen, at the center of the screen, what could be missing, what about height and width, do you want your image to stay in a particular size. Let's go add it.

1. *Control* + drag from the `imageView` back to the `imageView` and release (drag sideways) if you want to add the width.

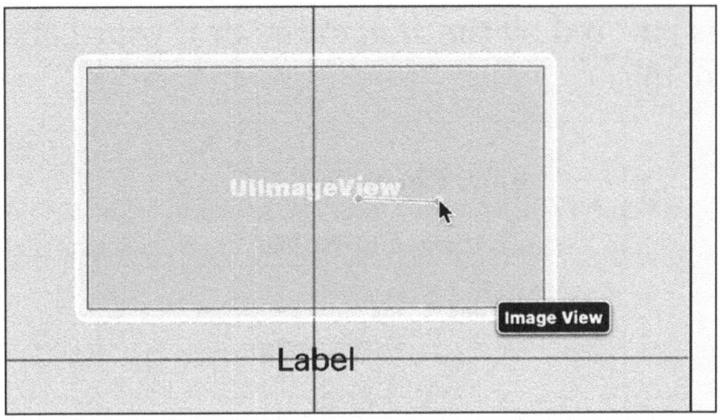

Figure 1.24: *Adding width constraint to the imageView*

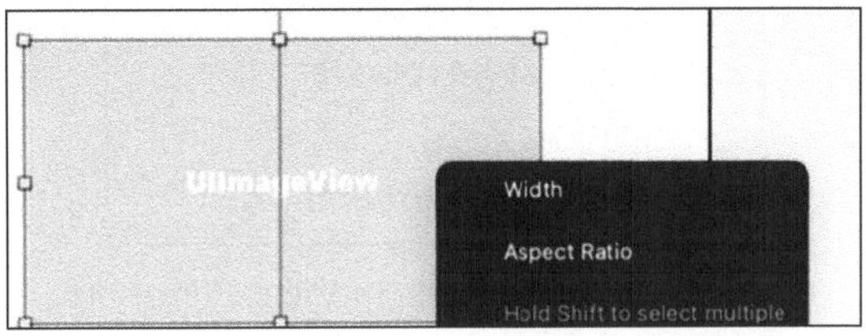

Figure 1.25: *Adding width constraint to the imageView*

2. If you drag it vertically it just shows height.

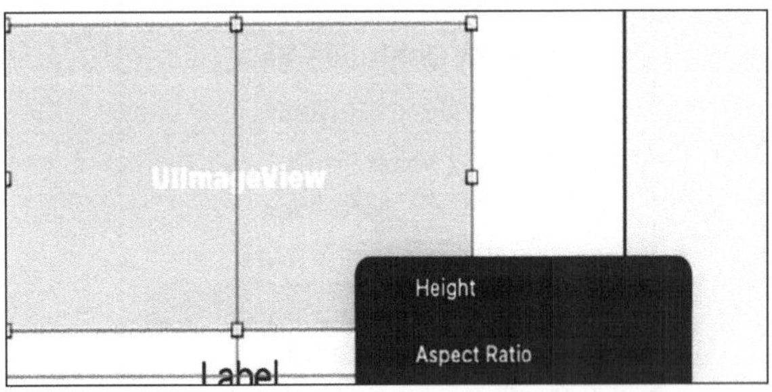

Figure 1.26: *Adding height constraint to the imageView*

3. As you can see, the red lines are gone.

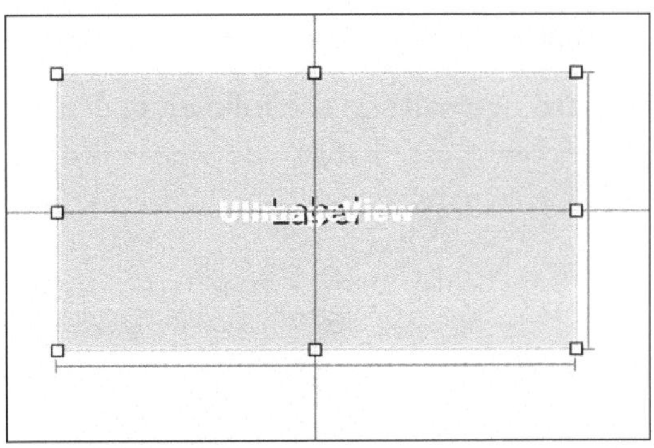

Figure 1.27: *Adding height constraint to the imageView*

4. If your label is covered by the `imageView` or if your Label is sitting above the `imageView` like this:

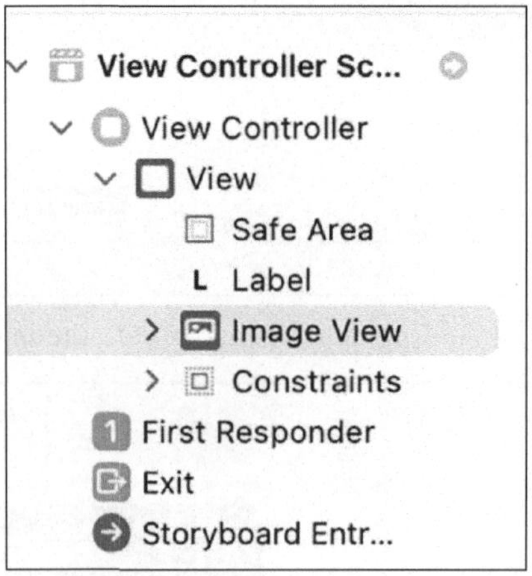

Figure 1.28: *ImageView in View Hierarchy*

5. Click the **'Label'** and drag it underneath the **'Image View'** and you should see in view hierarchy as follows:

Figure 1.29: *Label in the View hierarchy*

6. And in the storyboard, we will see the following:

Figure 1.30: *Label on top of UIImageView*

So, we want our label to go underneath the `UIImageView` and the gap between them, let's say maybe 10 points.

1. Just like while we were adding constraints for `UIImageView` and Safe Area we are *Control* + dragging from `UIImage` to Safe Area and release, here we are adding the constraints between `UIImageView` and Label. Click the `ImageView` and *Control* + Drag to the `UILabel`.

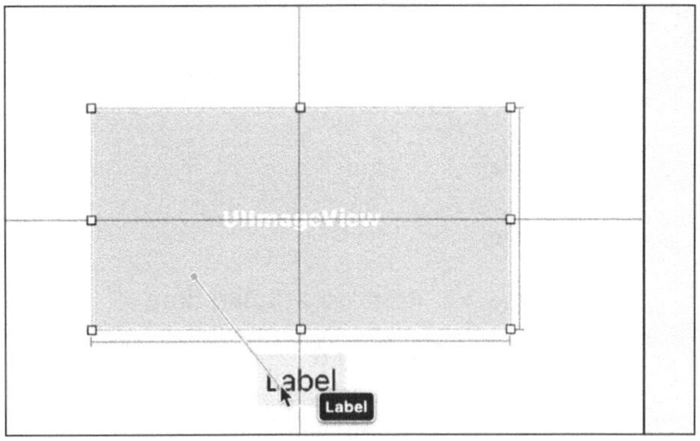

Figure 1.31: *Adding constraints between UIImageView and Label*

2. And then release it, you should see something like the following:

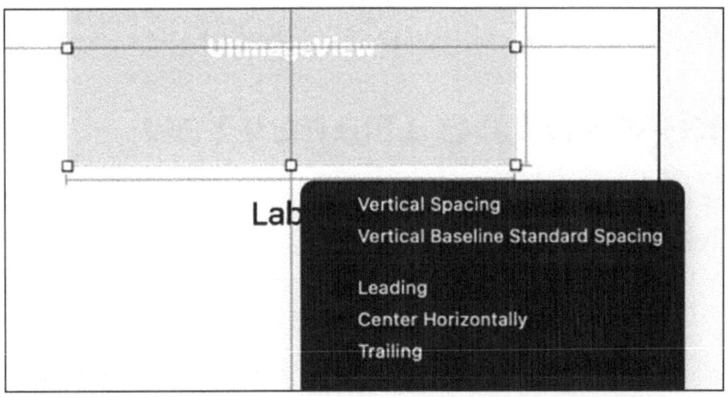

Figure 1.32: *Adding vertical spacing between UIImageView and Label*

3. Click the **`Vertical Spacing`**. You see something like the following in the size inspector when you click `ImageView`, which says the bottom space to label is **`14.33`** but just needs 10.

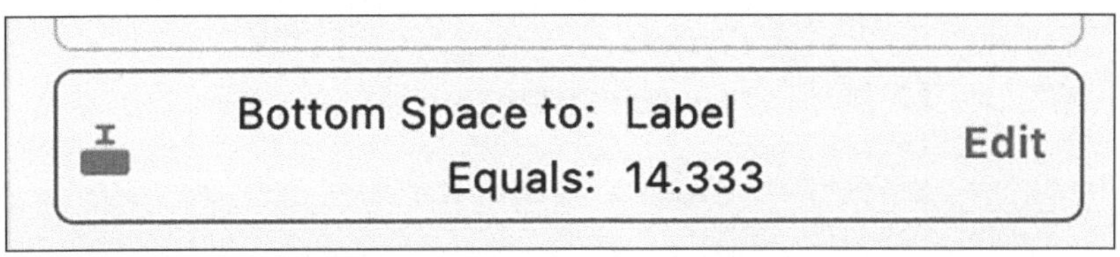

Figure 1.33: *Bottom space from UIImageView to Label constraint (in other words vertical spacing)*

4. Click the constraint and you should be able to see the following:

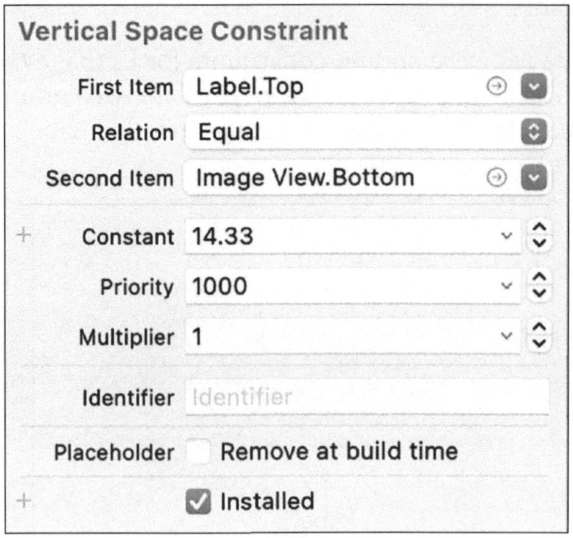

Figure 1.34: *Vertical spacing constraint*

5. Edit the constant to **`10`**.

Now we want our label to be at the center of the screen horizontally. So, we will add it. If you can't do it, refer to how we centered the `ImageView`.

Adding Image to the `ImageView`

1. Usually, the Image is given by the designer to fit all resolution sizes, just to get the Idea click the **`Assets`** in your project navigator.

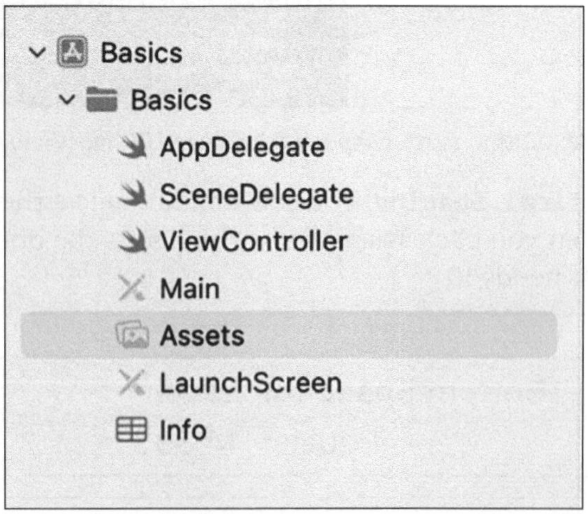

Figure 1.35: *Assets in View Hierarchy*

2. When you click **`Assets`** you should see the following screen:

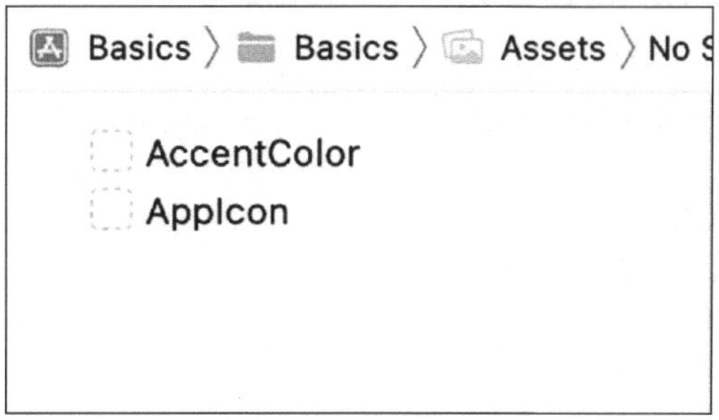

Figure 1.36: Assets

3. Let's not worry about the App icon right now. Below it, you will see **'+-'** beside the filter, click the **'+'** icon.

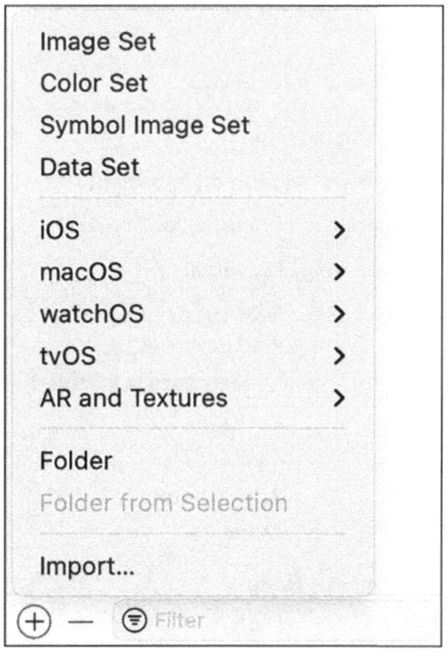

Figure 1.37: *Adding Image Set*

4. Click the **`ImageSet`** and the following screen will show up.

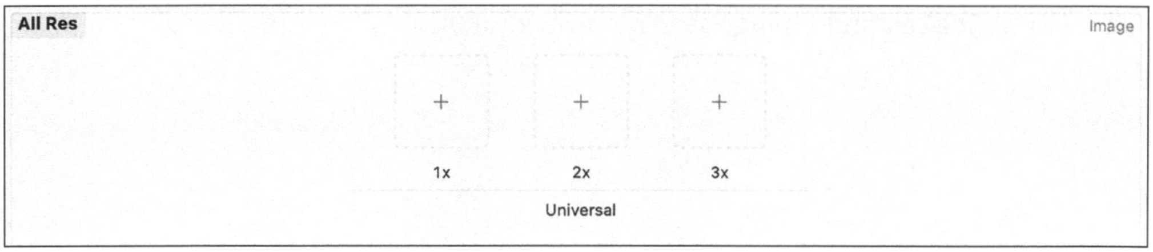

Figure 1.38: *Image Set*

1x, 2x and 3x, the designer should provide the images for different resolutions. This will help images stay sharp in all screen sizes. That's how you will have no blurry images in the Apps.

The Story Behind the Scales

There is not much story behind the scales, if your device is like an older Apple device, such as an old iPhone or iPad device which is of low resolution then the 1x images are used, if your device is a retina device then 2x images are used and if it is with much higher resolution, then 3x images are used. It's all about saving the user's device space. This concept is called app slicing, where the user's device will only do the things that are required. For example, if the user's device is a non-retina old iPhone, it will not download retina images at 2x resolution.

In some cases, the designer gives a vector image, one image for all the resolutions.

1. To add vector, select your image and go to the attribute inspector, to the left.

Figure 1.39: *Image Set attributes*

2. Go to **`Scales`** and change it from individual scales to a single scale.

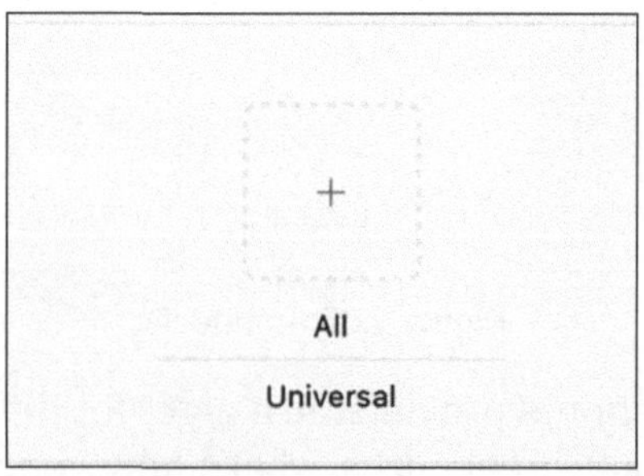

Figure 1.40: *Vector image single scale*

This image will be used in all the resolutions. Just keep in mind we, the designer, need to provide the vector image for this to work.

3. Get your favorite image ready. Now go to assets and click the first image. Since we were using it as a single scale earlier, we will have to revert to using individual scales as we don't have a vector image right now. After that, you can either click the `+` icon in that `imageSet` for 2x (this would be roughly compatible with most devices), which opens up your folders.

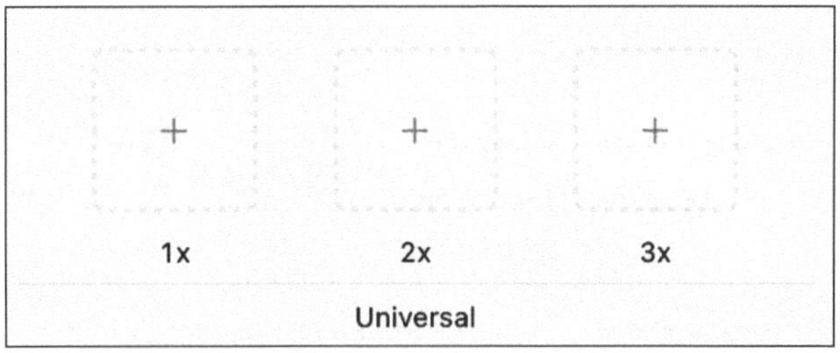

Figure 1.41: *Adding an image to the Image Set*

4. Or you can drag the image from your folders to this **+** icon. It should look like this.

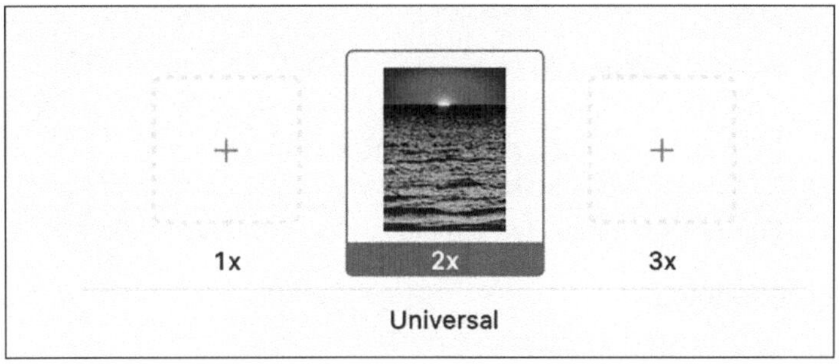

Figure 1.42: *Added image to the Image Set*

5. Now, go to your screen and click `imageView`. In the attribute inspector to your left, in the image field, type in the `imageSet` name. In our case, it is **`'First Image'`**.

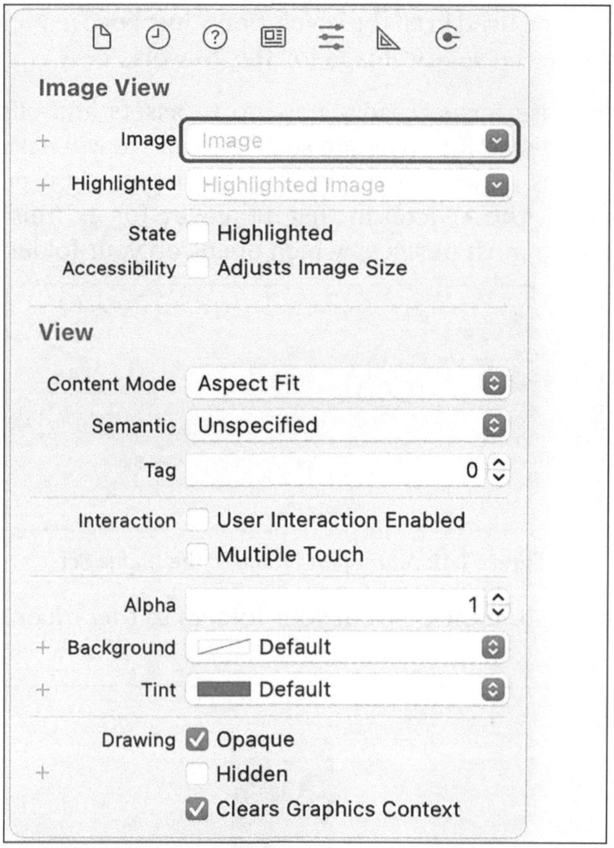

Figure 1.43: *ImageView's Image in the attribute inspector*

Mine looks like the following:

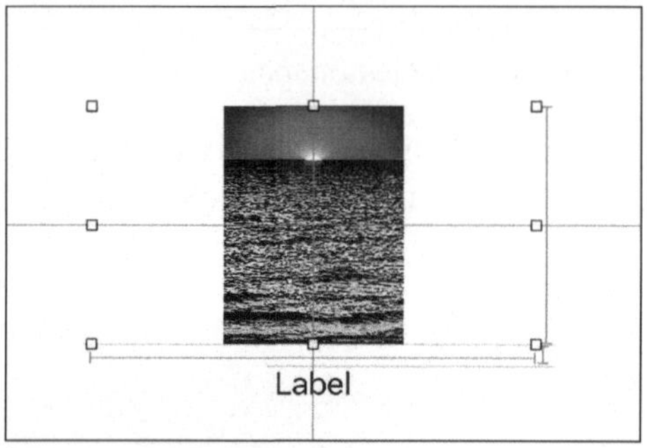

Figure 1.44: *Image added to the ImageView*

Since this is a portrait image and we gave the `imageView` specific constraints of height and width that do not match to our image, it looks odd. Let us change it so that the image looks good. (refer to steps of adding constraints to the `imageView` and playing with numbers).

Let us change the height to **280** and the width to **210**.

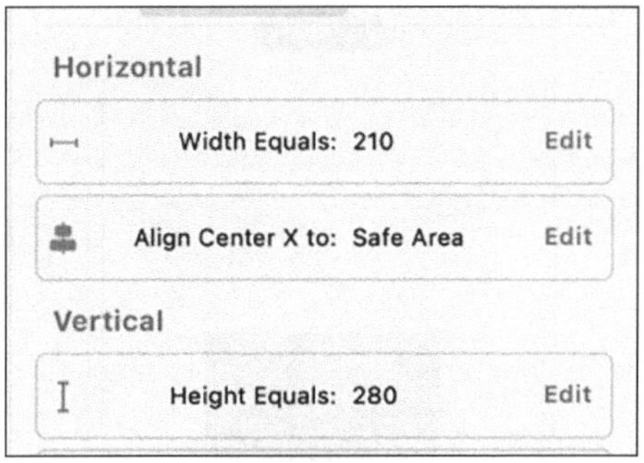

Figure 1.45: *Constraints in the Size Inspector*

It looks as follows:

Figure 1.46: *ViewController after modifying constraints*

You can arrange your `imageView` width and height accordingly.

Let's edit the label. Double click the **`Label`** in your storyboard and write what you want to have as the caption of the Image, for example, **`'Good Morning'`**.

Figure 1.47: ViewController with Image and Label

Adding Code References

Adding code references will help us modify the label and add an image to `imageView` in code rather than in the storyboard. Adding code references will help us while debugging and we can change the label's text during runtime.

1. To easily add the reference outlet, click the [+] icon, it will open two editors or storyboard windows.

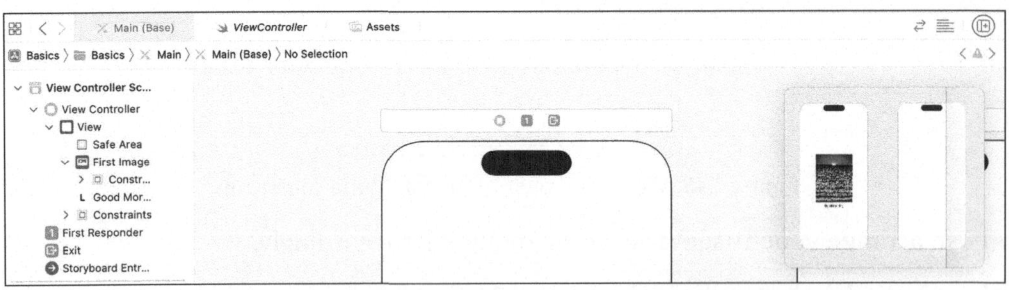

Figure 1.48: Adding additional window

2. Here you need to open the Storyboard and `ViewController` window side by side as shown in the following figure:

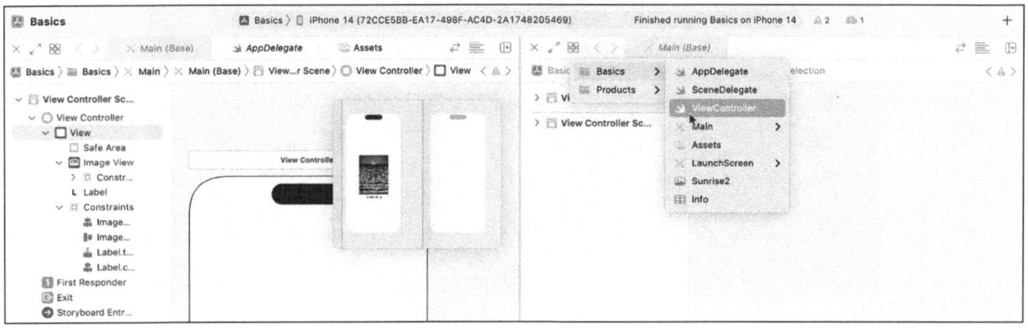

Figure 1.49: *Opening ViewController*

3. Now select the `ImageView` in the storyboard and click '*Control*' and drag that blue line to the `viewController`.

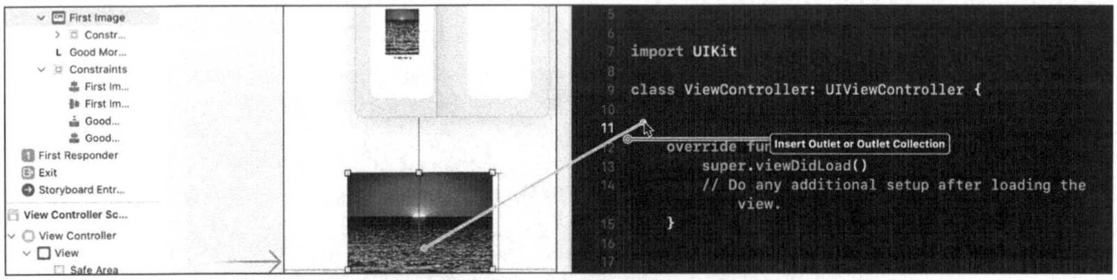

Figure 1.50: *Creating ImageView outlet in ViewController*

It will look as follows:

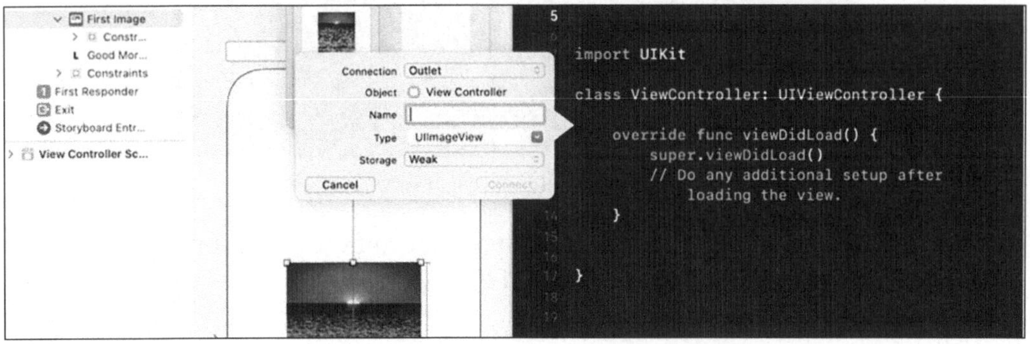

Figure 1.51: *Creating ImageView outlet*

4. Give the name **'imageView'** and do the same thing for the label as well.

```
import UIKit

class ViewController: UIViewController {

    @IBOutlet weak var imageView: UIImageView!
    @IBOutlet weak var label: UILabel!

    override func viewDidLoad() {
        super.viewDidLoad()
        // Do any additional setup after loading the view.
    }


}
```

Figure 1.52: *ViewController with UIImageView and UILabel outlets*

ViewDidLoad

This function gets called after the view is loaded. So, when you want to change your label's text after the screen is loaded, you can do it here.

```
import UIKit

class ViewController: UIViewController {

    @IBOutlet weak var imageView: UIImageView!
    @IBOutlet weak var label: UILabel!

    override func viewDidLoad() {
        super.viewDidLoad()

        label.text = "Have a Great day"
    }


}
```

Figure 1.53: *Adding text to the label in ViewController*

Something like the preceding code snippet, you can edit the text property of the label. Do it as it will be useful for the next topic of debugging.

Before jumping to the next topic, run it. Here, we will run in the iPhone 14 simulator.

Figure 1.54: *Screen with overridden text*

This is how the screen looks, where the label's text is overridden by the text that's given the **`viewDidLoad`** function.

To better understand how this overwriting is happening and where our first Label's text **`'Good Morning'`** went, let's debug the issue.

Debugging

Xcode provides excellent debugging tools, let's jump into debugging and add the debug pointer on the line where we are assigning the label's text inside the **`ViewDidLoad()`** function.

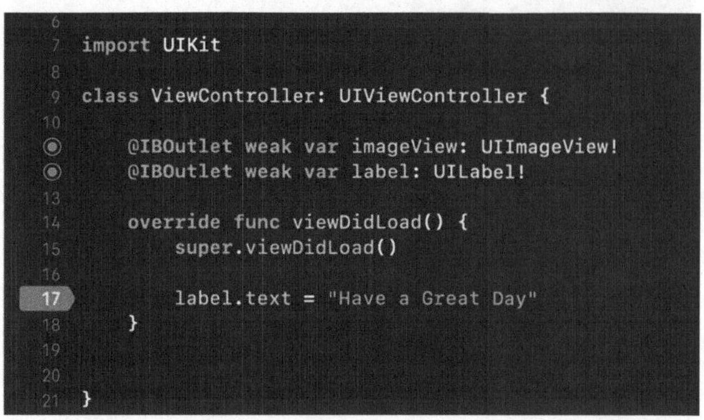

Figure 1.55: *ViewController with Debug pointer*

The blue pointer is the debug pointer. Now run it. If you see the simulator, it will show a white blank screen. In Xcode, you will see the debug pointer lightening up, indicating the compiler stopped there. This suggests that the Label's text has not been overridden by **'Have a Great Day'**. To confirm that, let's go to the console and type **"po label.text"**. The command **"po"** means **'print object'**.

***Figure 1.56:** Compiler reached the debug point and printed out the label's text*

If you see the label's text, it will still display **'Good Morning'** as the code where we are assigning **'Have a Great Day'** is not executed yet. Now let go of the debug pointer by clicking the second icon in the debug menu.

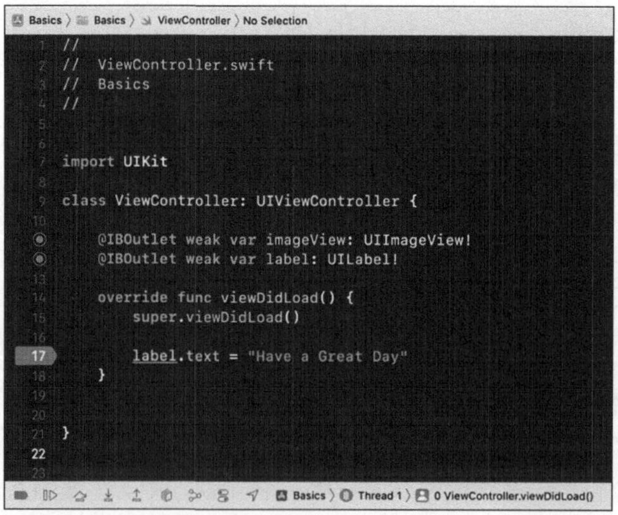

***Figure 1.57:** To let go of the debug pointer, click the second icon from the left*

Now you can see the app screen loaded with an overridden message.

Let's finish this simple chapter by exploring other Icons in debug menu.

Figure 1.58: *Debugging menu*

- If you want to disable the debugging for certain builds, you don't have to remove all the debug points but instead, click the icon and disable all the debug pointers.
- If you want to continue past a certain debug line, click the icon. We used this in the previous scenario, so you are already familiar with it.
- If you want the debugger to step over to the next line, click the icon. You will see the debugger move to the next line.

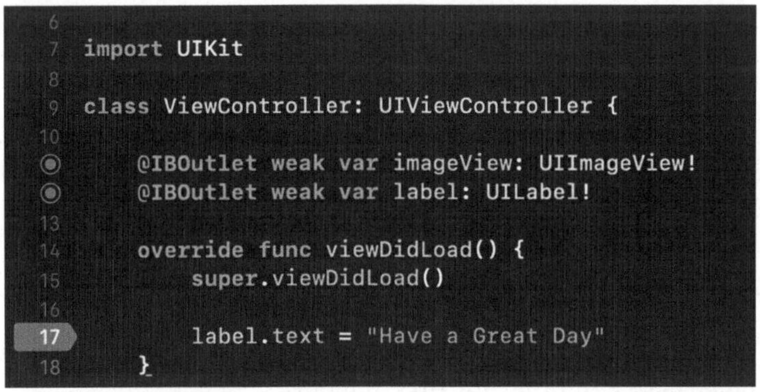

Figure 1.59: *Debugger stepping over to next line*

- For example, if you have to go into certain functions while debugging, then you click the icon which allows you to step into the function, if you want to step out then use icon.
- This icon allows you to see the View hierarchy. By clicking it, you will see the following:

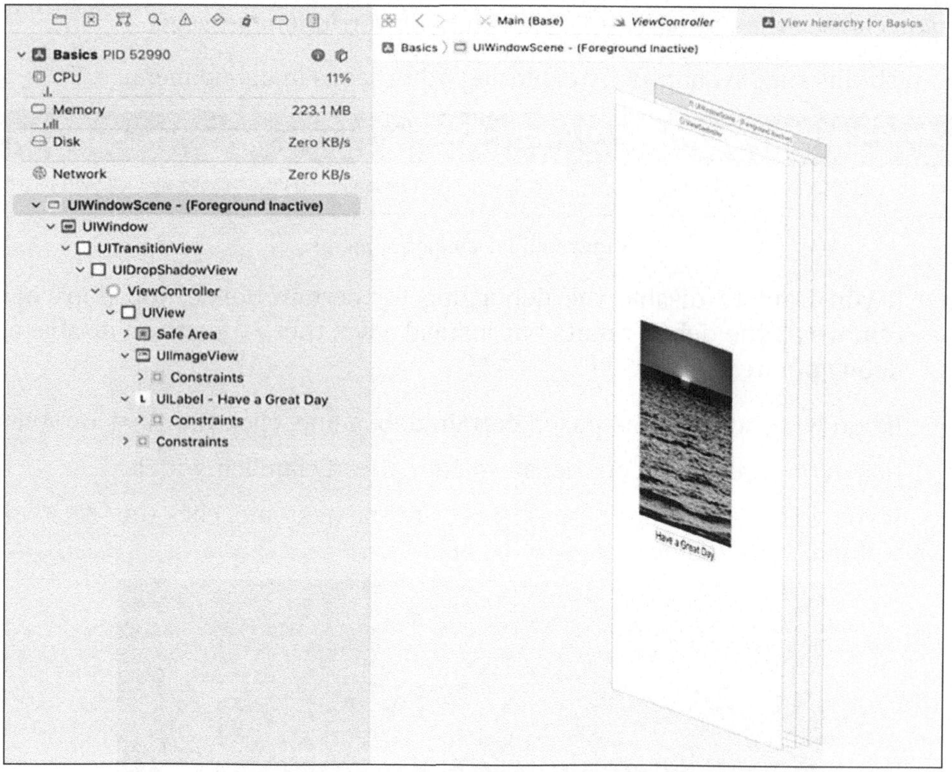

Figure 1.60: *View hierarchy of ViewController*

You will see how all your views are arranged on the screen.

(**Note**: *My debug pointer is on the next line of* **`'Label.text = "Have a Great Day."'`** *Debugger should be active in order for this to work.)*

- If you want to simulate the dark mode, bold text, or dynamic text in the storyboard, this feature is useful. We will explore it more in upcoming chapters .
- If you want to simulate a certain location, this icon is used. In this app, it's not useful, but in the upcoming chapters, we will use them.

Conclusion

This chapter sums up all you need to learn to build a simple app. Hope you enjoyed this chapter. It is the first step to being an awesome app developer. We learnt about how to use Xcode, how to build screens, running the App in different simulators and how to debug. After this chapter, you can experiment by adding other elements to our initial `viewController` and setting constraints accordingly. After experimenting, we will level up in the next chapter by exploring the app development process and how to use `UITableView` in your app.

Points to Remember

- `UIKit` is a framework provided by Apple that supplies all the UI elements used in our screens.
- Constraints let UI elements stay in a particular place and a particular size.
- Autolayout will arrange the UI elements on the screen according to the constraints given.
- You use `UIImageView` if you want to display a single image or series of animated images.
- Safe Area is the area that is uninterrupted by a status bar, navigation bar or toolbar.
- Adding code references of UI elements helps us to modify them during runtime and also aids in debugging.

CHAPTER 2
App Process and TableViews

Introduction

To go up a level, let's learn how apps are developed in the real world. Most of the apps that you use, such as Instagram, Facebook, Twitter, and the new Threads use `TableViews`. So, let's learn about `TableViews` in this chapter, a fun and important concept to learn and implement.

Structure

In this chapter, we will discuss the following topics:

- App development process
- `TableViews`
- Function
- Protocol
- Delegate
- `UITableViewDataSource`
- `UITableViewDelegate`
- Sections
- `UITableViewCell`
- `CGRect`
- Array
- Adding Header to the Table view
- Footer
- Footer for section
- `didSelectRowAt`

- `UIAlertController`
- Dictionary

App Development Process

App developers make people's lives a lot easier with Apps. Keep in mind App development is not about just writing code for the screen but providing the best user experience for the end-user. For that very reason, every app developer should know the intention of the app they are building. Firstly, let's get to know the App development process, that is, from having an App Idea to becoming Mark Zuckerberg.

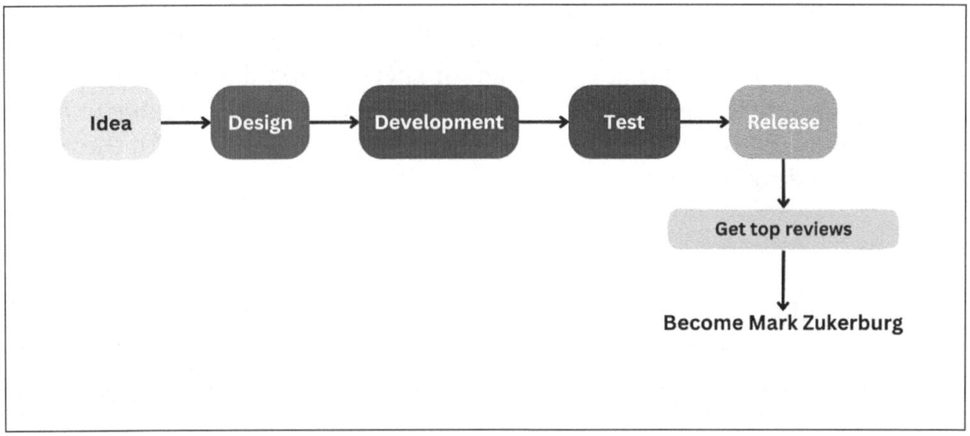

Figure 2.1: *App Development Process*

Idea

Not just all apps but everything starts with an Idea. Some Ideas come up to solve the problems around you, some come up because you want to be that cool kid in the street and some other ideas come up because you want to make the world a better place. For example, Mark Zuckerberg got the idea of Facebook when he was just trying to connect people in colleges and a few schools.

Design

Now that you have a wonderful idea, the next step is design, which is crucial. We just can't go 'Oh, I need an app to connect the people, let's go create one'. One should foresee how the app should look, how the user interacts with the app, how each element should look, and how each element works. Sometimes you can be your own designer and do all the things, but most companies have a designer or designers to design the app. You tell them the idea and the designer designs the whole app. The designer also provides images, icons, and button images that are of better resolution for the app. The designer also designs how each interaction of UI element should be. The designer designs primarily to provide the best user experience for the App.

Of course, the rough app design or wireframe starts with drawing on paper. There are also a lot of wonderful tools available for prototyping the App, for example, Sketch, Abstract, and InVision.

Development

Now that you have the design for each screen and each feature, you can start the development. You will develop each feature as specified in the design and in companies you have the business analysts who specify what each screen does and will specify each feature in detail. These specifications will be done in, for example, Jira cards. While developing if you find that the design or specification doesn't make sense, you can always go back to the designer or business analyst to make the changes, so you can provide the best user experience. Developers always communicate with the designers at every stage of development.

Test

Even if you are the world's top App developer, you need a testing phase. Normally companies have testers to test each feature you develop. A tester is someone who tests each feature manually and runs automated tests. Manual testing is nothing but the tester similarly testing the feature as how the user uses the app. Automated testing is where the tester writes the scripts and UI tests according to requirements given by the analyst and designer and runs the whole test. If at any point the tests fail in automated tests or manual tests, the tester comes back to the developers and asks them to fix it.

One more thing to keep in mind while developing is that to write unit tests for the code you write, as you send different parameters and test different scenarios in unit testing.

After the testers test the feature and give the green light to go ahead, we do user testing, where random people are asked to test the feature. This helps us to understand user's reactions to our App feature.

Release

After development, the tester tested the app, raised some bugs and developers fixed them. Now that everything is working well and good, it is time to release it. To make the release, you need to submit the app to the App Store. The app store reviews it and then the app is released for the world to use. You can release certain features in the next versions too. Some companies have new releases with new feature updates or iOS version-compatible updates. Some companies do scheduled monthly releases.

After releasing the App, all you need to do is keep an eye on the App Store for reviews or if any user has reported any bugs. In case of any bugs, we fix them and then we will have wonderful reviews and top App ratings. Eventually, our App will be the best app that's been ever used and then we become another Mark Zuckerberg.

TableViews

`TableViews` took over the App world, no matter what the app is, most of the apps you use have `TableViews`. Just unlock your phone and have a look, when you are scrolling through Instagram, what you are touching while scrolling is `TableView`. Check Facebook, Twitter, or LinkedIn; everything uses `TableView`.

Not all the Apps you are scrolling through use `TableView`; it could be a `ScrollView` or a `CollectionView` too. But if you are scrolling through linear repeated patterned items, then you are scrolling through a `TableView`. In our code, we can build a `TableView` using `UITableView`.

UITableView

`UITableView` is a view that has a single column with multiple rows and each row will have the content with the data you supply. As you probably know, it is provided by `UIKit`.

Even the contacts and settings app in your iPhone are the `UITableViews`.

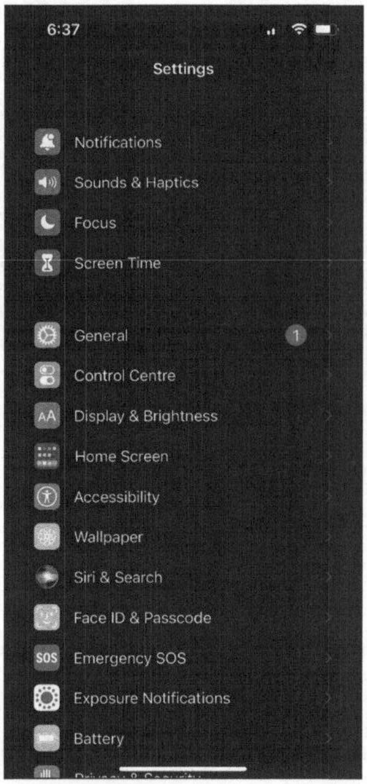

***Figure 2.2**: UITableView in Settings app*

As mentioned, the `UITableView` has multiple rows and a single column, and each row's content is managed by a specialized view known as `UITableViewCell`.

For example: In the following screenshot, the highlighted ones are `UITableViewCells`.

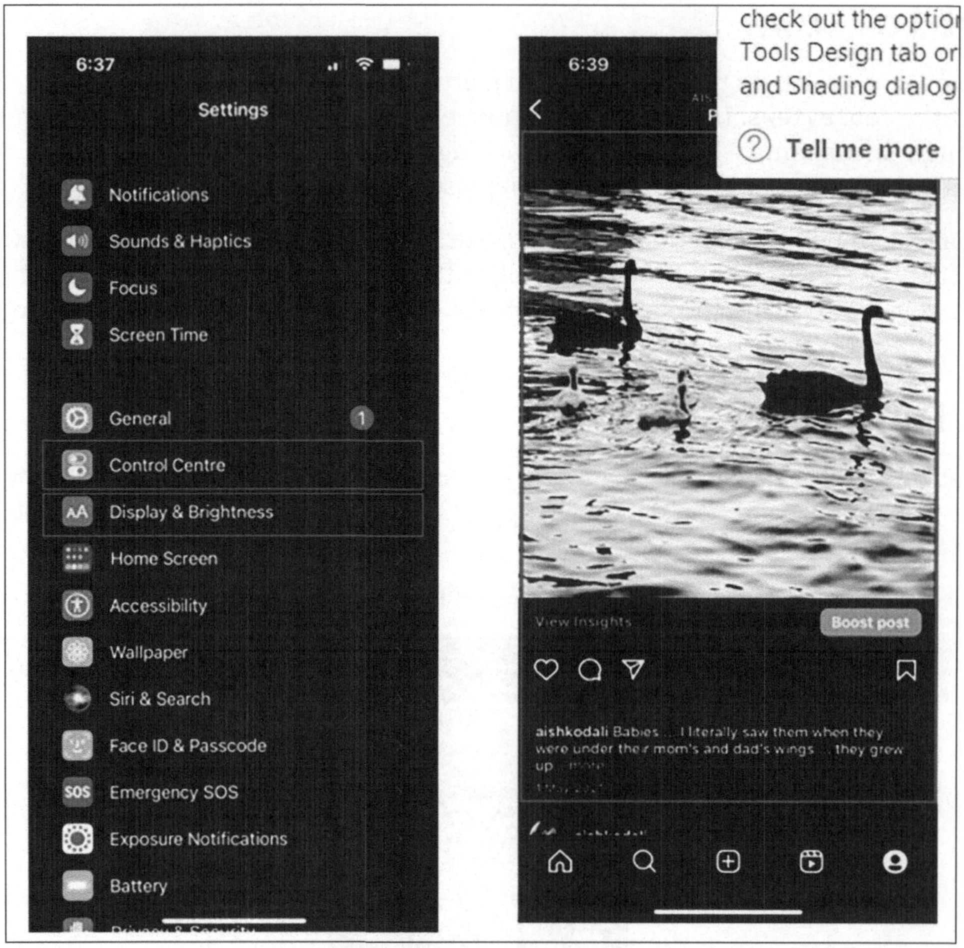

Figure 2.3: *Different apps showing cells*

Now let's put `UITableViews` into implementation. What's a better way to learn than to implement?

1. Open Xcode, and create a new project called `TableViewExample`.
2. Go to **`Main.storyboard`**. If you don't know how to, then please refer to *Chapter 1, Getting Started*.
3. You will see a `ViewController` in the storyboard as follows, which is also an `intialViewController`.

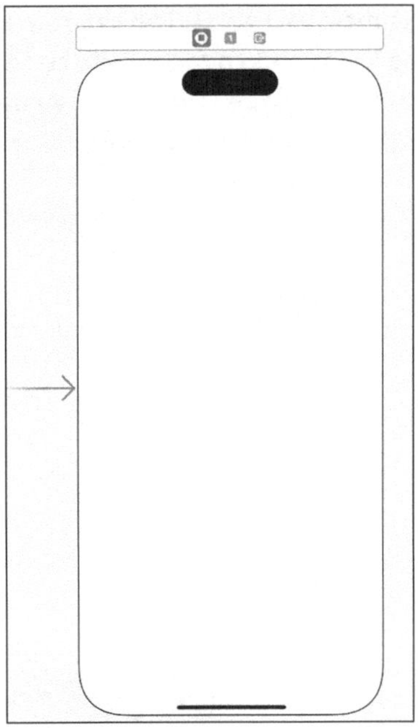

Figure 2.4: *ViewController in the Storyboard*

4. Now add the `UITableView` to the `ViewController`, by clicking the **'+'** on the top-right of the storyboard. If not sure how to add the elements to the storyboard, then please refer to *Chapter 1, Getting Started.*

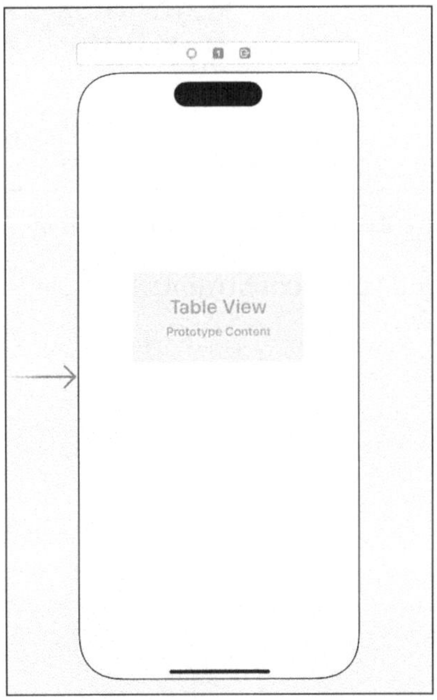

Figure 2.5: *ViewController with TableView*

5. Now let's add constraints to the `UITableView` to Safe Area. **`Add 'Leading Space to Safe Area'`**, **`'Trailing Space to Safe Area'`**, **`'Top Space to Safe Area'`**, and **`'Bottom Space to Safe Area'`**. For reference, on how to add constraints between elements and Safe Area, please refer to the previous chapter.

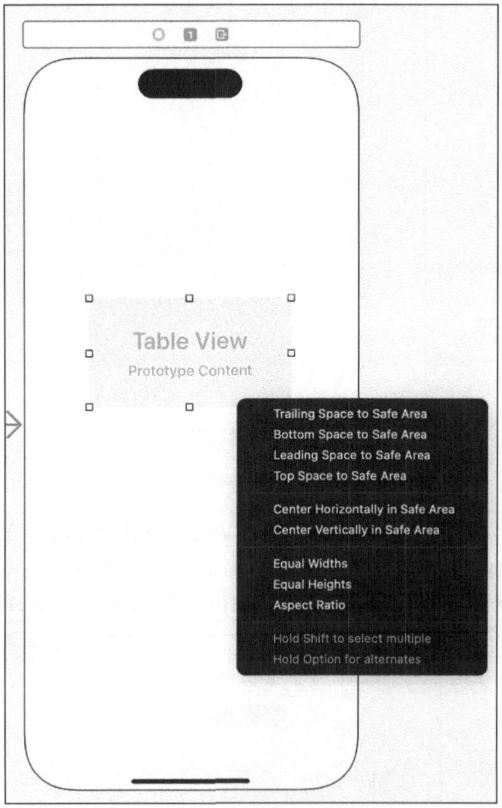

Figure 2.6: *Adding constraints to Table View*

6. When you have added these constraints, you can see as follows:

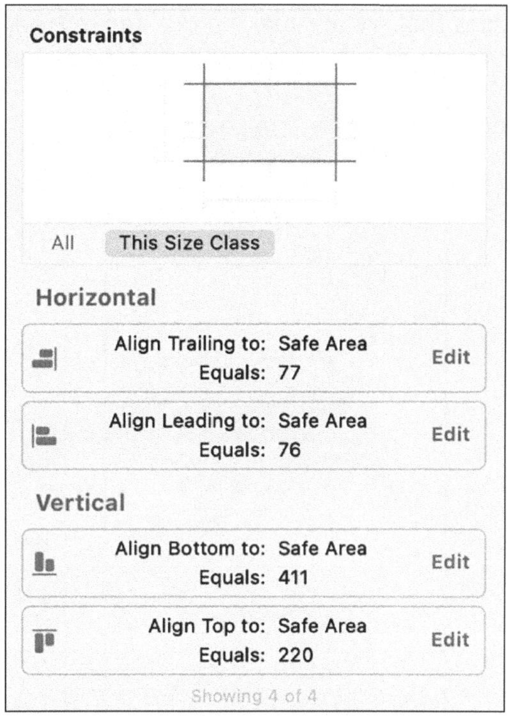

***Figure 2.7**: Constraints in size inspector*

7. Make the constants for four of these constraints zero.

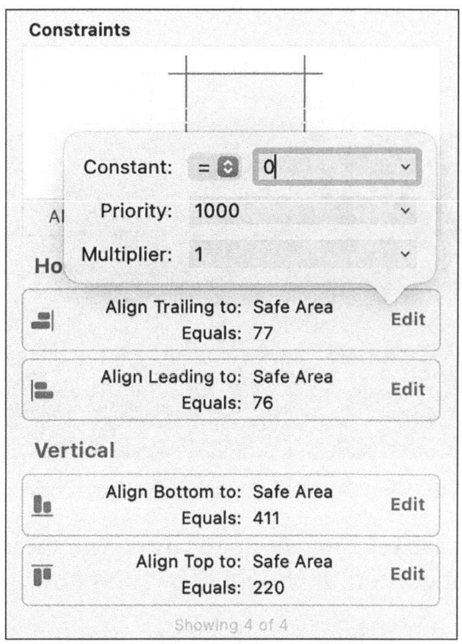

***Figure 2.8**: Editing constraints*

8. What this means is that we are making our `TableView`, the same frame as the safe area. After modifying the constraints, this is what you will see in *Figure 2.9*.

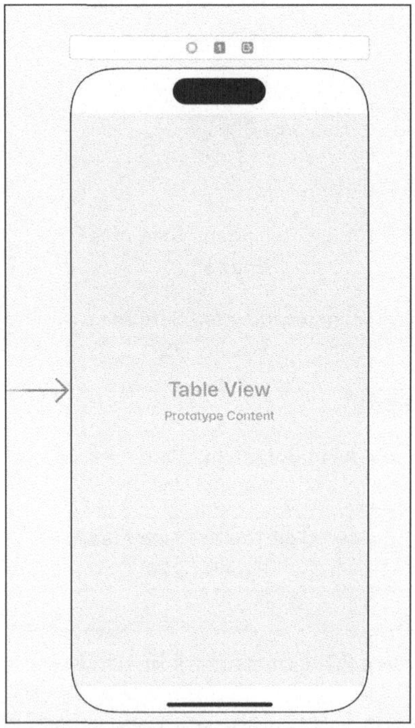

***Figure 2.9**: Table View with the same frame and size as the Safe area*

9. Now add the code reference of your `tableview` in the `ViewController`. If any doubts, please check the previous chapter.

```
import UIKit

class ViewController: UIViewController {

    @IBOutlet weak var tableView: UITableView!

    override func viewDidLoad() {
        super.viewDidLoad()
        // Do any additional setup after loading the view.
    }

}
```

***Figure 2.10**: ViewController with tableView code reference*

10. As we added the `TableView`, we need to tell the table view how many rows it should have, what content it should show, and how it should show.

For that very reason, we got delegate and data source functions. Before getting into them, let's learn a few terms for better understanding.

Function

Just like all other coding languages, such as C and Objective-C – C, we have functions in Swift, which are blocks of code that perform a certain task. If you want to declare a function, then you can declare it with the keyword **'func'**. For reference, check the following syntax.

```
func funcName(parameters) -> return type {
return returnType.
}
```

Protocol

Protocol, as the name says it, is a set of rules or a contract. So, if an object conforms to a specific protocol, it means it needs to implement certain functions and include the variables that are defined in the protocol.

Delegate

What is meant by delegation? Assigning the tasks or responsibilities to an individual. Similarly, here delegate means assigning responsibilities to an instance of another class.

UITableViewDataSource

This is a protocol that has functions, providing Cells and managing data for a table view.

UITableViewDelegate

This is a protocol that has functions, such as managing cell selections, configuring section headers and footers, deleting cells, re-ordering cells, and many others for our table view.

Now that you know what is delegate and `dataSource`, we are assigning that `tableView`'s delegate and `dataSource` as our `ViewController`, which also means that our `ViewController` should also conform to `UITableViewDelagate` and `UITableViewDataSource` protocols. This means our `ViewController` should implement `UITableViewDelagate` and `UITableViewDataSource` protocol functions, which tell how many rows our `tableView` should show, what it should, and how it should show.

Also, note that if we want to assign any object as delegate and `dataSource`, the following is the way to do it.

```
import UIKit

class ViewController: UIViewController, UITableViewDelegate, UITableViewDataSource {

    @IBOutlet weak var tableView: UITableView!

    override func viewDidLoad() {
        super.viewDidLoad()

        tableView.delegate = self
        tableView.dataSource = self
    }

}
```

***Figure 2.11**: ViewController with Table View delegate and dataSource*

Don't worry about that red line showing up when you are assigning that `viewController` is of type `UITableViewDelegate` and `UITableViewDataSource`; it is just an alert to implement protocol functions.

If you click the 'red bullet' of the red line, it will show as in *Figure 2.12*,

```
class ViewController: UIViewController, UITableViewDelegate, UITableViewDataSource {

    @IBOutlet weak var tableView: UITableView!

    override func viewDidLoad() {
        super.viewDidLoad()
```

Type 'ViewController' does not conform to protocol 'UITableViewDataSource' ×
Do you want to add protocol stubs? Fix

***Figure 2.12:** ViewController showing that it is missing protocol functions*

It says **'Type 'ViewController' does not conform to protocol 'UITableViewDataSource' '** and if you click the fix, the protocol function should appear.

```
func tableView(_ tableView: UITableView, numberOfRowsInSection section: Int) -> Int {
    code
}
```

***Figure 2.13:** UITableViewDataSource protocol function in the ViewController*

Then the red line appears again as we are not implementing another required `UITableViewDataSource` function. If you click the fix, the function should appear as shown here.

```
class ViewController: UIViewController, UITableViewDelegate, UITableViewDataSource {
    func tableView(_ tableView: UITableView, numberOfRowsInSection section: Int) -> Int {
        code
    }

    func tableView(_ tableView: UITableView, cellForRowAt indexPath: IndexPath) -> UITableViewCell {
        code
    }
```

***Figure 2.14:** UITableViewDataSource protocol functions in the ViewController*

Note: *Instead of clicking the fix on the red line, we can directly add the methods and the red lines will disappear.*

So, what are these methods, and why we should implement them?

One of the methods is `numberOfRowsInSection`, when you implement this you are telling the `tableView` the number of rows, it needs to show up.

For example, if we want 10 rows to show up, we return 10 from the function as shown in *Figure* 2.14. But later in the chapter, we can return a dynamic count rather than a hard-coded **'10'**:

```
func tableView(_ tableView: UITableView, numberOfRowsInSection section: Int) -> Int {
    10
}
```

Figure 2.15: *Returning 10 in numberOfRowInSection function*

Sections

You might wonder by the preceding function name **'numberOfRowsInSection'**, especially **'InSection'**? A Section is nothing but a grouping of rows. For example, check your settings app.

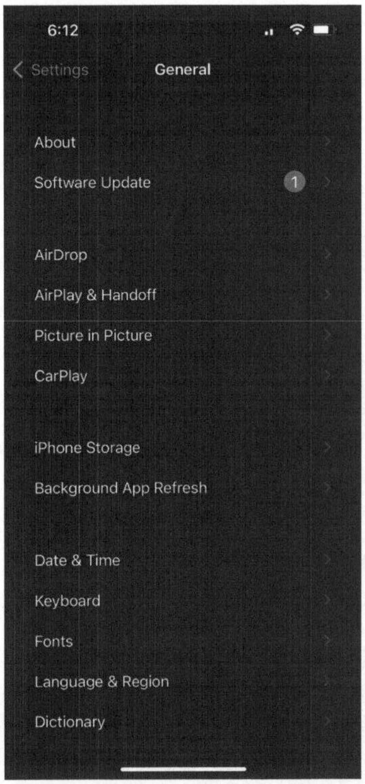

Figure 2.16: *Settings app with sections*

In *Figure* 2.16, we have four sections.

You can specify the number of sections using the `DataSource` method.

```
func numberOfSections(in tableView: UITableView) -> Int
```

The default value for this function is '1', so if you don't implement this method, then your `tableView` will have one section.

The next method we need to implement is `cellForRowAtIndexPath` which returns `UITableViewCell`.

UITableViewCell

We can say that `UITableViewCell` is a special view that manages the content of a single row. In other words, we can say that `UITableViewCell` is like the content view of each row.

IndexPath

In simple terms, we can say `IndexPath` is nothing but the location of the section and row in your `tableView`.

Formally, `IndexPath` is the list of indexes, which represent the path to a specified item in a tree of nested arrays.

So, all we are doing is returning a view(content) for each row of the `TableView`.

The `UITableViewCell` can have anything as `subViews`, such as `imageViews`, Labels or `Textfields`, or anything.

For now, let's have a label in each row. Let's publish the top 10 programming languages in our `tableView`.

So, for better understanding, in each row, we will have a label which will be the name of the programming language.

Here is how we create `TableViewCell` instance in a simple way:

```
Let cell = UITableViewCell()
```

`Let` allows you to create immutable variables, which means once you create them you can't modify them. If you want to create mutable variables, then use **`Var`**.

`UITableViewCell()` means `UITableViewCell.init()` which means we are initializing `UITableViewCell`, and we are creating the instance of `UITableViewCell`. Some initializing functions do have parameters, which means we are creating instances of that object with certain requirements.

Before iOS 14, the code to have text in our cell used to be **`cell.textLabel?.text = "Swift"`** but **`cell.textLabel`** is deprecated after iOS 14.

Deprecation

If you see something is deprecated or will be deprecated, it means you won't be able to use it any further in any future versions. When there is an iOS update, all code bases need to be updated as well so that we are using non-deprecated code and staying up-to-date.

After iOS 14, the `UITabeViewCell` doesn't have the `textLabel`, instead, the cell got `contentConfiguration`. So, we should create the content configuration and assign it to it.

Let's do something awesome now, treat it like a life hack.

If you want to open any file in Xcode, the shortcut to it is '*Command + Shift + O*' and type in the class or file name you want to open.

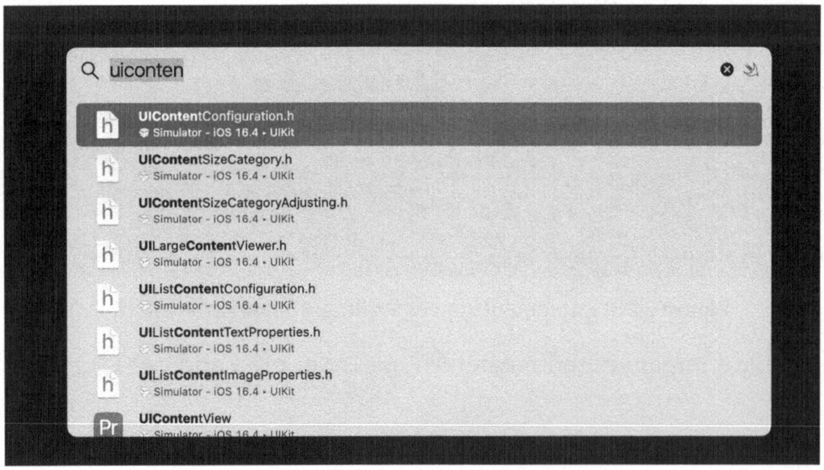

Figure 2.17: *Shortcut showing class name*

The file or class name shows up, select the file or class you want to open. Thats it.

The cell's `contentConfiguration` is of type `UIContentConfiguration`, if you open the `UIContentConfiguration` using the preceding shortcut, you won't find text property in it.

If you open the `UITableViewCell` class and go to the property `'textLabel'`, you will comment that as an alternative, we should be using `UIListContentConfiguration`.

```
@available(iOS, introduced: 3.0, deprecated: 100000, message: "Use UIListContentConfiguration instead, this property will be
    deprecated in a future release.")
open var textLabel: UILabel? { get } // default is nil.  label will be created if necessary.
```

Figure 2.18: *textLabel deprecated*

If you open `UIListContentConfiguration`, you can see that it conforms to the `UIContentConfiguration` protocol and it got the text variable.

```
UIKIT_EXTERN API_AVAILABLE(ios(14.0), tvos(14.0), watchos(7.0)) NS_SWIFT_UI_ACTOR
@interface UIListContentConfiguration : NSObject <UIContentConfiguration, NSSecureCoding>
```

Figure 2.19: *UIListContentConfiguration*

Now that you know these, let's put them into implementation. The `UITableViewCell` does have the `defaultContentConfiguration` which returns `UIListContentConfiguration` which is good, as it comes with default configuration; let's use it or else you can initialize a new one too. Let's create a cell first and use its default configuration.

```
let cell = UITableViewCell()
var contentConfig = cell.defaultContentConfiguration()
contentConfig.text = "Swift"
cell.contentConfiguration = contentConfig
```

Now that we have our cell and its `contentConfiguration`, let's return this cell for the `cellForRowIndexPath` as shown here.

```
func tableView(_ tableView: UITableView, cellForRowAt indexPath: IndexPath) -> UITableViewCell {

    let cell = UITableViewCell()

    var contentConfig = cell.defaultContentConfiguration()
    contentConfig.text = "Swift"
    cell.contentConfiguration = contentConfig

    return cell
}
```

Figure 2.20: *Implementing cellForRowAtIndexPath function*

Now that we have implemented `numberOfRowsInSection` and `cellForRowIndexPath`, let's run it.

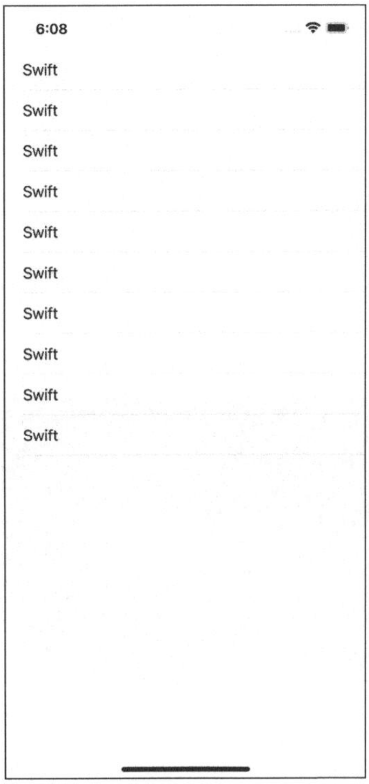

Figure 2.21: *Simulator showing cells with given text*

As you might have noticed, the `tableView` is showing ten rows as per the number we returned for `numberOfRowsInSection` and showing the same static text as per the text value we provided in `contentConfiguration` **`'contentConfig.text = "Swift"'`**.

Now that you understand these functions, let's make our `tableView` publish dynamic content.

The very first thing we need to publish the dynamic data is the data itself.

Let's get data, we want to publish the 10 programming languages in our `tableView`.

Ruby, Python, Rust, Swift, Kotlin, Java, Objective – c, JavaScript, C, SQL.

To hold these 10 programming language's names, we need a data structure.

Array

An array is an ordered collection of items of the same type. You can save any kind of elements in the Array, and you can randomly access any element in the array.

This is how we create an array.

```
let progLanguages = ["Ruby", "Python", "Rust", "Swift", "Kotlin",
"Java", "Objective - c", "JavaScript", "C", "SQL"]
```

Here we are creating an array of Strings.

We are using let here because this array will not be changed in the later part of the code; it is immutable.

We will be fetching names of programming languages from this array for our `tableView` in `cellForRowIndexPath` method as shown here:

`contentConfig.text = progLanguages[indexPath.row]`

We are replacing the preceding code in place of **`contentConfig.text = "Swift"`**. As we are fetching it from the array, we don't need static text anymore.

```
func tableView(_ tableView: UITableView, cellForRowAt indexPath: IndexPath) -> UITableViewCell {

    let cell = UITableViewCell()

    var contentConfig = cell.defaultContentConfiguration()
    contentConfig.text = progLanguages[indexPath.row]
    cell.contentConfiguration = contentConfig

    return cell
}
```

Figure 2.22: *Assigning dynamic text to content configuration*

Even for `numberOfRowsInSection` function, we make it return as per our array instead of returning static **`'10'`**.

```
func tableView(_ tableView: UITableView, numberOfRowsInSection section: Int) -> Int {

    progLanguages.count
}
```

Figure 2.23: *Assigning dynamic count*

Go ahead and run it.

You should be able to see the result as in the following figure:

***Figure 2.24:** Simulator showing the content from the given Array*

Now add one more language name to your array and see what happens. So, here you are not editing any of your protocol functions, but changing your Array.

```
let progLanguages = ["Ruby", "Python", "Rust", "Swift", "Kotlin",
"Java", "Objective - c", "JavaScript", "C", "SQL", "Pearl"]
```

Add **`"pearl"`** at the end of the array, and now go ahead and run it. You should see the updated `tableView`.

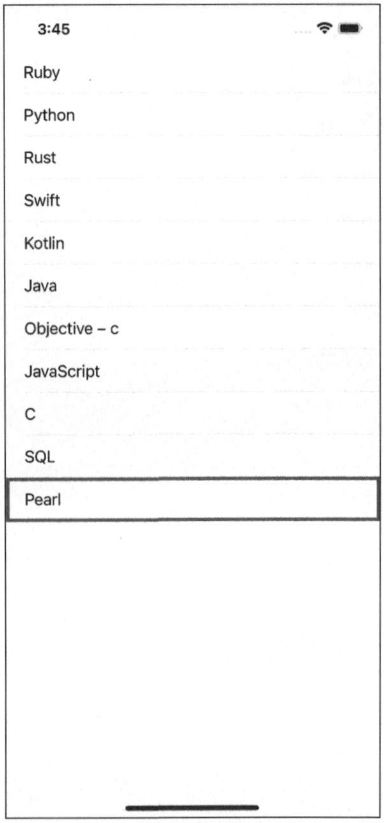

***Figure 2.25**: Simulator showing Pearl, an updated array item*

By now, you should know that it is happening because we are loading the data from the array and not giving it any static content.

Now that we learned a little about `TableView`, let's learn about `TableViewHeader` and `TableViewFooter`.

Adding Header to the `TableView`

We can add headers to any `tableView` using multiple functions and in multiple ways, and for the 'keep-it-simple' purpose, we will be using `tableView(_:viewForHeaderInSection:)`.

In fact, we are adding the header to the `TableView`'s section. As we got only one section it looks like `tableView`'s Header.

We must return a view to display the header for the section and that returning view can have anything as `subviews` like labels, images, or even different background colors. Let's get into implementation.

Let's add a label that says, **"Programming languages"**.

So first, implement the delegate method `tableView(_:viewForHeaderInSection:)`

```
func tableView(_ tableView: UITableView, viewForHeaderInSection section: Int) -> UIView? {
        }
```

As we have to return the view, let's create the **View**,

```
let headerView = UIView.init(frame: CGRect.init(x: 0, y: 0, width: tableView.frame.width, height: 50))
```

Here we are giving a frame to our view while creating because we are not creating this view in the storyboard with constraints. If we don't give the frame, then we might see nothing on the screen.

CGRect

The `CGRect` is the structure that carries the dimension and location of the rectangle. In the above code, we are creating the `headerView`, which is the `UIView` with a frame of the rectangle, which is with the preceding location and dimensions specified.

Let's return that view for our delegate function as shown here.

```
func tableView(_ tableView: UITableView, viewForHeaderInSection section: Int) -> UIView? {

    let headerView = UIView.init(frame: CGRect.init(x: 0, y: 0, width: tableView.frame.width, height: 50))

    return headerView
}
```

***Figure 2.26**: ViewForHeaderInSection with headerView*

Now let's add a label as a `subView` to our view.

```
let label = UILabel()
label.frame = CGRect.init(x: 20, y: 5, width: headerView.frame.width ,
height: headerView.frame.height )
label.text = "Programming Languages"
label.font = .systemFont(ofSize: 21, weight: .bold)
```

We created the `UILabel` and gave the frame, otherwise, your label's text won't be visible. We gave the text as **"Programming Languages"**, you can give the text whatever you want. As this label is a header, the Label's font should be bold and bigger than the other labels in our `TableView`. So that's the reason we gave the **"System font size 21"** and with weight **"bold"**.

Now add this label as the `subView` to your View.

```
headerView.addSubview(label)
```

```
func tableView(_ tableView: UITableView, viewForHeaderInSection section: Int) -> UIView? {

    let headerView = UIView.init(frame: CGRect.init(x: 0, y: 0, width: tableView.frame.width, height: 50))

    let label = UILabel()
    label.frame = CGRect.init(x: 20, y: 5, width: headerView.frame.width , height: headerView.frame.height )
    label.text = "Programming Languages"
    label.font = .systemFont(ofSize: 21, weight: .bold)

    headerView.addSubview(label)

    return headerView
}
```

***Figure 2.27**: headerView with label as a SubView*

Now go ahead and run it.

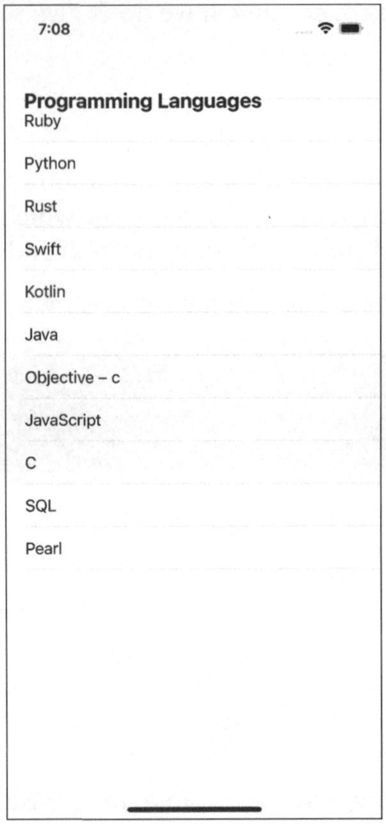

***Figure 2.28**: Simulator with header*

The reason why we got the header looking like how it is because we did not specify the height for the header of `tableView`'s section. If you look at the code, then you can see that the height for View and Label are given, but not the header height. The `tableView`'s section will know that it has a view as a header, but does not know how much height the header should be, and for that, we need to use another delegate method.

```
func tableView(_ tableView: UITableView, heightForHeaderInSection
section: Int) -> CGFloat {

        50.0
}
```

```
func tableView(_ tableView: UITableView, viewForHeaderInSection section: Int) -> UIView? {

    let headerView = UIView.init(frame: CGRect.init(x: 0, y: 0, width: tableView.frame.width, height: 50))

    let label = UILabel()
    label.frame = CGRect.init(x: 20, y: 5, width: headerView.frame.width , height: headerView.frame.height )
    label.text = "Programming Languages"
    label.font = .systemFont(ofSize: 21, weight: .bold)

    headerView.addSubview(label)

    return headerView
}

func tableView(_ tableView: UITableView, heightForHeaderInSection section: Int) -> CGFloat {

    50.0
}
```

Figure 2.29: *Implementing heightForHeaderInSection*

Now go ahead and run it.

Figure 2.30: *Simulator with fixed header*

That fixed it.

Footer

Now that we have the header, let's add a footer as well. You can add the footer to the `TableView` and you can add the footer to the `TableView`'s section.

First, let's try adding the footer to the `TableView` and see, then we will add the footer to the section so that you will know the difference.

In the `viewDidLoad()` function after assigning the delegate and `dataSource` to our `tableView`, let us create the footer and add the label as a subview that says, "`The above programming languages are really useful to build awesome applications, websites and wonderful software products.`"

```
let tableViewFooterView = UIView(frame: CGRect(x: 0, y: 0, width:
tableView.frame.width-5, height: 150))
let titleLabel = UILabel(frame: CGRect(x:10,y: 5 ,width:tableViewFooter-
View.frame.width,height:150))
titleLabel.numberOfLines = 0;
titleLabel.lineBreakMode = .byWordWrapping
titleLabel.backgroundColor = UIColor.clear
titleLabel.textColor = .black
titleLabel.font = UIFont(name: “Montserrat-Regular”, size: 12)
titleLabel.text  = “The above programming languages are really useful to
build awesome applications, websites and wonderful software products.”
tableViewFooterView.addSubview(titleLabel)
```

Now assign this `tableViewFooterView` to the `tableView`'s `footerView`.

```
tableView.tableFooterView = tableViewFooterView
```

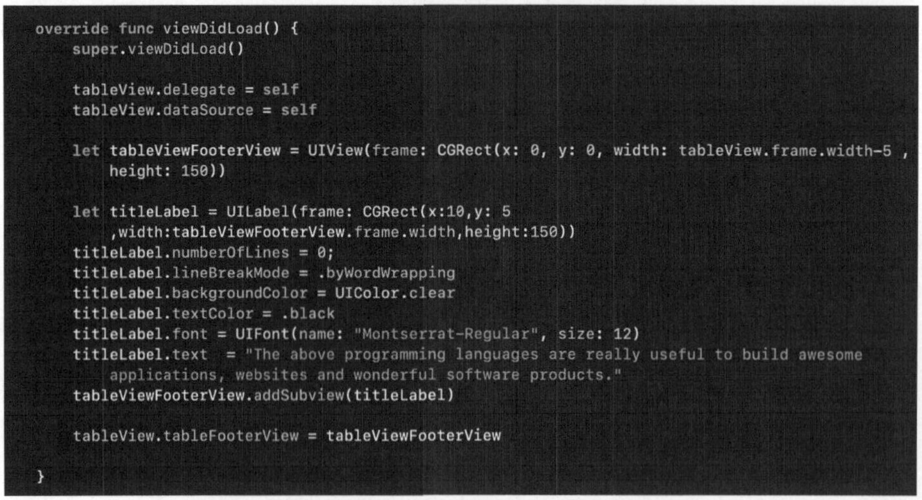

```
override func viewDidLoad() {
    super.viewDidLoad()

    tableView.delegate = self
    tableView.dataSource = self

    let tableViewFooterView = UIView(frame: CGRect(x: 0, y: 0, width: tableView.frame.width-5 ,
        height: 150))

    let titleLabel = UILabel(frame: CGRect(x:10,y: 5
        ,width:tableViewFooterView.frame.width,height:150))
    titleLabel.numberOfLines = 0;
    titleLabel.lineBreakMode = .byWordWrapping
    titleLabel.backgroundColor = UIColor.clear
    titleLabel.textColor = .black
    titleLabel.font = UIFont(name: "Montserrat-Regular", size: 12)
    titleLabel.text  = "The above programming languages are really useful to build awesome
        applications, websites and wonderful software products."
    tableViewFooterView.addSubview(titleLabel)

    tableView.tableFooterView = tableViewFooterView

}
```

***Figure 2.31**: Adding footer to the tableView*

Now run the project and you will see the `tableView`'s footer.

***Figure 2.32**: Simulator with tableView footer*

Footer for Section

We don't want any labels for our section footer but a gray color view, which defines the end of our section content.

Just like we have delegate functions for adding headers to our section, we have them for footers too.

`tableView(_:viewForFooterInSection:)`

Let's implement this method and give our `tableViewSection` a `FooterView`.

```
func tableView(_ tableView: UITableView, viewForFooterInSection section: Int) -> UIView? {
 let footerView = UIView(frame: CGRect(x: 0, y: 0, width: tableView.frame.size.width, height: 50))
       return footerView
   }
```

In the preceding method, we created a `footerView` and returned it as we need to tell the `tableView` as `sectionFooter`.

Let's add the background color of this footer to gray.

```
   func tableView(_ tableView: UITableView, viewForFooterInSection
section: Int) -> UIView? {
       let footerView = UIView(frame: CGRect(x: 0, y: 0, width:
tableView.frame.size.width, height: 50))
       footerView.backgroundColor = .gray
       return footerView
   }
```

Remember to give the height for the section's footer.

```
 func tableView(_ tableView: UITableView, heightForFooterInSection
section: Int) -> CGFloat {
        50.0
    }
```

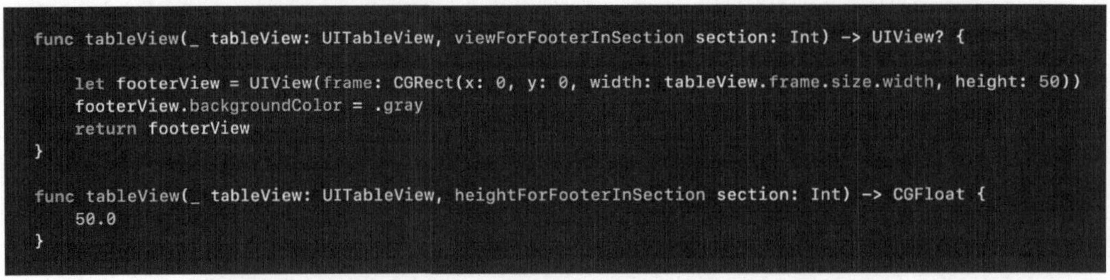

```
func tableView(_ tableView: UITableView, viewForFooterInSection section: Int) -> UIView? {

    let footerView = UIView(frame: CGRect(x: 0, y: 0, width: tableView.frame.size.width, height: 50))
    footerView.backgroundColor = .gray
    return footerView
}

func tableView(_ tableView: UITableView, heightForFooterInSection section: Int) -> CGFloat {
    50.0
}
```

Figure 2.33: *ViewController implementing Protocol functions for adding section footer*

Now you know what to do, go ahead and run it.

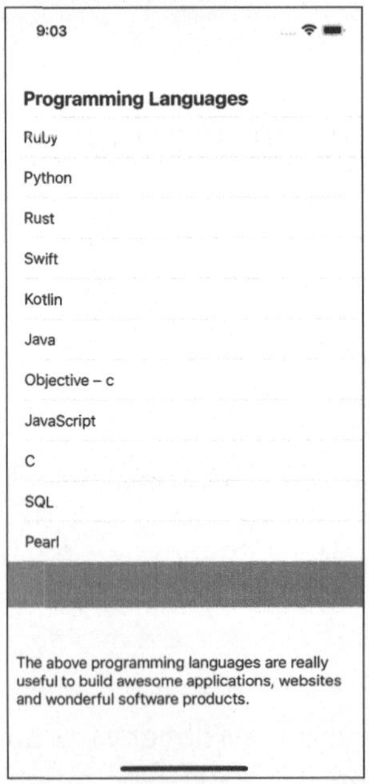

Figure 2.34: *Simulator with section footer*

Now you know the difference, the `tableView` footer stays at the end of the `tableView`, section's footer is at the end of the section.

So far, we have learned how to use `TableViews` using delegate and `dataSource` methods, how to publish data in `tableView` rows, and how to have `tableView`'s section header and footers and `tableView footer`.

didSelectRowAt:

Finally, one interesting concept and useful concept, `tableView(_:didSelectRowAt:)`, this delegate function gets called when the user taps on `tableView`'s row.

So, if you want your app to do anything when the row is tapped, then you need to implement this function.

In our case, when the user taps on a certain row/certain programming language, it should show what that programming language does and what it is used for.

The first step is, obviously, to implement the delegate method.

There is a little hack to implement to get the delegate methods instead of copying and pasting what is written here.

Go to your `ViewController` file and start typing the delegate method you want to implement, in this case, it is `didSelectRowAt`, and you will be able to see a pop-up with our delegate function as follows.

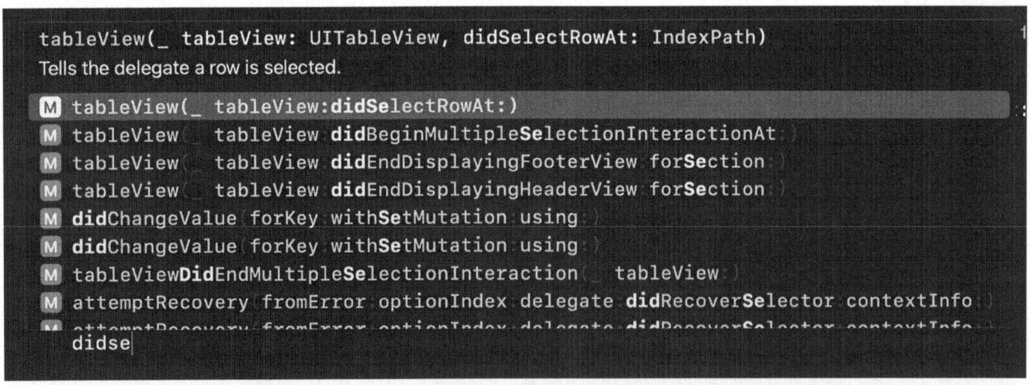

Figure 2.35: *Shortcut showing protocol functions*

Click the first method as that's what you want to implement and then you will be able to see as follows:

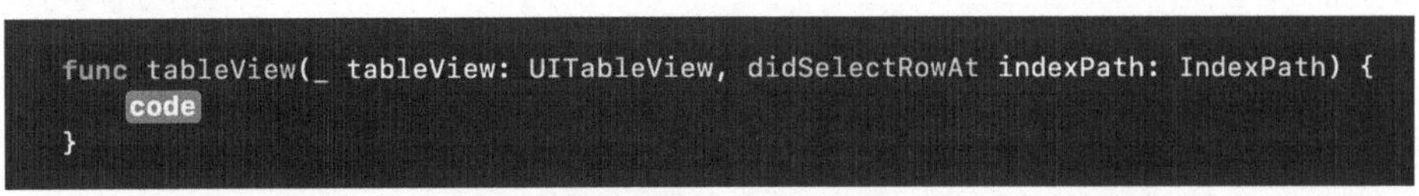

Figure 2.36: *The function that gets called when the user taps on a row*

Just in case, if you didn't understand the preceding technique, here is the delegate function.

```
func tableView(_ tableView: UITableView, didSelectRowAt indexPath:
IndexPath)  {
    }
```

When the user taps on the row, our idea is to show the user what each programming language does in an alert. Let's use `UIAlertController`.

UIAlertController

`UIAlertController` is the object of type `UIViewController` that displays the Alert with message and buttons.

Let's implement `AlertController` inside our delegate method,

```
let alert = UIAlertController(title: "Title", message: "Message", pre-
ferredStyle: UIAlertController.Style.alert)
```

We want our `ViewController` to show the `AlertViewController`:

```
self.present(alert, animated: true, completion: nil)
```

Here the self is our `ViewController`, which has a method to present the `ViewController`. So, here we are presenting the `alertViewController` with animation turned on. More on the navigation and presentation are discussed in further chapters.

When you publish a `UIAlertController`, the interaction with the content in the background is blocked. A transparent overlay of `AlertController` is presented with `Alert` at the center.

Check here for a reference.

```
func tableView(_ tableView: UITableView, didSelectRowAt indexPath: IndexPath) {

    let alert = UIAlertController(title: "Title", message: "Message", preferredStyle:
        UIAlertController.Style.alert)

    self.present(alert, animated: true, completion: nil)

}
```

Figure 2.37: *Creating AlertController and presenting it*

Go ahead and run your project.

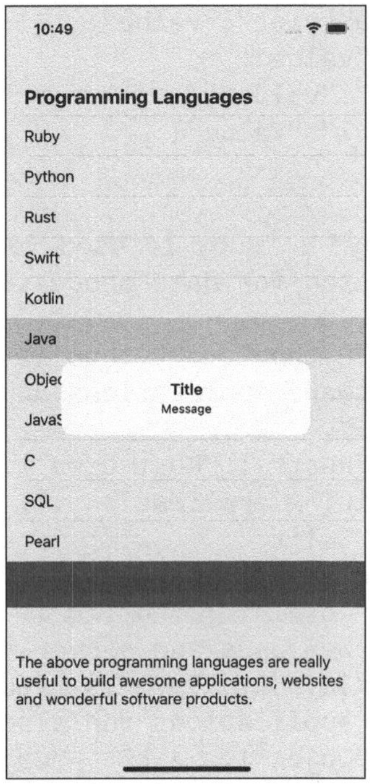

Figure 2.38: *Simulator with AlertController*

You will see the alert with the title and message. So, here the title will be the programming language name and the message should be about our programming language.

In order to publish the message about our programming language, we need one more data structure. Let's create a dictionary.

Dictionary

The Dictionary is nothing but a collection of unordered items. It stores the items in key/value pairs. Like an Array to fetch an Item, we don't have to provide the Index, rather we fetch the element using a key, which is a unique identifier for its value.

Let `progLangsDefs = ["key":"value"]` this is how you create a dictionary. The **`'Keys'`** will be programming language names and the **`'values'`** will be what these languages do. Our dictionary would look like this.

```
let progLangsDict = ["Ruby":"value",
                     "Python":"value",
                     "Rust":"value",
                     "Swift":"value",
                     "Kotlin":"value",
                     "Java":"valuc",
                     "Objective - c":"value",
```

```
                    "JavaScript":"value",
                    "C":"value",
                    "SQL":"value",
                    "Pearl":"value"]
```

Let's go add values now.

```
let progLangsDict = ["Ruby" : "Ruby is used for building web servers
and websites.Can be also used for data processing, automation tools and
devOps. ",
                         "Python" : "Python is wonderful for building
the IoT applications, software applications and used in data visualisa-
tion and in data analysis.",
                         "Rust" : "Rust used to for building operating
systems, games and data mining applications.",
                         "Swift" : " Swift is used for building iOS,
Mac, Apple watch and Apple TV applications.",
                         "Kotlin" : "Kotlin is used for building Android
applications, client-side web apps and server-side applications.",
                         "Java" : "Java is used for building software
applications, server-side applications and also mobile applications.",
                         "Objective - c" : "Objective c is used for
building applications for iOS and macOS platforms",
                         "JavaScript" : "Javascript is used for building
interactive and dynamic web applications.",
                         "C" : "C is used for building for operating
systems, complicated applications, gaming applications and data mining
applications.",
                         "SQL" : "SQL is used for fetching data from
databases and for manipulating databases.",
                         "Pearl" : "Pearl can be used in building graph-
ical user interface development, web development and used for common
interface gateway scripts."]
```

Creation of a dictionary should be done inside the `ViewController`, but not in any function. By doing that, we will have access to the dictionary within the whole class.

```
class ViewController: UIViewController, UITableViewDelegate, UITableViewDataSource{

    @IBOutlet weak var tableView: UITableView!

    let progLanguages = ["Ruby", "Python", "Rust", "Swift", "Kotlin", "Java", "Objective - c", "JavaScript", "C", "SQL", "Pearl" ]

    let progLangsDict = ["Ruby" : "Ruby is used for building web servers and websites.Can be also used for data processing,
        automation tools and devOps. ",
                         "Python" : "Python is wonderful for building the IoT applications, software applications and used in data
                            visualisation and in data analysis.",
                         "Rust" : "Rust used to for building operating systems, games and data mining applications.",
                         "Swift" : "Swift is used for building iOS, Mac, Apple watch and Apple TV applications.",
                         "Kotlin" : "Kotlin is used for building Android applications, client-side web apps and server-side
                            applications.",
                         "Java" : "Java is used for building software applications, server-side applications and also mobile
                            applications.",
                         "Objective - c" : "Objective c is used for building applications for iOS and macOS platforms",
                         "JavaScript" : "Javascript is used for building interactive and dynamic web applications.",
                         "C" : "C is used for building for operating systems, complicated applications, gaming applications and data
                            mining applications.",
                         "SQL" : "SQL is used for fetching data from databases and for manipulating databases.",
                         "Pearl" : "Pearl can be used in building graphical user interface development, web development and used for
                            common interface gateway scripts."]
```

Figure 2.39*: ViewController with Dictionary*

While fetching the data from this dictionary, all we need to do is send the **'key'**. Let's get the key first. This should be done inside the `didSelectRowAt` function.

```
let key = progLanguages[indexPath.row]
```

We are getting the key from our `progLanguages` array and sending that to the dictionary as a key reference.

```
let value = progLangsDict[key]
```

```
func tableView(_ tableView: UITableView, didSelectRowAt indexPath: IndexPath) {

    let key = progLanguages[indexPath.row]

    let value = progLangsDict[key]

    let alert = UIAlertController(title: "Title", message: "Message", preferredStyle: UIAlertController.Style.alert)

    self.present(alert, animated: true, completion: nil)

}
```

Figure 2.40*: Fetching key and value*

Replace the **'Title'** with **'key'** and **'Message'** with **'value'** for our `AlertViewController` as shown here.

```
func tableView(_ tableView: UITableView, didSelectRowAt indexPath: IndexPath) {

    let key = progLanguages[indexPath.row]

    let value = progLangsDict[key]

    let alert = UIAlertController(title: key, message: value, preferredStyle: UIAlertController.Style.alert)

    self.present(alert, animated: true, completion: nil)

}
```

Figure 2.41*: Assigning key and value in UIAlertController as title and message*

Now go ahead and run it. Click any row, and you will see something like this.

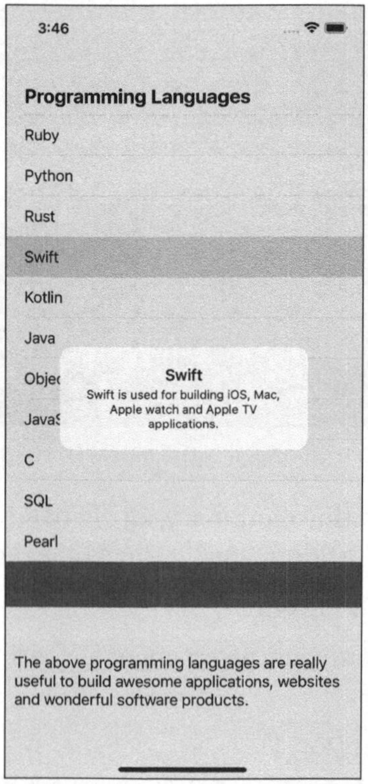

***Figure 2.42:** Simulator showing alert with values from the dictionary*

Everything is looking good, but after the alert popped up, the user will be stuck, as the user can't dismiss the alert. The user can't even click any other row as the `UIAlertController` blocks the interaction with background objects.

Let's add a button, which allows the user to dismiss the alert.

UIAlertAction

`UIAlertAction` is the action that will be taken when the user presses a specific button.

So, here we are adding `UIAlertAction` while creating it.

```
alert.addAction(UIAlertAction(title: "OK", style: UIAlertAction.Style.
default, handler: nil))
```

`UIAlertAction(title: "OK", style: UIAlertAction.Style.default, handler: nil)`, this part of code creates and returns an action and title with the given title and specified behavior. When you assign this `UIAlertAction` to `UIAlertController` using action, it configures the button with a specified title.

We can give a different handler instead of nil, which gives a different functionality for our button.

The preceding line of code should be written before presenting the Alert as follows.

```
func tableView(_ tableView: UITableView, didSelectRowAt indexPath: IndexPath) {
    let key = progLanguages[indexPath.row]
    let value = progLangsDict[key]
    let alert = UIAlertController(title: key, message: value, preferredStyle: UIAlertController.Style.alert)
    alert.addAction(UIAlertAction(title: "OK", style: UIAlertAction.Style.default, handler: nil))
    self.present(alert, animated: true, completion: nil)
}
```

***Figure 2.43**: Adding action to AlertController*

Let's run the project and see what happens.

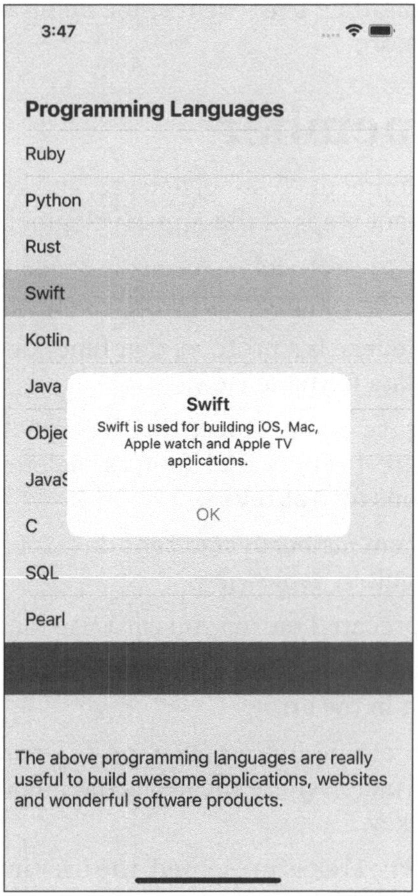

***Figure 2.44:** Alert with 'OK' button*

Now if you click any programming language you should see an alert with an **'OK'** button. When you click it, the alert dismisses and you can select a different language.

Conclusion

This chapter acts as an important stepping stone. In this chapter, you have learned about the App development process, useful to know if you are working for a company, building your own App, or starting your own start-up. Next, in this chapter, you learned a variety of interesting and important concepts including, `UITableViews`, conforming to protocols, `UITableViewCells`, how to create a `UITableView` with dynamic data, how to add sections headers and footers, Table view footers, and what to do when users select a row. Just keep in mind we have multiple ways to create the `UITableViewCells` and `tableView`'s section's header and footer, and we used the simplest ways to create these in this chapter. Going further we will be using other ways of creating `UITableViewCells` and section headers/footers. In the next chapter, you will learn more about other `UIelements`, including `UIScrollView`, `UIButtons`, `UIPickerView`, and many more.

Points to Remember

- Idea, Design, Development, Testing, Release, and keeping an eye on App store reviews are important steps of the App development process.
- If a class conforms to protocol, it means it needs to implement the required functions and have the required variables specified in the protocol.
- `UITableViewDataSource` is a protocol that functions, which provides cells and then can manage data for table view.
- `UITableViewDelegate` is a protocol that has functions and can manage cell selections, configure headers and footers, delete cells, re-order cells, and many other functions for `TableView`.
- If you don't implement `numberOfsections` `dataSource` function, you will have one section by default in Table View.
- If something is deprecated means you can't use it any further.
- An array is an ordered collection of items of the same type. You can randomly access any element in the array.
- The Dictionary is nothing but a collection of unordered items. It stores the items in key/value pairs, where the key is the unique identifier. You can fetch the value using its key.
- When `UIAlertController` is presented, the user interaction with the items in the background is blocked.

CHAPTER 3
The Other UI Elements

Introduction

In this chapter, you are going to learn a lot more exciting stuff that is required for building wonderful apps, including important UI elements, such as `UIScrollViews`, `UIButtons`, `UITextFields`, `UITextViews`, `UIStackViews`, `UIPageControl`, and `UIPickerViews`.

Structure

In this chapter, we will discuss the following topics:

- `UIScrollView`
- `UIButton`
- `UITextField`
- `UITextView`
- `UIStackView`
- `UIPageControl`
- `UIPickerView`

`UIScrollView`

Now that you have learned about `UITableView` in the previous chapter, let's learn about its parent, the `UIScrollView`. You must have seen apps containing an image, followed by some text, and then when you want to read the hidden text, you scroll up.

So, in such scenarios our `UIScrollView` comes into play.

A scroll view is a view with an origin that is movable over the content view, allowing the user to scroll.

Let's jump into implementation:

1. Open XCode and create a project called **`ScrollViewExample`**.
2. Go to your Storyboard and add `UIScrollView` to your `ViewController`.
3. Add constraints to `UIScrollView` to Safe Area:

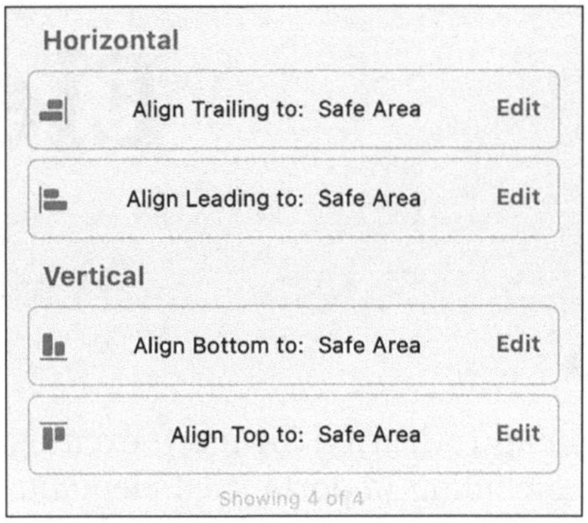

Figure 3.1: *UIScrollView Constraints*

Don't worry if you see the red lines and `scrollView` not expanding; you will understand as you progress further:

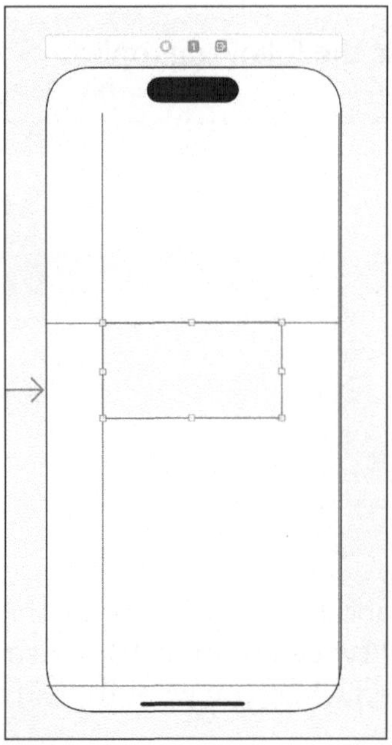

Figure 3.2*: UIScrollView on ViewController*

However, for now, to avoid confusion, drag the `UIScrollView` to the same frame and size as the Safe Area:

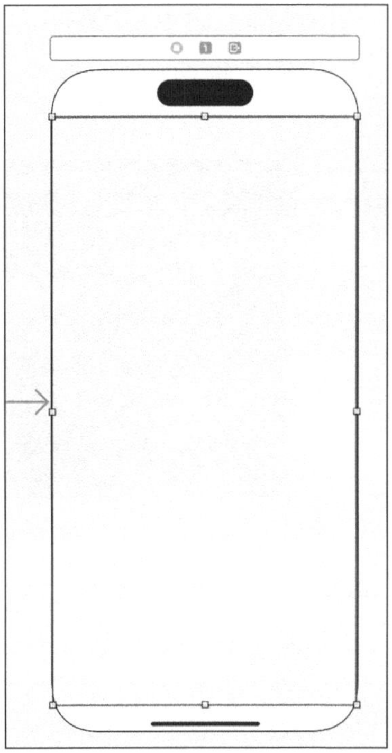

Figure 3.3: *UIScrollView dragged to the same frame as Safe Area*

Now, here comes the fun part: `ScrollView` needs a `contentView`.

The `ScrollView` takes the shape of the `contentView`. The `contentView` is nothing but a view that you add as a `subView` to the `scrollView`.

If you want to add an image and a long text where the user needs to scroll to read the whole text, you add all these elements to this `contentView`, rather than to the `ScrollView`, as the `ScrollView` takes the shape of the `contentView`.

Let's add the View (`contentView`) to the `UIScrollView` in your Storyboard.

Adding the constraints to our `View` and `ScrollView` is a bit tricky here.

Add these four constraints (see *Figure* 3.4) to your View to the `UIScrollView`'s '**`Content Layout Guide`**':

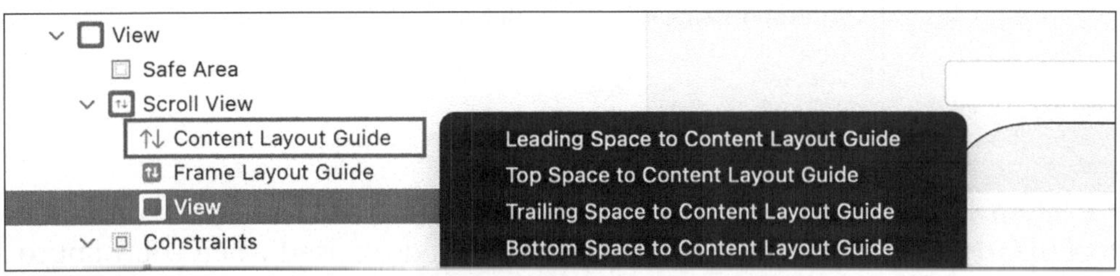

Figure 3.4: *UIScrollView's content layout guide*

Then, add **'Equal Heights'** and **'Equal widths'** to the `ScrollView`'s '**Frame Layout Guide**':

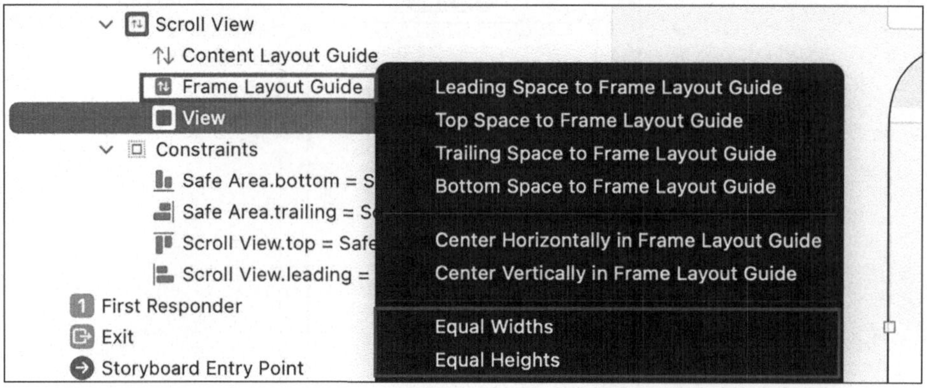

***Figure 3.5**: UIScrollView's frame layout guide*

All these constraints' constants must be set to zero.

The screenshot of the view's constants should also be set to zero:

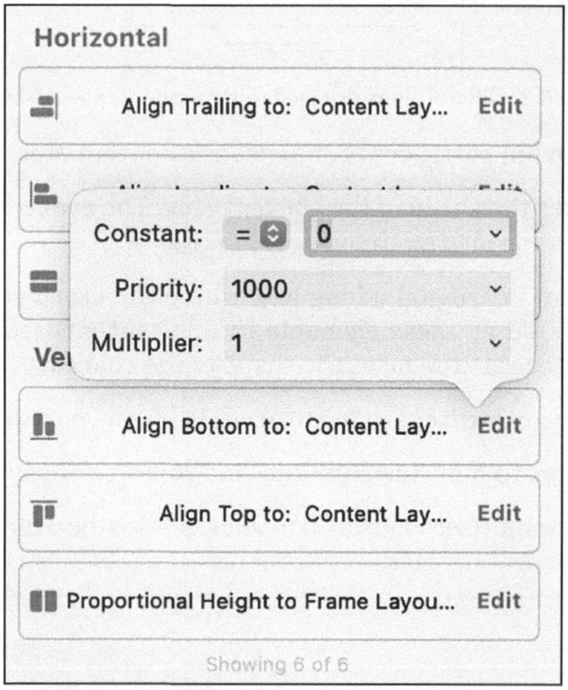

***Figure 3.6**: Setting constraint's constant value to 0*

The content layout guide is used when you add constraints related to the content area of the `UIScrollView`, while the frame layout guide is used when you want to add constraints that involve the frame rectangle of `UIScrollView`.

Now, you can see that the red lines are gone:

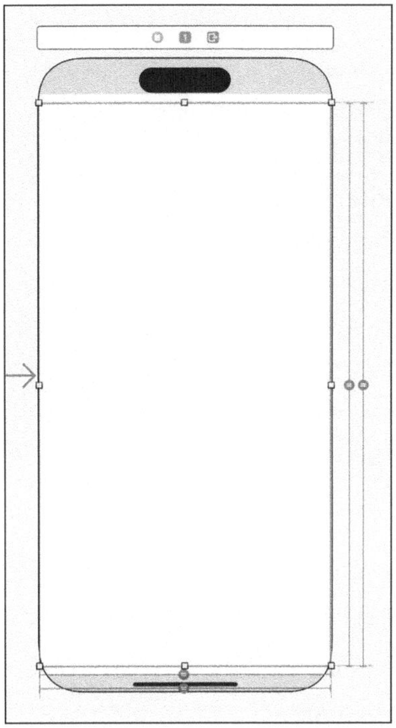

Figure 3.7: *UIScrollView with constraints*

If your view is not dragged as full frame as your screen in your Storyboard, please ensure that the constraint's priority and multiplier are the same as shown in *Figure* 3.8:

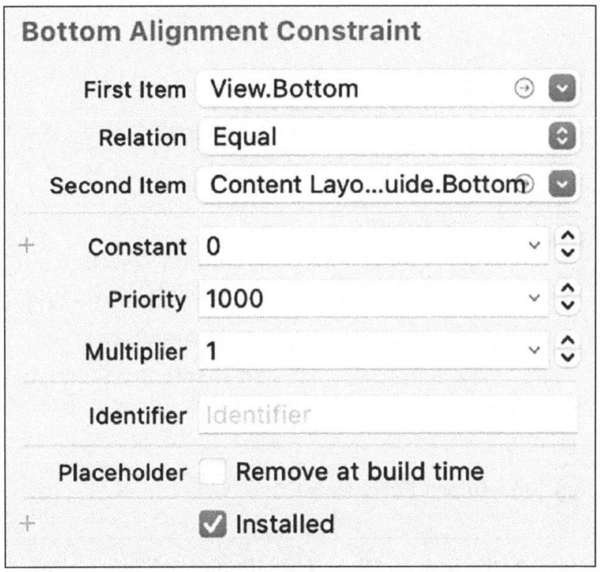

Figure 3.8: *Constraint with priority and multiplier*

For better understanding, let's rename our view inside the `Scroll View` to `Content View`:

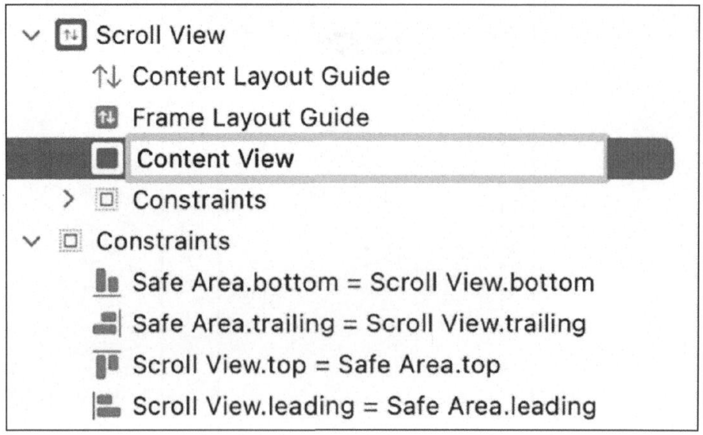

***Figure 3.9**: Renaming View to Content View in the View hierarchy*

Now, let's add an `imageView` and a label to our `Content View`. This is how your View hierarchy should look like, as shown in *Figure 3.10*:

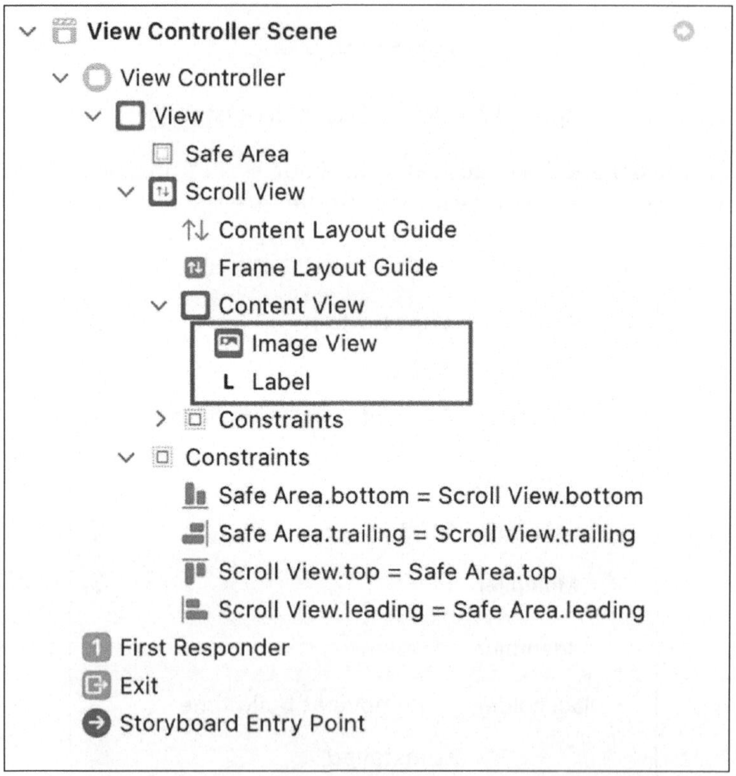

***Figure 3.10**: UIImageView and UILabel in View hierarchy*

Let's add constraints to our `ImageView` as shown in *Figure 3.11*:

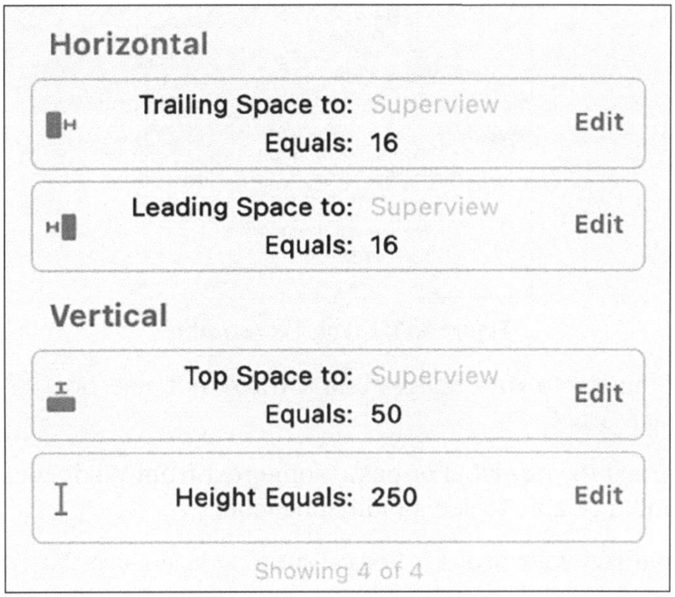

Figure 3.11: *UIImageView constraints*

Here, the label is single line, but what you want is multi-line text. So, before adding constraints to the label, you need to click the label and go to the attribute inspector. In the attribute inspector, you will find the attribute **`'Lines'`**.

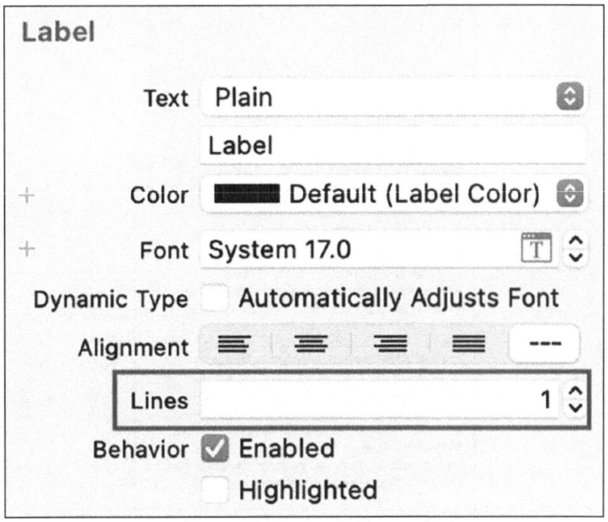

Figure 3.12: *UILabel in the attribute inspector*

Change the **`'Lines'`** from **`'1'`** to **`'0'`**; this will allow the label to become multi-line.

Now, let's add constraints to the label:

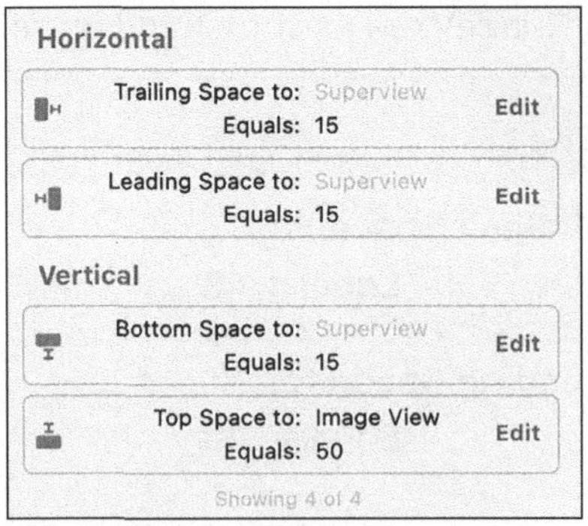

Figure 3.13: *UILabel constraints*

Add your favorite image to your `imageView`. If you're not sure how to do this, refer to *Chapter 1, Getting Started.*

Then, add a long text to your label or paste some text from Wikipedia. Once you have pasted it, you should be able to see a multi-line label.

Now go ahead and run your project. Before running it, ensure that you have enough text so that you can scroll. If you don't have enough text to write, run it on a smaller screen size device.

Figure 3.14: *Screen with UIScrollView, UIImageView, and multi-line label*

You might notice that your text has been cut off, and it's not scrolling. The reason for this is the height of the content view, which is stopping it from expanding as per the label.

To fix this, all you need to do is change the `contentView`'s height constraint's priority to 250:

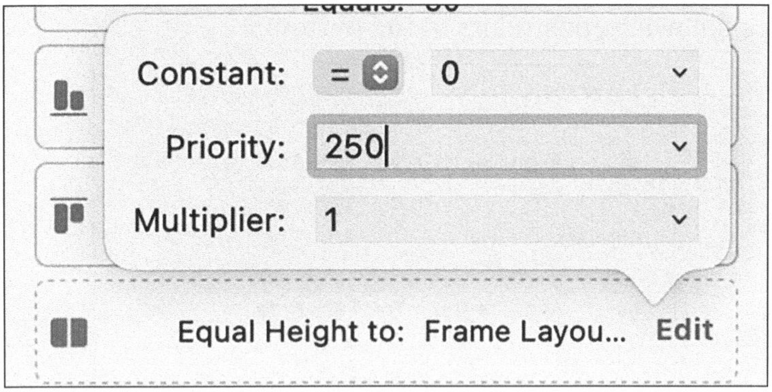

Figure 3.15: *ContentView's height constraint's priority*

The priority of a constraint, as the name implies, says how important a constraint is. By default, it is 1000, which means it is highly important and cannot escape the constraint. In our case, if the `contentView`'s height constraint's priority is 1000, it can't break it as per our text, resulting in the text being cut off. However, if you change the priority, it expands as per the text without cutting it off.

Now, let's run it.

See, now you can scroll as the priority is changed.

UIButton

You know all the apps that you use have buttons, and you use them from time to time. For example, when you want to post a story on Instagram, you click the button with the **'+'** image on it. When you want to transfer money to different accounts, you click the **'send'** button. Sometimes, a button doesn't look like a typical button in some apps. For example, the **'like'** button on Instagram; when you tap on it feels like you are just filling a heart symbol, but it is a typical button with a change of images and some animation.

In programming terms, a button is nothing but a component that executes a bunch of code in response to user interaction.

`UIButton` is a subclass of `UIControl`, which is the parent class of all the controls that perform a specific action in response to the user interaction. Some examples of `UIControls` include `UIButtons`, `UITextfields`, and `UISliders`.

Now, let's get into the implementation:

1. Create a new project in Xcode called **`ButtonExample`**.
2. Go to your **`Main.storyboard`** and add a button to your Default `ViewController`.
3. Add **`'Button'`** to your `ViewController`.
4. Add the following constraints to the button:

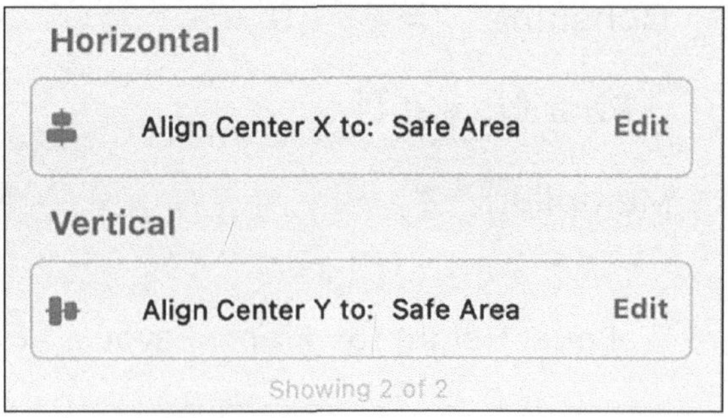

Figure 3.16: *Button's constraints*

5. Add an `IBOutlet`/code reference to the button in the `ViewController`:

```
class ViewController: UIViewController {

    @IBOutlet weak var button: UIButton!

    override func viewDidLoad() {
        super.viewDidLoad()

    }
```

Figure 3.17: *Code reference of UIButton*

Now, we need a specific action to be performed when the user taps the button. To achieve that, we need to add IBAction.

`@IBAction` allows us to connect or trigger certain functions to the Storyboard elements.

To add **`IBAction`**: Right-click the button and then a menu should pop up, as shown in *Figure 3.18*:

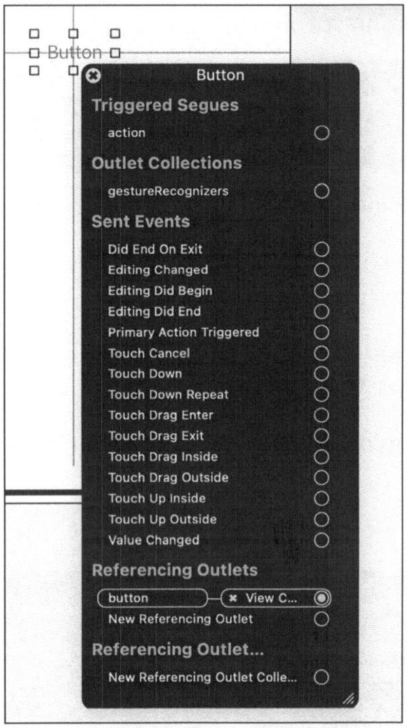

Figure 3.18: *UIButton's events*

Just like `IBOutlet` was added by dragging from the Storyboard to the `ViewController` and releasing it, you need to click the icon beside **"`Touch up Inside`"** in the menu and drag to the `ViewController` and release it. This will give you the pop-up in the `ViewController`, as shown in *Figure* 3.19:

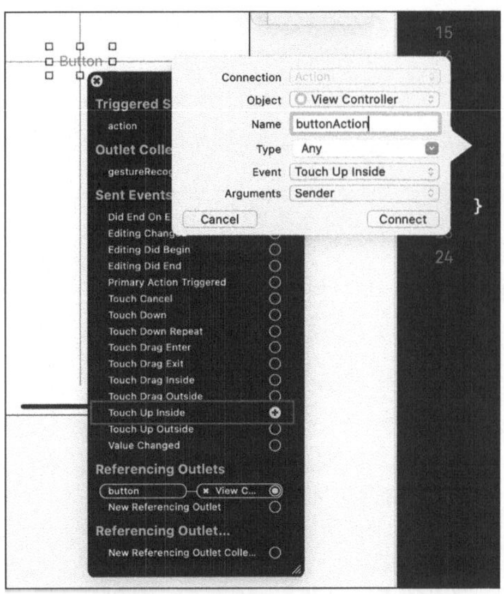

Figure 3.19: *Adding UIButton's action*

This should create the `buttonAction` function, as shown in *Figure* 3.20:

```
@IBAction func buttonAction(_ sender: Any) {
}
```

***Figure* 3.20**: *IBAction of the UIButton*

So whatever task you want to perform when the user taps on the button, that code should be written inside this function.

Here, let's add a simple task: whenever the user taps on the button, let's change our button's background color to **`'lightGray'`**.

As we already got the button's code reference, do the following inside your `IBAction` function:

```
button.backgroundColor = .lightGray
```

```
@IBAction func buttonAction(_ sender: Any) {

    button.backgroundColor = .lightGray
}
```

***Figure* 3.21**: *Changing background color*

Go ahead and run it. When you tap on the button, you should see the change in the button's background color, as shown in *Figure* 3.21:

***Figure* 3.22**: *Screen showing UIButton*

Now, let's do something fun. When the user long taps the button, let's change the button color to a different color. To do this, we need to add a `UILongPressGestureRecognizer` as a `gestureRecognizer` to the button.

A gesture recognizer, as the name implies, recognizes the gestures that can be made. There are different gestures, such as Tap Gesture, Long Press Gesture, Pan Gesture, and more.

Let's get into implementation.

Let's create the function that needs to be called when the user long presses the button and adds **'@objc'** in front of the function declaration, as shown in *Figure* 3.23.

```
@objc func longPressAction() {

}
```

Figure 3.23: *func with @objc*

The reason we are using **@objc** in front of our function is that to interact with Objective-c during runtime. It's like telling the Swift code what to do. The UIKit is Objective-c runtime, so to interact with it, we need to add **@objc**.

Now, let's create the `UILongPressGestureRecognizer` in `ViewDidLoad()` function as follows:

```
let longPressGR = UILongPressGestureRecognizer(target: self, action:
#selector(longPressAction))
longPressGR.minimumPressDuration = 0.5
longPressGR.delaysTouchesBegan = true
```

Add this `longPressGesture` to the button as follows:

```
override func viewDidLoad() {
    super.viewDidLoad()

    let longPressGR = UILongPressGestureRecognizer(target: self, action: #selector(longPressAction))
    longPressGR.minimumPressDuration = 0.5
    longPressGR.delaysTouchesBegan = true

    button.addGestureRecognizer(longPressGR)
}
```

Figure 3.24: *Adding gesture recognizer to button*

Here, we are setting the `minimumPressDuration` as 0.5 secs, which means the user has to press and hold the button for at least 0.5 secs for our button to call the `longPressAction`.

Setting `delaysTouchesbegan` to truc allows us to dclay scnding touchcs in the beginning phase.

Now, let's add some code to our `longPressAction` function:

```
@objc func longPressAction() {
      button.backgroundColor = .red
 }
```

All we did was change the background color to red, this happens only when the user long-presses the button.

Now, go ahead and long-press the button; you should be able to see the button's background color turning red.

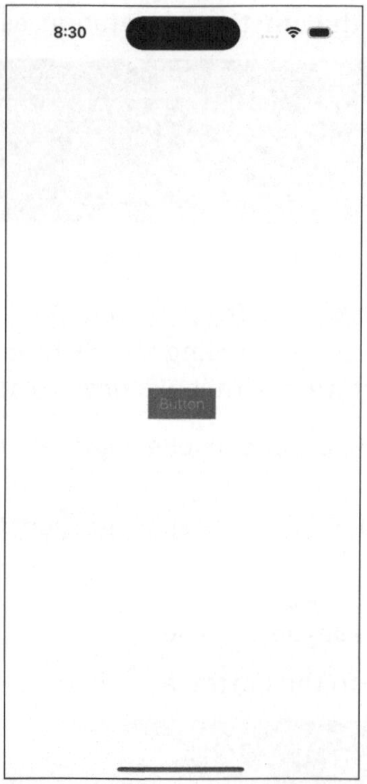

Figure 3.25: *Screen showing button*

UITextField

Nowadays, we can open bank accounts and book flight details through apps. While doing these things, you might have noticed that there are forms you need to fill, which have editable text areas, such as for collecting your name and other details. The text area that you see in those apps where you enter your name and fill in your data is `UITextField`. Keep in mind that `UITextField` is specifically one-line data only.

Similar to how you used `UITableViewDelegate` and `UITableViewDataSource` functions in the previous chapter, you will be using these `UITextFieldDelegate` protocol functions, this time for text validation, for controlling the editing process, and for custom and specific interactions with the keyboard.

Let's jump into implementation and learn more about these delegate methods as well.

1. Let's create a project called `TextFieldExample`, and `initialViewController`/ default `ViewController`, and drag the `TextField` element.

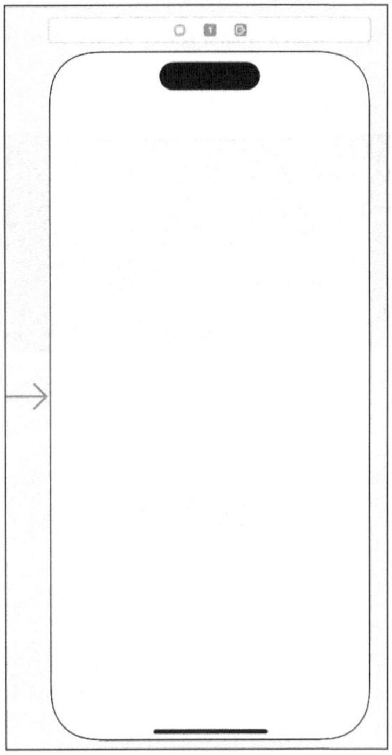

***Figure 3.26**: ViewController with UITextField*

2. Now, add the following constraints to `UITextField` to Safe Area:

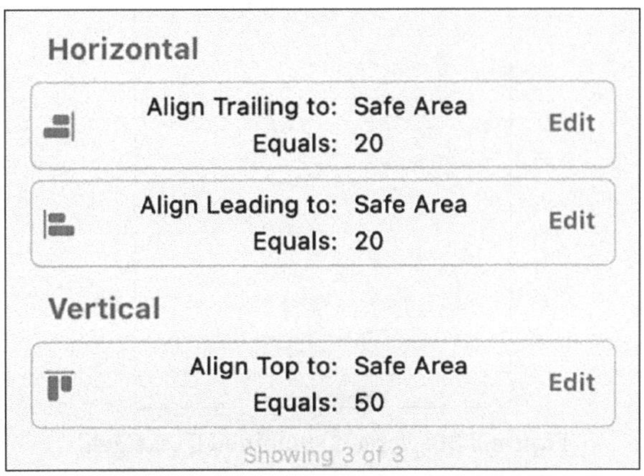

***Figure 3.27**: UITextField's constraints*

If not sure how to add constraints, please refer to *Chapter 1, Getting Started.*

3. Now, let's add a code reference to our `textField` in `ViewController`.
4. Next, set `UITextFieldDelegate` to your `ViewController`:

```
class ViewController: UIViewController, UITextFieldDelegate {
```

***Figure 3.28**: Assigning UITextFieldDelegate to ViewController*

5. Set your `textField`'s delegate:

```
override func viewDidLoad() {
    super.viewDidLoad()

    textField.delegate = self

}
```

***Figure 3.29**: Setting textField's delegate*

Now go ahead and run it:

***Figure 3.30**: Screen showing UITextField*

You can see your screen with text field. When you tap on it, the cursor blinks, and you can type from your computer keyboard. However, if you want the keyboard to appear on the simulator, type '*Command + k*'.

Figure 3.31: *Screen with UITextField with Keyboard*

Imagine you have entered a page with a form, and you want the keyboard to appear for the first `textField`. Add the following piece of code to the `ViewDidLoad` function after assigning the `textField` delegate:

```
textField.becomeFirstResponder()
```

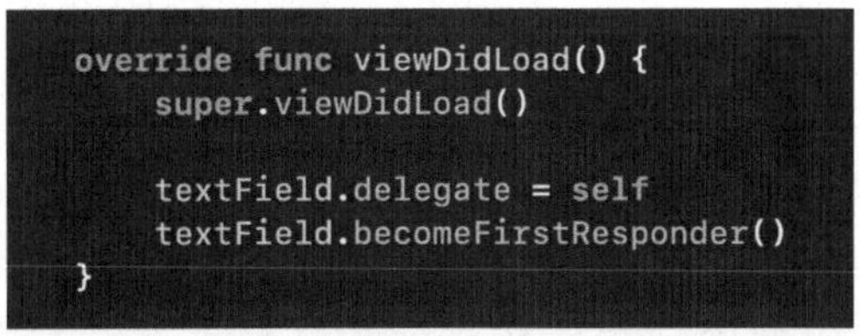

```
override func viewDidLoad() {
    super.viewDidLoad()

    textField.delegate = self
    textField.becomeFirstResponder()
}
```

Figure 3.32: *Calling becomeFirstResponder*

What we are doing here is, immediately after the view is loaded, we are telling our `textField` to be the first responder.

Usually, when a user clicks a certain object, it becomes the first responder, which is the first object to receive an action message or event in a responder chain. So here, we are setting the `textField` as the first responder so that the user doesn't have to touch the `textField` to get the keyboard, but it appears as soon as the screen is loaded.

Go ahead and run your project. You should be able to see the `textField` and keyboard soon after the screen appears.

Now, let's implement some delegate methods, and we can also save the user-entered data.

We need a variable to save our `textField` data. Let's say we are storing the user's name in the `textField`:

```
var username: String?
```

You might wonder what the `var username: String?` with a question mark at the end of the variable means.

`?` at the end of the variable means that we are suggesting the value of this variable can be nil sometimes.

`!` at the end of the variable or an object or an `IBoutlet` means it can't be nil anytime.

`textField(_:shouldChangeCharactersIn:replacementString:)`

This delegate function gets called whenever the user types a single character into `textField`:

```
func textField(_ textField: UITextField, shouldChangeCharactersIn range: NSRange, replacementString string: String) -> Bool {
return true
}
```

This asks the delegate if it must change the specific text or not. Here, the replacing string would be the newly entered character, and the range would be the range of characters of the string that have to be replaced.

Keep in mind that when the user types a character, this method gets called first and then it gets displayed in the `textField`. If you want to try it, put a debug pointer in the preceding function at the return true line. Type a character in the simulator, and you will see the debug pointer appear at this line. You will not see the typed character in the simulator; when you let go of the debug pointer, you will see the character appearing in the `textField`. Now, let's continue saving the text from this `textField` by adding the following code inside our delegate function:

```
func textField(_ textField: UITextField, shouldChangeCharactersIn range: NSRange, replacementString string: String) -> Bool {

    let textFieldText = (textField.text ?? "") as NSString
    let wholeString = textFieldText.replacingCharacters(in: range, with: string)
    print(wholeString)

    return true
}
```

Figure 3.33: *Getting the updated string in shouldChangeCharactersIn function*

So, what we are doing in the preceding code is getting the `textField` in the first line and typecasting it as NSString. Remember that when you get `textField.text`, you will get the characters that are already visible in the `textfield`. For example, if the user wants to type the word **`'cat'`** and previously typed **`'ca'`**, and now the user typed 't', this function gets triggered. When you print `textField.text`, you will be able to see only **`'ca'`**.

If you want, you can add `print(textField.text)` on top of those three lines inside the delegate function for better understanding.

In this line, let `wholeString = textFieldText.replacingCharacters(in: range, with: string)`, we are actually taking the text from the `textfield` and adding the character that the user has typed at the end.

`replacingCharacters(in:with:)`

This function replaces the string with the given string in the provided range. To better understand this, put a debug pointer in the preceding line and check on the range.

In this way, we will get the whole string that the user has typed, and we can save it in our app.

Now, if you print the `wholeString`, you will get the whole string. You can even assign the `wholeString` to your username variable.

```
func textField(_ textField: UITextField, shouldChangeCharactersIn range: NSRange, replacementString string: String) -> Bool {

    let textFieldText = (textField.text ?? "") as NSString
    let wholeString = textFieldText.replacingCharacters(in: range, with: string)
    print(wholeString)

    username = wholeString

    return true
}
```

***Figure 3.34**: Assigning an updated string to Username*

Now you have the `textField` and the keyboard, but there may be occasions where you want to dismiss the keyboard. There were cases where some functionalities of the apps got disabled because the keyboard was not dismissed.

In this case, we can dismiss our keyboard when the user clicks **'return'**.

When the user clicks return on the keyboard, the following delegate functions get called:

```
func textFieldShouldReturn(_ textField: UITextField) -> Bool {
return true
}
```

So, when we need to show the keyboard, we use `becomeFirstResponder()`. To dismiss the keyboard, we need to use `resignFirstResponder()`. It's that easy.

```
func textFieldShouldReturn(_ textField: UITextField) -> Bool {
textField.resignFirstResponder()
return true
 }
```

Here, the first responder is `textField`, and we are telling it to resign its status as the first responder, which will cause the keyboard to be dismissed.

Now, go ahead and run it. Enter something in the `textField` and click **`return`**; you will see the keyboard being dismissed.

Let's make it a little more complicated by adding one more `textField` to our screen.

To differentiate between `textFields` on our screen, let's add labels in front of them.

To add the label in front of our `textField`, remove the **"`Align leading to: Safe Area`"** constraint:

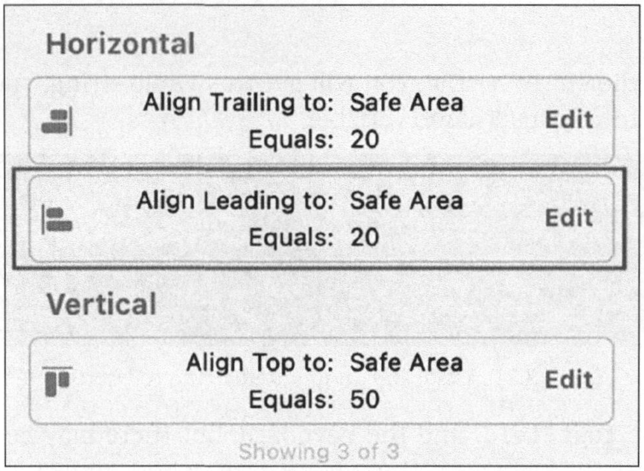

***Figure 3.35**: Showing the constraint to be removed*

Following are the two labels **'`name and email`'** that are added, along with an additional `textField`. To avoid confusion, I have named the `textFields` in the view hierarchy of the Storyboard:

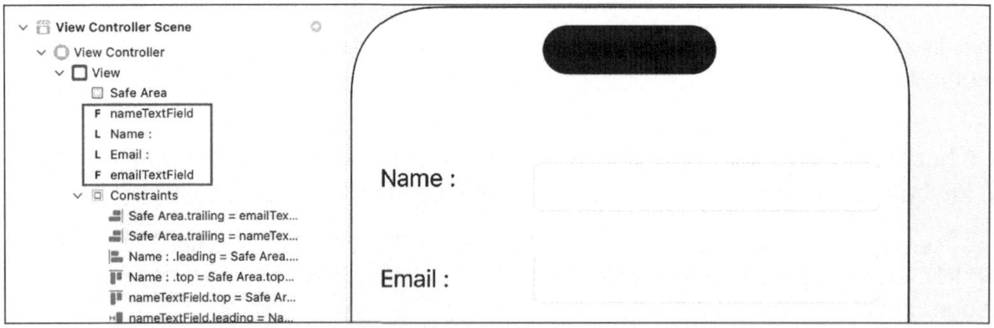

***Figure 3.36:** View hierarchy with added Name UILabel, Name UITextfield, Email UILabel, and email UITextField*

Please add the following constraints for `Name UILabel`:

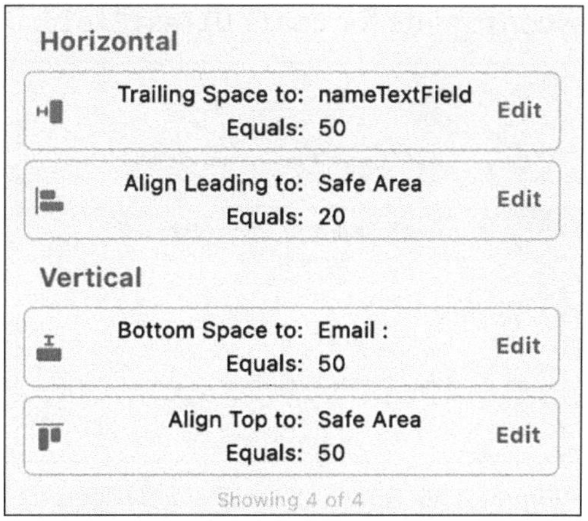

Figure 3.37: *Name UILabel constraints*

Please add the following constraints for `Name UITextField:`

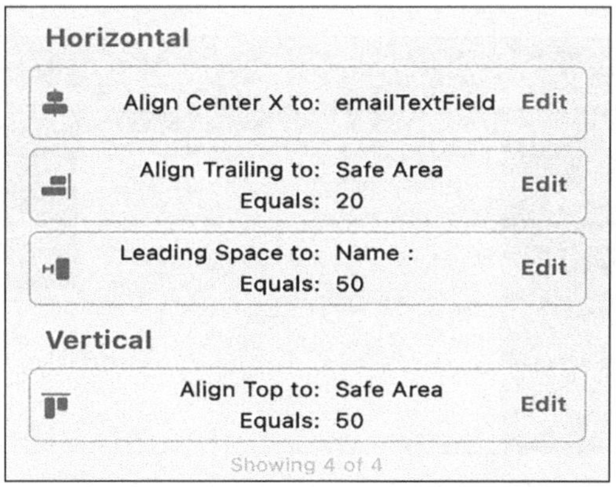

Figure 3.38: *Name UITextField constraints*

Please add the following constraints for `Email UILabel`:

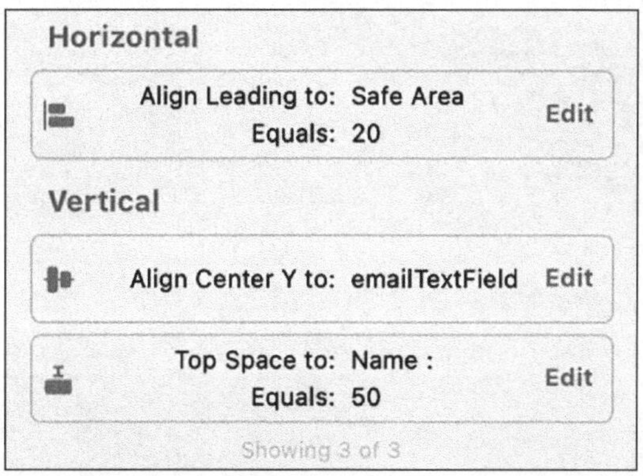

Figure 3.39: *Email UILabel constraints*

Please add the following constraints for `Email UITextField`:

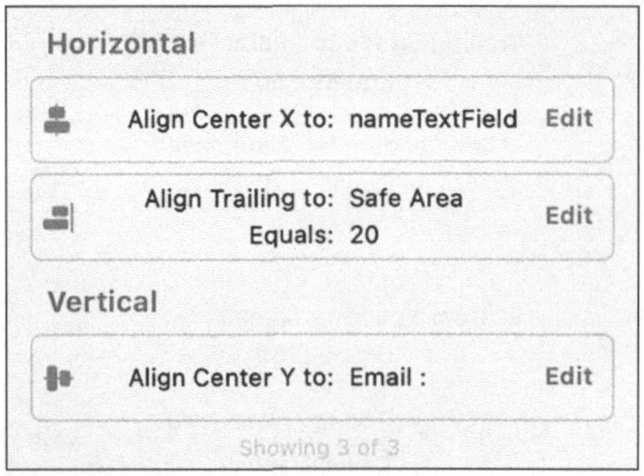

Figure 3.40: *Email UITextField constraints*

To avoid confusion in our code, let's rename our first `textField` in `ViewController` to **'nameTextField'**. To rename, right-click the variable and then click **`refactor`** -> **`rename`**, as shown in *Figure* 3.40.

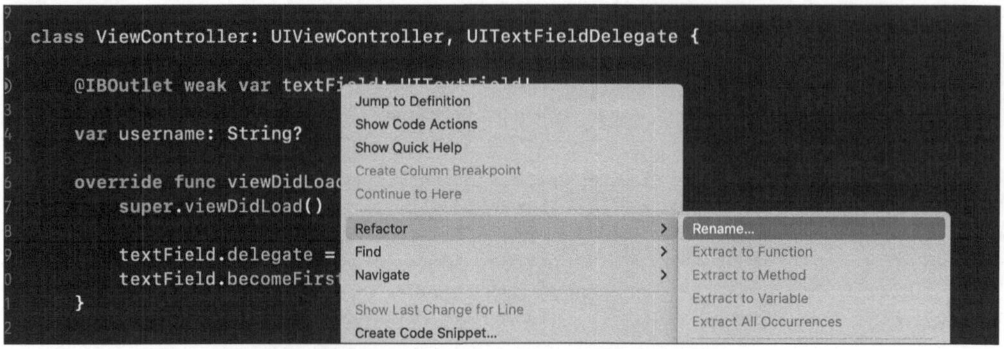

Figure 3.41: *Renaming UITextField*

Xcode shows us all the references of our variable as shown in *Figure* 3.41:

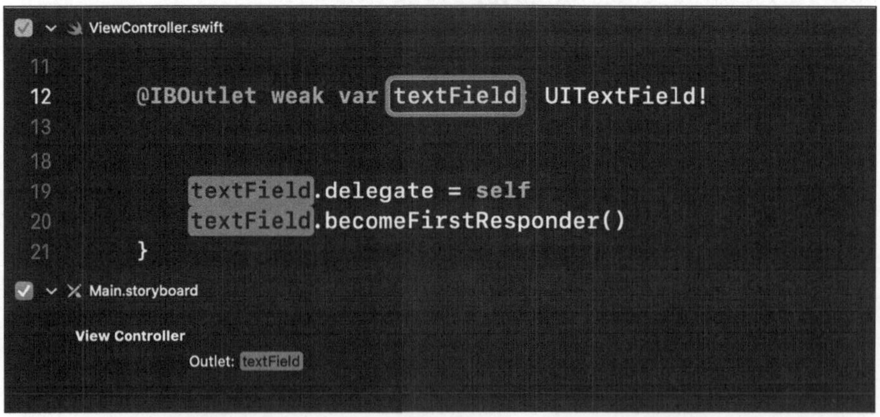

Figure 3.42: *Renaming UITextField code reference*

It will be renamed as `nameTextField` as shown in *Figure 3.42*:

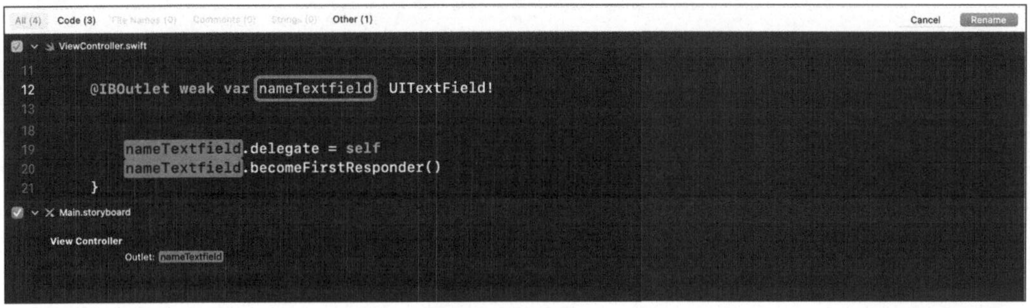

***Figure 3.43**: Renamed UITextField*

You can see that while typing its references also change. After typing the desired name, click the **'rename'** button at the top right.

Now, add the code reference of another `UITextField` as well, and let's call it `emailTextField`. Add another variable to save the user's email address too:

```
class ViewController: UIViewController, UITextFieldDelegate {

    @IBOutlet weak var nameTextfield: UITextField!
    @IBOutlet weak var emailTextField: UITextField!

    var username: String?
    var email: String?
```

***Figure 3.44**: Code reference to the emailTextField*

Assign the `emailTextField`'s delegate as well, as follows:

```
emailTextField.delegate = self
```

Now, when you click `emailTextField`, we want the keyboard to be compatible with an email address. To do that, all you need is assign the `keyboardType` to `emailAddress` as follows:

```
emailTextField.keyboardType = .emailAddress
```

Go ahead and run it; tap on the second `textField`, which is the `emailTextfield`.

As you can see, the keyboard is a little different; special characters, such as **'@'** and **'.'** appear on the keyboard, which are the most used characters in email.

For example, if you want your user to enter an OTP, you can change the `keyboardType` to `numberPad`, and then the keyboard will only have numbers. To understand it better, let us change the keyboard type `emailTextField` or `nameTextField` and then change it back to its original setting.

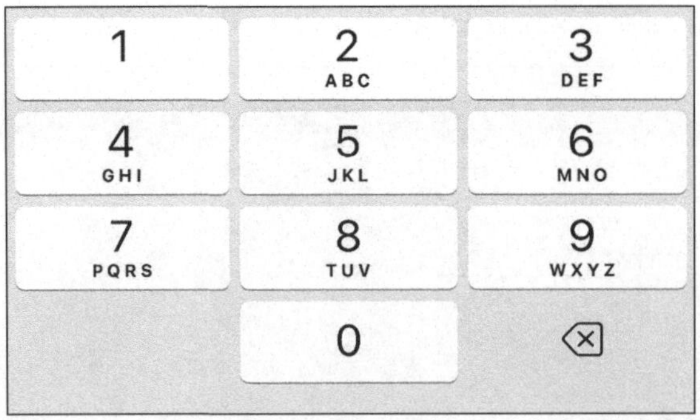

***Figure 3.45**: Number pad*

Now, let's see how to store multiple **`textField`**'s texts in our app in the `textField(_:shouldChangeCharactersIn:replacementString:)` delegate function.

The problem here is that no matter which `textField` is, this function gets triggered. If we execute the following code and if the user types in the `emailTextField`, then our variable **'`username`'** will have an email address rather than the name.

```
func textField(_ textField: UITextField, shouldChangeCharactersIn range: NSRange, replacementString string: String) -> Bool {

    let textFieldText = (textField.text ?? "") as NSString
    let wholeString = textFieldText.replacingCharacters(in: range, with: string)
    print(wholeString)

    username = wholeString

    return true
}
```

***Figure 3.46**: Showing the wrong part of the code*

To fix the problem, we need to do the validation of **`textFields`** and then assign the text to our username and email variables, as follows:

```
func textField(_ textField: UITextField, shouldChangeCharactersIn range: NSRange, replacementString string: String) -> Bool {

    let textFieldText = (textField.text ?? "") as NSString
    let wholeString = textFieldText.replacingCharacters(in: range, with: string)
    print(wholeString)

    if textField == nameTextfield {
        username = wholeString
    } else if textField == emailTextField {
        email = wholeString
    }

    return true
}
```

***Figure 3.47**: Code showing the validations between UITextFields*

`UITextView`

`UITextView` is also an editable text area but with the bonus of multi-line text and also scrollable. You will see the `UITextView` in forms that ask for feedback or any comments.

Let's jump into implementation. Instead of creating a new project, let's use the project created for `UITextFields`.

1. Open the `TextFieldExample` project, and let's add `UITextView` to the same Storyboard and the same `ViewController` with the two textfields. Add the label **`'About me'`** in front of it.

   It should look like the following:

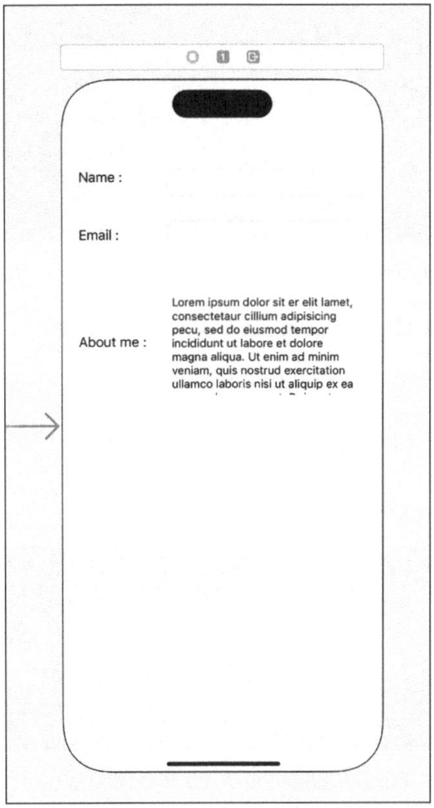

***Figure 3.48:** UITextView added to ViewController in Storyboard*

2. Create an `IBOutlet` for the `textView` in your `ViewController`. One more thing we need to do here is to assign `ViewController` as `UITextViewDelegate` and then assign it to `textView` as delegate:

```
class ViewController: UIViewController, UITextFieldDelegate, UITextViewDelegate {

    @IBOutlet weak var nameTextfield: UITextField!
    @IBOutlet weak var emailTextField: UITextField!

    @IBOutlet weak var aboutMeTextView: UITextView!

    var username: String?
    var email: String?

    override func viewDidLoad() {
        super.viewDidLoad()

        nameTextfield.delegate = self
        emailTextField.delegate = self

        aboutMeTextView.delegate = self

        emailTextField.keyboardType = .numberPad

        nameTextfield.becomeFirstResponder()
    }
```

***Figure* 3.49:** *Setting UITextView's delegate*

3. Please ensure that the default text of `UITextView` is deleted.
4. Implement `UITextViewDelegate` function `textViewDidChange(_:)`,

   ```
   func textViewDidChange(_ textView: UITextView) {
   }
   ```

5. Now print the `textView`'s text as follows:

```
func textViewDidChange(_ textView: UITextView) {
    print(textView.text)        ⚠ Coercion of impli
}
```

***Figure* 3.50:** *Printing textView's text*

6. The yellow lines shown here are just warnings that `textView.text` could return nil, and in this case, it is asking what should I return.

   You can fix it as follows:

   ```
   print(textView.text ?? "there is no text")
   ```

   `??` – This operator is used for providing a default value. If the value of optional is nil, it is called Nil-Coalescing Operator.

7. Now, go ahead and run it. You won't see any trace of `textView` as we did not give any borders or background color to differentiate. However, go ahead and tap on it, and you will see the cursor blinking as shown in *Figure* 3.51:

***Figure 3.51**: Screen with UITextView*

8. Go ahead and type in the `textView`, you will see the exact letters typed by the print statement given inside our `textViewDidChange(_:)` function in the Xcode console.

9. Let's add the border to our textView so that we can differentiate it from the screen.

   Add the following code in `viewDidLoad()`:

   ```
   aboutMeTextView.layer.borderWidth = 0.2
   aboutMeTextView.layer.borderColor = UIColor.gray.cgColor
   aboutMeTextView.layer.cornerRadius = 5.0
   ```

   The Layer here is the Core Animation layer, which is not only for `UITextView` but also for `UIViews` and many other `UIElements` when you want to add a border. You can use this Core Animation Layer for rendering.

   So here, we are adding the rounded corners, the same as our preceding textfields, by giving `cornerRadius`. We are also giving the same `borderWidth` the same as for `textfields`. Additionally, we need to provide the border color because if not, the `borderWidth`, the border's corner radius, and the border itself will not be visible.

10. Now, go ahead and run it.

***Figure 3.52:** Screen with UITextView with border*

UIStackView

`UIStackView` is an amazing interface for laying out multiple views vertically or horizontally.

When you add views to the `UIStackview`, it magically aligns the views as per the preferences specified, and you don't have to add constraints to the views, which is the actual magic.

Now, let's jump into implementation.

1. Open Xcode and create a new project called `StackViewExample`. Go to the **`Main.storyboard`** and add the vertical `stackView` to your `ViewController` in the Storyboard.

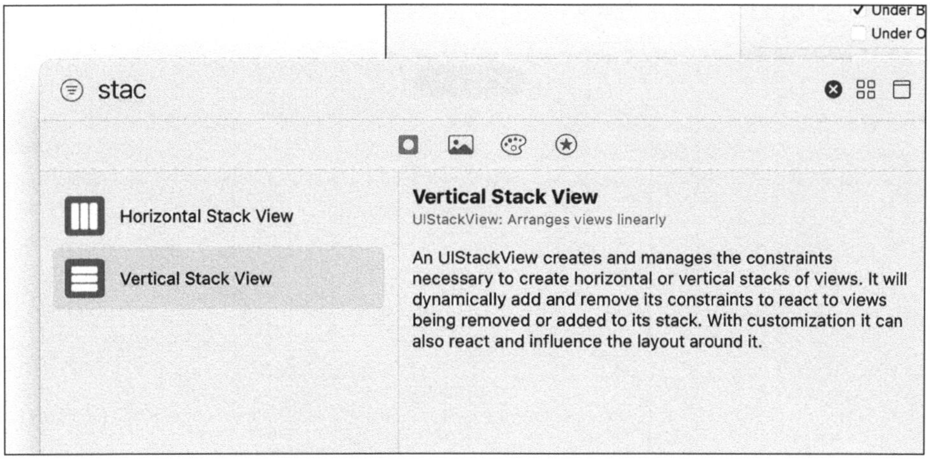

Figure 3.53: *Types of UIStackViews*

You can add a horizontal `stackView` if you want to lay out the views horizontally, but for this example, let's add a vertical `stackview`.

2. Go ahead and add the following constraints to your `stackView`:

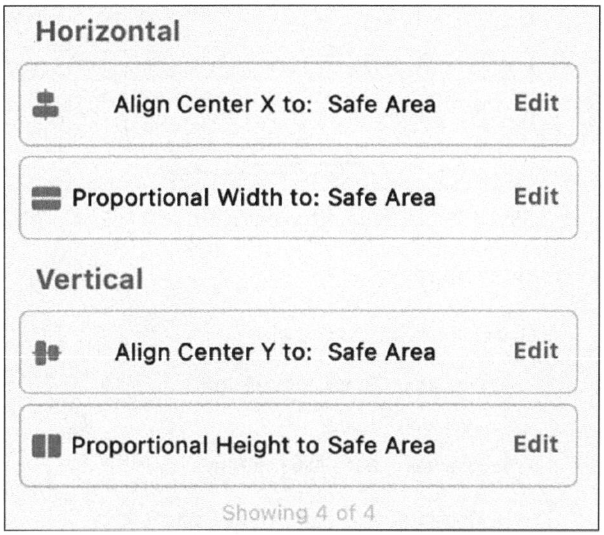

Figure 3.54: *UIStackView Constraints*

3. If you look at the constraints, you might notice that the same height and width are given as the safe area, but the `ViewController` looks as follows:

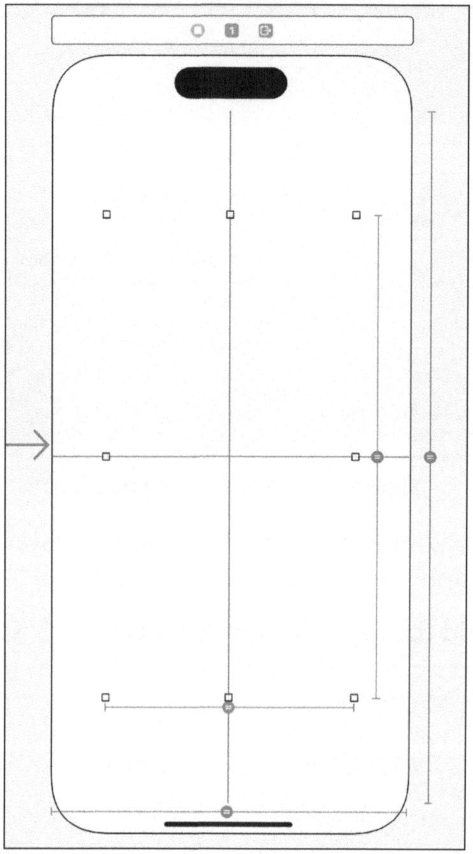

Figure 3.55: *UIStackView with constraints on ViewController*

This is the trick that made it happen.

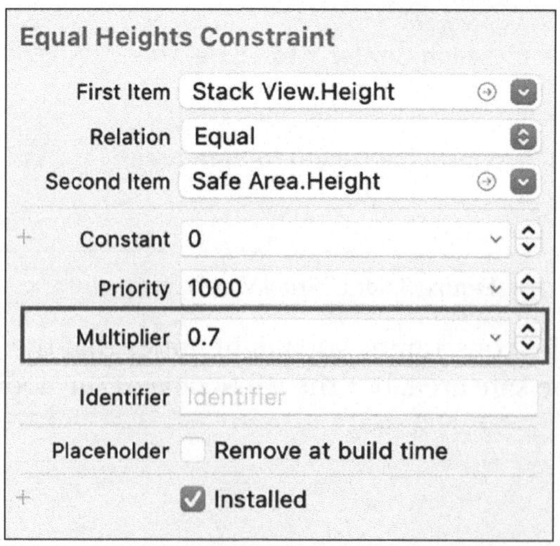

Figure 3.56*: UIStackView height constraint with updated Multiplier*

The `StackView`'s height is the same as the Safe Area, but the multiplier is 0.7. If the multiplier were 1, we would get the same height. Now, as we have given it 0.7, it is multiplying whatever the height of the Safe Area is to 0.7 and setting that as the height of `StackView`. For example, if the height of the safe area is, let's say 100, then 100*0.7 = 70 will be the height of `stackView`'s. There are a lot of ways to manipulate constraints, which you will learn as we go forward.

The same can be done with width constraint too.

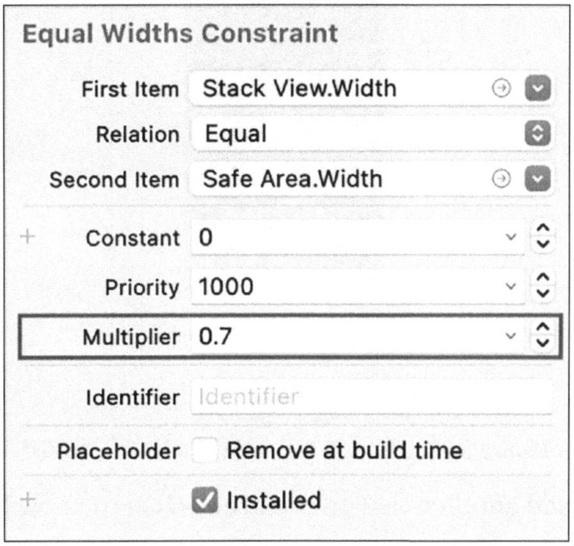

***Figure 3.57**: UIStackView width constraint with updated Multiplier*

Add a view into the `stackView`, and you must see the view spread across the `stackView`. To see, add a background color to the view in the attribute inspector.

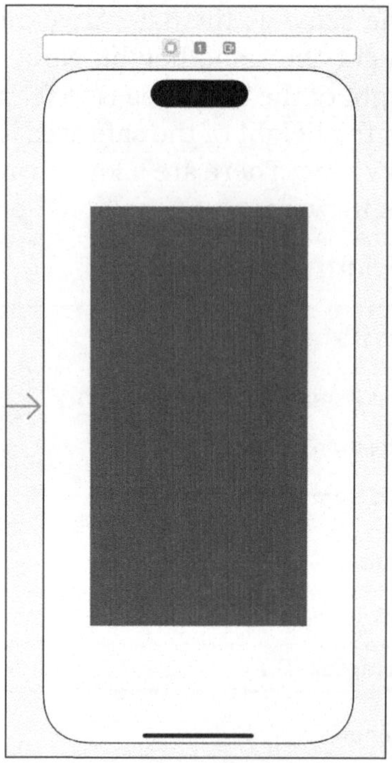

Figure 3.58: *UIStackView with single view added*

Now, go ahead and add another view to the `stackView`, to know how these views are laid out.

When you have added the second view to the `StackView`, it might have been added as a `subView` to the first view we have added. You can fix this by rearranging in the View hierarchy:

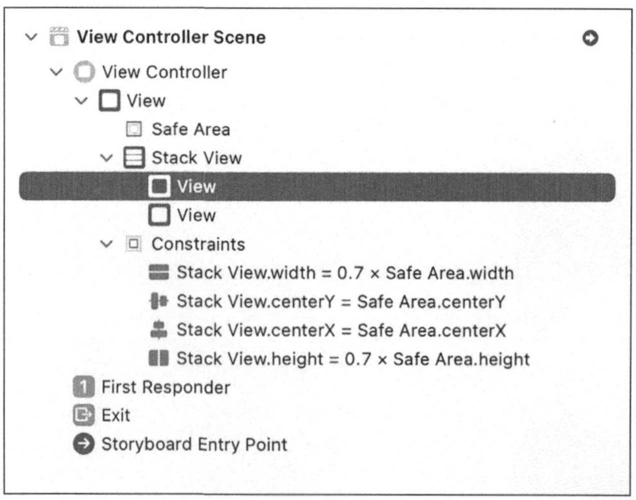

Figure 3.59*: Multiple Views inside the UIStackView in View Hierarchy*

You might see that the view's constraints are complaining about height constraints. Before fixing this, you must understand about `stackView`'s distribution.

If you click the `stackView` in the view hierarchy and attribute inspector, you will see the following:

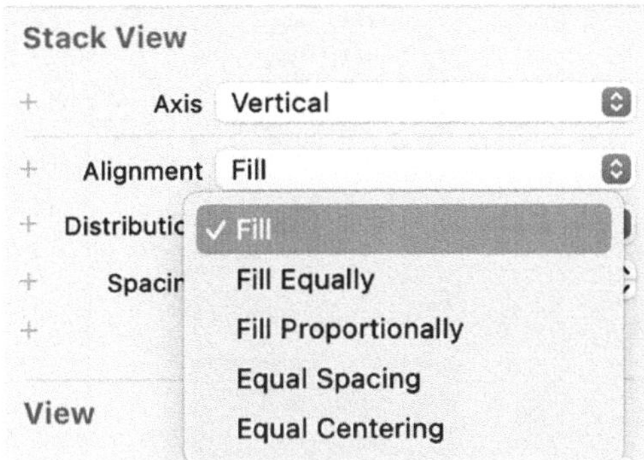

Figure 3.60: *Changing UIStackView's distribution in the attribute inspector*

The default for distribution is `.fill`, which means it fills the `UIStackView` with the views that you provided. However, if that's the case, why are we getting complaints about the view's height? It is because it does not know how to fill it or in what way to fill it. We will fix this later.

However, for now, let's change the distribution to **`Fill Equally`**:

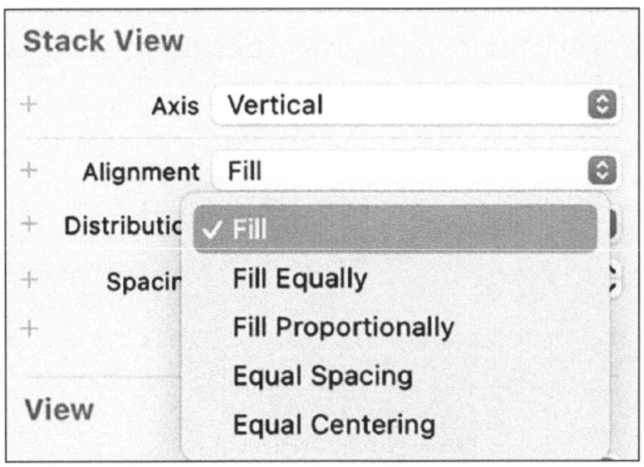

Figure 3.61: *Changing UIStackView's distribution to 'Fill Equally'*

After the change, you might see that the constraint complaints are gone, and the views are filled equally.

What is happening here is when you set the distribution to **`'fill equally'`**, the `stackView` also gives equal heights to the views, that's the reason the complaints are gone. Now go ahead and add another view to the `stackView`, and don't forget to add the background color.

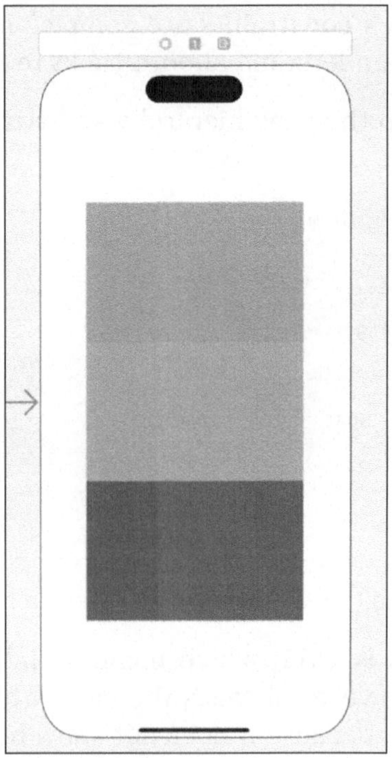

***Figure 3.62**: UIStackView with added additional Views*

Here, the height of the `stackView` is divided between its three `subViews` equally.

Now, let's change the distribution to Fill proportionally to see what it does. Change the top view's height to 100 in the Size Inspector:

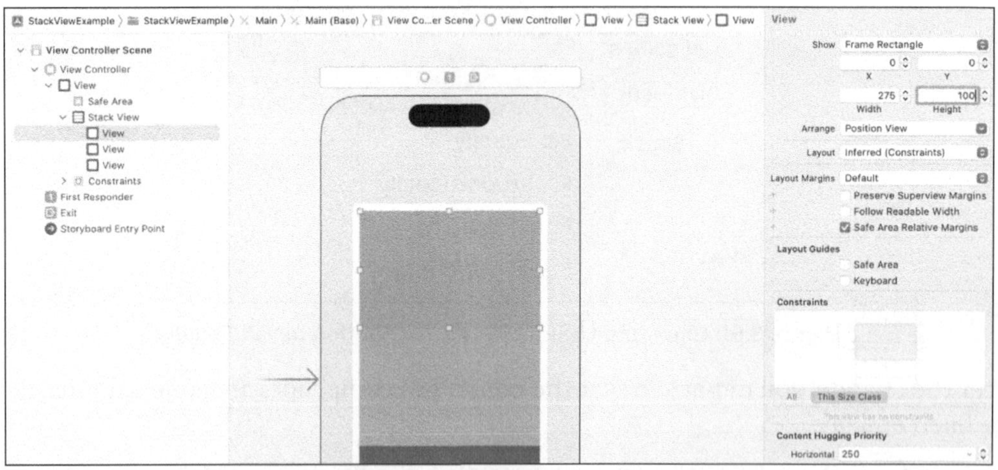

***Figure 3.63:** Changing the SubView's height*

You can see that after doing this, the other view's height changed/increased proportionally, filling the remaining height/space of the `UIStackView`.

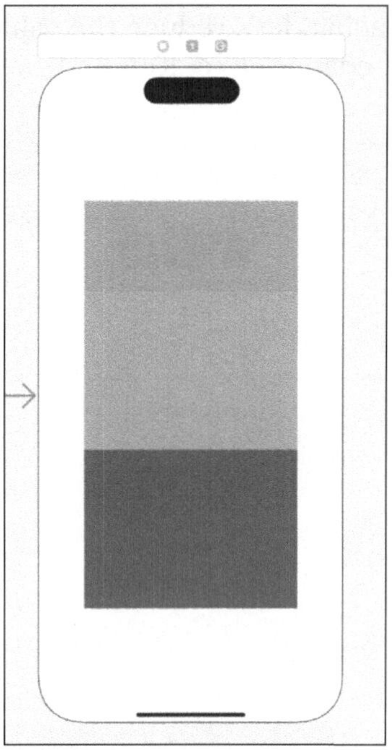

Figure 3.64: *UIStackView proportionally filling the Views*

Go ahead and change the height of the third view, and you will see the other view getting adjusted proportionally.

Let's change the distribution to Equal Spacing. For this, you need to provide the height constraint for these three views.

No need to change any constraint; just add the constraint.

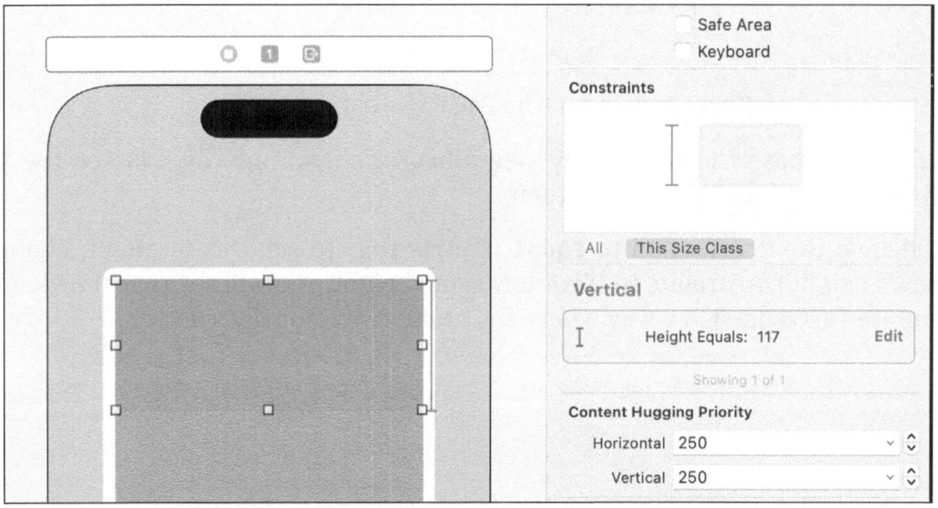

Figure 3.65: *Providing Height Constraint to the Views*

Now, as you can't see any spacing, let's reduce the value of view 1. In the preceding example, it was 117 and let's change it to 100, and now you will see white spaces appearing between views:

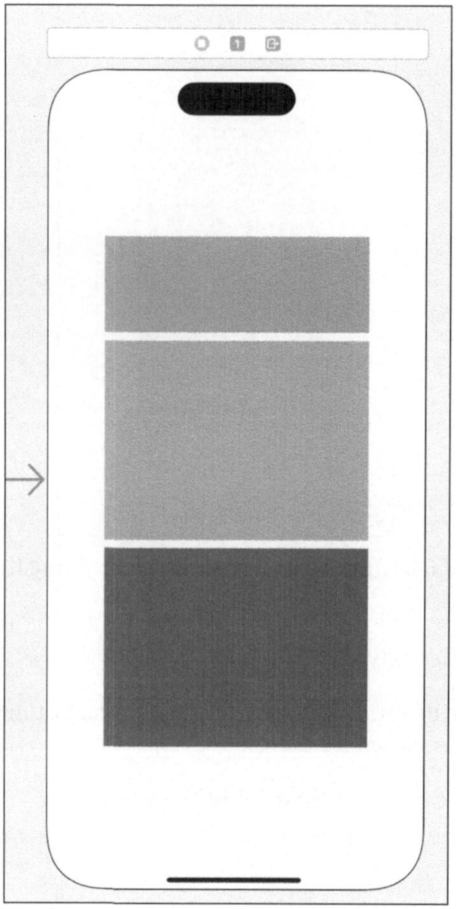

***Figure 3.66**: Views with Equal spacing between them*

When you decrease the size of any view's height constraint you will see the views adjust with equal spacing between them.

Now, change the distribution to **`Equal Centering`**. To see this in effect, change all the view's height constraints to 117 or any same height, you will see that the views and spacing are rearranged in a way where the centers are equally spaced.

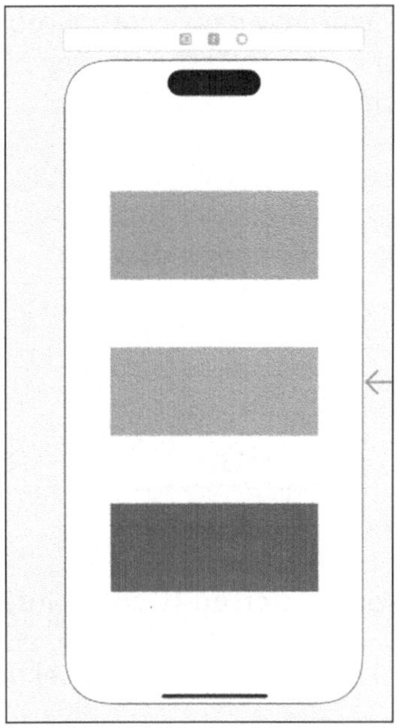

Figure 3.67: *Views with Equal Centering*

Now, let's get back to fill. For fill, the problem we face is that the `StackView` does not know how to fill it. To fix this, we need to provide the height for the first two views, and you will see the third view filling the remaining space.

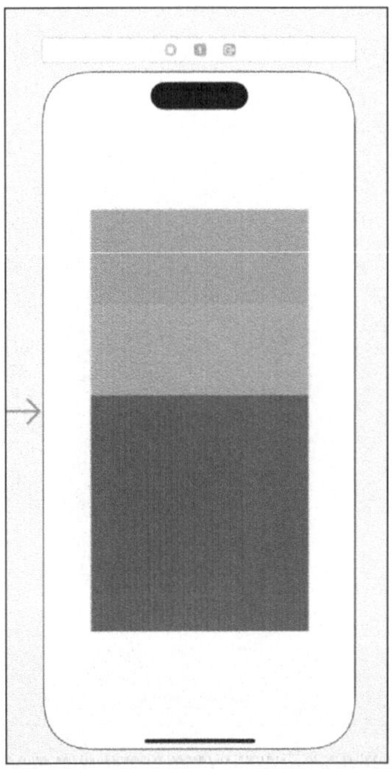

Figure 3.68: *UIStackView with fill distribution*

`StackView`'s alignment is an easy concept compared to distribution. The default alignment is Fill, which fills the `stackView` with views horizontally. To see this, try reducing the width of all the views in the Size Inspector.

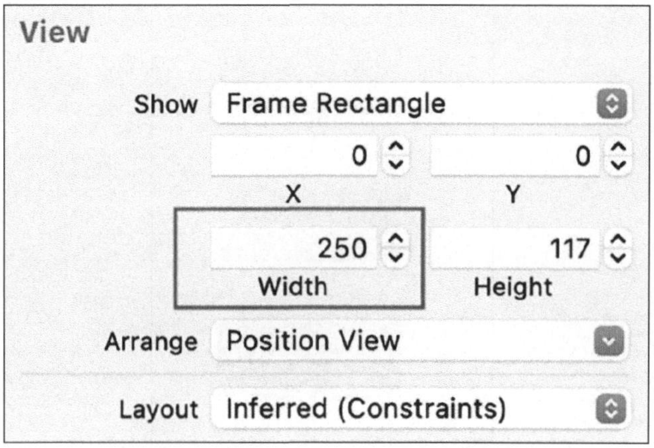

Figure 3.69: *Changing the width of the View*

The width won't change as the alignment is set to **`'fill'`**. You will see that the widths have been, and here, the widths are filling the horizontal space that is available.

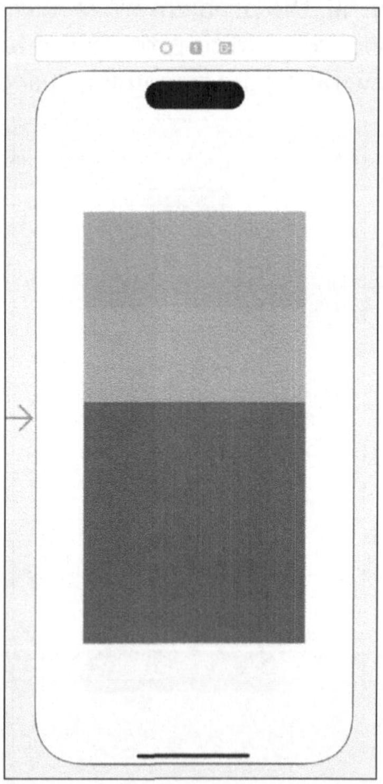

Figure 3.70: *UIStackView with fill alignment*

Now, change the alignment to **'Leading'**, decrease the widths of the first two views, and leave the third one with the same height. You should be able to see something like this:

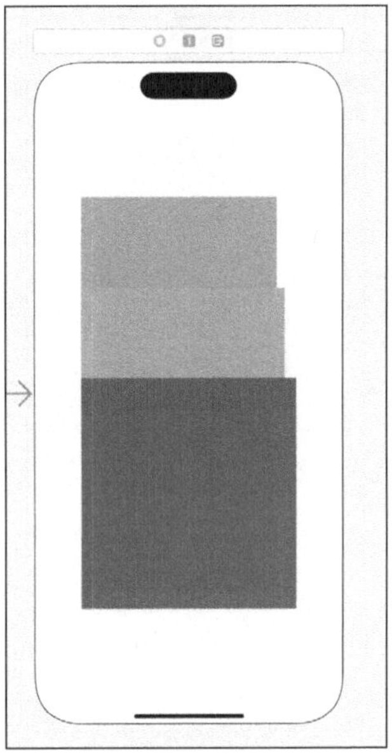

Figure 3.71: *UIStackView with Leading alignment*

Change the alignment to **'center'**, and you should be able to see that the views are aligned in the center.

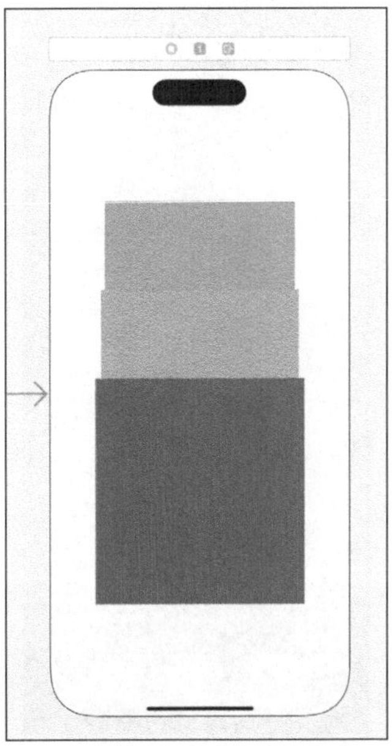

Figure 3.72: *UIStackView with center alignment*

Now, change the alignment to **'trailing'**, and you should be able to see something like this, where views are aligned to the right:

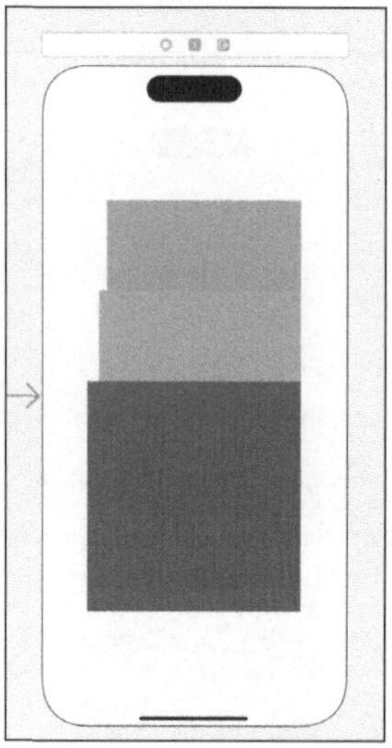

Figure 3.73: *UIStackView with Trailing alignment*

UIPageControl

You can find the page control when you are scrolling through app menu pages on your iPhone.

Figure 3.74: *Screen with UIPageControl*

`UIPageControl` is that horizontal series of dots that you saw in the preceding screenshot, which can show us how many pages are there before and after the current page.

Let's jump into implementation straight away.

1. Create a project called `PageControlExample`. Go to your **`Main.storyboard`** and add a `ScrollView` to your default `ViewController`.

   Add the following constraints:

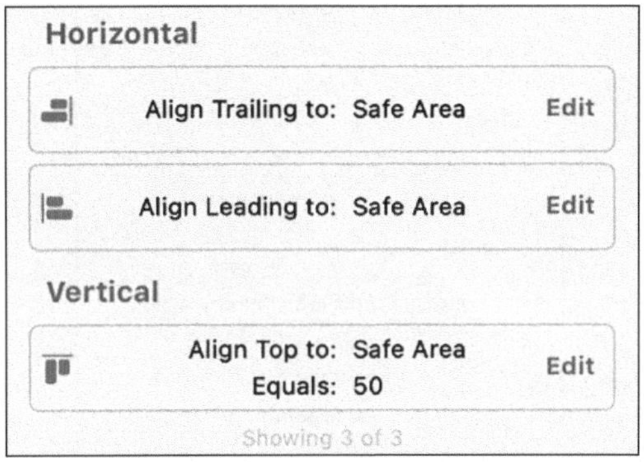

Figure 3.75: *UIScrollView Constraints*

2. If the `ScrollView` is not updating the frames as per the constraints given(which happens sometimes), you can drag it by yourself to make sense. It should look like something as follows:

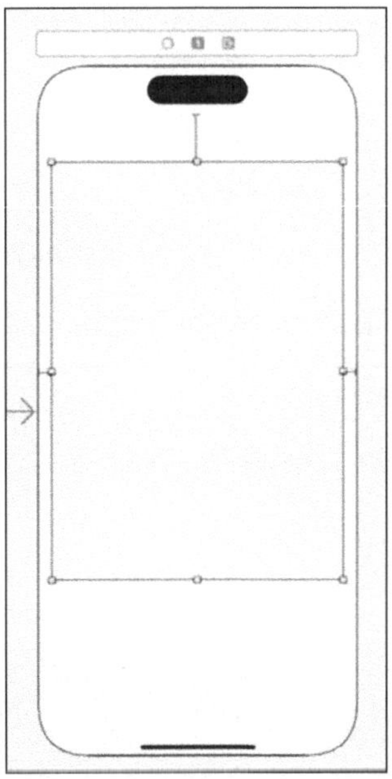

Figure 3.76: *UIScrollView with Constraints*

3. Next, add the page control to the `ViewController`. It should be outside and below the `UIScrollView`. To be able to see the page control, change the background color of the page control to any color you like, other than the default or white in the attribute inspector.

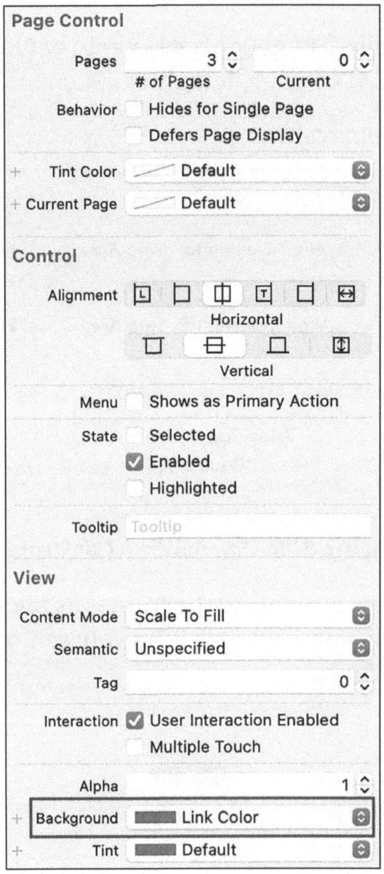

Figure 3.77: *UIPageControl's attribute Inspector*

4. Give the following constraints to the page control:

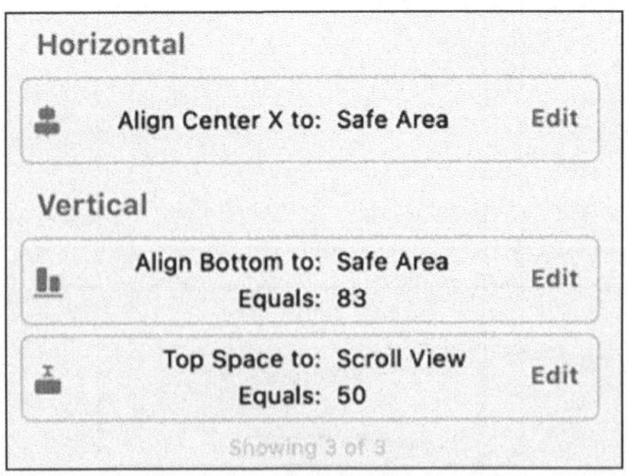

Figure 3.78: *UIPageControl constraints*

5. Don't worry about the constraints' warnings. We are going to add some UI elements using code rather than in the Storyboard. Your `ViewController` in the Storyboard should look like as shown here:

Figure 3.79: *UIViewController with UIScrollView and UIPageControl*

6. Give the code references to the `UIPageControl` and `UIScrollView`. Add these two variables as well, which gives the screen width and height:

```
var screenWidth : CGFloat = UIScreen.main.bounds.size.width
var screenHeight : CGFloat = UIScreen.main.bounds.size.height  -
code
```

Now, let's set the `contentSize` of the `scrollView` inside the `ViewDidLoad()`:

```
scrollView?.contentSize = CGSizeMake((screenWidth * 3), (screen-
Width * 0.67))
```

7. Calculate the required height. Remember that the `scrollView` takes the shape of the content provided or the content size provided.

   Setting the content size of `UIScrollView` is nothing but telling `UIScrollView` how much it can scroll through. We are giving the scrollable area.

8. Now, assign your `ViewController` as `UIScrollViewDelegate` and set it as your `scrollView`'s delegate as follows:

```
scrollView.delegate = self
```

9. Next, set the `scrollView`'s `isPagingEnabled` to `true`.

   So, when the `UIScrollView`'s paging is enabled, the `scrollView` stops at multiples of `UIScrollView` bounds when the scrolling happens, rather than scrolling through all the way.

   This is how your `ViewController` should look like:

```
class ViewController: UIViewController, UIScrollViewDelegate {

    @IBOutlet weak var scrollView: UIScrollView!
    @IBOutlet weak var pageControl: UIPageControl!

    var screenWidth : CGFloat = UIScreen.main.bounds.size.width
    var screenHeight : CGFloat = UIScreen.main.bounds.size.height

    override func viewDidLoad() {
        super.viewDidLoad()

        scrollView?.contentSize = CGSizeMake((screenWidth * 3), (screenWidth * 0.67))

        scrollView.delegate = self
        scrollView.isPagingEnabled = true

    }
```

***Figure 3.80**: ViewController reference*

For the user to be able to scroll through three views, give the `contentSize` of `scrollView`, and the width as (`scrollWidth * 3`). Let's create some views for the user to scroll:

```
for i in 0...2 {
            let contentView = UIView()
            contentView.frame = CGRect(x: screenWidth * CGFloat (i), y:
0, width: screenWidth,height: screenHeight)

            scrollView?.addSubview(contentView)
        }
```

Here we add three views and we add them as `subViews` to the `scrollView`. But we should be able to differentiate between them so that we know actually we are scrolling through them.

So for that, let's add the following code before adding the `contentView` as a `subView` to the `scrollView`:

```
if i == 0 {
contentView.backgroundColor = UIColor.green
 }
if i == 1 {
contentView.backgroundColor = UIColor.blue
 }
```

```
if i == 2 {
contentView.backgroundColor = UIColor.red
 }
```

So, we are adding different background colors to the view for differentiation.

This is how `ViewDidLoad()` should look like:

```
override func viewDidLoad() {
    super.viewDidLoad()

    scrollView?.contentSize = CGSizeMake((screenWidth * 3), (screenWidth * 0.67))

    scrollView.delegate = self
    scrollView.isPagingEnabled = true

    for i in 0...2 {
        let contentView = UIView()
        contentView.frame = CGRect(x: screenWidth * CGFloat (i), y: 0, width: screenWidth,height: screenHeight)
        if i == 0 {
            contentView.backgroundColor = UIColor.green
        }

        if i == 1 {
            contentView.backgroundColor = UIColor.blue
        }

        if i == 2 {
            contentView.backgroundColor = UIColor.red
        }
        scrollView?.addSubview(contentView)
    }
```

***Figure 3.81**: Adding different views to the scrollView*

Now, let's set the page indicator by adding the following function:

```
func setIndiactorForCurrentPage()  {
let page = (scrollView.contentOffset.x)/screenWidth
pageControl.currentPage = Int(page)
}
```

Here we are getting the page by calculating the offset divided by the `screenWidth`. This means that when the user scrolls to the second page, the content offset will be two times the screen width.

And we are setting that as a `pageControl`'s current page. This should happen after the user has ended the scrolling to the next page. For this, we got `UIScrollView` delegate function that gets called when the scroll view ends decelerating after scrolling:

```
func scrollViewDidEndDecelerating(_ scrollView: UIScrollView) {
 }
```

Call `setIndicatorForCurrentPage()` inside this function because, for example, when scrolling to the second page has ended, that's when the page control should show that it's on the second page.

Go ahead and run it. You should see something as follows:

***Figure 3.82**: Screen with First View with UIPageControl*

Now, scroll our colored view to the right, and you should see a blue-colored view with page control showing the updated position/second position.

`UIPickerView`

`UIPickerView` can be seen in situations where the user has to select the input from the options provided using a spinning-wheel metaphor, instead of the user entering random custom values. This can be seen in the clock app on your iPhone:

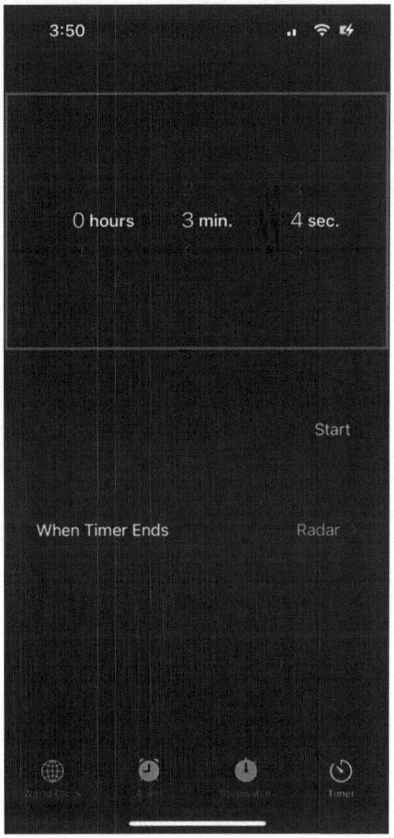

Figure 3.83: *UIPickerView example*

Let's jump into implementation directly.

1. Open Xcode and create an Xcode project called **`PickerViewExample`**. Go to your **`Main.storyboard`** and add the `UIPickerView` to the `Viewcontroller`.

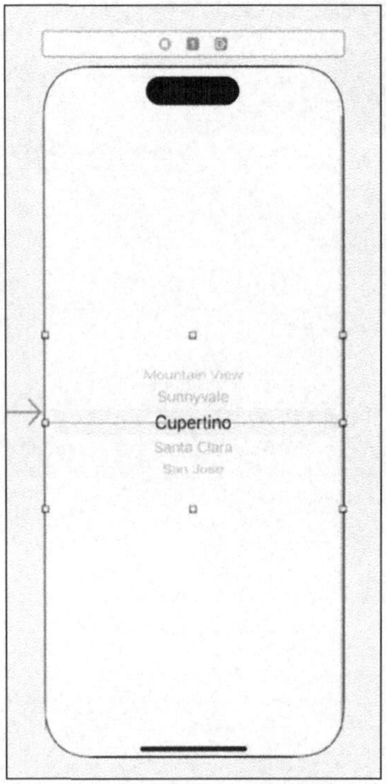

***Figure 3.84**: UIPickerView added to the UIViewController*

2. Add the following constraints to the `UIPickerView`:

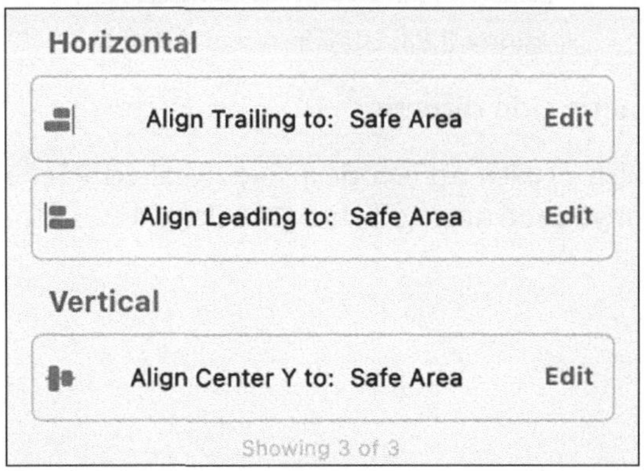

***Figure 3.85**: UIPickerView Constraints*

Add the code reference of our `UIPickerView`. Assign the `ViewController` as the `UIPickerViewDataSource` and `UIPickerViewDelegate`.

Just like in the previous chapter about `tableViews`, here the `Viewcontroller` shows the warning about missing protocol stubs of `UIPickerViewDataSource`. Simply add them. If not sure how to add, please refer to the previous chapter, as it is described in detail there.

There are two required protocol stubs as shown in the following image. Now assign the `pickerView` its delegate and data source in `viewDidLoad()`

This is how your `ViewController` should look like:

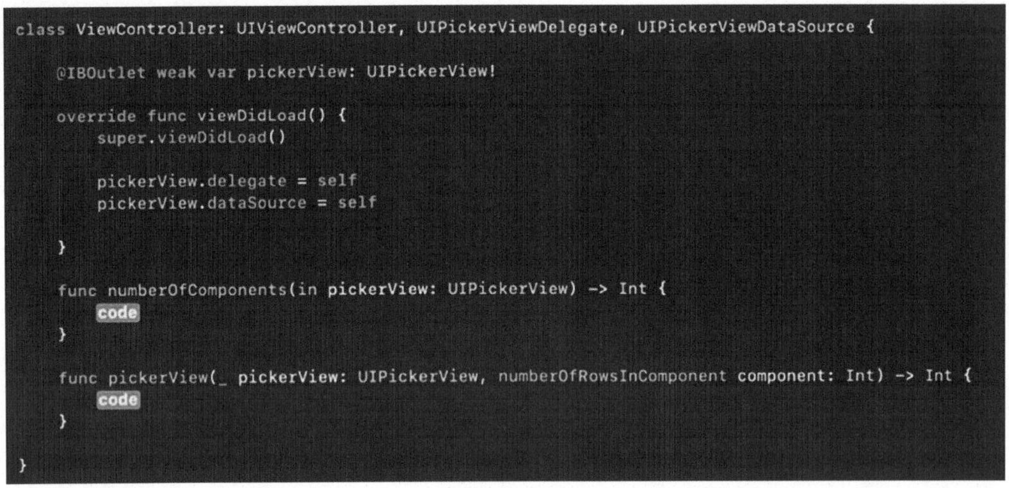

Figure 3.86: *UIPickerView's DataSource functions*

The idea here is that when the user chooses the color, the screen should change its color accordingly.

Let's add the colors array. You can add your favorite colors:

```
let colours = ["Red", "Blue", "Green", "Gray"]
```

Now, return the colors count for the '**`pickerView(_:numberOfRowsInComponent:)`**' function.

To get the title for a row, add the following `UIPickerViewDelegate` function:

```
func pickerView(_ pickerView: UIPickerView, titleForRow row: Int,
forComponent component: Int) -> String? {
colours[row]
}
func numberOfComponents(in pickerView: UIPickerView) -> Int {
1
}
```

Here, we are returning the title from colors array, and the number of components we are returning is 1, as we just want to show the color name in the `UIPickerView`.

Now, go ahead and run it. You should see something like this:

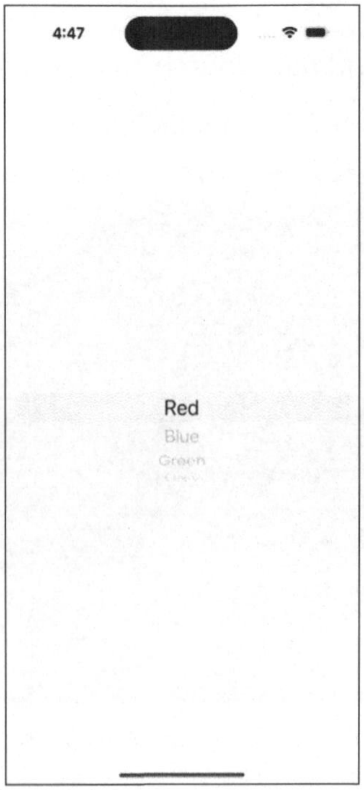

Figure 3.87: *Screen with UIPickerView*

Now, let's add some functionality for the user to select the row and for changing the screen color.

When the user clicks the row, the following function is called:

```
func pickerView(_ pickerView: UIPickerView, didSelectRow row: Int,
inComponent component: Int) {
}
```

Following are the `UIPickerViewDelegate` and `UIPickerViewDataSource` functions that are required to be your `ViewController`:

```
func numberOfComponents(in pickerView: UIPickerView) -> Int {

    1
}

func pickerView(_ pickerView: UIPickerView, numberOfRowsInComponent component: Int) -> Int {
    colours.count
}

func pickerView(_ pickerView: UIPickerView, titleForRow row: Int, forComponent component: Int) -> String? {

    colours[row]
}

func pickerView(_ pickerView: UIPickerView, didSelectRow row: Int, inComponent component: Int) {

}
```

Figure 3.88: *UIPickerView Delegate and DataSource functions*

Inside didSelectRow function, to keep it simple, no validations are done on the colors array. If the user selects the second row, change the view's background color to Blue.

```
func pickerView(_ pickerView: UIPickerView, didSelectRow row: Int,
inComponent component: Int) {
       if row == 0 {
self.view.backgroundColor = .red
       } else if row == 1 {
self.view.backgroundColor = .blue
} else if row == 2 {
self.view.backgroundColor = .green }
else {
self.view.backgroundColor = .gray
}
 }
```

Now go ahead and run it, and you can see that as you change the color, the screen color changes as well.

***Figure 3.89**: Screen with UIPickerView*

Now, let's learn how to add more components so that you can build something you have seen in the Clock app.

Let's add the data array as follows:

```
let data = [["1","2","3","4"], ["A", "B","C","D"]]
```

Return 2 to numberOfComponents function as follows:

```
func numberOfComponents(in pickerView: UIPickerView) -> Int {
2
}
```

Change the 'pickerView(_:numberOfRowsInComponent:)' function as follows:

```
func pickerView(_ pickerView: UIPickerView, numberOfRowsInComponent component: Int) -> Int {
    data[component].count
}
```

Figure 3.90: *UIPickerView's numberOfRowsInComponent function*

Change the 'pickerView(_:titleForRow:forComponent:)' function as follows:

```
func pickerView(_ pickerView: UIPickerView, titleForRow row: Int, forComponent component: Int) -> String? {
    data[component][row]
}
```

Figure 3.91*: UIPickerView's titleForRow function*

Now go ahead and run it. You should see something like this:

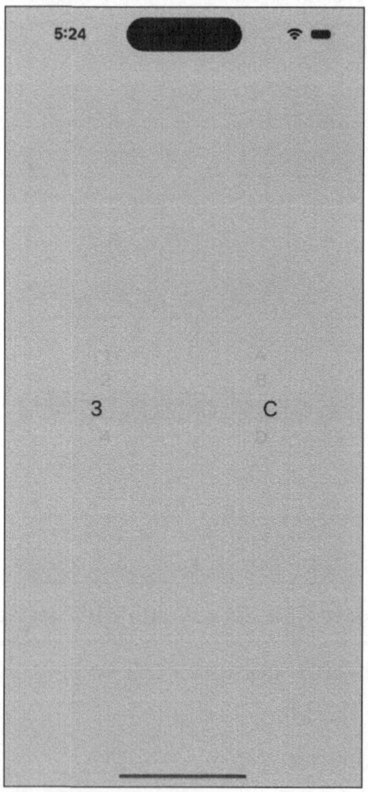

Figure 3.92: *Screen with UIPickerView with multiple components*

Since we did not change the `pickerView(_:didSelectRow:inComponent:)` function when we changed the rows in the picker view, it changed the screen color as per the previous implementation.

Conclusion

In this chapter, we have learned a lot about different things that are really essential for our App development, without these elements, there won't be an App. So play with these things we have learned in this chapter, the more you use these elements, the better you get at improving user experience and making more beautiful Apps. In the next chapter, we will learn the most important part of App development: Navigation.

Points to Remember

- A scroll view is a view with an origin that's adjustable over the content view, which allows the user to scroll.
- `ScrollView` takes the shape of the `contentView`.
- Content layout guide is used when you add constraints related to the content area of the `UIScrollView`.
- Frame layout guide is used when you want to add constraints that involve the frame rectangle of `UIScrollView`.
- Changing the '**`Lines`**' of the Label from **'`1`'** to **'`0`'** will allow the label to go multi-line.
- Priority of constraint, as the name implies, says how important a constraint is.
- Some examples of **`UIControls`** are **`UIButtons`**, **`UITextfields`**, and **`UISliders`**.
- **`@IBAction`** allows us to connect or trigger certain functions to the Storyboard elements.
- The reason we are using **`@objc`** in front of our function is that we want to interact with Objective-c during runtime.
- If you want the keyboard to appear on the simulator, type '`Command + k`'.
- `?` – Means that the value of this variable can be nil sometimes.
- `!` – If you have **"`!`"** at the end of the variable or an object or an `IBoutlet`, it means it can't be nil anytime.
- The `textField(_:shouldChangeCharactersIn:replacementString:)` delegate function gets called whenever the user types a single character into `textField`.
- `UITextView` is also an editable text area, but with the bonus of multi-line text and is also scrollable.

- `??` – This operator is used for providing a default value. If the value of optional is nil, it is called Nil-Coalescing Operator.
- `UIStackView` is an amazing interface for laying out multiple views vertically or horizontally.
- `UIPageControl` is the horizontal series of dots that you see on your iPhone menu screen, which can show us how many pages are there before and after the current page.
- `UIPickerView` can be seen in situations where users have to select the input from the options provided using a spinning-wheel metaphor, instead of the user entering random custom values.

Chapter 4
Navigation

Introduction

In this chapter, you will learn about Navigation. You might think navigation is only the second priority when compared to other things in the app, but it's the most important part of any app. It allows you to navigate to different screens and close the screens. Some actions of navigation would make users' lives easier. So, this chapter is all about it.

Structure

In this chapter, we will discuss the following topics:

- Navigation
  - Navigation controller
  - Navigation bar
  - Navigating programmatically

Navigation

You will see navigation in all the apps unless it is a single-screen app. For example, open Instagram and click the account of any post you saw. When you navigate to their account screen, you will see a back button on the top left, which is also an action of navigation.

So, what we are waiting for? Let's learn and implement.

`NavigationController`

Apple provides us with a wonderful `UINavigationController`. If you open the `UINavigationController`, you can see it is the `UIViewController`(what this means is that it's the subclass of `UIViewController`, in other words, inherited from `UIViewController`). This `NavigationController` is a container view controller, that can manage child view controllers in the navigation interface.

1. Now that we have learned what it is, let's go build it. You must know the steps by now. Go to Xcode -> create a project called **`NavigationVCExample`**.

2. Now go to **`Main.Storyboard`** -> Add `UINavigationController` to your storyboard.

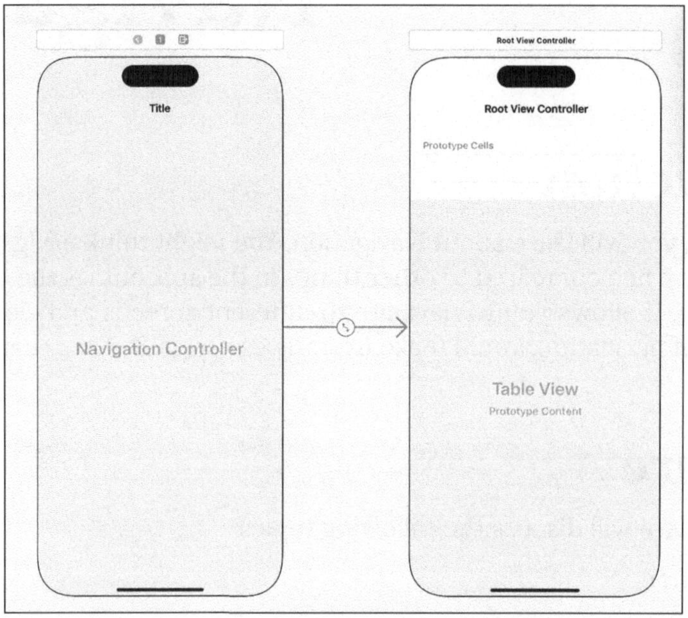

Figure 4.1: *Navigation Controller in storyboard*

3. You might have noticed that it comes with `RootViewController` in which, if you see the type of the class of the Root View Controller in the identity inspector, you will see that `UITableViewController`.

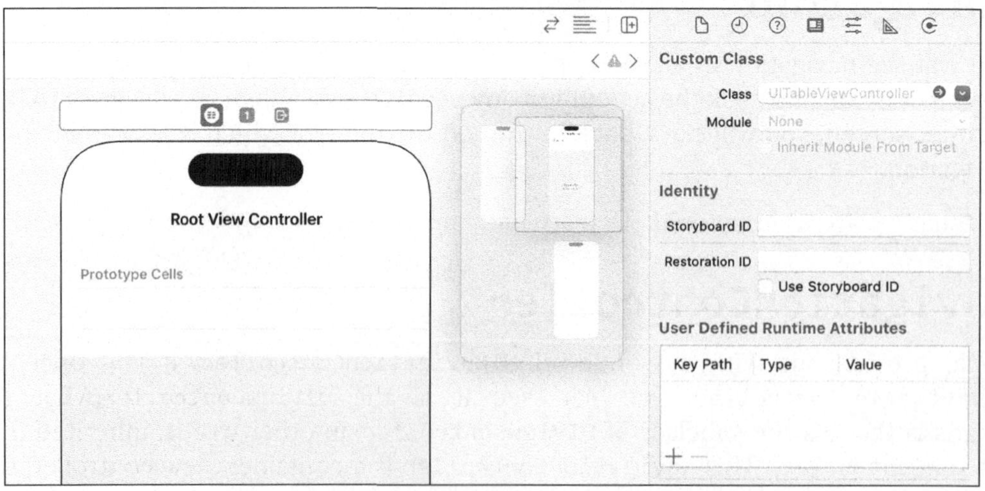

Figure 4.2: *RootViewController's identity inspector*

`RootViewController` is nothing but the base view controller or the initial view controller in our navigation stack. When you perform any navigation actions on this `rootViewController`, for example, navigating to different screens, in that case, the root view controller sits at the bottom of the navigation stack and the child view controller will be added on top of this root view controller.

You might also wonder when you drag `UINavigationController` to the storyboard it comes with the default `UITableViewController`, one of the reasons could be most of the apps use it in that way, maybe that's the reason Apple is giving it to the developers by default to decrease the additional work.

We don't need `UITableViewController` for now. So, let's break the connection between `UINavigationController` and `UITableViewController` and add the connection to our default `UIViewController`.

1. To break the connection, all you have to do first is to select the connection.

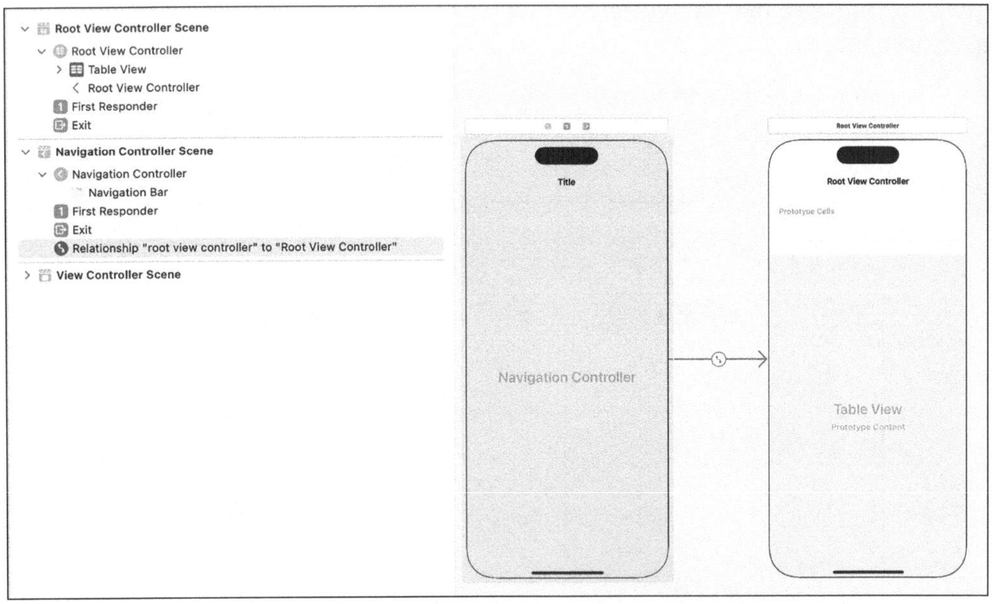

Figure 4.3: *NavigationController's segue*

2. And if you go to the Attributes Inspector, you will see that it is a `Relationship Segue`.

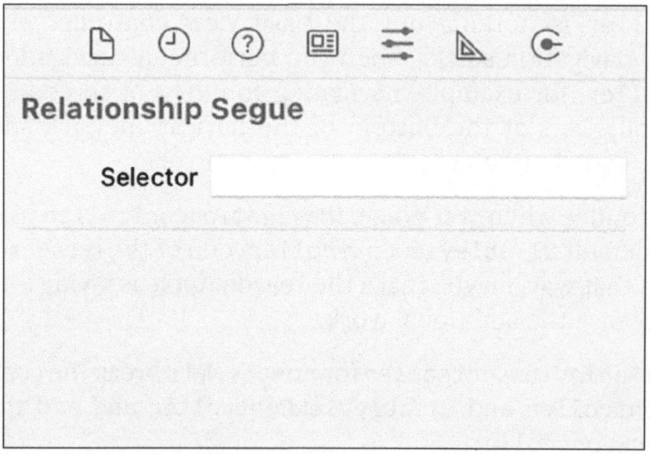

***Figure 4.4**: Segue's attributes inspector*

Segues are nothing but the visual connectors between your `UIViewControllers` on your Storyboards.

3. So, all we need to do is delete that segue to destroy the relationship between them. To delete it, simply click that segue and click the delete button on your keyboard.

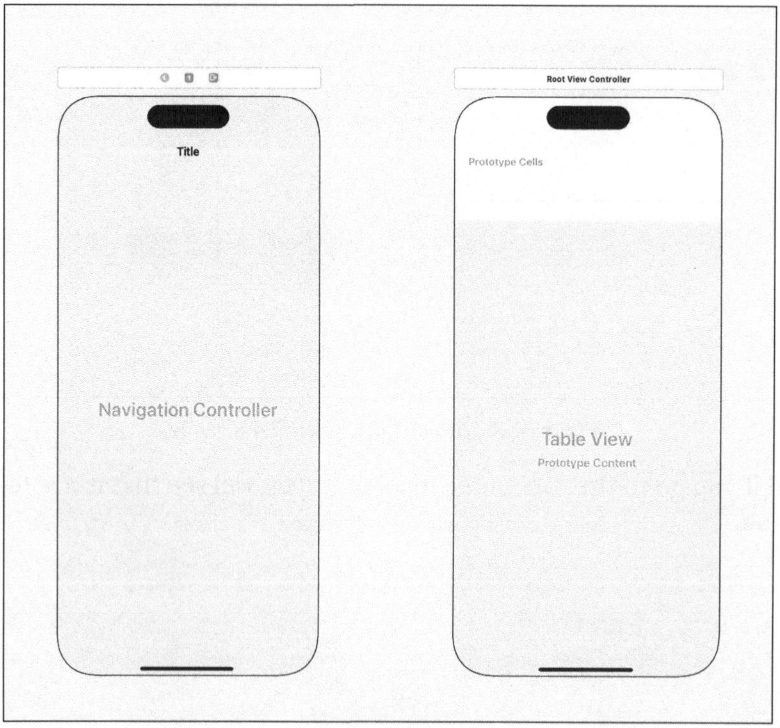

***Figure 4.5**: Navigation controller's segue deleted*

As you can see, the segue is deleted. Let's add the segue between `UINavigationController` and our default `UIViewController`.

1. To do that, delete the useless `UITableViewController` and bring our default `UIViewController` beside the `UINavigationController` so that it will be easy for us to give the segue between them.
2. Now click the `UINavigationController` + *Control*, drag it to `UIViewController`, and release it.

   You should see something as follows, which gives options about the type of segue ways you want to use.

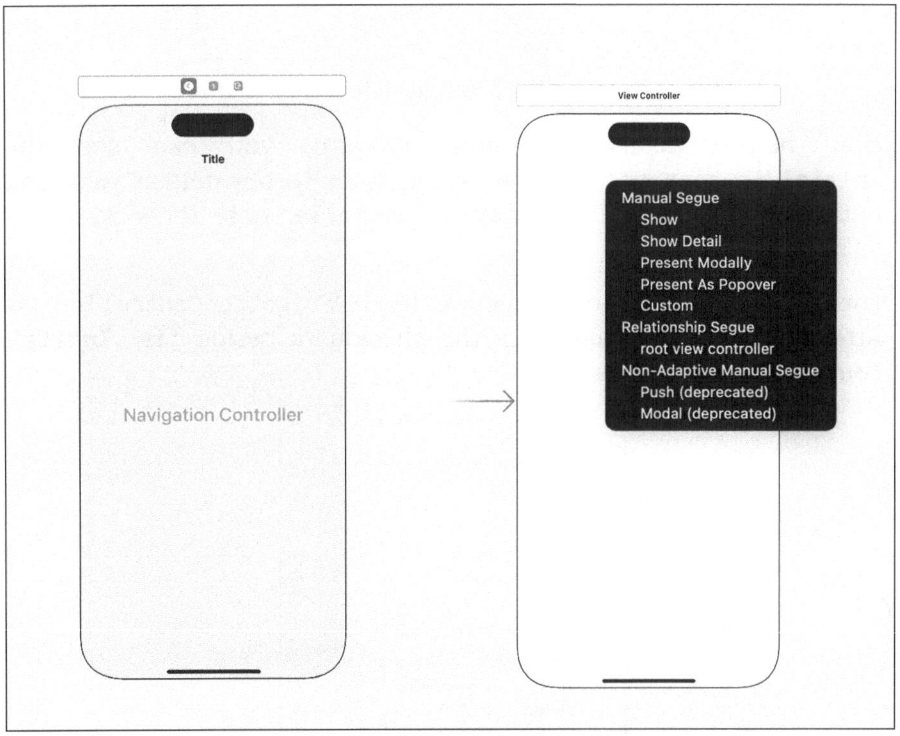

Figure 4.6: *Navigation controller's segues*

3. Click the **'Relationship Segue - Root View controller'** which is highlighted in the preceding screenshot.

   You should see something as follows.

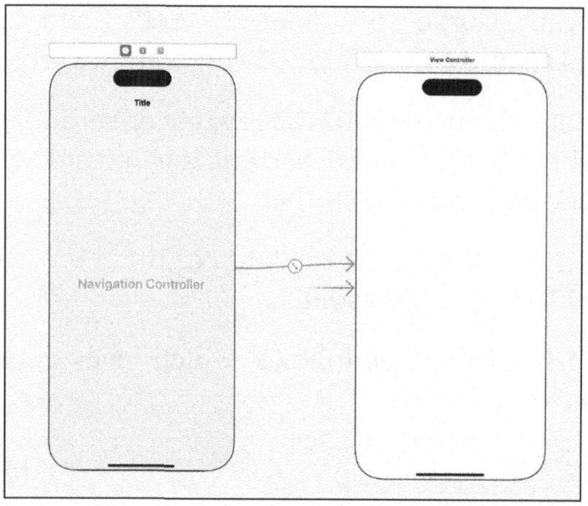

Figure 4.7: *Navigation controller's root view controller*

Now before taking any step forward, you can see that the `initialViewcontroller` arrow is still stuck to our default view controller, but here we want our `UINavigationController` to be the kickstart point, so let's change it.

4. For that all you need to do is, click the `UINavigationController`, go to the Attributes Inspector, and click the checkmark beside **'`is Initial View Controller`'** as follows.

Figure 4.8: *Making the initial view controller*

The result will be as follows:

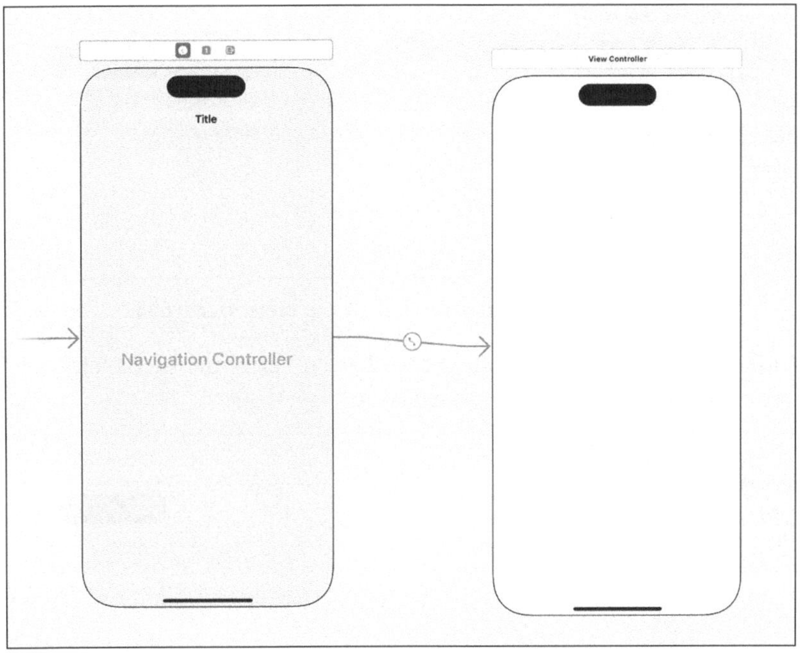

Figure 4.9: *Navigation controller as the initial view controller*

You might wonder why the Xcode is not complaining even if we make the `UINavigationController` the initial `ViewController`. The reason is that `UINavigationcontroller` is a subclass of `UIViewController`, technically a `UIViewController`. If you want to check for yourself, then open Xcode, click '*Command + Shift* + 0', and type `UINavigationController`. This is what you get:

```
UIKIT_EXTERN API_AVAILABLE(ios(2.0)) NS_SWIFT_UI_ACTOR
@interface UINavigationController : UIViewController
```

Figure 4.10: *Navigation controller's parent class*

We are doing this as we want our `UIViewController` to use the full benefits of `UINavigationController`.

We can't add any content to our `UINavigationController` as `UINavigationController` is just for controlling the navigation of controllers. If you want to add any content like buttons or views, then it should be done on `UINavigationController`'s `rootViewController`.

In our case, it's our `ViewController` in the storyboard.

1. If you click the **`UINavigationController`** in the View hierarchy, you can see it comes with a **`Navigation Bar`** with the title as follows:

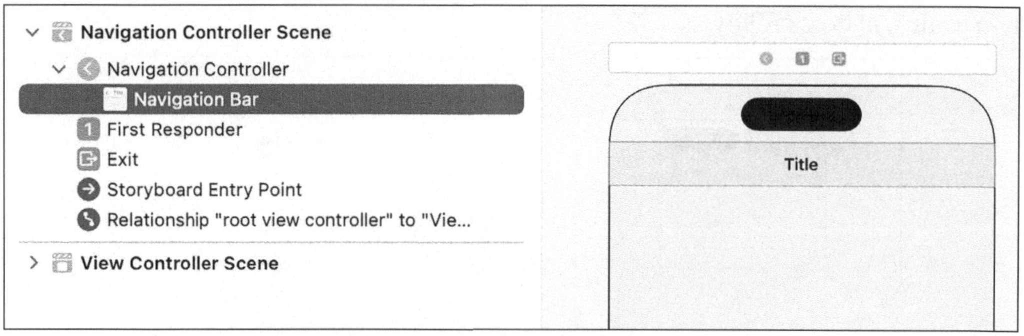

Figure 4.11: *Navigation bar in the view hierarchy*

2. Now if you expand the `ViewController` in the view hierarchy, you can see it got the **'`Navigation Item`'** as follows.

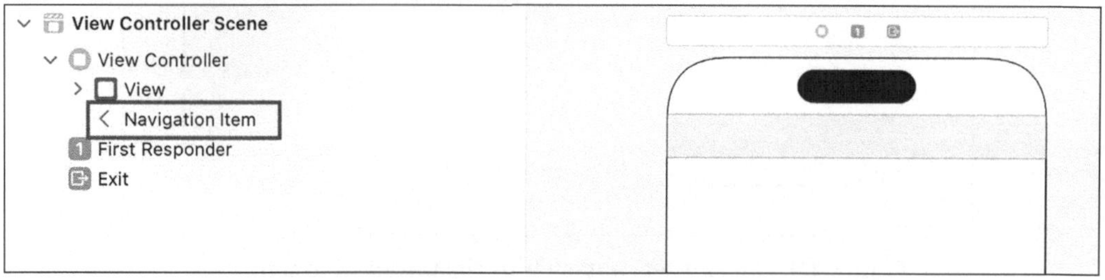

Figure 4.12: *Navigation item selected*

3. Click the **'`Navigation Item`'**, open the Attributes Inspector, and this is what you will see:

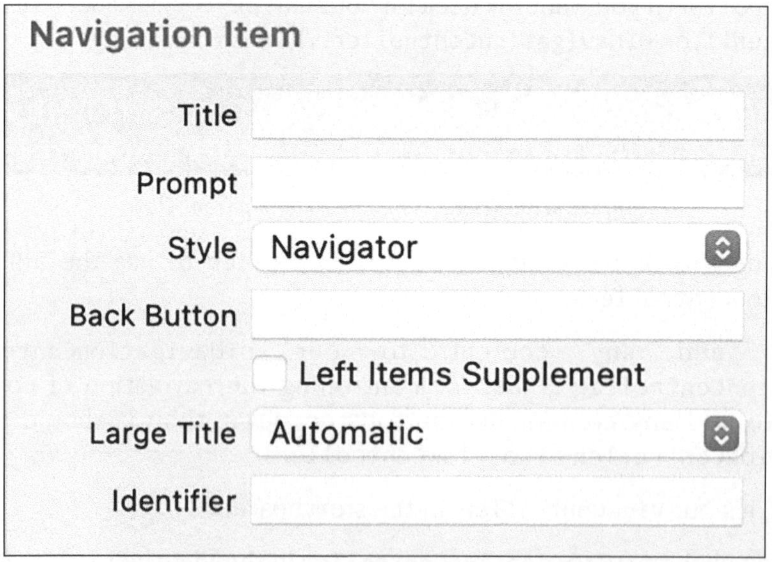

Figure 4.13: *Navigation item's attributes inspector*

4. Let's give the title in the attributes inspector as **`Screen 1`**. After that, you will notice the title on the screen as follows:

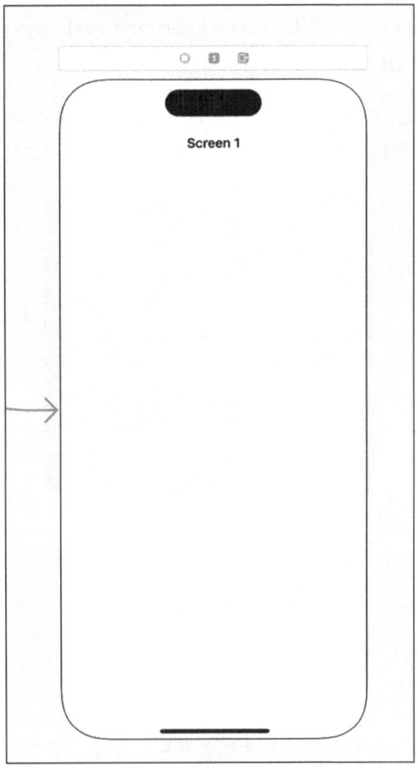

***Figure 4.14**: Screen 1 in the storyboard*

5. Go ahead and run it. You should see your screen with the Navigation/Screen Title **`Screen 1`**.

6. Now let's add a button at the center of our screen. Add the following constraints to the button:

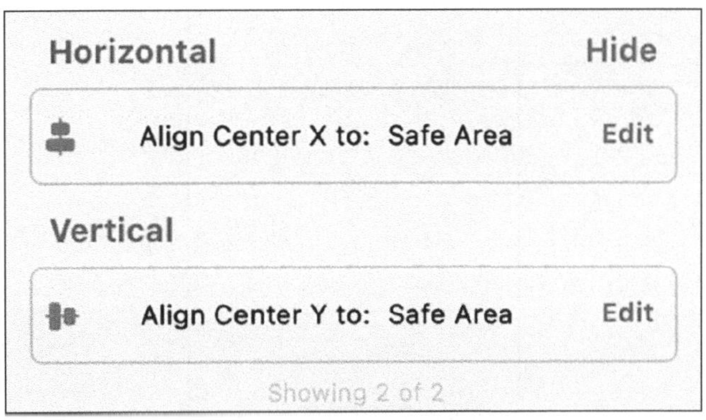

***Figure 4.15:** Button's constraints*

7. To see how the navigation works, let's add a new `UIViewController` to our storyboard.
8. Take a look at the newly added `UIViewController` in View Hierarchy. There is no navigation item on it.
9. Now click + *Control* + drag from the button to the newly added View Controller and release it, you should see something as follows:

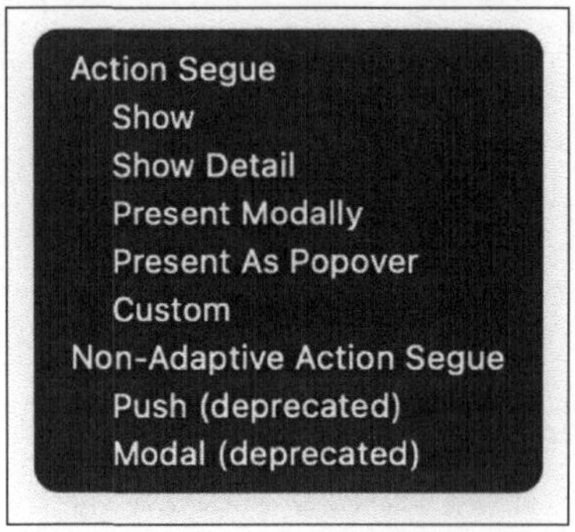

Figure 4.16: *Navigation segues*

10. Click the **`Show under Action`** Segue.
11. Let's run it. Click the button and you will land on your second screen which looks as follows.

Figure 4.17: *Screen2 in simulator*

12. When you click the back button on the top left of the screen **`'< Screen 1'`** it should take you back to screen 1.

You can change the style of the back button. Also, let's add the title to our second screen too.

1. Go to your second `ViewController` in the view hierarchy and select the **`Navigation Item`**. Open the attributes inspector and you should see the screen as follows:

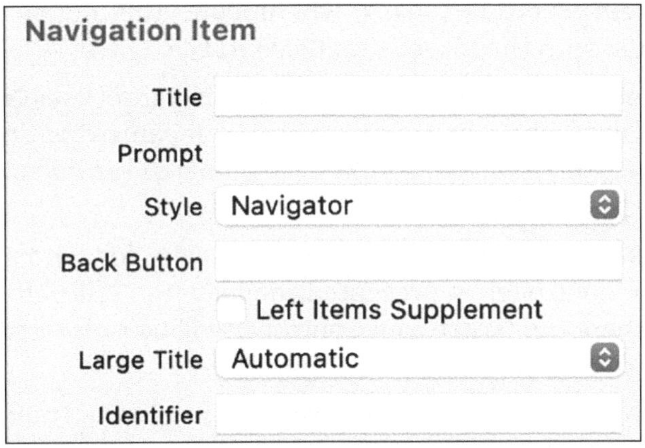

Figure 4.18: *Navigation item in the attributes inspector*

2. Let's give it the title **`Screen 2`** and if you want the Instagram style back button, change the **`'Style'`** to **`'Editor'`**; for reference check as follows:

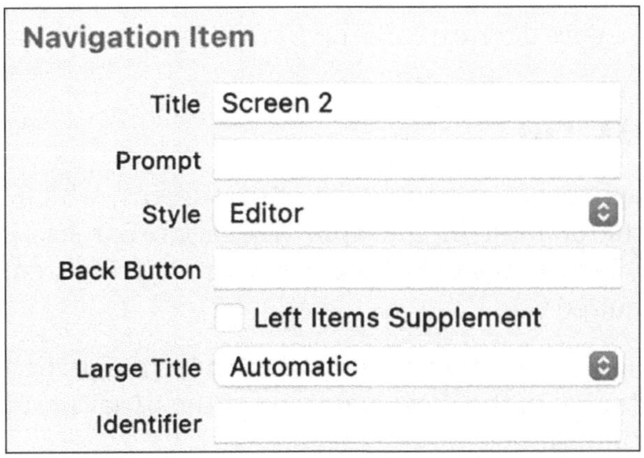

Figure 4.19: *The navigation item's title changed*

You can see the changes in the storyboard itself. Go ahead, run it, and experiment with it.

As you saw navigation working in action, let me explain to you in detail, what we have done.

Action Segues:

Firstly, let's learn about action segues. As discussed earlier, the segues are visual connectors between view controllers, but we need to learn the types of action segues. Depending on the segue you select, the view controllers will be presented accordingly,

- **Show**: When you have a show segue, this will push the target view controller to the top, that is the target view controller will present with the back button.
- **Show Detail**: This is used when `ViewControllers` are in `UISplitViewController`. This will update the detail view side of the `UISplitView` with the target `ViewController`.
- **Present Modally**: When you use this segue, the target `ViewController` modally, you don't get a **`'back'`** button with this. You can swipe down to dismiss this target `ViewController`. This target `ViewController` doesn't have to be a part of the navigation stack.
- **Present As Popover**: When you use this segue for iPhone, you will see the target view controller is presented modally, the true effect can be seen in the iPad, where the target ViewController will be presented as the popover at the center of the screen.
- **Custom:** You can use this custom segue and get the transition to the target **`ViewController`** in your own way.

An exciting exercise for you would be to try each of these segues and run it in the simulator. You will understand better when you try it for yourself.

Now that you know what we have done with the button, adding segues, and learning the types of action segues, let's explore the Navigation bar and Navigation items.

Navigation Bar

`UINavigationBar` appears at the top of the App screens, which allows the users to navigate through the content of the App. Navigation Bar has `UINavigationItems` that get displayed when associated `ViewController` is presented; they even allow to perform actions required too.

We don't have to create a new project for this. Let's open the preceding project if closed and open the storyboard. In the View hierarchy of the `UINavigationController`, you will find the navigation bar.

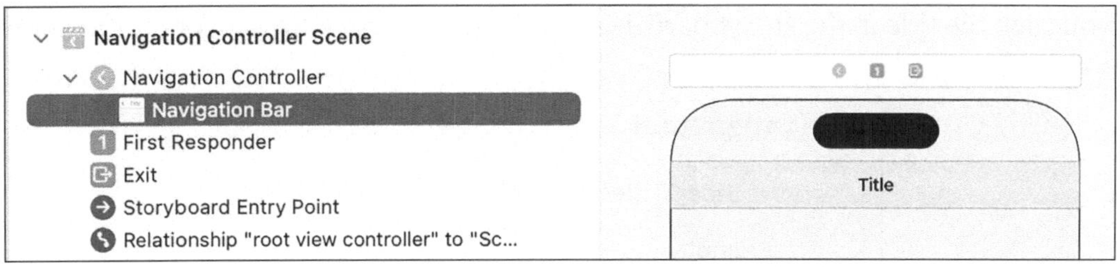

***Figure 4.20**: Navigation Bar selected in the view controller*

You can even add the Navigation bar to your view controllers, for example, if you want to have the title for your screen.

To check that, all we need to do is add a new `UIViewController` to the storyboard and make it `intialViewController` by checking the **`'is initial View Controller'`** in the attribute inspector of the View Controller.

Add the Navigation Bar to this `ViewController`, and it should look as follows.

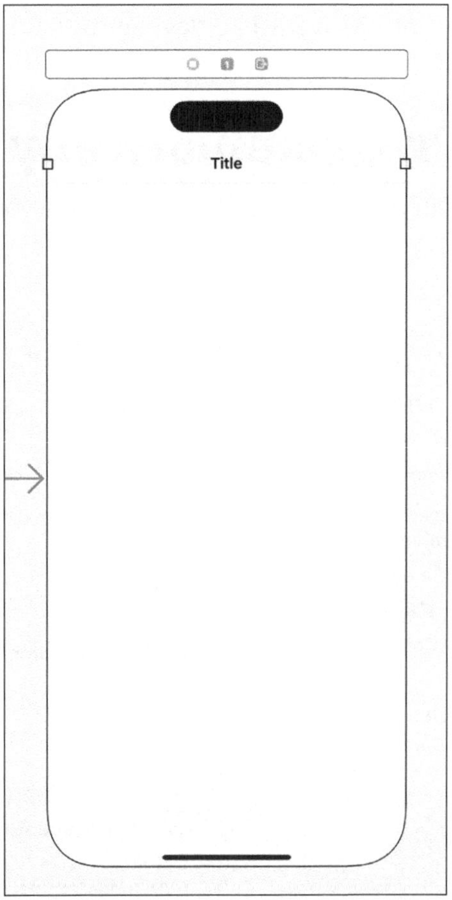

***Figure 4.21:** Navigation bar in the view controller*

If you click the title in the storyboard, it should open the attributes inspector as shown here.

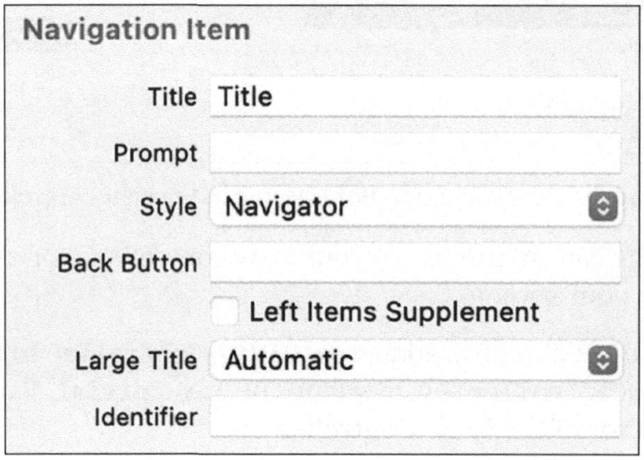

Figure 4.22: *Navigation item in attributes inspector*

Change the title as you want or give it like `NavBarView`. Run it. You should see your screen with its title on the Navigation bar.

Navigating Programmatically

Now that you have had fun with navigation from the storyboard, let's try presenting screens programmatically.

Let's create a new project.

1. Go to the **`Main.storyboard`** and add a second/new `viewController`.
2. On the project navigator, right-click the project as shown in the following figure.

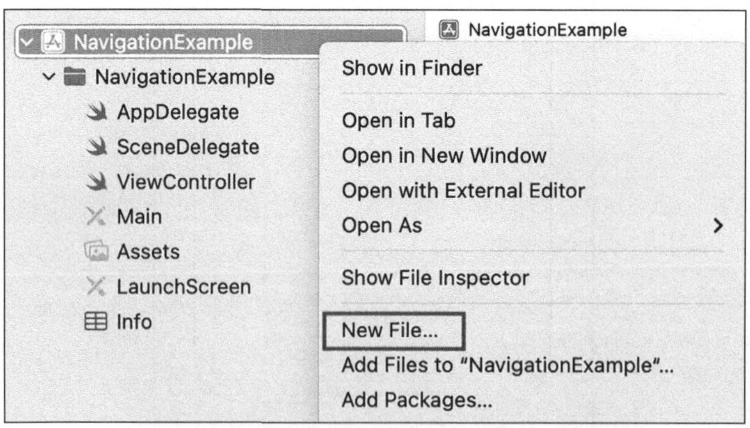

Figure 4.23: *Creating a new file in the project*

3. Click the **'New File'**, choose **'Cocoa Touch Class'**, and click **'Next'**; for reference check *Figure 4.24*.

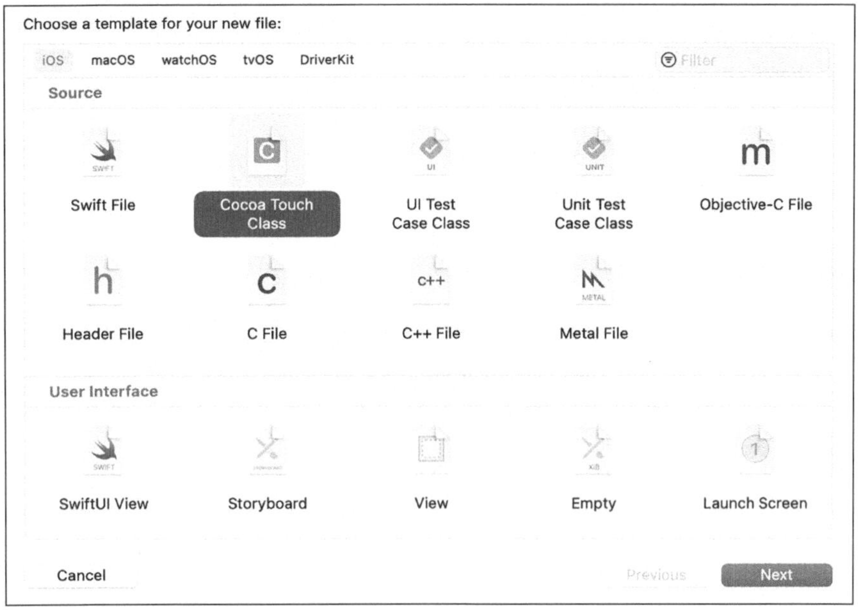

Figure 4.24: *Selecting cocoa touch class for choosing a template*

4. Choose the **'Subclass of'** as **'UIViewController'** and give the class as **'SecondViewController'** as shown in the following figure.

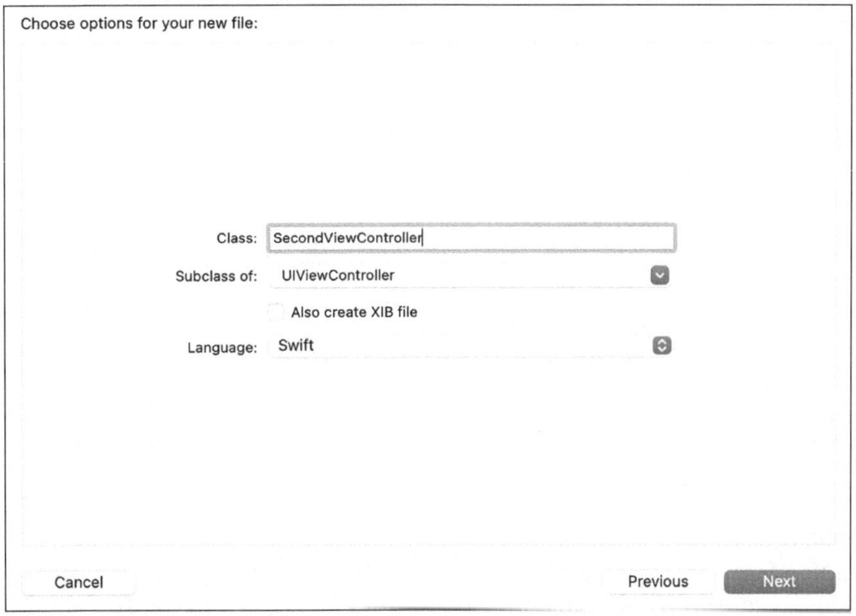

Figure 4.25: *Choosing the subclass of SecondViewController*

5. Click **'Next'** and it shows the location of your project and file. Click **'Create'** and you will see the `SecondViewController` in the project navigator as shown in the following figure. If you want to change the position of a newly created file in the project navigator, then you can do it by dragging it and placing it in the position you want.

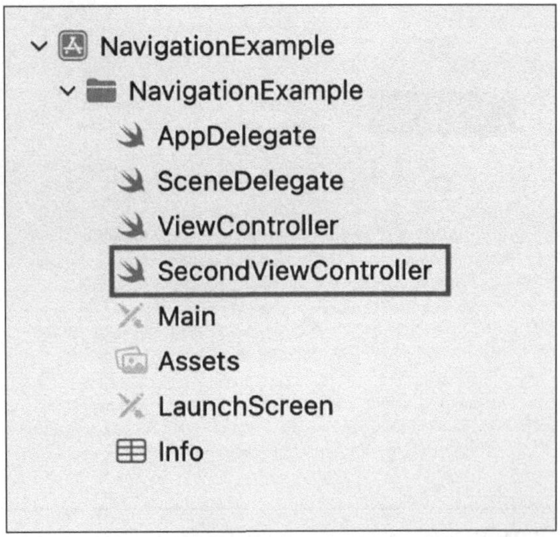

Figure 4.26: *SecondViewController in project navigator*

6. Now go to your storyboard, click your newly added `UIViewController`, and open **`Identity Inspector`**. There you will find **'Class'** under the **'Custom Class'** section, type `SecondViewController` for the class as follows.

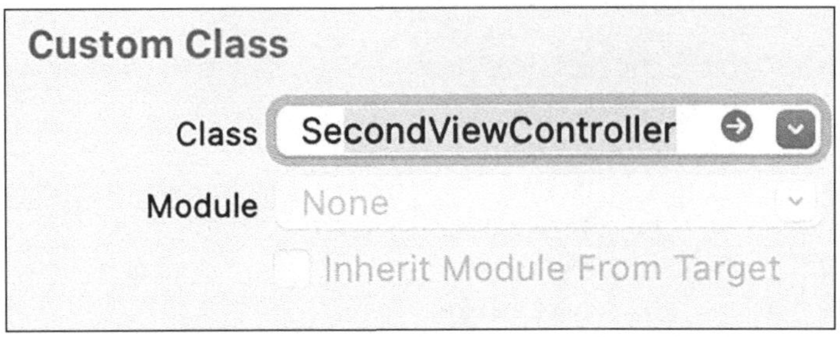

Figure 4.27: *Assigning the custom class*

Here we are linking the `SecondViewController.swift` to the newly added `UIViewController` in the Storyboard, which is a coding reference.

When we create a project, we get a default `UIViewController` in the storyboard which is already linked to the `ViewController.swift`. So, it is all done for us. Going forward, we might need to get used to creating a lot of `ViewController` files. Sometimes, we don't need a `UIViewController` in the storyboard; a swift file is enough.

7. Now, add the **'Storyboard ID'** in the identity section as well, as shown in the following figure:

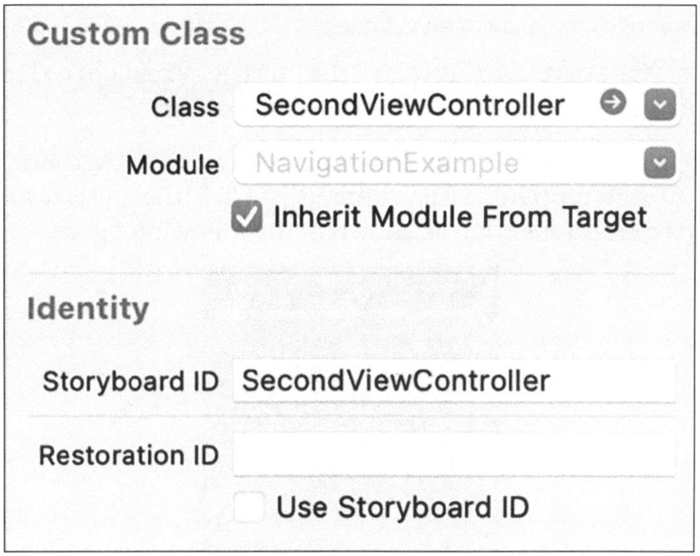

Figure 4.28: *Assigning the Storyboard ID*

This will allow you to identify your `ViewController` while instantiating.

1. Let's add the button on the first `ViewController` at the center of the screen. We did this in the previous section. If you do not know what constraints to add, please refer to that section.

2. Next, add the code reference `IBAction` in its `ViewController` file as shown in the following figure:

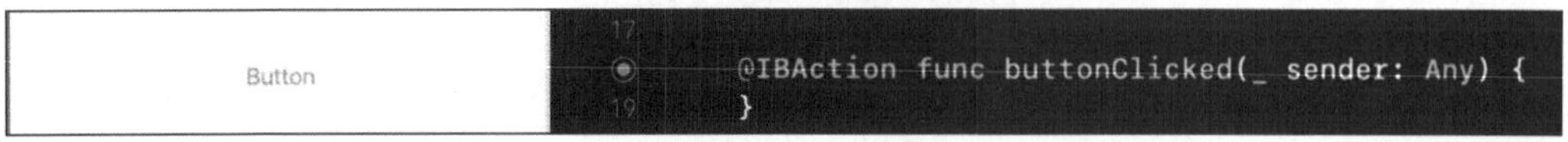

Figure 4.29: *Giving an IBAction to the button*

So, what we want here is when the button is clicked, the second screen should appear, just like we did previously, but here we want to do it programmatically.

Inside button `IBAction`, what we want is our `SecondViewController`. Let's get it by adding the following code inside our `IBAction`.

```
let secondVc = self.storyboard?.instantiateViewController(withIdentifier:
"SecondViewController") as! SecondViewController
```

Here we create an instance of our `SecondViewController`, by getting it from the current storyboard, which our default/current `ViewController` is in, with the Storyboard ID we have given in the Identity inspector.

Now, you can present our `SecondVC` from our `ViewController` by adding the following code.

```
self.present(secondVc, animated: true)
```

When you use **'present'** to display the target `ViewController`, the target `ViewController` is present over the base `ViewController`.

Before running it, give your `SecondViewController` a background color so that it will be easy to differentiate. After running it, click the button and you will see `SecondViewController` appearing as shown in the following figure:

Figure 4.30: *SecondViewController appearing*

If you drag down the `secondViewController`, it goes away.

But we want to present the `SecondViewController` in a way that it comes with a 'back button' and full screen.

To achieve that, instead of presenting it using `UIViewController`, we need to push it using `UINavigationController`.

Let's remove or comment the following line,

```
self.present(secondVc, animated: true)
```

And add the following line,

```
self.navigationController?.pushViewController(secondVc, animated: true)
```

For reference, check the following figure:

```
@IBAction func buttonClicked(_ sender: Any) {
    let secondVc = self.storyboard?.instantiateViewController(withIdentifier: "SecondViewController") as! SecondViewController
    self.navigationController?.pushViewController(secondVc, animated: true)
}
```

Figure 4.31: *The buttonClicked function*

Now go ahead, run it and click the button.

As you can see, after clicking the button nothing happens because our `ViewController` does not have `UINavigationController`. If you check the code, you might wonder why Xcode is not complaining.

```
self.navigationController?.pushViewController(secondVc, animated: true)
```

We are saying that the `navigationController` is optional, which means it could be Nil too. The preceding code says if the `navigatonController` then pushes the `secondVc.`

Let's go add `UINavigationController` to the storyboard.

Please refer to steps of adding `UINavigationController` to the storyboard, which includes steps, such as adding the `UINavigationController` to the storyboard, deleting the default `RootViewController`, adding our `intialViewController/ViewController` with button as `rootViewController` to our `UINavigationController`, and finally making the `UINavigationController` as `intialViewController`.

Now go ahead, run it, and click the button.

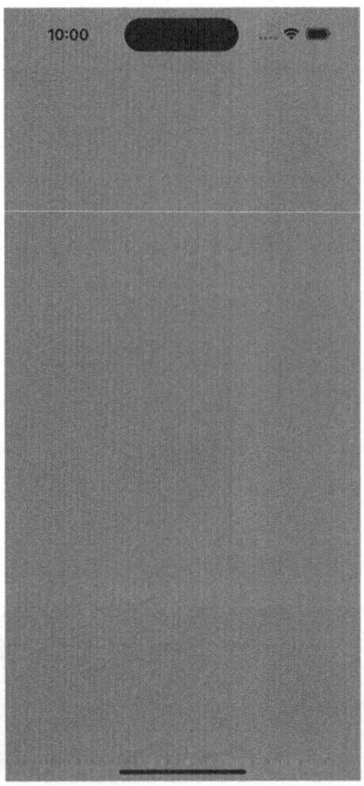

Figure 4.32: *SecondViewController with back button*

Now you can see your second screen appearing with the back button.

Let's see another functionality of `UINavigationController`, and for that, you need more `UIViewControllers` in the storyboard. Let's call them `ThirdViewController` and `FourthViewController` and give them different background colors to differentiate between them. Create `ThirdViewController.swift` and `FourthViewController.swift`.

Now select the `ThirdViewController` in the storyboard, go to **`Identity Inspector`**, and give the class as **`'ThirdViewController'`** which refers to `ThirdViewController.swift`. Also, ensure that the Storyboard ID is given, which could be anything, but here it is given as **`'ThirdVC'`**.

Refer to the following figure to understand it better:

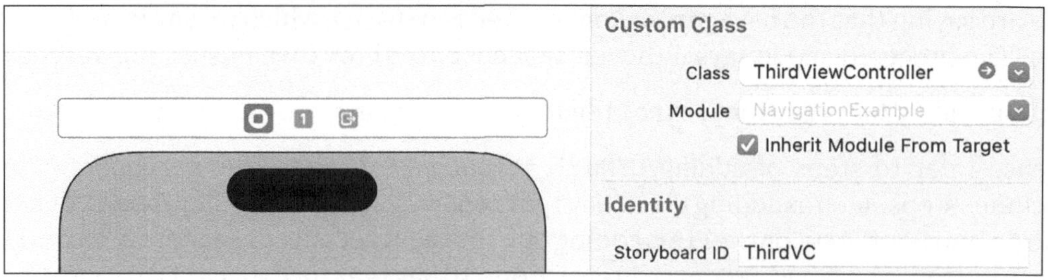

***Figure 4.33**: Assigning the custom class to the view controller*

Do the same for the `FourthViewController` and the Storyboard ID given here is **`'FourthVC'`**.

Now add a button at the center of the screen for the `SecondViewController`.

Add `IBAction` of the button **`'Touch Up Inside'`** in `SecondViewController.swift`; if not sure how to do, then please refer to the steps we did for `FirstViewController`.

The next step is to instantiate the `ThirdViewController` inside the `IBAction` using the following code.

```
let thirdVc = self.storyboard?.instantiateViewController(withIdentifier:
"ThirdVC") as! ThirdViewController
```

Please ensure that the correct **`'Storyboard ID'`** is given in the preceding code, otherwise, it won't be recognizable.

Push it using `navigationController`; for reference, check the following figure:

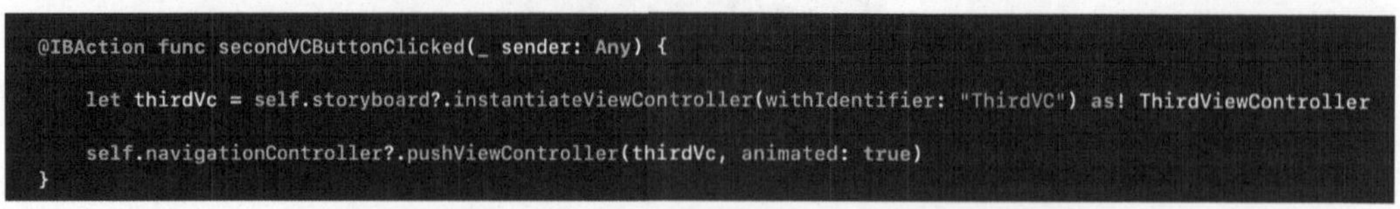

***Figure 4.34**: IBAction of a button in SecondViewController*

Run it. Click the button on your `FirstViewController` -> it takes you to the `SecondViewController` -> Click the button on your `SecondViewController` -> it takes you to the `ThirdViewController`.

***Figure 4.35**: ThirdViewController appearing on screen*

You might wonder why we did not make `SecondViewController` as `RootViewController` of `UINavigationController`, and so, how does the `SecondViewController` get it `NavigationController`?

The answer to this is that we have `UINavigationController` and we add our `FirstViewController` as Root `ViewController`, and then we push our `SecondViewController` from `FirstViewController` using `UINavigationController`. The `SecondViewController` is added on top of the Navigation stack. So, if you click **`'Debug View Hierarchy'`**, then you can see in the background there is UINavigationController.

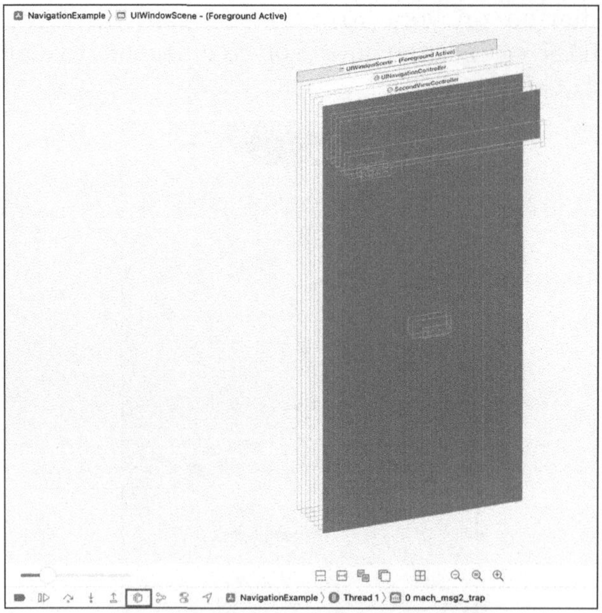

Figure 4.36: *Screens in Debug view hierarchy*

It's time to reveal another awesome functionality of `UINavigationController`. Now you are on `ThirdViewController` on the simulator, long-press the back button. You will see something like the following figure:

Figure 4.37: *Screen with long-pressed back button*

If you click the first **'back'** button, it takes you to the second screen, and if you click the second **'back'** button, it takes you to the first screen.

Instead of just having **'back'** when long pressed on the back button, we can also have a title of the screen. For that, all you need to do as follows in `ViewDidLoad()`.

`self.navigationItem.title = "First Screen"`

Refer the following figure to understand it better:

```
override func viewDidLoad() {
    super.viewDidLoad()

    self.navigationItem.title = "First Screen"
}
```

Figure 4.38: *Assigning navigation item title*

Give the `navigationItem .title` for `SecondViewController` and `ThirdViewController` too.

Now run it and you will see the screen as follows. When you click the screen name, it takes you to that screen.

Figure 4.39: *Long-pressed back button with previous screen names*

Before jumping to the next section, let's learn that we can also present `ViewController` from `UINavigationController`.

To do that, go to your `SecondViewController`, inside your `IBAction`, and comment the following line.

```
self.navigationController?.pushViewController(thirdVc, animated: true)
```

Now let's present our `thirdVC` using the following line.

```
self.navigationController?.present(thirdVc, animated: true)
```

To refer to the whole `IBAction` function in `SecondViewController`, check the following figure:

```
@IBAction func secondVCButtonClicked(_ sender: Any) {

    let thirdVc = self.storyboard?.instantiateViewController(withIdentifier: "ThirdVC") as! ThirdViewController

    //self.navigationController?.pushViewController(thirdVc, animated: true)

    self.navigationController?.present(thirdVc, animated: true)

}
```

Figure 4.40: *Presenting a view controller*

Run it. Go to the **`'Second Screen'`** by clicking the center button on the First Screen, then click the center button on the **`'Second Screen'`**, you should be able to see the **`'Third Screen'`** presented in the following figure. To dismiss this screen all you have to do is simply drag the screen down, and you will be back on the **`'Second Screen'`**.

Figure 4.41: *Presenting third screen*

Conclusion

In this chapter, we have covered Navigation, which is important for any app development. Different types of navigation will give the users smooth navigation, which increases the app's usability. In the next chapter, you will develop a TODO list sample app with all the knowledge we acquired from this chapter and the previous chapters and this is going to be our first App.

Points to Remember

- `NavigationController` is a container view controller, that can manage child view controllers in the navigation interface.
- Segues are nothing but the visual connectors between your `UIViewControllers` on your storyboards.
- `UINavigationBar` appears at the top of the App screens, which allows the users to navigate through the content of the App.

CHAPTER 5
Sample App

Introduction

This is the most exciting chapter, where we get to put all the knowledge that we acquired from previous chapters to test and build a sample app and a TODO list app. While building the app we will also get to learn some more new topics like Structs, `DispatchQueue`, `UIBarButtonItem`, and many more. So let's get going.

Structure

In this chapter, we will discuss the following topics:

- Sample app
    - Idea
    - Design
    - Development
    - Structs
    - `DispatchQueue`
    - `beginUpdates()`
    - `endUpdates()`
    - `UIBarButtonItem`
    - `UIDatePicker`
    - If let
    - Guard let

Sample App

Now that we have learned important concepts of app development, let's develop a sample app using the concepts we have learned until now.

Let's develop an app using some steps of the app development process.

Idea

Here the Idea is to develop a **TODO** list App.

Design

The **TODO** list app should have a list; a list of TODO items. You can use any of the prototyping tools available. For now, we will be using the **'Proto.io'** website, but please feel free to use any other prototyping tool for designing. You can even design on paper to design the App.

The following screen is designed using **'Proto.io'**:

Figure 5.1: *Screen 1 prototype*

In the preceding design, we have a list of TODO items and a button named **'details'**. When the user clicks it, it takes to another screen where additional details like date and time can be added. When a user finishes the task, the user can click the icon beside the title and it will become yellow and the title turns gray, which tells the user that the task has been done. Check the prototype for the **'Details'** screen.

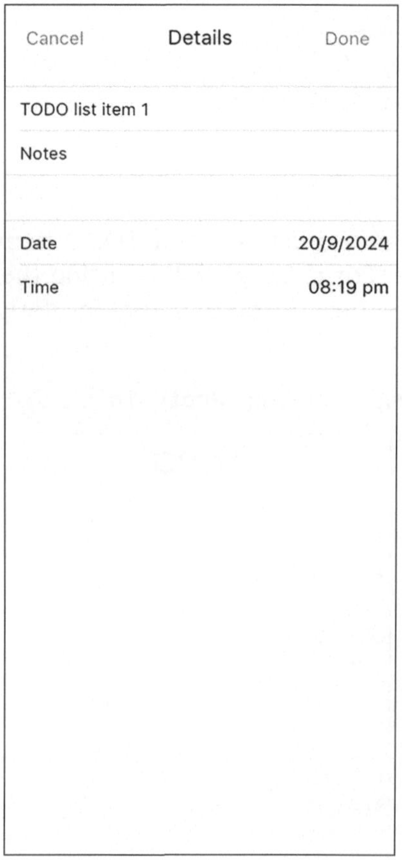

Figure 5.2: *Screen 2 prototype*

Now that we have our designs, let's get into development.

Development

Go to Xcode and create an Xcode project **`'TODO List'`**. This will be our app name. You can give your own app name, it doesn't have to be **`'TODO List'`**.

1. Go to your **`Main.storyboard`** and delete the default `ViewController`. Add the `UINavigationController` with its default `rootViewController` to the storyboard. Refer to the following figure to understand how your storyboard should look like:

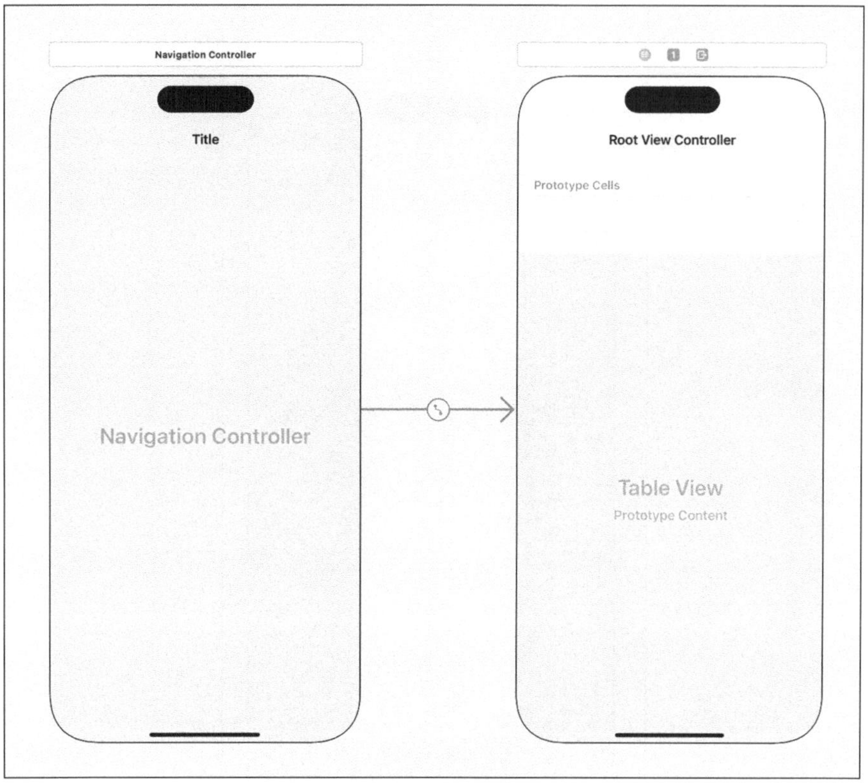

Figure 5.3: *Navigation controller in storyboard*

2. Let's prototype the cell first.

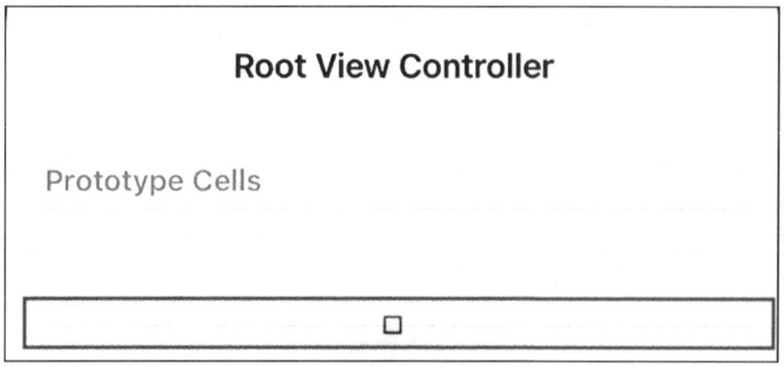

Figure 5.4: *Prototype cell's separator*

3. Let's increase the height of the cell by dragging the separator so that we can add other UI elements to the cell comfortably.
4. Add a button to the prototype cell, as shown in the following figure:

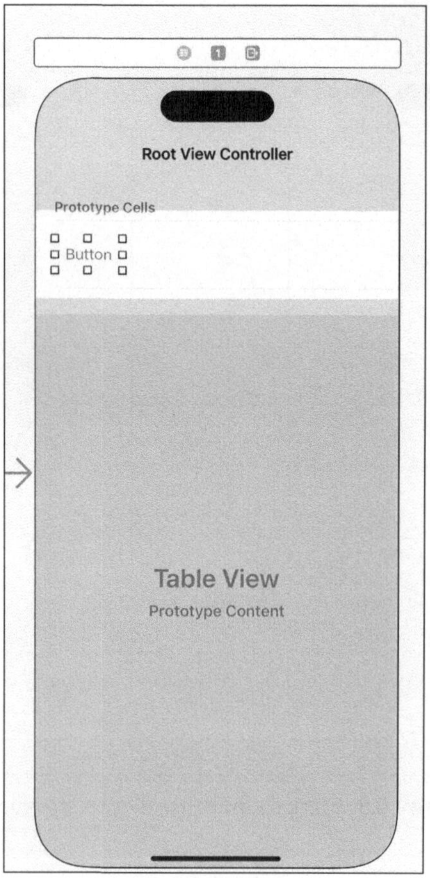

Figure 5.5: *Button added to the cell*

5. As we don't have a designer handy to give the button Icons, we need to be resourceful ourselves. There is a website called https://icons8.com/ where you can search for any icons and download them. Let's download an icon that is similar to the following figure, or you can choose Apple's SFSymbols too. Most companies use third-party or use in-house designers as mentioned earlier.

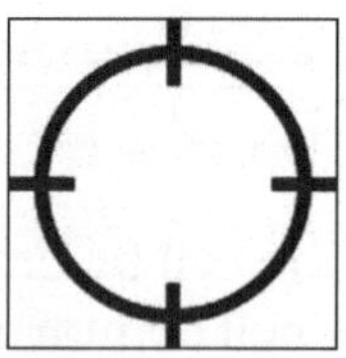

Figure 5.6: *Checkmark icon*

6. Please ensure that you download the better resolution. In the preceding prototype cell, we must remove the button title and add the image in the Attributes Inspector as shown in the following figure:

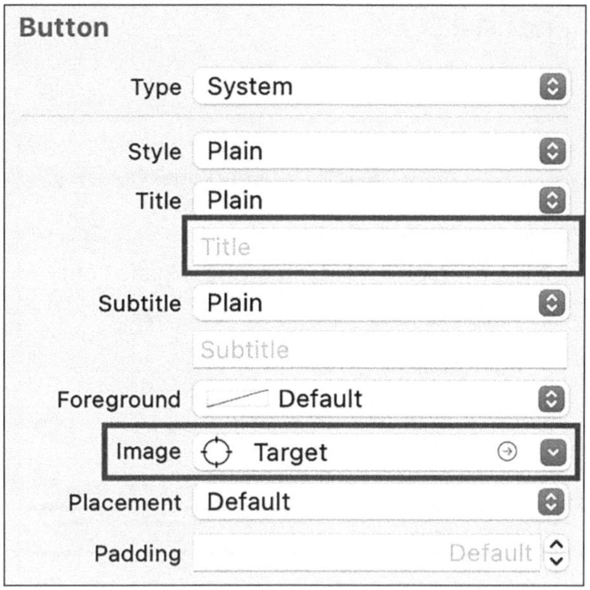

Figure 5.7: *Button's attributes inspector*

7. Before adding an image to the button, don't forget to add the image to the new **`ImageSet`** in the Assets.
8. Add the following constraints to the button in the prototype cell:

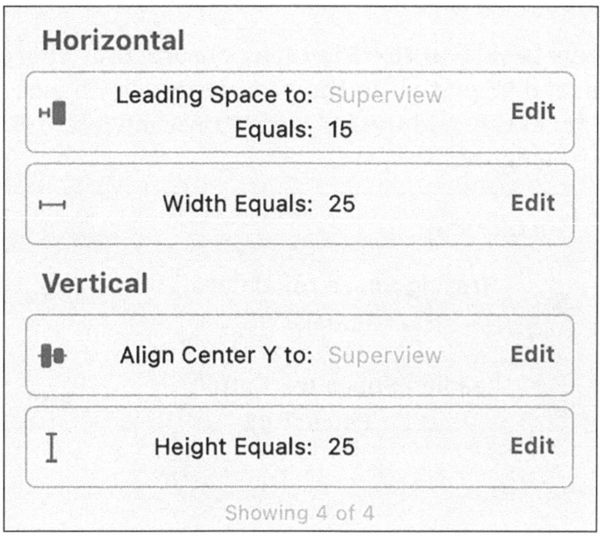

Figure 5.8*: Button's constraints*

9. Next, add the `UITextField` with no borders to the prototype cell, beside your button. You can change the border style in the attributes inspector as shown in the following figure:

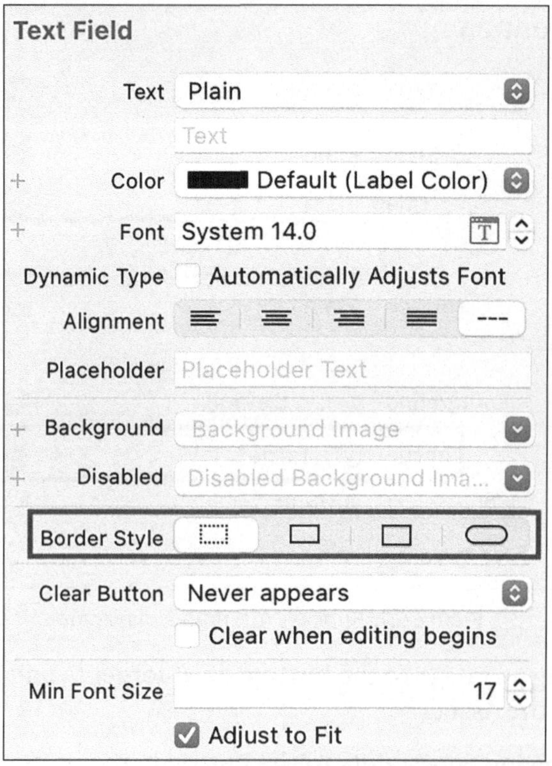

Figure 5.9: *TextField's border style*

10. Add a button beside `UITextField` to ensure that the order is `UIButton`, `UITextfield`, and `UIButton` in the prototype cell. Change the title of the last button to **`'details'`**. Add the following constraints to `UITextField` as shown in the following figure:

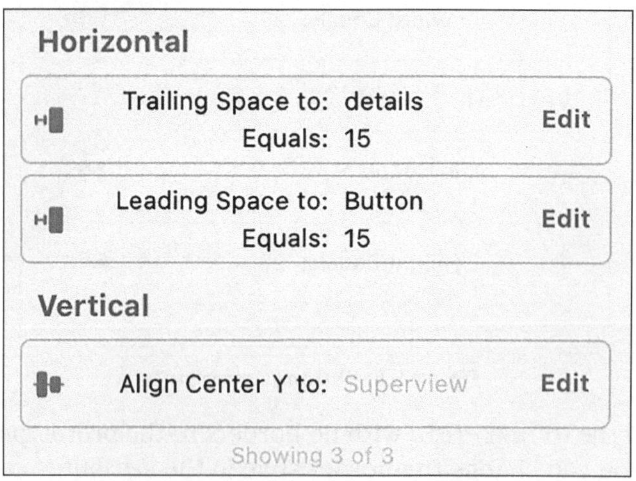

Figure 5.10*: TextField's constraints*

Here the **'details'** is the button with the title **'details'**, which is placed to the right of the `UITextField`, and the **'button'** is the button with the target icon.

11. Add the following constraints to the **'details'** button:

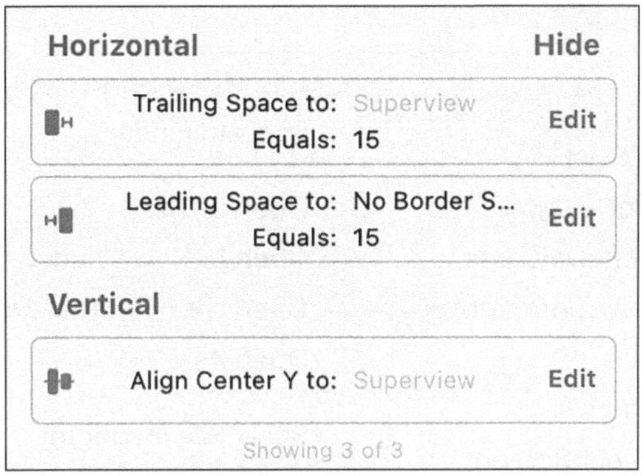

Figure 5.11: *DetailsButton's constraints*

12. Let's change the details button appearance, by selecting the **details** button and going to attributes inspector, changing the background color and tint color as shown in the following figure:

Figure 5.12: *DetailsButton's background color*

To understand the prototype cell with the preceding UI elements, check the following figure:

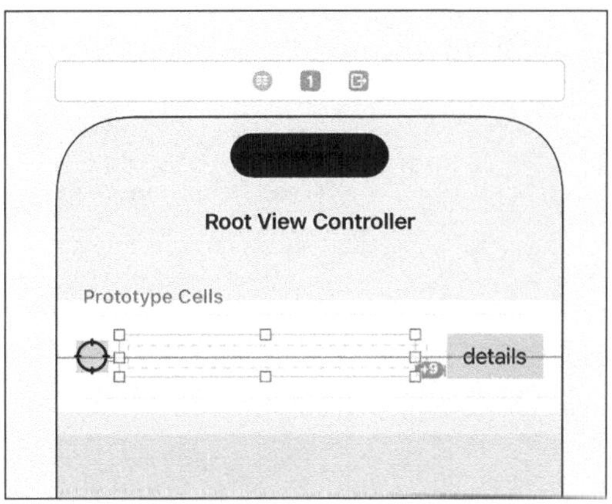

Figure 5.13: *Prototype cell*

13. Now let's create a code reference of our `RootViewController`. Here we are not creating a subclass `UIViewController` but a subclass of `UITableViewController`.

Right-click the project and click the **'New File'**. For reference, check the following figure:

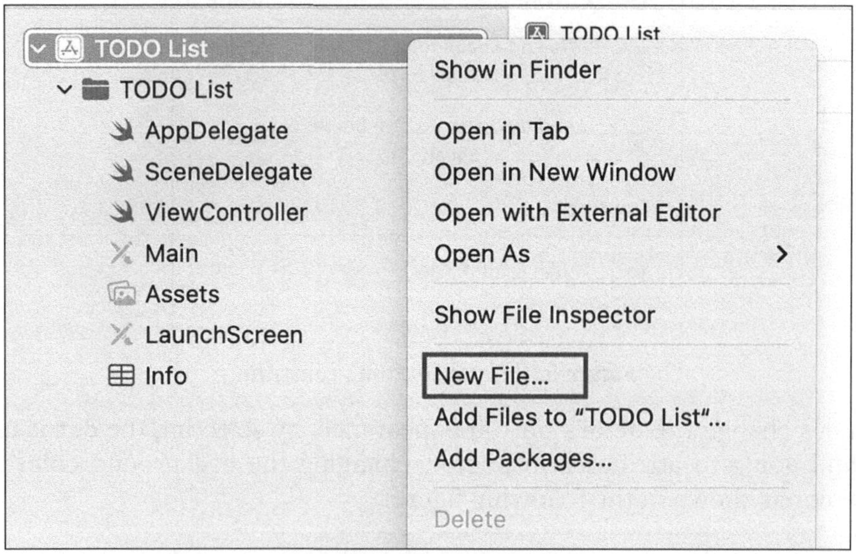

Figure 5.14: *Adding a new file*

14. Select **'Cocoa Touch Class'** as shown in the following figure and click **Next**:

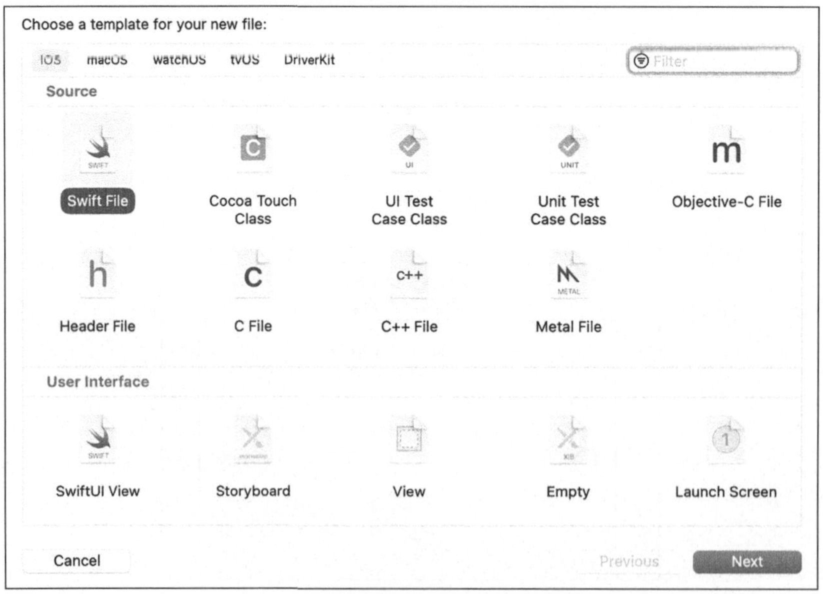

Figure 5.15: *Selecting cocoa touch class for template*

15. Change the subclass from `UIViewController` to `UITableViewController` and then click **'Next'**.
16. Choose the location for the file and then click **'Create'**.
17. If you check the `TableViewController.swift`, it comes with Data Source functions.

    Go to your `Main.storyboard`, click `RootViewController`, go to **'Identity Inspector'**, and give the **'Class'** as **'TableViewController' and 'Storyboard ID'** as **'TableViewController'**. You may check the **'Use Storyboard ID'** too.

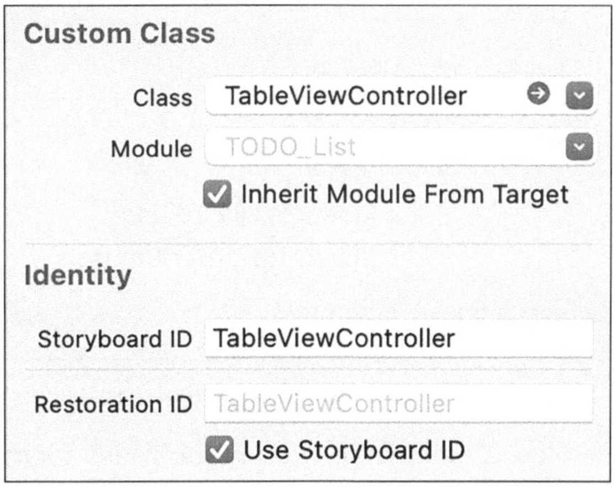

Figure 5.16: *Assigning custom class and storyboard ID*

18. Now go to Storyboard View hierarchy and select **'Table View Cell'** as shown in the following figure:

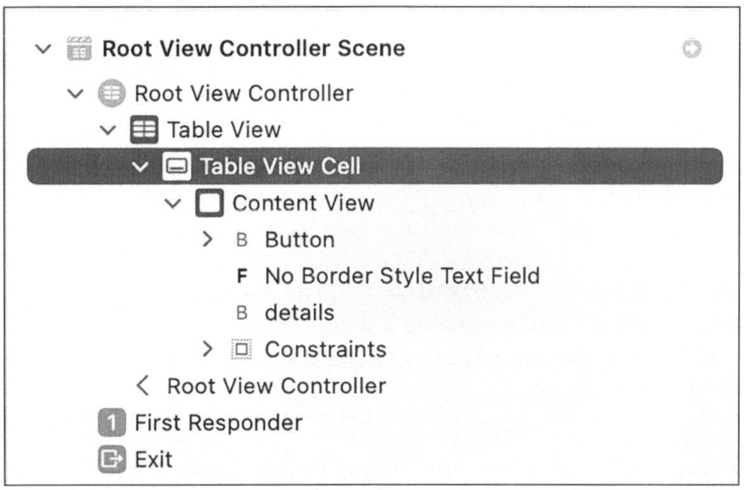

Figure 5.17: *Table View Cell in View Hierarchy*

19. Go to attributes inspector and give the **'Identifier'** as shown in the following figure:

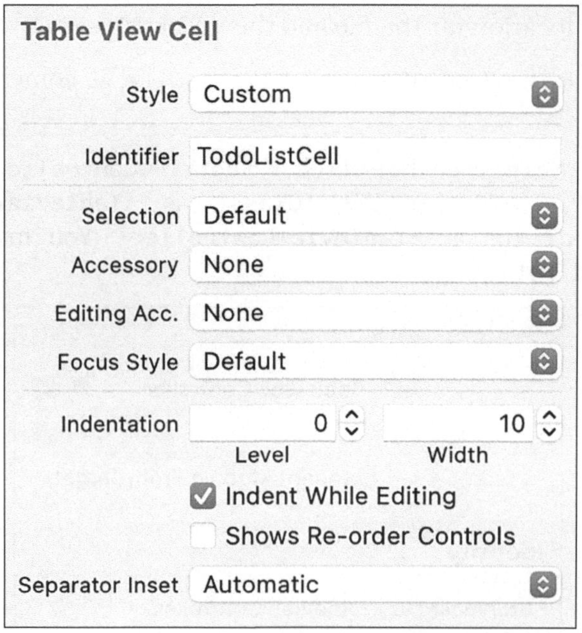

***Figure* 5.18:** *Table View Cell's attributes inspector*

Every cell of the table view should have the unique reuse identifier assigned to the prototype table view cell as shown in the attribute inspector. This reuse identifier allows us to create and recycle our table view cells.

Now let's go to **TableViewController.swift** and modify the Data source functions as follows.

```
override func numberOfSections(in tableView: UITableView) -> Int {
        return 1
}

override func tableView(_ tableView: UITableView, numberOfRowsInSection
section: Int) -> Int {
        return 2
}
override func tableView(_ tableView: UITableView, cellForRowAt index-
Path: IndexPath) -> UITableViewCell {
let cell = tableView.dequeueReusableCell(withIdentifier: "TodoListCell",
for: indexPath) return cell
}
```

Remember, if you don't implement the `numberOfSections`, then it will return the **'1'** by default.

In the preceding storyboard, I changed the background color of the button to yellow with the target icon as you can see in the following figure:

Figure 5.19: *Screen with prototyped cells*

The size of the details button looks a little big. To reduce it, give the Height constraint as **'75'** and the Width constraint as **'30'**.

Let's give the row height too by adding the following function:

```
override func tableView(_ tableView: UITableView, heightForRowAt index-
Path: IndexPath) -> CGFloat {
      50
}
```

Run it and the result you will see is as follows:

***Figure 5.20:** Screen with prototyped cells*

Now let's create a code reference for our custom prototype cell. This will help us customize our cell even more, for example, adding rounded corners for buttons.

1. All you have to do is go to your `TableViewController.swift`. In this, you already have the class called **'`TableViewController`'**, which is the subclass of `UITableViewController`. Let's add one more class to it. The class `TODOListCell` is the subclass of `UITableViewcell`. It should be as follows:

```
import UIKit

class TODOListCell: UITableViewCell {

}

class TableViewController: UITableViewController {

    override func viewDidLoad() {
        super.viewDidLoad()
```

***Figure 5.21:** TODOListCell class*

2. Go to your storyboard and select your cell, if you are not able to select in your storyboard(because sometimes the content view gets selected), go to **View hierarchy** and select your cell, open the **Identity Inspector**, and give the class as **TODOListCell**(your cell class name) under custom class as shown in the following figure:

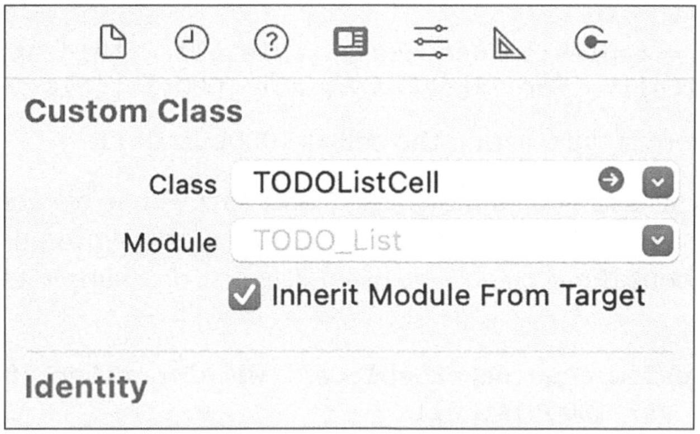

Figure 5.22: *Customer class for prototype cells*

3. It's time to create `IBOutlets` for the UI elements on your cell in your `TODOListCell` Class; if not sure how, please refer to *Chapter 1, Getting Started.* It is the same way of creating `IBOutlet` for any UI element in your storyboard. Your `TODOListCell` class should look as follows:

```
class TODOListCell: UITableViewCell {

    @IBOutlet weak var checkMarkButton: UIButton!
    @IBOutlet weak var textField: UITextField!
    @IBOutlet weak var detailsButton: UIButton!
```

Figure 5.23*: TODOListCell class with UI elements reference*

4. If you look at our cells, we must have rounded corners for our buttons, for both `checkMarkButton` and `detailsButton`. We can do that in our special function called `configureCell`. We can call this `configureCell()` in the `cellForRowAtIndexPath()` function in our `TableViewController`.

```
func configureCell() {
        // configure checkMarkButton
        checkMarkButton.layer.cornerRadius = 15

        // configure detailsButton
        detailsButton.layer.cornerRadius = 5
}
```

5. Now go to your `TableViewController` class, go to your `'cellForRowAtIndexPath:'`, and modify this line,

   ```
   let cell = tableView.dequeueReusableCell(withIdentifier:
   "TodoListCell", for: indexPath)
   ```

   to this

   ```
   let cell = tableView.dequeueReusableCell(withIdentifier:
   "TodoListCell", for: indexPath) as! TODOListCell
   ```

All we are doing here is typecasting the cell as `TODOListCell`.

Here we forced typecasting by adding **`as! TODOListCell`** as we are sure that the cell we will get is of type `TODOListCell`, but here we can do optional typecasting when we are not sure about the type we get back; it is just one simple trick to do optional typecasting.

```
let cell = tableView.dequeueReusableCell(withIdentifier: "TodoListCell",
for: indexPath) as? TODOListCell
```

Here the 'cell' will not be nil if the cell is of type '`TODOListCell`', but if `tableView.dequeueReusableCell` returns a different type, we will get nil. In that case, we have to do a null check.

6. Now call your cell's function `configureCell()`. Check the following figure for reference:

```
override func tableView(_ tableView: UITableView, cellForRowAt indexPath: IndexPath) -> UITableViewCell {

    let cell = tableView.dequeueReusableCell(withIdentifier: "TodoListCell", for: indexPath) as! TODOListCell
    cell.configureCell()

    return cell
}
```

Figure 5.24: *cellForRowAtIndexPath: function*

7. Run it and the result will be as follows:

***Figure* 5.25**: *Simulator with cells*

Let's get some requirements straight, the background color `checkMarkButton` should be 'yellow' only when the user taps on it, let's say, after finishing the task. We want a new row to appear when the user taps on our `TableView`; it's like adding a new `TODOList` item when the user taps on the `tableView`.

1. Firstly, go to your storyboard, select your `checkMarkButton`, and in Attributes inspector change the background to **'Clear Color'**.
2. Next, add the variable `noOfRows` in our `TableViewController` class. For now, let's say it's 2. Later on, we can make it according to the data the user will add. Refer to the following code:

```
var noOfRows = 2
```

3. Now, let's add `UITapGestureRecognizer` to our `tableView` in our `viewDidLoad()` function.

```
override func viewDidLoad() {
       super.viewDidLoad()
```

```
        let tapOnTableView: UITapGestureRecognizer = UITapGesture-
Recognizer(target: self, action: #selector(self.handleTap(_:)))

        tableView.addGestureRecognizer(tapOnTableView)
    }
```

4. Add the `handleTap` function to handle the tap,

```
@objc func handleTap(_ sender: UITapGestureRecognizer? = nil) {

        noOfRows += 1
        tableView.reloadData()

    }
```

What we are doing here is, whenever the user taps on the `TableView`, the `noOfRows` variable increases by 1. For example, if it is 2, when the user taps on our `TableView`, the `noOfRows` increases to 3.

5. Next, we call `UITableView`'s `reloadData` function; it reloads our `UITableView`, by calling all our `UITableView`'s data source and delegate functions.

   Let's change the `numOfRows` data source function as follows:

```
override func tableView(_ tableView: UITableView, numberOfRowsIn-
Section section: Int) -> Int {
        return noOfRows
    }
```

6. Run it, and the result will be as shown in the following figure:

Figure 5.26: *Simulator screen*

7. Now tap on the `tableView`, and you will see the newly added row as shown in the following figure:

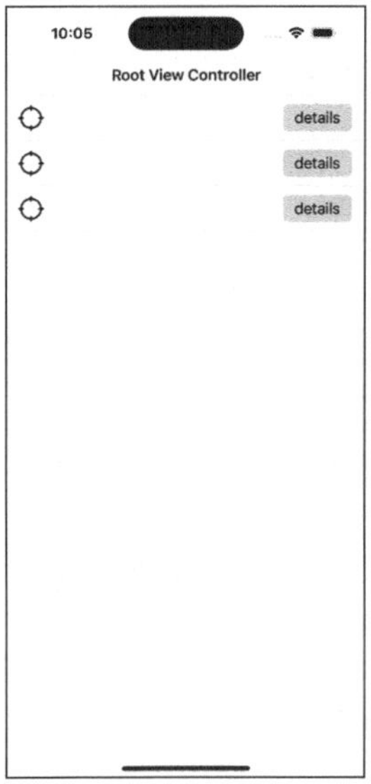

***Figure 5.27**: Simulator screen with an added row*

The next step is to create a struct so that we can save the data and load our `TableView` dynamically.

1. Right-click the project, click **'New File'**, and select **'Swift File'** as shown in the following figure and give **'Save As'** as **'TODOListItem'**.

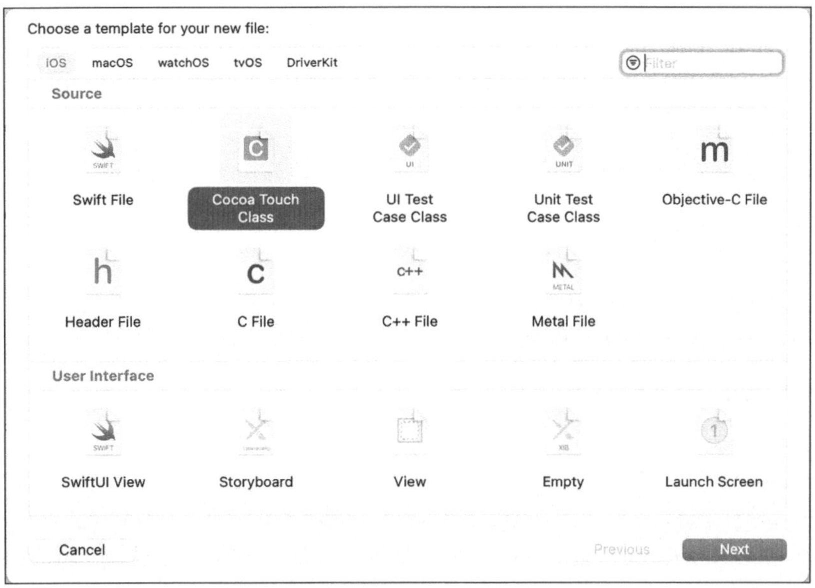

***Figure 5.28**: Creating a new Swift file*

2. Open the file and create a struct **'TODOListItem'** with variables as follows.

```
struct TODOListItem {

    var item: String

    var notes: String?
    var date: Date?
    var time: Date?
}
```

Structs

Structs are data types that can store multiple variables of different data types. You can have properties and methods in your struct. You might wonder if we could have created 'class' instead of 'struct', but we need to know the difference before proceeding to delete this struct. A 'struct' is a value type, not a reference type, which means the runtime deals directly with the struct's underlying data, which can be very efficient. Coming to a 'Class' it is the reference type, not the value type. The 'structs' can be used to make an object's unique copy without saving the state. If you don't have to control an object's identity, then use the 'structs'. The structs are lightweight and high-performance data types. These are some of the wonderful reasons why and when we should use a struct.

Coming back to our code, whenever the user adds a new list item, it will be a `TODOListItem`. These items will be added to the array in our `TableViewController`. Let's create an array of `TODOListItems` in our `TableViewController`.

```
var toDoListItemsArray: [TODOListItem] = []
```

We created an empty array. Whenever the user adds a new item, it will be added to this.

Add the following variable `cellIsEditing`, this variable will be used in our `handleTap` function.

```
var cellIsEditing: Bool = false
```

Using this variable, we will be either adding a new row when the user taps on the screen which we are already doing, or dismissing the keyboard, which we will be doing.

Two more variables that are required in our `TableViewController` are as follows.

```
var theToDoItemString: String?
var selectedItem: TODOListItem?
```

The **'theToDoItemString'** is used to capture what has been typed in our cell and for other convenient coding practices. The **'selectedItem'** is used to capture the item that is selected by the user.

Before going any further, change back the **'noOfRows'** to 0, as we gave **'noOfRows = 2'** earlier.

Now let's deal with the **'handleTap'** function, as discussed earlier when the user taps on the screen, it should add a new row; if a user is already typing on the row and when the user taps on the screen, it should end editing, which dismisses the keyboard. To do that, we need to add the 'if' condition that checks on variable **'cellIsEditing'** as follows.

```
if cellIsEditing == false {
      noOfRows += 1
      tableView.reloadData()
}
```

'cellIsEditing' will become true when the user is editing which we will be doing in the later part of our code, but let's write the code for when it is true in the else condition as follows.

```
if cellIsEditing {

    cellIsEditing = false
    view.endEditing(true)

} else {
    noOfRows += 1
    tableView.reloadData()
}
```

Check the following screenshot for a better understanding of the 'handleTap' function:

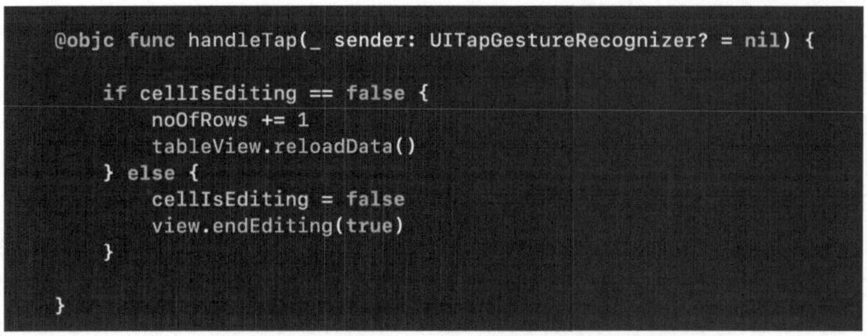

Figure 5.29: *handleTap function*

We should make 'cellIsEditing' false as we are ending the editing, and 'view.endEditing(true)' ends all the editing on the screen.

Let's get our cell requirements straight. We have two requirements here.

- If it is a new cell, the textField text should be empty and the textField should become the first responder too, which means the keyboard should appear.

- If it is an old `todo` list item, it means there will be text in `textField` and you get this data from our `toDoListItemsArray`.

Let's get that working. In our `tableView(_:cellForRowAt:)` function, after configuring our cell, add the following code.

```
cell.textField.text = nil

// making the new item as selected item
let id: Int = toDoListItemsArray.count + 1
let todoListItem = TODOListItem(id: id)
selectedItem = todoListItem
DispatchQueue.main.async {
    cell.textField.becomeFirstResponder()
 }
```

As this is the new cell that appears when the user wants to enter a new `ToDo` Item, the `textField.text` should be nil, which made it. Next, we create a variable id based on our `toDoListItemsArray.count`, which will be our new item's id and is very useful for identifying our `TodoListItems` in the later part of our App.

Using the preceding `'id'`, we are initializing `'TODOListItem'` and assigning this item to our `TableViewController's selectedItem`, as this will be the item that the user is currently editing and finally, we are making our cell's `textField` as a first responder and making this on the main thread.

DispatchQueue

`DispatchQueue` is built on top of the Grand Central Dispatch(GCD) queue, which is an API used for managing concurrent operations in your app. The `DispatchQueue` helps to execute the app's tasks concurrently and serially. This can help us to improve the efficiency of your app. Here we are using `DispatchQueue.main.async`, which we are saying to execute the code given concurrently on the main thread.

The preceding code should be implemented only if it is a new row, which means only for the `ToDo` list item. If there are no items in our `TableViewController`, then the new row would be the first row. If there are items already in our list, then the newly added row will be the last row. So, let's add our preceding code into an 'if' condition as follows:

```
if indexPath.row == noOfRows - 1 {

    cell.textField.text = nil

    let id: Int = toDoListItemsArray.count + 1
    let todoListItem = TODOListItem(id: id)
    selectedItem = todoListItem
```

```
    DispatchQueue.main.async {
        cell.textField.becomeFirstResponder()
    }

}
```

The preceding `'if'` condition says that if `indexPath.row == noOfRows - 1`, which means, for example, there is already one old row, and the user taps on the screen. A new row is added, where the new cell is added, and where the preceding code will be implemented. Here, `indexPath.row` is 1 which means it is the second row and in this case, the `noOfRows` is 2 and 2-1 =1. This means the preceding code gets implemented for the new row.

Let's implement the second requirement, that is, if it is an old `ToDo` list item, then we should get the data from our `toDoListItemsArray` and populate the data in the required fields.

After calling the cell's configure cell function and before the preceding if condition, write the following code.

```
let todoListItem = toDoListItemsArray[indexPath.row]
cell.textField.text = todoListItem.item
cell.textField.endEditing(true)

DispatchQueue.main.async {
    self.view.endEditing(true)
}
```

Here we are getting the `todoListItem` from our `'toDoListItemsArray'` and assigning our `todoListItem`'s item to our `textField`. We are ending the editing of our `textField` and editing our view.

There is a chance that this code could fail when there are no items in our array or no item in our array at `indexPath.row`. So, let's add the preceding code in the 'if' condition as follows.

```
if indexPath.row <= toDoListItemsArray.count - 1 {

    // Existing item
    let todoListItem = toDoListItemsArray[indexPath.row]
    cell.textField.text = todoListItem.item
    cell.textField.endEditing(true)

    DispatchQueue.main.async {
        self.view.endEditing(true)
    }
}
```

The preceding condition will ensure that our code executes only when our array has items at `indexPath.row`. Now let's add the 'else if' condition and add the code of our first requirement of adding a new row. Do it as given here.

```
if indexPath.row <= toDoListItemsArray.count - 1 {

    // Existing item
    let todoListItem = toDoListItemsArray[indexPath.row]
    cell.textField.text = todoListItem.item
    cell.textField.endEditing(true)

    DispatchQueue.main.async {
        self.view.endEditing(true)
    }

} else if indexPath.row == noOfRows - 1 {

    cell.textField.text = nil

    let id: Int = toDoListItemsArray.count + 1
    let todoListItem = TODOListItem(id: id)
    selectedItem = todoListItem
    DispatchQueue.main.async {
        cell.textField.becomeFirstResponder()
    }

}
```

Your whole `tableView(_:cellForRowAt:)` should look as follows:

```
override func tableView(_ tableView: UITableView, cellForRowAt indexPath: IndexPath) -> UITableViewCell {

    let cell = tableView.dequeueReusableCell(withIdentifier: "TodoListCell", for: indexPath) as! TODOListCell
    cell.textField.delegate = self
    cell.configureCell()

    if indexPath.row <= toDoListItemsArray.count - 1 {

        // Existing item
        let todoListItem = toDoListItemsArray[indexPath.row]
        cell.textField.text = todoListItem.item
        cell.textField.endEditing(true)

        DispatchQueue.main.async {
            self.view.endEditing(true)
        }

    } else if indexPath.row == noOfRows - 1 {

        cell.textField.text = nil

        let id: Int = toDoListItemsArray.count + 1
        let todoListItem = TODOListItem(id: id)
        selectedItem = todoListItem
        DispatchQueue.main.async {
            cell.textField.becomeFirstResponder()
        }
    }

    return cell
}
```

Figure 5.30: *cellForRowAtIndexPath: function with added code for the new row*

If you check the preceding screenshot, before calling the `configureCell()` function, we are also assigning the cell's `textfield`'s delegate as our `TableViewController`. We should assign that our `TableViewController` is `UITextFieldDelegate` as follows.

```
class TableViewController: UITableViewController, UITextFieldDelegate {
```

Let's think of something as per our requirements. When the user adds a new `ToDoListItem` or a new row, the user should be able to delete the row or `ToDoListItem` that is no longer needed. We can do it by using our `UITableViewDataSource` functions `tableView(_:canEditRowAt:)` and `tableView(_:commit:forRowAt:)`. Implement them as follows:

```
override func tableView(_ tableView: UITableView, canEditRowAt index-
Path: IndexPath) -> Bool {
     true
}
override func tableView(_ tableView: UITableView, commit editingStyle:
UITableViewCell.EditingStyle, forRowAt indexPath: IndexPath) {
    if editingStyle == .delete {
        self.tableView.beginUpdates()
        self.toDoListItemsArray.remove(at: indexPath.row)
        noOfRows -= 1
        self.tableView.deleteRows(at: [IndexPath(row: 0, section: 0)],
with: .automatic)
        self.tableView.endUpdates()
    }

}
```

If you don't implement `tableView(_:canEditRowAt:)` the code that we wrote in `tableView(_:commit:forRowAt:)` might not work. In `tableView(_:commit:forRowAt:)` we got if condition **'`if editingStyle == .delete`'**, this will allow us to have the feature where when the user swipes the row to the left from the right end, it shows the delete option. Under this 'if' condition, we begin updates for our `TableView`.

`beginUpdates()`

It starts a series of method calls that select, delete, and insert rows and sections of your table view.

Then we need to modify our array(our data) and `noOfRows` accordingly before deleting the row in our `TableView`, otherwise, our `TableView` will update accordingly. You can delete the row in `TableView` by calling `UITableView`'s `deleteRows` function as follows:

```
self.tableView.deleteRows(at: [IndexPath(row: 0, section: 0)], with:
.automatic)
```

Then we call `UITableView`'s `endUpdates` function.

endUpdates()

As the name implies, it ends a series of method calls that delete, select, insert, and reload rows and sections of your table view. All of your changes will be animated by the table view simultaneously.

Before going forward with implementing any more features, let's implement the UITextField delegate function as the user needs to enter the cell's text field and the text `textField(_:shouldChangeCharactersIn:replacementString:)`. Firstly, let's get the following `textfield`'s text and user-entered text inside our delegate function.

```
func textField(_ textField: UITextField, shouldChangeCharactersIn range:
NSRange, replacementString string: String) -> Bool {

    let textFieldtext: NSString = (textField.text ?? "") as NSString
    let endToDOString = textFieldtext.replacingCharacters(in: range,
    with: string)
    print("the end string is", endToDOString)

}
```

Now implement the following code.

```
theToDoItemString = endToDOString
selectedItem?.item = theToDoItemString
cellIsEditing = true
```

We assign the end user entered string to our `TableViewController`'s **'theToDoItemString'** variable, then we modify our `TableViewController`'s `selectedItem`'s item, which is a `ToDo` list item that the user entered. And don't forget our `TableViewController`'s `selectedItem` gets assigned in `tableView(_:cellForRowAt:)`.

For a new row, the preceding code works wonderfully, but if the user wants to modify the old ToDo list item, then we must modify the 'item' in our `toDoListItemsArray`, and for that, implementation is as follows.

```
if textField.text?.count != 0 {

    if let itemIntheArray = toDoListItemsArray.first(where: { $0.item ==
textField.text}) {

        var editingItem = itemIntheArray
        editingItem.item = theToDoItemString
```

```
        toDoListItemsArray = toDoListItemsArray.map { $0.item == text-
Field.text ? editingItem : $0 }
        print("the array",toDoListItemsArray)
    }

}
```

Here we check if the `textField`'s text count is not 0, as we don't have to implement the preceding code. Next, we check if there is a `TODOListItem` with an 'item' that already exists as `textField`'s text. If the `TODOListItem` exists, we assign that item to the new variable **'editingItem'**, and then we assign the editing Item. Item with the modified string. Then we modify this item in the array using a map.

```
toDoListItemsArray = toDoListItemsArray.map { $0.item == textField.text
? editingItem : $0 }
```

Here we map `TODOListItem` with already existing `textField`'s text, then we replace that item with the **'editingItem'**. Finally, we print the array to check if the item has been replaced or modified.

The next task is if it is a new row or new `TODOListItem` and the editing has ended, that item should be added to our **'toDoListItemsArray'**. For that, let's implement another `UITextField`'s delegate method **'textFieldDidEndEditing(_:)'**.

```
func textFieldDidEndEditing(_ textField: UITextField) {

    if let itemIntheArray = toDoListItemsArray.first(where: { $0.item ==
textField.text}) {
        toDoListItemsArray = toDoListItemsArray.map { $0.item == theTo-
DoItemString ? itemIntheArray : $0 }
        print("the array",toDoListItemsArray)
    } else {
        if let theNewItem = selectedItem {
            toDoListItemsArray.append(theNewItem)
            selectedItem = nil
        }
    }
}
```

We are checking if the item exists in our array `TodListItemsArray`; if it exists, we are modifying the item and if not, we are adding it as a new item to the array.

Go ahead, run it, and experiment with it. You should see something similar as follows:

***Figure 5.31**: Simulator screen with new row*

Let's add another awesome functionality. When the user is done with the task, the user clicks the checkmark button, as shown in the following figure:

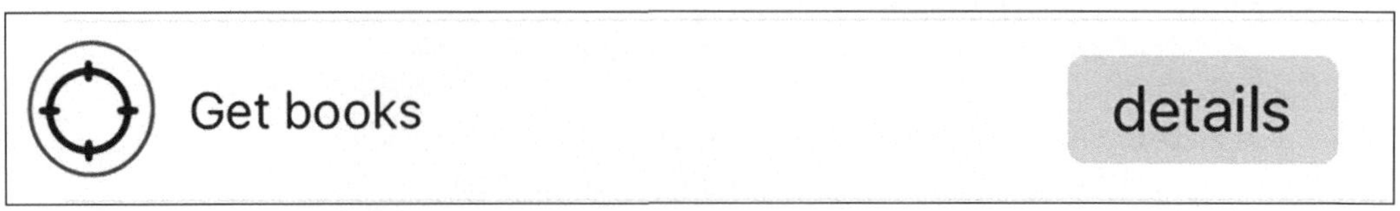

***Figure 5.32**: Cell with checkmark button highlighted*

When the user clicks that button, the text should turn grey for two seconds and then the row or `TODO` List Item should be deleted. That `TODOListItem` should be deleted from our `toDoListItemsArray` too which means this functionality should be done in our `TableViewController`.

The first thing to do here is to create the `IBAction` for your `checkMarkButton` in your `TODOListCell` as shown in the following figure:

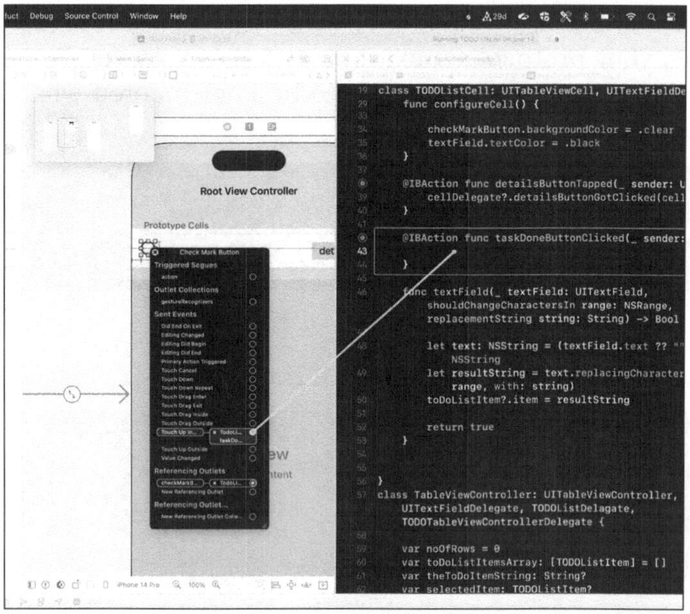

Figure 5.33: *Assigning IBAction to the checkmark button*

When a user clicks the `checkMarkButton`, the button's background should also turn yellow, which gives the user indication that the user has clicked the button.

So, inside our `@IBAction` **`'taskDoneButtonClicked'`**

```
checkMarkButton.backgroundColor = .systemYellow
textField.textColor = .lightGray
```

We also made `textField`'s text color gray. Your **`'taskDoneButtonClicked'`** should look as follows:

```
@IBAction func taskDoneButtonClicked(_ sender: Any) {
    checkMarkButton.backgroundColor = .systemYellow
    textField.textColor = .lightGray
}
```

Figure 5.34: *IBAction of checkmark button*

We got our `IBaction` for this button in the `TODOListCell` class, but this cell class does not know anything about our `TableViewController` or our array; so how do we delete the rows in our `tableView` and delete items from the array and how do we solve this problem? This is where delegates come into action. Let's create our very first protocol in our app. On top of your `TODOListCell` class, add the following protocol:

```
protocol TODOListDelagate {
}
```

Inside this protocol, declare a function **'func taskDoneButtonGotClicked(cell: TODOListCell)'**, your protocol should look as follows. As you know what protocol is, we just define the function that needs to be implemented when you assign this protocol to your class.

```
protocol TODOListDelagate {
    func taskDoneButtonGotClicked(cell: TODOListCell)
}
```

***Figure 5.35**: TODOListDelegate*

Inside your `TODOListCell` declare your `TODOListDelegate` as follows:

```
class TODOListCell: UITableViewCell, UITextFieldDelegate {

    @IBOutlet weak var checkMarkButton: UIButton!
    @IBOutlet weak var textField: UITextField!
    @IBOutlet weak var detailsButton: UIButton!

    var cellDelegate: TODOListDelagate?
```

***Figure 5.36:** TODOListDelegate in TODOListCell*

Now inside your **'taskDoneButtonClicked'** call your delegate's function **'taskDoneButtonGotClicked'** as shown in the following figure:

```
@IBAction func taskDoneButtonClicked(_ sender: Any) {
    checkMarkButton.backgroundColor = .systemYellow
    textField.textColor = .lightGray
    cellDelegate?.taskDoneButtonGotClicked(cell: self)
}
```

***Figure 5.37:** Calling delegate function*

The idea here is whichever class is declared as `TODOListDelegate` needs to implement this delegate function **'taskDoneButtonGotClicked'**. Next, we will make our `TableViewController` as `TODOListDelegate` and implement this delegate function and this delegate function gets triggered whenever the cell's `checkMarkButton` gets clicked as we are calling this delegate function inside `checkMarkButton`'s `IBAction` **'taskDoneButtonClicked'**.

So, let's go and make our `TableViewController` a `TODOListDelegate` as follows:

```
class TableViewController: UITableViewController, UITextFieldDelegate, TODOListDelagate {
```

***Figure 5.38**: Making the TableViewController as TODOListDelegate*

Then, in our `tableView(_:cellForRowAt:)` assign the cell's `cellDelegate` as `TableViewController` as follows:

```
override func tableView(_ tableView: UITableView, cellForRowAt indexPath: IndexPath) -> UITableViewCell {

    let cell = tableView.dequeueReusableCell(withIdentifier: "TodoListCell", for: indexPath) as! TODOListCell
    cell.textField.delegate = self
    cell.cellDelegate = self
    cell.configureCell()
```

***Figure* 5.39:** *Assigning cellDelegate*

Now let's implement our delegate function, **'`taskDoneButtonGotClicked`'**. Before implementing, let's get the requirements straight. When this **'`checkMarkButton`'** is clicked we want the background color of the button to turn yellow and `UITextField`'s text color to turn gray, which we are doing in our `IBAction` in our `TODOListCell`. Next, after two seconds, we should delete the row. Let's implement this in our delegate function implementation in our `TableViewController`.

```
func taskDoneButtonGotClicked(cell: TODOListCell) {

    DispatchQueue.main.asyncAfter(deadline: .now() + 2) {
        if let indexPath = self.tableView.indexPath(for: cell) {
            if indexPath.row == self.toDoListItemsArray.count - 1 {
                self.tableView.beginUpdates()
                self.toDoListItemsArray.remove(at: indexPath.row)
                self.noOfRows -= 1
                self.tableView.deleteRows(at: [indexPath], with:
                .automatic)
                self.tableView.endUpdates()
            }
        }
    }
}
```

`DispatchQueue.main.asyncAfter`: `DispatchQueue.main.asyncAfter` will do the same as `DispatchQueue.main.async`, that is, executing your code concurrently on the main thread, but only after the deadline you have provided, which in our case is two seconds.

Here we are deleting the row from our `TableView` after two seconds. Also, we are modifying our `toDoListItemsArray` and `noOfRows` accordingly.

Run it, and you should be able to see it as follows:

Figure 5.40: *Simulator screen with completed task*

Now that we dealt with `checkMarkButton`, we have another button in our cell, `detailsButton`. Similarly, let's create an `IBAction` for our `detailsButton`(check how it was done for `checkMarkButton` earlier), the `IBAction` function is **'detailsButtonTapped'**.

When the **'detailsButton'** gets clicked, it should take the user to the 'details' screen. Since we can't do that from **'TODOListCell'**, we need to do this from `TableViewController`; so we need a delegate function just like we did for `checkMarkButton`. So, let's declare one more function in our `TODOListDelegate` as follows:

```
protocol TODOListDelagate {
    func detailsButtonGotClicked(cell: TODOListCell)
    func taskDoneButtonGotClicked(cell: TODOListCell)
}
```

***Figure 5.41**: TODOListDelagate with detailsButtonGotClicked function*

In our `IBAction` **'detailsButtonTapped'**, let's call our **'detailsButtonGotClicked'** as follows:

```
@IBAction func detailsButtonTapped(_ sender: UIButton) {
    cellDelegate?.detailsButtonGotClicked(cell: self)
}
```

Figure 5.42: *IBAction detailsButtonTapped*

Now it is time to implement this delegate function in our `TableViewController` as follows:

```
func detailsButtonGotClicked(cell: TODOListCell) {

}
```

The requirement of this function is it should take the user to the details screen. But, we don't have the details screen yet. Before creating the screen, let's meet certain requirements first.

The requirements of the details screen are the user should be able to enter the date, time, and any notes for this `ToDo` Item.

Go to your **`Main.storyboard`** and drag `UITableViewController` to the storyboard. You might wonder why there is no data to populate in repeating patterns in the details screen. Why are we using `UITableViewController`? The reason is until now we used `UITableViewController` or `UITableViews` with dynamic prototypes, but now we are using static cells.

We will not use the same cell prototype for all the cells rather we will design each cell individually. You will learn more while implementing.

1. As you dragged the `UITableViewController` to the **`Main.Storyboard`**, let's create a code reference for this `UITableViewController`, and name it `DetailsTableViewController`. Go to **`Main.Storyboard`**, click your newly added `UITableViewController`, and then go to **`Identity Inspector`**, give the Class and Storyboard ID as **`'DetailsTableViewController'`**, and click use **`'Storyboard ID'`**.

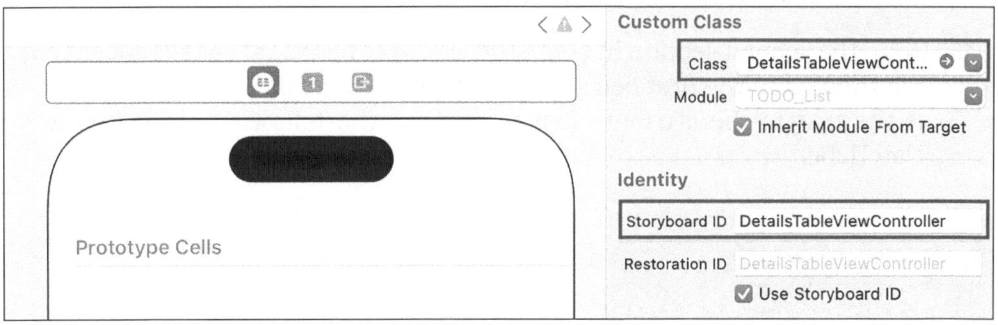

Figure 5.43: *Assigning the custom class view controller*

2. Now go to the view hierarchy, click the '**`Details Table View Controller Scene`**', and click the **`'Table View'`** as shown in the following figure:

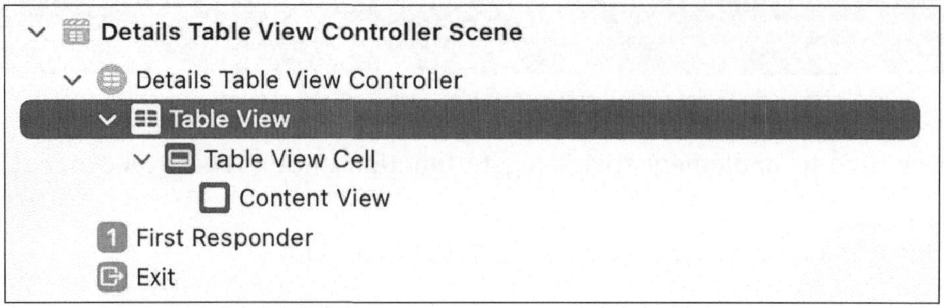

Figure 5.44: *Selection Table View in the view hierarchy*

3. Go to the Attributes Inspector, change the **`'Content'`** to **`'Static Cells',`** and change the other attributes as shown in the following figure:

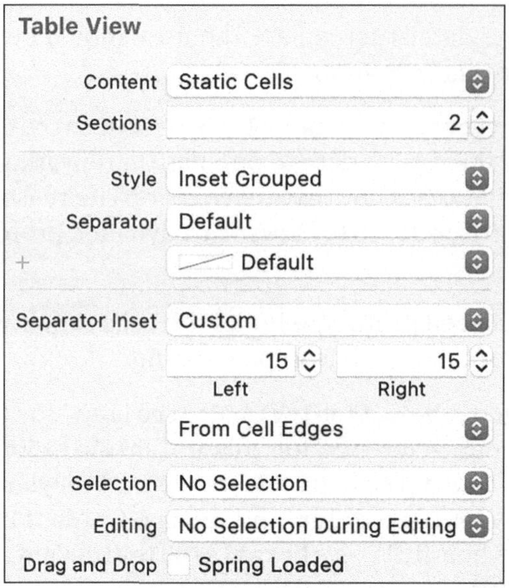

Figure 5.45*: Changing the TableView's content to Static Cells*

4. Go to the second section in your storyboard of **`DetailsTableViewController`** and then go to the first cell and add a label to the cell. Give the label and date as the text in the attribute inspector. Give the following attributes to your 'Date' label.

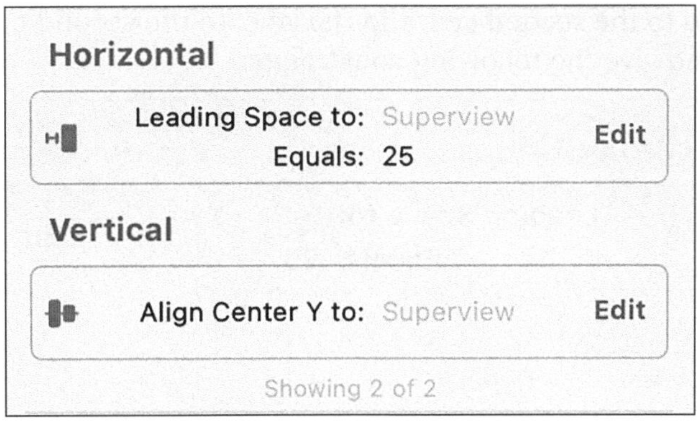

Figure 5.46: *Date label attributes*

5. Add the `UITextField` to the same cell with the following attributes:

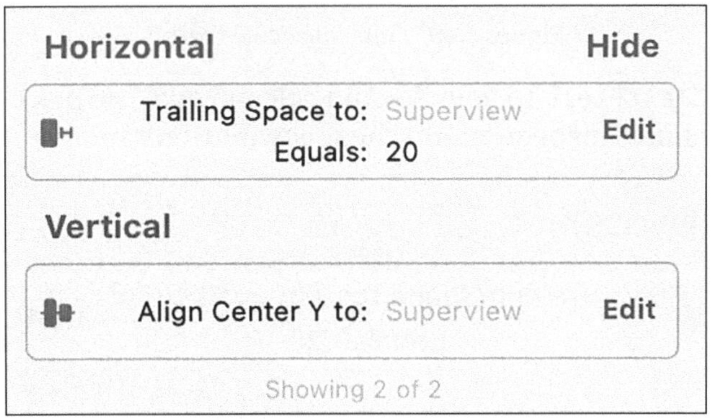

Figure 5.47: *Date textField attributes*

6. Now go to the attributes inspector and give the placeholder as **'DD/MM/YYYY'**. To understand better, check the following figure:

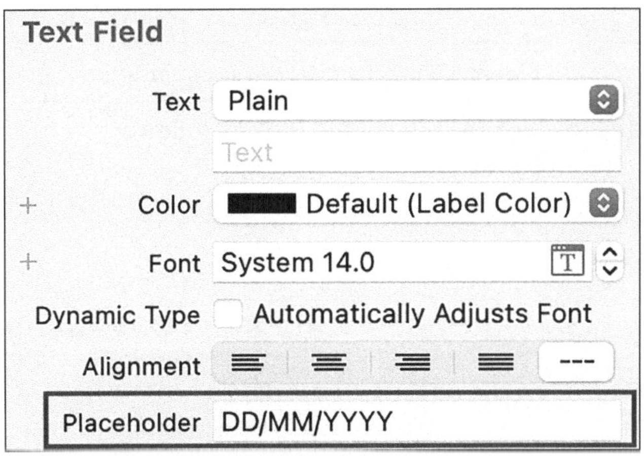

Figure 5.48: *Date textField's placeholder*

7. Time to go to the second cell; add the label to the second cell, give the text as **'Time'**, and give the following constraints:

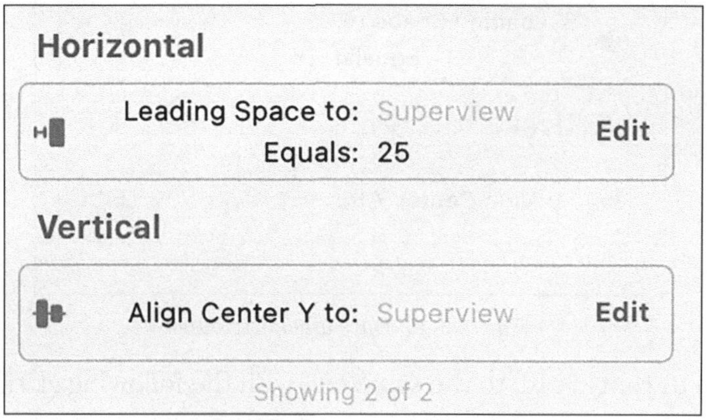

***Figure* 5.49**: *Time label constraints*

8. Add the `UITextField` to your second cell and give the placeholder as **'HH:MM'** in the attributes inspector. Add the following constraints:

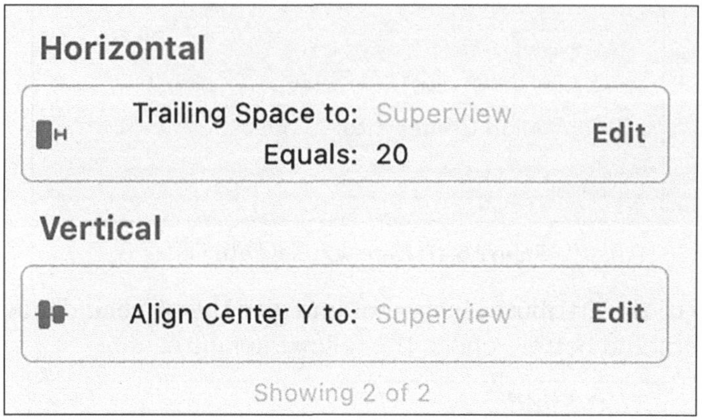

***Figure* 5.50**: *Time textField's constraints*

Your `DetailsTableViewController` should look as follows:

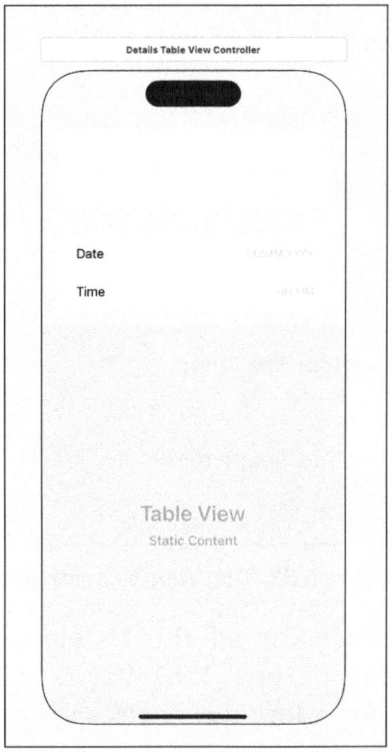

Figure 5.51: *DetailsTableViewController*

9. Now let's go to the first section. Add a `UITextField` to the first cell with the following constraints:

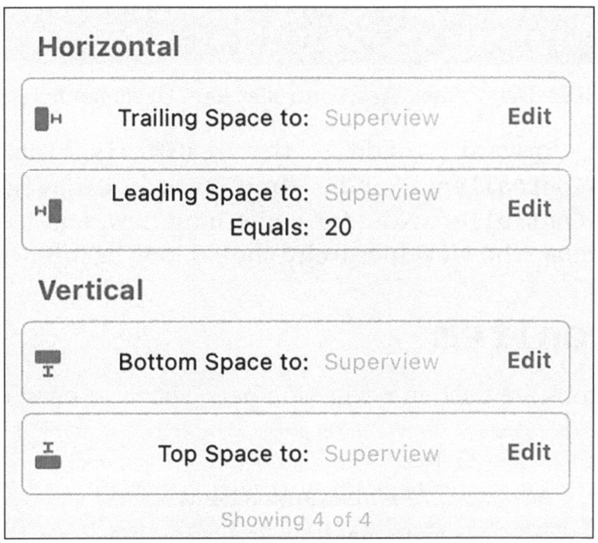

Figure 5.52: *First cell's constraints*

10. Add the `UITextView` to the second cell with the following constraints:

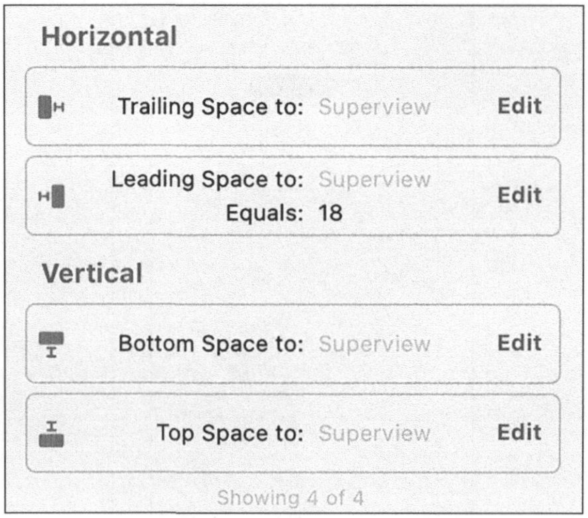

***Figure* 5.53:** *TextView's constraints*

11. Give the code reference for all the UI elements we have added to the `DetailsTableViewController`'s `TableView`'s cells; you can give whatever names you want, but for reference, check the following figure:

```
class DetailsTableViewController: UITableViewController {

    @IBOutlet weak var todoItemTextField: UITextField!
    @IBOutlet weak var notesTextView: UITextView!
    @IBOutlet weak var dateTextField: UITextField!
    @IBOutlet weak var timeTextField: UITextField!
```

***Figure* 5.54**: *DetailsTableViewController with UI elements references*

Before going forward, add the `UINavigationBar` to your `DetailsTableViewController`, and drag the `UINavigationBar` to `DetailsTableViewController`. Now for something new, add `UIBarButtonItem` to your `UINavigationBar`, the view hierarchy should look as follows.

UIBarButtonItem

These kinds of buttons are used in navigation bars, shortcut bars, or toolbars.

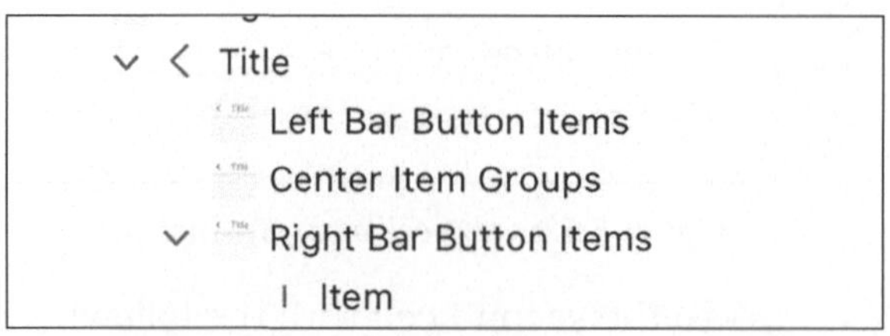

***Figure* 5.55**: *Right bar button item added*

Now add one more `UIBarButtonItem` under **'Left Bar Button Items'** as follows:

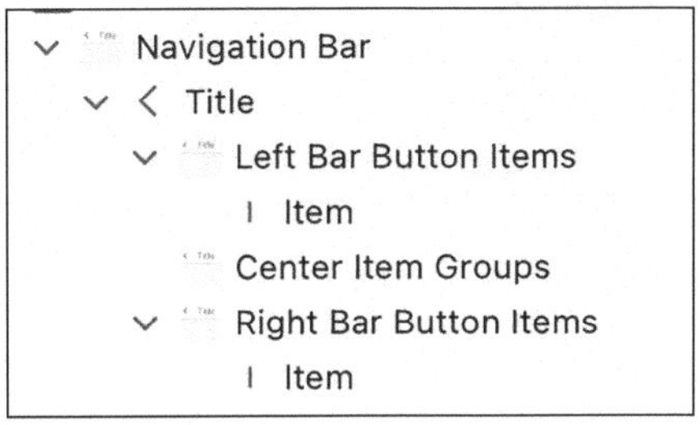

***Figure* 5.56**: *Left bar button item added*

1. Click the **'Title'** under **'Navigation Bar'**, go to attributes Inspector, and change the title to **Details** as shown in the following figure:

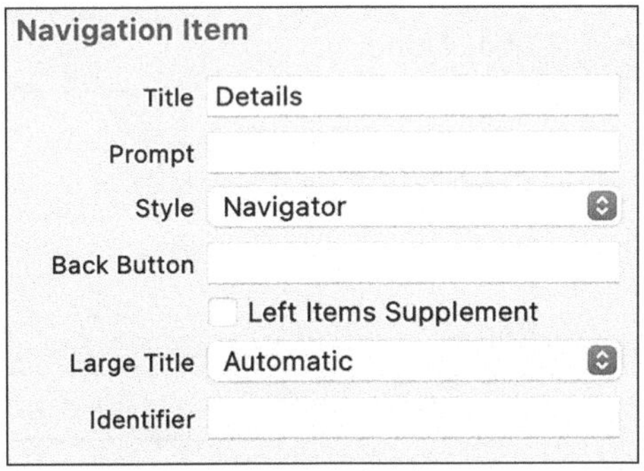

***Figure* 5.57:** *Navigation item's attributes inspector*

2. Click the **'Item'** under **'Left Bar Button Items'** and in the attributes Inspector, change as follows:

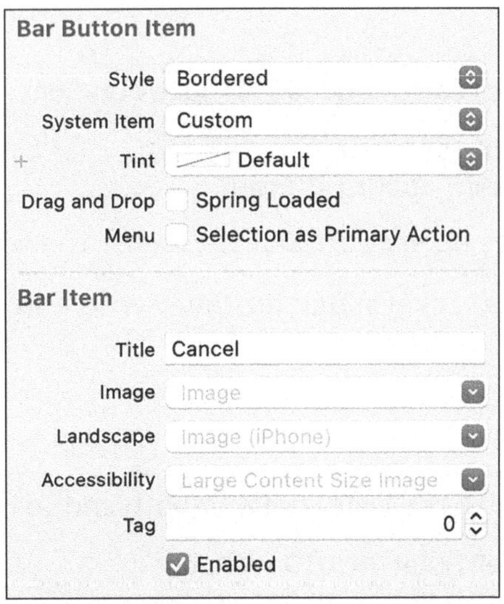

***Figure* 5.58:** *Bar button item's attributes inspector*

3. Click the **'Item'** under **'Right Bar Button Items'** and in the attributes Inspector, change as follows:

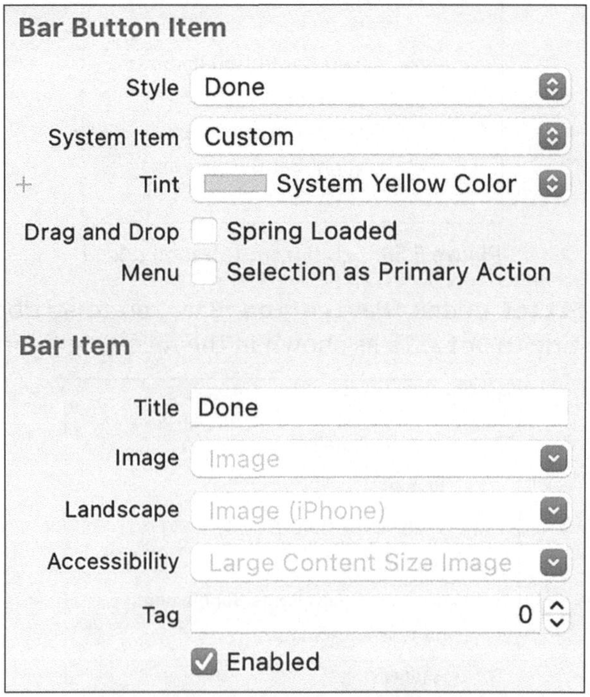

***Figure 5.59**: Bar button item's inspector*

Now that we got **'Cancel '** and **'Done'** on our navigation bar, create the `IBActions` for these `UIBarButtons` in your `DetailsTableViewController`, it's the same we create for `UIButtons`, the `IBActions` could be **'doneButtonTapped'** and **'cancelButtonTapped'** as simple as that.

Add the following variables to your `DetailsTableViewController`:

```
var toDoListItem: TODOListItem?
var modifiedToDoListItem: TODOListItem?
```

You might wonder why we need two `TODOListItems`. You will know later.

Next, we need two `UIDatePickers`, one for the user to enter the Date and another to enter the Time.

UIDatePicker

UIDatePicker is used to pick the Date, time, or both and to enter the time interval.

```
var datePicker: UIDatePicker = UIDatePicker()
var timePicker: UIDatePicker = UIDatePicker()
```

We need these `UIDatePickers` to appear when users click respective `UITextFields`. To do that, go to your **'viewDidLoad()'** function and configure the `UIDatePickers` as follows:

```
datePicker.preferredDatePickerStyle = .inline
datePicker.addTarget(self, action: #selector(handleDatePicker(sender:)),
for: .valueChanged)
dateTextField.inputView = datePicker

timePicker.datePickerMode = .countDownTimer
timePicker.preferredDatePickerStyle = .wheels
timePicker.addTarget(self, action: #selector(handleHoursPicker(send-
er:)), for: .valueChanged)
timeTextField.inputView = timePicker
```

Here we pick the `UIDatePicker`'s styles and add functions to be triggered when the user selects the Date and Time. Finally, we set `UIDatePicker` as `inputViews` to respective `textFields`; this allows the `DatePicker` to appear on the screen when the user taps on the `TextField`. Next, add the target functions as follows:

```
@objc func handleDatePicker(sender: UIDatePicker) {

}


@objc func handleHoursPicker(sender: UIDatePicker) {

}
```

Next, make your `DetailsTableViewController` as `UITextFieldDelegate` and `UITextViewDelegate`. Assign your `UITextField`'s and `UITextView`'s delegate as your `DetailsTableViewController`.

Remember, we have two `TODOListItems`, the **'toDoListItem'** is the item we will get from the previous **'TableViewController'** and the **'modifiedToDoListItem'** is the item that will be modified and will be sent back to **'TableViewController'**, when the 'Done' button is clicked. When the **'Cancel'** button is clicked, the original, unmodified **'toDoListItem'** will be sent back to the `TableViewController`.

Now let's imagine that we got **'toDoListItem'** from the previous `TableViewController` when the user clicked the 'details' button. Let's deal with it as follows:

```
if let id = toDoListItem?.id {
    modifiedToDoListItem = TODOListItem(id: id)
}

if toDoListItem?.item != nil {
    todoItemTextField.text = toDoListItem?.item
```

```
            modifiedToDoListItem?.item = toDoListItem?.item
        } else {
            todoItemTextField.text = "New ToDoList item"
            modifiedToDoListItem?.item = "New ToDoList item"
        }

        if let notes = toDoListItem?.notes {
            notesTextView.text = notes
            modifiedToDoListItem?.notes = notes
        } else {
            notesTextView.text = "Notes"
            notesTextView.textColor = UIColor.lightGray
        }
```

Here we assign the **'id'** that we got from **'toDoListItem'** to `modifiedToDoListItem`'s id. We get the `toDoListItem.item` as nil when the user taps on the screen on the previous `TableViewController` and the row is added without adding any `TODOListItem`'s item but by clicking the details button. In that case, we assign the "New ToDoList item" to our **'todoItemTextField'** and `modifiedToDoListItem`'s item. If we get `toDoListItem`'s item, then we assign that to **'todoItemTextField'** and **'modifiedToDoListItem'**.

IF Let

In the preceding code, you will see that we are using **"if let id = toDoListItem?.id {"** and then we are assigning it to the `modifiedToDoListItem`; this is optional binding. What we are saying here is, if the `toDoListItem?.id` is not nil, we are assigning the value of toDoListItem?.id to the new variable 'id' and only if we get the value from `toDoListItem?.id`, then only we are executing this part of code `modifiedToDoListItem = TODOListItem(id: id)`. We can also do forced unwrapping too, which might cause the crash if the value is nil.

For a better understanding of the forced unwrapping, check the following example.

```
let idString: String? = "1234"
```

Given here is an optional string, but for optional binding, we could write as follows:

```
if let id = idString {
  print(id)
}
```

We will check if `idString` is not nil and then print it only if it is not nil.

But for forced unwrapping, we could just do something as follows:

```
let idString: String? = "1234"
print(idString!)
```

Since we are sure that the value of `idString` is not nil and printing it to tell the compiler we use "!"; Beware, if the value is nil, it could crash the app. To save us from these kinds of scenarios we got **'guard let'**.

Guard Let

Let's do the preceding example using Guard let,

```
let idString: String? = "1234"

guard let id = idString else {
  print("Error: Id missing")
  return
}
print(id)
```

'Guard let' is similar to **'If let'**, except for one thing, that is, in **'If let'**, if it is not nil, the code inside **'if block'** gets executed and the life of the variable created using **'if let'** is limited to the **'if block'**. But coming to the **'guard let'**, as shown earlier, if the `idString` is not nil, then do nothing and go ahead and print it. But if it is nil, we print the error or in the real app we can show the respective error. **'Guard let'** is designed in a way that we should exit the condition if the check fails. We either need to use **'return'** to exit or use **'throws'** to throw the error. The advantage of using 'guard let' is the life of the variable created using 'guard let' stays around even after the check as you have seen earlier.

So mostly we have used **'If let'** in our project as it serves the better purpose. If we get the 'notes', we assign that to our `notesTextView` and `modifiedToDoListItem`. If the **'notes'** is nil, we assign the `notesTextView`'s text as **'Notes'** and change the text color to gray; this will make it look like a placeholder for our `notesTextView`.

Now coming to **'date'** and **'time'**, if you check the `TODOListItem`, the **'date'** and **'time'** are of type **'Date'**, so we need the **'DateFormatter'** to change from **'Date'** type to **'String'** type and publish it in our `UITextFields`.

```
if let date = toDoListItem?.date {
    let dateFormatter = DateFormatter()
    dateFormatter.dateFormat = "dd/MM/yyyy"
    modifiedToDoListItem?.date = date
    dateTextField.text = dateFormatter.string(from: date)
}

if let time = toDoListItem?.time {
    let dateFormatter = DateFormatter()
    dateFormatter.dateFormat = "HH:mm"
    modifiedToDoListItem?.time = time
    timeTextField.text = dateFormatter.string(from: time)
}
```

Here we do the same as we did for other variables of **'TODOListItem'**, if we get the variables, we assign them to the **'modifiedToDoListItem'** and publish them in the respective `UITextFields`. The only difference is we use **'DateFormatter'** to format it.

You use the same code while handling the `UIDatePicker`, so go to your **'handleDatePicker'** function and add the following code:

```
@objc func handleDatePicker(sender: UIDatePicker) {
    let dateFormatter = DateFormatter()
    dateFormatter.dateFormat = "dd/MM/yyyy"
    modifiedToDoListItem?.date = sender.date
    dateTextField.text = dateFormatter.string(from: sender.date)

}
```

When the user selects the date, in `UIDatePicker`, we get the date component, format it, and assign it to the **'dateTextField'**.

We do the same for handling the `timePicker`. See the following:

```
@objc func handleHoursPicker(sender: UIDatePicker) {
    let dateFormatter = DateFormatter()
    dateFormatter.dateFormat = "HH:mm"
    modifiedToDoListItem?.time = sender.date
    timeTextField.text = dateFormatter.string(from: sender.date)
}
```

Now let's deal with `UITextField` and `UITextView`'s delegate functions, the `textField` here is the **'todoItemTextField'**, the very first `UITextField` in our `DetailsTableViewController` and the `UITextView` is the **'notesTextView'**.

Let's go implement **'textField(_:shouldChangeCharactersIn:replacementString:)'** as follows:

```
func textField(_ textField: UITextField, shouldChangeCharactersIn range:
NSRange, replacementString string: String) -> Bool {

    let text: NSString = (textField.text ?? "") as NSString
    let resultString = text.replacingCharacters(in: range, with: string)

    if textField == todoItemTextField {
        self.modifiedToDoListItem?.item = resultString
    }

    return true
}
```

Here we get the text from `UITextField` and user-entered text and assign this to our `modifiedToDoListItem`. No `textField` validations are done in this function because we assigned the `TextFieldDelegate` to only **'todoItemTextField'**, which means the preceding function gets called only when the user edits the **'todoItemTextField'**.

Next, let's implement the `UITextView's textViewDidBeginEditing(_:)` function as follows:

```
func textViewDidBeginEditing(_ textView: UITextView) {
    if textView.textColor == UIColor.lightGray {
        textView.text = nil
        textView.textColor = UIColor.black
    }
}
```

Previously, we changed our '**notesTextView'** text color to gray to make it look like a placeholder, so when the user taps on **'notesTextView'**, the placeholder should disappear, and the text color should change back to black; we have done the same here.

Just like we got `'textField(_:shouldChangeCharactersIn:replacementString:)'` which gets called when the user starts typing on `UITextField`, we got `textView(_:shouldChangeTextIn:replacementText:)` for `UITextView`, which gets called when the user starts typing on it; let's implement it now.

```
func textView(_ textView: UITextView, shouldChangeTextIn range: NSRange,
replacementText text: String) -> Bool {

    let textViewText = textView.text ?? ""
    guard let updatedRange = Range(range, in: textViewText) else { re-
turn false }
    let resultingUpdatedText = textViewText.replacingCharacters(in: up-
datedRange, with: text)
    modifiedToDoListItem?.notes = resultingUpdatedText

    return true
}
```

We are doing the same as we did for `UITextField`; getting the `notesTextView`'s text and user-typed text and assigning it to our **'modifiedToDoListItem'**.

Now we have two more UI elements to deal with on our screen: **Cancel** and **Done** button actions. Before going any further, let's get the requirements straight.

When the user clicks the **Cancel** button, even though the user modified the details and added extra details, if the user clicks the Cancel button, then it should go back to `TableViewController` with unmodified `TODOListItem`.

When a user clicks the **Done** button, it should go back to `TableViewController` with the modified `TODOListItem`. Now you know why we got `TODOListItems` in our `DetailsTableViewController`.

Note that we are sending the information from `DetailsTableViewController` to the `TableViewController`. Here delegates come into action. Let's have a protocol in which the function gets called when **'Cancel'** and **'Done'** are clicked, and this function should be implemented in **'TableViewController'** as it needs the information from **'DetailsTableViewController'**.

```
protocol TODODetailsTableViewControllerDelegate {
    func modifiedItemDetails(toDoListItem: TODOListItem?)
}
```

Define this protocol on top of your `DetailsTableViewController` with the function **'modifiedItemDetails(toDoListItem:)'**.

Now go to `DetailsTableViewController` and add **'detailsTableViewController Delgate'** as follows:

```
class DetailsTableViewController: UITableViewController {

    var datePicker: UIDatePicker = UIDatePicker()
    var timePicker: UIDatePicker = UIDatePicker()

    var toDoListItem: TODOListItem?
    var modifiedToDoListItem: TODOListItem?

    @IBOutlet weak var todoItemTextField: UITextField!
    @IBOutlet weak var notesTextView: UITextView!
    @IBOutlet weak var dateTextField: UITextField!
    @IBOutlet weak var timeTextField: UITextField!

    var detailsTableViewControllerDelgate: TODODetailsTableViewControllerDelegate?
```

Figure 5.60: *DetailsTableViewController with TODODetailsTableViewControllerDelegate*

Now call this function `detailsTableViewControllerDelgate`'s when the user taps on the Cancel button; go to your **'cancelButtonTapped'** `IBAction` function as follows.

```
@IBAction func cancelButtonTapped(_ sender: Any) {
    view.endEditing(true)
    detailsTableViewControllerDelgate?.modifiedItemDetails(toDoListItem:
toDoListItem)
    self.dismiss(animated: true)
}
```

An extra thing we are doing here is ending the editing, as it will dismiss the keyboard if it is on screen and dismiss our `DetailstableViewController` after sending the unmodified **'TODOListItem'** as discussed earlier. **'self.dismiss(animated:true)'** allows us to dismiss the current View Controller we are on and takes us back to the previous `ViewController`, that the current view controller is being presented on.

Now let's call our `detailsTableViewControllerDelgate`'s function when **'Done'** is tapped. So go to your `IBAction` **'doneButtonTapped'** and add the code as follows:

```
@IBAction func doneButtonTapped(_ sender: Any) {
    view.endEditing(true)
    detailsTableViewControllerDelgate?.modifiedItemDetails(toDoListItem:
modifiedToDoListItem)
    self.dismiss(animated: true)
}
```

We do the same as we did when the 'Cancel' button was tapped like ending the editing and dismissing the current view controller. The only thing we did differently is sending **'modifiedToDoListItem'** which sends modified data to the `TableViewController` or the view controller that implements the **'TODODetailsTableViewControllerDelegate'** function.

Now we will make our **'TableViewController'** as **'TODODetailsTableViewControllerDelegate'**; for reference, check the following figure:

```
class TableViewController: UITableViewController, UITextFieldDelegate, TODOListDelagate, TODODetailsTableViewControllerDelegate {
```

Figure 5.61: *TableViewController as TODODetailsTableViewControllerDelegate*

Go to your **'detailsButtonGotClicked'** function and add the following line to assign the `DetailsTableViewController's` `detailsTableViewControllerDelgate` as `self(TableViewController)`:

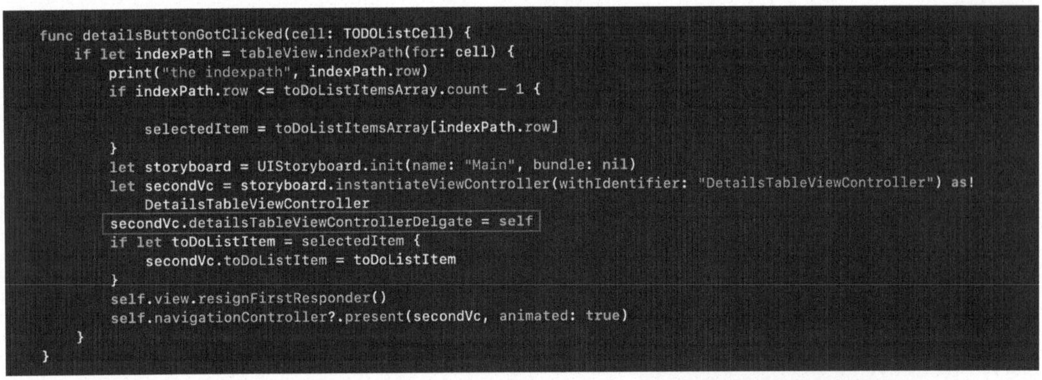

```
func detailsButtonGotClicked(cell: TODOListCell) {
    if let indexPath = tableView.indexPath(for: cell) {
        print("the indexpath", indexPath.row)
        if indexPath.row <= toDoListItemsArray.count - 1 {

            selectedItem = toDoListItemsArray[indexPath.row]
        }
        let storyboard = UIStoryboard.init(name: "Main", bundle: nil)
        let secondVc = storyboard.instantiateViewController(withIdentifier: "DetailsTableViewController") as!
            DetailsTableViewController
        secondVc.detailsTableViewControllerDelgate = self
        if let toDoListItem = selectedItem {
            secondVc.toDoListItem = toDoListItem
        }
        self.view.resignFirstResponder()
        self.navigationController?.present(secondVc, animated: true)
    }
}
```

Figure 5.62: *Assigning detailsTableViewControllerDelegate*

Implement `detailsTableViewControllerDelgate`'s function as follows:

```
func modifiedItemDetails(toDoListItem: TODOListItem?) {

    if let updatedToDoListItem = toDoListItem {

        // if item exist in the array then modify it
        if let itemIntheArray = toDoListItemsArray.first(where: { $0.id
== updatedToDoListItem.id }) {
            toDoListItemsArray = toDoListItemsArray.map { $0.id ==
updatedToDoListItem.id ? updatedToDoListItem : $0 }
```

```
        } else {
            // if item doesnot exist in the array then add it to the array
            toDoListItemsArray.append(updatedToDoListItem)
            selectedItem = nil
            noOfRows = toDoListItemsArray.count
        }
        self.tableView.reloadData()
    }
}
```

In the preceding function, we are checking if the item exists in our `toDoListItemsArray` based upon the **`'id'`** variable because no matter what the user changes, then the user can't change the 'id' of the element. If the element exists in our array, then we are modifying that element. If the element doesn't exist, then we are adding the element to the array. Finally, we are reloading our `tableView`.

We need to cover three more features to complete our app development process.

- Changing the navigation bar title of our `TableViewController`
- Limiting our `TableViewController`'s `ToDo` list item's character count to 25
- Showing the **`'Done'`** button on the Navigation Bar when the `ToDo` list item `UITextField` is edited.

1. Let's do it one by one; firstly, change our navigation bar title to **`To Do`**. Go to your **`Main.storyboard`**, select your `TableViewController`, and go to view hierarchy, select Navigation Item as follows:

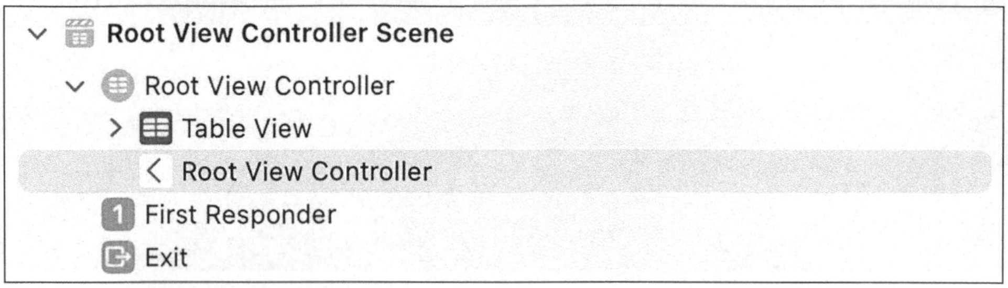

***Figure 5.63**: Selecting the navigation item in the view hierarchy*

2. Open Attributes inspector and change the **`'Title'`** to **`'To Do'`** as follows:

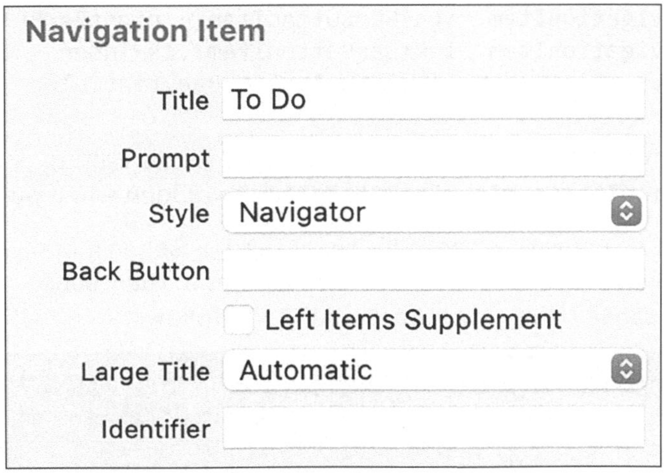

Figure 5.64: *Navigation item's attributes inspector*

3. Secondly, limit our cell's `textField`'s text to 25 characters as follows:

```
func textField(_ textField: UITextField, shouldChangeCharactersIn range: NSRange, replacementString string: String) -> Bool {

    let maxStringCount = 25
    let textFieldtext: NSString = (textField.text ?? "") as NSString
    let endToDOString = textFieldtext.replacingCharacters(in: range, with: string)
    print("the end string is", endToDOString)

    theToDoItemString = endToDOString
    selectedItem?.item = theToDoItemString
    cellIsEditing = true

    if textField.text?.count != 0 {

        if let itemIntheArray = toDoListItemsArray.first(where: { $0.item == textField.text}) {
            print("the item is", itemIntheArray)

            var editingItem = itemIntheArray
            editingItem.item = theToDoItemString
            toDoListItemsArray = toDoListItemsArray.map { $0.item == textField.text ? editingItem : $0 }
            print("the array",toDoListItemsArray)
        }

    }
    return endToDOString.count <= maxStringCount
}
```

Figure 5.65: *Limiting the UItextField's character count*

Here we define **'maxStringCount'** to 25. Usually, we return **'true'** to the preceding function, which allows the user to type, but now we are only returning **'true'** if the `endToDOString`'s count is less than or equal to 25. The user can't type if the count reaches above 25 characters.

4. Finally, let's add the **'Done'** button when the user is editing our table view as follows in the `viewDidLoad()` function.

```
let rightBarButtonItem = UIBarButtonItem(title: "Done", style:
.done, target: self, action: #selector(self.doneButton-
Tapped(sender:)))
```

```
self.navigationItem.rightBarButtonItem = rightBarButtonItem
self.navigationItem.rightBarButtonItem?.isHidden = true
self.navigationController?.navigationBar.tintColor = .systemYel-
low
```

This button will be hidden when the user is not editing, so we are setting `navigationItem's rightBarButtonItem` to hidden when our view is loaded.

5. Now, if it is a new cell, the cell's `textField` is set as a first responder, which means the editing is on, and we should show the **'Done'** button. So, let's modify `'tableView(_:cellForRowAt:)'` as follows:

```
override func tableView(_ tableView: UITableView, cellForRowAt indexPath: IndexPath) -> UITableViewCell {

    let cell = tableView.dequeueReusableCell(withIdentifier: "TodoListCell", for: indexPath) as! TODOListCell
    cell.textField.delegate = self
    cell.cellDelegate = self
    cell.configureCell()

    if indexPath.row <= toDoListItemsArray.count - 1 {

        // Existing item

        let todoListItem = toDoListItemsArray[indexPath.row]
        cell.textField.text = todoListItem.item
        cell.textField.endEditing(true)

        DispatchQueue.main.async {
            self.view.endEditing(true)
        }

    } else if indexPath.row == noOfRows - 1 {

        cell.textField.text = nil
        self.navigationItem.rightBarButtonItem?.isHidden = false

        // making the new item as selected item
        let id: Int = toDoListItemsArray.count + 1
        let todoListItem = TODOListItem(id: id)
        selectedItem = todoListItem
        DispatchQueue.main.async {
            cell.textField.becomeFirstResponder()
        }
    }
```

Figure 5.66: *Showing the rightBarButtonItem in cellForRowAtIndexPath: function*

6. In other places, we want to show the **'Done'** button when the `textField` begins editing; let's do it as follows:

```
func textFieldDidBeginEditing(_ textField: UITextField) {
    self.navigationItem.rightBarButtonItem?.isHidden = false
    cellIsEditing = true
}
```

And we will hide it when textField ends editing.

```
func textFieldDidEndEditing(_ textField: UITextField) {

    if selectedItem?.item != nil {
        if let itemIntheArray = toDoListItemsArray.first(where: { $0.item == textField.text}) {
            toDoListItemsArray = toDoListItemsArray.map { $0.item == theToDoItemString ? itemIntheArray : $0 }
            print("the array",toDoListItemsArray)
        } else {
            if let theNewItem = selectedItem {
                toDoListItemsArray.append(theNewItem)
                selectedItem = nil
            }
        }
    }
    self.navigationItem.rightBarButtonItem?.isHidden = true
}
```

Figure 5.67: *Hiding the rightBarButtonItem when textField ends editing*

Now let's implement our **'Done'** button functionality as follows:

```
@objc func doneButtonTapped(sender: UIBarButtonItem) {
    if cellIsEditing == true {
        cellIsEditing = false
        view.endEditing(true)
    }
}
```

We check if `cellIsEditing` is true and we end the editing, which calls `textFieldDidEndEditing(_:)` when view ended editing, and this does the required tasks.

We met all the requirements, ran it, experiment with it, and found bugs because no app is perfect. After finding bugs, fix them by yourself, which is a good learning experience.

Conclusion

In this chapter, we learned about developing our own sample app using the knowledge we acquired from previous chapters and also gaining additional knowledge by developing a ToDo List App. We covered the Idea, design, and development phases of the app process. The app developers can do unit testing, which will be covered in further chapters. UI testing is usually done by the tester in the company, which includes manual testing as well. We did not discuss the Release phase as we are not releasing the app to the Appstore yet. In the next chapter, you will learn about networking and fetching data from APIs.

Points to Remember

- Structs are data types that can store multiple data types.
- A struct is a value type, not a reference type, which means the runtime deals directly with the struct's underlying data, which can be very efficient.
- `DispatchQueue` is built on top of the Grand Central Dispatch(GCD) queue, which is an API used for managing concurrent operations in your app.

- The reuse identifier allows us to create and recycle our table view cells.
- `beginUpdates()` starts a series of method calls that select, delete, and insert rows and sections of your table view.
- `endUpdates()` ends a series of method calls that delete, select, insert, and reload rows and sections of your table view.
- `UIBarButtonItems` buttons are used in navigation bars, shortcut bars, or toolbars.
- `UIDatePicker` is used to pick the Date, time, or both and to enter the time interval.

Chapter 6
Networking

Introduction

In this chapter, you will learn about Networking. Just like the name says, networking is nothing but talking to each other. Just imagine you went to a networking event, all you did was talk to each other, get the information from the other person, and tell your information to the other person. Just like that, we will learn how to make our app talk to the APIs, post the information to the API, get the information from the API, and publish it in our app.

Let us take an example of a well-used app, Instagram. When you open the app, the app talks to the API, which fetches the data from the database, which includes all your posts, likes, and comments.

Unless and until the data is saved locally, like our sample we built in the previous chapter, almost most of the apps talk with APIs to fetch the data or to post the data to the database.

Structure

In this chapter, we will discuss the following topics:

- `URLSession`
- `URLSession.shared`
- Closures
- URL
- `URLRequest`
- `URLSessionDataTask`
- `URLSessionUploadTask`
- `URLSessionDownloadTask`
- Codables
    - Encodable
    - Decodable

- JSONDecoder
- JSONEncoder

Introduction to `URLSession`

`UrlSession` is a wonderful tool for networking that allows developers to interact with the web to send and fetch data. Using `URLSession`, we can download audio, video, and image files. With `URLSession`, we can make foreground and also background network requests.

`URLSession.shared`

`URLSession.shared` is a shared singleton object that gives developers the ability to perform default actions such as fetching the contents of your URL.

Now that you know how important `URLSession` is for connecting to the URL in theory, let us get into the implementation.

Create a new project. You can give any name to your project, let us say `URLSessionExample`.

Before going any further, let us learn an important topic in Swift, that is, Closures.

Closures

Closures are nothing but a block of code; you can see a closure as a function but without a function name. Closures are like blocks on objectives C and C. It can be called a variable that holds blocks of code. It can be as simple as the following:

```
{
  print("Have a good day")
}
```

Following is the way you declare a closure:

```
{ (parameters) -> returnType in
   // your code
}
```

Just like the preceding code, a closure can be as simple as printing **"Have a good day,"** but we should be able to call this closure anywhere in our code. As discussed in the previous section, it is a variable that holds the chuck of code, so an example closure will look as follows:

```
var goodDayGreet = {
    print("Have a good day")
}
```

Then, calling closure is simple:

```
goodDayGreet()
```

Closures with Parameters and Return Type

Just like functions, we can pass on the parameters and have return types for Closures as follows:

```
var add = { (num1: Int, num2: Int) -> (Int) in
  var sum = num1 * num2
  return sum
}

var findSum = add(3,2)
```

You can pass a closure as a parameter to a function, which is quite an awesome usage of closure. Consider the following example:

```
let multiplication = {(num1: Int, num2: Int) -> Int in
    return num1 * num2
}

let addition = {(num1: Int, num2: Int) -> Int in
    return num1 + num2
}

func calculate(a: Int, b: Int, calculationType: (Int, Int) -> Int) ->
Int {
    return calculationType(a, b)
}

let performCal = calculate(a: 2, b: 3, calculationType: multiplication)
```

Here all we are doing is defining closures that multiplies its parameters and another closure that adds its parameters. Then we have a function 'calculate' that accepts two numbers and closure as parameters.

Finally, we call the function, sending the required parameters. You can execute the aforementioned code in playgrounds of Xcode or in `viewDidLoad()`. You can send addition closure instead of multiplication closure while calling the calculate function.

Implicit Returns

We can have implicit returns too. Let us take the aforementioned addition closure; it can be written with implicit returns as follows:

```
let addition: (Int, Int) -> Int  = {
      return $0 + $1
}
```

Shorthand Arguments

We can send the shorthand arguments to any function just like the following:

```
let square: (Int) -> (Int) = {
    print($0)
    return $0 * $0
}
```

If you have noticed, the definition of closure changed a little while using the shorthand arguments and implicit returns.

Closure Types

Let us learn about different types of closures so you can make better use of them.

Trailing Closures

The trailing closure is nothing but when the closure is passed as the final argument of the function. When calling the function, the trailing closure is written after the parentheses, and you do not send the argument label for the closure in the function call. Checkout the following example:

```
func cube(num:Int,onSuccess clos:(Int)->Void) {
    clos(num * num * num)
}
```

The following code is used to call the function:

```
cube(num: 3) { (cubeOfNum) in
    print(cubeOfNum)
}
```

Escaping Closures

An escaping is a closure that lives outside the function's life that closure was passed to so that it can be used in your different parts of your code.

Check out the following example:

```
var identityClosure: ((Bool) -> Void)?

func findIdentitytoken(completeionHandler: @escaping (Bool) -> Void) {
    identityClosure = completeionHandler
}
```

Non-Escaping Closures

A non-escaping closure is, as the name specifies, cannot escape the function; the closure cannot be alive outside the function's life.

Now that we have learned about closures, which is an important topic in Swift, let us move forward in the project we have previously created.

Let us create a function `fetchData().` In this function, we will fetch the data by connecting to the URL.

An image has been uploaded at the following URL: https://i.imgur.com/HYh8Zif.jpg

Let us use URLSession to connect to this URL and get the image from it.

URL

A URL identifies the location of your resource. It can be a web server or the path to your local file.

Inside our `fetchData()` function, let us create the URL from the string we got "https://i.imgur.com/HYh8Zif.jpg."

```
let url = URL(string: "https://i.imgur.com/HYh8Zif.jpg")!
```

URLRequest

`URLRequest` allows developers to make the configuration of the HTTP request. To send a request to the web server, we need to use the other class, such as `URLSession`. `URLRequest` got an HTTP method, where we can configure if it is POST, GET, or many other, and we can configure HTTP headers as well.

Let us create the `URLRequest` using the aforementioned URL.

```
var request = URLRequest(url: url)
```

The `URLRequest`'s default `httpMethod` is **`'GET'`**, so you do not have to specifically specify it. But for 'post' you need to specify the httpMethod.

`URLSession` has different types of `URLSessionTasks` that can allow you to perform different types of tasks such as download, upload, and fetch.

URLSessionDataTask

This allows us to fetch the data from the web service, and we can use this for post request as well by attaching the `httpBody` to our request.

URLSessionUploadTask

This allows us to, as the name suggests, upload the data to the web service using POST or PUT httpMethods.

URLSessionDownloadTask

This task allows developers to download the files from the web services. You can use this for downloading, for example, images.

You can access the respective tasks by URLSession.shared.dataTask, URLSession.shared.uploadTask, and URLSession.shared.downloadTask.

Here in our scenario, we want to fetch the data from the URL with dataTask:

```
let task = URLSession.shared.dataTask(with: request) { data, response,
error in
            if let data = data {
                let image = UIImage(data: data)
            } else if let error = error {
                print("HTTP Request Failed \(error)")
            }
        }
```

All we are doing here is executing our request; if we get the data from our request, we are creating an image using it, or else if we get the error, we are simply printing it in this scenario.

As you can see in the preceding code, you do not have to create a shared session; you can access it by using URLSession's **'shared'** property directly.

The final task is to resume the task as follows:

```
task.resume()
```

If you look at the previous section, all we are doing is creating URLSessionDataTask, but to move forward and to begin to perform any operations, we need to call the URLSessionTask's functions. Here we need to call **'resume()'** to make our dataTask do the work.

You might wonder what resume() does, as the name says, it resumes the tasks.

Following is how your fetchData() function should look like:

```
func fetchData() {

    let url = URL(string: "https://i.imgur.com/HYh8Zif.jpg")!

    var request = URLRequest(url: url)

    let task = URLSession.shared.dataTask(with: request) { data, response, error in
        if let data = data {
            let image = UIImage(data: data)
        } else if let error = error {
            print("HTTP Request Failed \(error)")
        }
    }

    task.resume()

}
```

Figure 6.1: *fetchData() function*

Call the function in your `viewDidLoad()`, as shown in *Figure* 6.2.

```
override func viewDidLoad() {
    super.viewDidLoad()

    fetchData()
}
```

***Figure 6.2**: calling fetchData()*

Now, in order to know if our `fetchData()` function is working, let us have debug points at the following places:

```

func fetchData() {

    let url = URL(string: "https://i.imgur.com/HYh8Zif.jpg")!

    var request = URLRequest(url: url)

    let task = URLSession.shared.dataTask(with: request) { data, response, error in
        if let data = data {
            let image = UIImage(data: data)
        } else if let error = error {
            print("HTTP Request Failed \(error)")
        }
    }

    task.resume()

}
```

Figure 6.3: *fetchData() function with debug points*

Time to go head and run it. All we will see is a blank screen because we have not done anything on the screen. If the request went well, you must see your debug point reaching **'`if let data = data`'.**

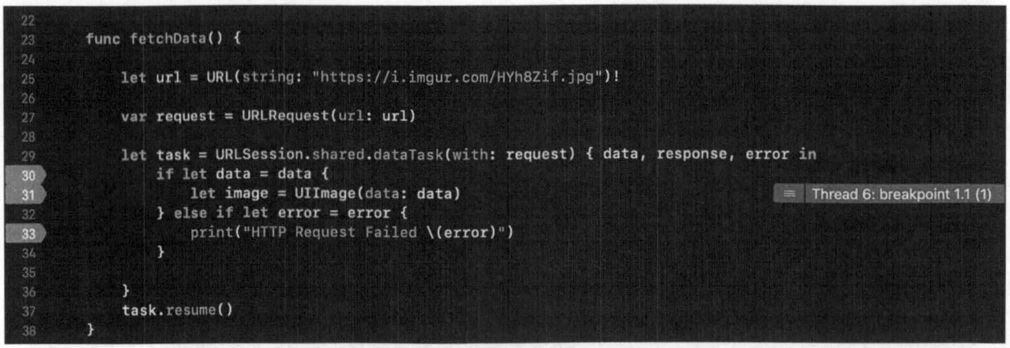

***Figure 6.4:** checking on image*

If you want to play a bit more with this, have an `UIImageView` at the center of your screen and assign this image to your `UIImageView`. It is suggested you go ahead and do it.

For the aforementioned request, the response we were getting was the data to create the image, but for most of the requests, we make in our apps, the responses come back with the JSON data. The JSON data comprises all of the data you need. For example, if you are making a request to an API to get customer details, such as name, date of birth, and address, you can get all of that in one go. You do not need to make different requests for just name alone or just the date of birth.

A simple JSON response could look like this:

```
{
    “name”: “Kate Hill”,
    “date_of_birth”: “23/05/1995”,
    “Address”: “Unit-609, 250 iOS street, Swift - 3006”

}
```

When we get the JSON response, we need to parse through the response, get the data, and update the screens according to the data we received.

This is where Codables comes to our rescue.

Codables

Codable was introduced in Swift 4.0, which helps us to parse through and converse from JSON to Swift data types and vice versa.

Encodable

Encodable is the process of converting the Swift data types to JSON or other external representation.

Decodable

Decodable is the process of converting the JSON or other external representations to Swift data types.

Let us jump into implementation for better understanding.

Create a new project, **`'Films'`**. Before going forward, let us explore a publicly available API: **https://swapi.dev/documentation#intro**.

This is the API that gives us the data regarding Star Wars movies. Have a read through the website.

After going through it, just write the URL https://swapi.dev/api/films/ in your browser. You must be able to see the API response, which gives all the Star Wars movies (all six movies).

Now, instead of using the aforementioned URL to fetch the data and use it in our codable example, let us fetch the data regarding just the first movie using this URL: https://swapi.dev/api/films/1/. Go head and use the URL in the browser. You should be able to see something like this:


```
{
    "title": "A New Hope",
    "episode_id": 4,
    "opening_crawl": "It is a period of civil war.\r\nRebel spaceships,
striking\r\nfrom a hidden base, have won\r\ntheir first victory again-
st\r\nthe evil Galactic Empire.\r\n\r\nDuring the battle, Rebel\r\nspies
managed to steal secret\r\nplans to the Empire's\r\nultimate weapon,
the DEATH\r\nSTAR, an armored space\r\nstation with enough power\r\nto
destroy an entire planet.\r\n\r\nPursued by the Empire's\r\nsinister
agents, Princess\r\nLeia races home aboard her\r\nstarship, custodian of
the\r\nstolen plans that can save her\r\npeople and restore\r\nfreedom
to the galaxy....",
    "director": "George Lucas",
    "producer": "Gary Kurtz, Rick McCallum",
    "release_date": "1977-05-25",
    "characters": [
        "https://swapi.dev/api/people/1/",
        "https://swapi.dev/api/people/2/",
        "https://swapi.dev/api/people/3/",
        "https://swapi.dev/api/people/4/",
        "https://swapi.dev/api/people/5/",
        "https://swapi.dev/api/people/6/",
        "https://swapi.dev/api/people/7/",
        "https://swapi.dev/api/people/8/",
        "https://swapi.dev/api/people/9/",
```

```
        "https://swapi.dev/api/people/10/",
        "https://swapi.dev/api/people/12/",
        "https://swapi.dev/api/people/13/",
        "https://swapi.dev/api/people/14/",
        "https://swapi.dev/api/people/15/",
        "https://swapi.dev/api/people/16/",
        "https://swapi.dev/api/people/18/",
        "https://swapi.dev/api/people/19/",
        "https://swapi.dev/api/people/81/"
    ],
    "planets": [
        "https://swapi.dev/api/planets/1/",
        "https://swapi.dev/api/planets/2/",
        "https://swapi.dev/api/planets/3/"
    ],
    "starships": [
        "https://swapi.dev/api/starships/2/",
        "https://swapi.dev/api/starships/3/",
        "https://swapi.dev/api/starships/5/",
        "https://swapi.dev/api/starships/9/",
        "https://swapi.dev/api/starships/10/",
        "https://swapi.dev/api/starships/11/",
        "https://swapi.dev/api/starships/12/",
        "https://swapi.dev/api/starships/13/"
    ],
    "vehicles": [
        "https://swapi.dev/api/vehicles/4/",
        "https://swapi.dev/api/vehicles/6/",
        "https://swapi.dev/api/vehicles/7/",
        "https://swapi.dev/api/vehicles/8/"
    ],
    "species": [
        "https://swapi.dev/api/species/1/",
        "https://swapi.dev/api/species/2/",
        "https://swapi.dev/api/species/3/",
        "https://swapi.dev/api/species/4/",
        "https://swapi.dev/api/species/5/"
    ],
    "created": "2014-12-10T14:23:31.880000Z",
    "edited": "2014-12-20T19:49:45.256000Z",
    "url": "https://swapi.dev/api/films/1/"
}
```

With the help of this structure, we need to create our Struct that can help parse our aforementioned JSON data.

So, let us create the Struct **'Film'** as follows:

```
struct Film {

    var title:String
    var episodeId: Int
    var openingcrawl: String
    var director: String
    var producer: String
    var releaseDate: String
    var characters: [String]
    var planets: [String]
    var starships: [String]
    var vehicles: [String]
    var species: [String]
 }
```

Were you able to see that the Struct we created got the variables and the data types according to the JSON data that we are getting from the URL? For example, in the aforesaid JSON, we are getting the **title** as a String type, so we have created the variable 'title' of the String type, and we are getting the **episode_id** as 4, which is of type Int, so we have created the variable **'episodeId'** of the Int type. Before going any further, let us declare that our Struct Film is `Codable`; just doing this will help us to serialize the JSON data to Swift data types and vice versa.

```
struct Film: Codable {

    var title:String
    var episodeId: Int
    var openingcrawl: String
    var director: String
    var producer: String
    var releaseDate: String
    var characters: [String]
    var planets: [String]
    var starships: [String]
    var vehicles: [String]
    var species: [String]

    }
```

We have created the Struct with variables of type according to the JSON we have received, but you should also notice that we have created some of the variable names that were not matching as per the data we received. For example, in JSON data, we are receiving `episode_id`, `opening_crawl` and `release_date`, but the variables we have created for them are `episodeId`, `openingCrawl`, and `releaseDate`. This could be a problem because variable names should be identical to the JSON data we received; otherwise, it will be difficult to parse. So, we solve this by having the nested enum `codingKeys`, which will be confirming to the protocol **'CodingKey'**; this will allow Swift to automatically utilize it as a key type. Let us implement it as follows:

```
enum CodingKeys: String, CodingKey {
    case title
    case episodeId = "episode_id"
    case openingcrawl = "opening_crawl"
    case director
    case producer
    case releaseDate = "release_date"
    case characters
    case planets
    case starships
    case vehicles
    case species
}
```

Just make sure the `enum` is inside your Struct, so your Struct **'Film'** should look similar to *Figure* 6.6. You can create this **'Struct'** in a separate file or can add in the same `ViewController` file outside the `ViewController` class.

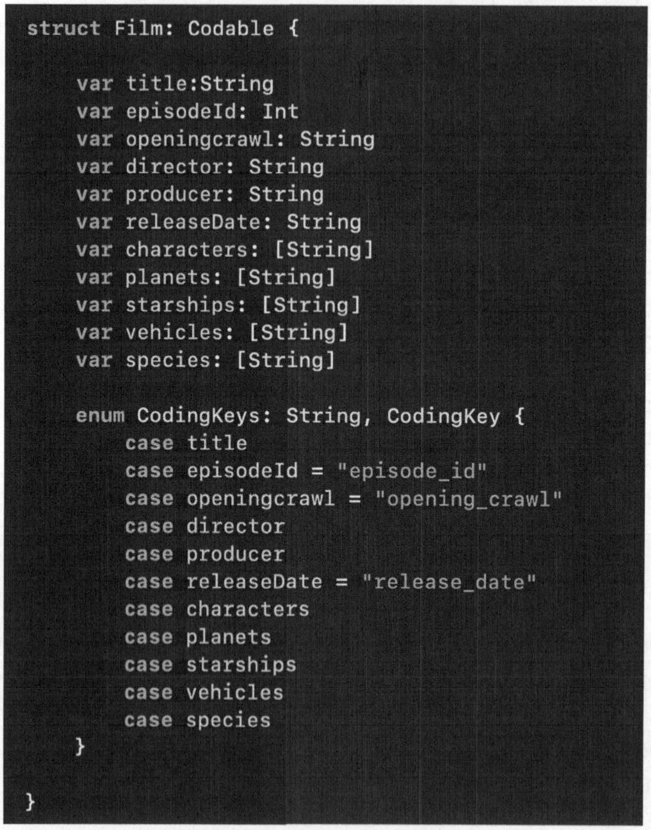

Figure 6.5: *Film Struct*

Now comes the exciting part of making the request, and when we get the response, we will decode the received data using the Codable object. You will see how the data is converted into our Film.

Let us go back to our `ViewController` class and add the `fetchData` function. Inside the `fetchData` function, let us make a request just like we did before, but this time to a different URL: `'https://swapi.dev/api/films/1/'`. Just take a look at the succeeding code:

```
func fetchData() {

    let url = URL(string: "https://swapi.dev/api/films/1/")!

    var request = URLRequest(url: url)

    let task = URLSession.shared.dataTask(with: request) { data,
response, error in
        if let data = data {
          // parse date here
        } else if let error = error {
            print("HTTP Request Failed \(error)")
        }

    }
    task.resume()
}
```

So before, we were creating image with the data we received for our request, but this time, we have to parse the data after receiving the data. Let us go ahead and add function **`'parseData'`** with the parameter for json of type Data. Following is what it should look like.

```
func parseData(json: Data) {

}
```

Inside this function, we need `JSONDecoder` with which we will use our codable Struct.

JSONDecoder

`JSONDecoder` will allow us to decode the JSON into our instances of data types.

Let us create the `JSONDecoder` and use it as follows:

```
    let decoder = JSONDecoder()

    if let film = try? decoder.decode(Film.self, from: json) {
    }
```

In the aforementioned code, **try?** is used. It is kind of like we are telling that this function we are calling can throw an error.

After decoding, we will get a film of type Film. We can even print our struct's properties, or else we can publish the properties on our screen. Right now, to keep it simple, let us print it as follows:

```
if let film = try? decoder.decode(Film.self, from: json) {
    print(film.title)
    print(film.director)
}
```

Following is how your `parseData` function should look like:

```
func parseData(json: Data) {

    let decoder = JSONDecoder()

    if let film = try? decoder.decode(Film.self, from: json) {
        print(film.title)
        print(film.director)
    }
}
```

Figure 6.6: parseData function

Now, time to call this `parseData` function in `fetchData` function, as shown in *Figure 6.8*.

```
func fetchData() {

    let url = URL(string: "https://swapi.dev/api/films/1/")!

    var request = URLRequest(url: url)

    let task = URLSession.shared.dataTask(with: request) { data, response, error in
        if let data = data {
            self.parseData(json: data)
        } else if let error = error {
            print("HTTP Request Failed \(error)")
        }

    }
    task.resume()
}
```

Figure 6.7: *Calling parseData(json: data) function inside fetchData() function*

Call the **'fetchData'** function in `viewDidLoad()`.

Time to hit the run button. You can have breakpoints in the `parseData` function to just make the code get executed as follows:

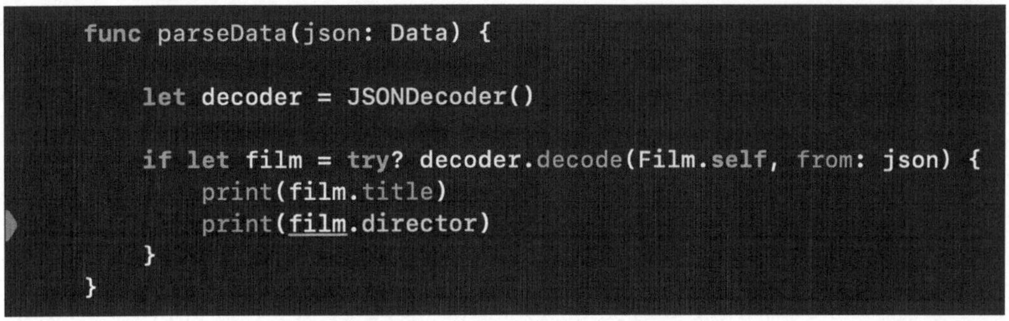

Figure 6.8: *Printing out Film properties*

You can also see the film name printed as follows:

Figure 6.9: *Film name printed in console*

So that is how easy it is to fetch the data from URL and parse the JSON data into Swift data type.

You might wonder what if you want to post request to the URL; it is super easy as well. All you need to do is get the JSON format from the backend team; for example, a sample request body could look like follows:

```
{
    "name": "Kate Hill",
    "date_of_birth": "23/05/1995",
    "address": "10600 N Tantau Ave, Cupertino, CA 95014, USA"

}
```

To send the aforementioned JSON in request body, you should create the struct as follows:

```
struct Customer: Codable{
    var name: String
    var dateOfBirth: String
    var address: String

    enum CodingKeys: String, CodingKey {
        case name
        case dateOfBirth = "date_of_birth"
        case address
    }
}
```

In the preceding case, when we were converting the JSON to Swift data type, we used `JSONDecoder`. Here we need to convert Swift data type to JSON, which means we need to encode, so here we use `JSONEncoder`.

JSONEncoder

`JSONEncoder` allows to encode the instances of our data types to JSON objects.

You can create the function `sendCustomerDetails()`. Inside this function, let us create a customer with the aforementioned properties. In a real app, these details, such as name, date of birth, and address, can be collected by user input, but as this is just a sample, we can create the **'Customer'** with hardcoded data like the following:

```
let customer = Customer(name: "Kate Hill",
                                    dateOfBirth: "23/05/1995",
                                    address: "10600 N Tantau Ave, Cuperti-
no, CA 95014, USA")
```

Now time to use the `JSONEncoder`, so that we can turn the above **'customer'** into data.

```
let data = try! JSONEncoder().encode(customer)
```

Let's create the `URLRequest`, using the URL as below,

```
var request = URLRequest(url: url)
```

You can create the URL using the URL string, as below,

```
let url = URL(string: "Sample URL here")!
```

If you got any API to do post request, you can post the preceding URL string.

Now, let us set the **'httpMethod'** of our request to **"POST"** and the body of our request to the **data** we got using `JSONEncoder` as follows:

```
request.httpMethod = "POST"
request.httpBody = data
```

We also need to make sure that we are telling the backend service we are passing JSON data; for that, we should send the detail as a header of our request, not just this detail in headers, but the other details that are required, which we will know by backend devs requirements. The headers can be set as follows:

```
request.setValue("application/json", forHTTPHeaderField: "Content-Type")
```

Now that we got everything to make a post request, let us do it.

```
let task = URLSession.shared.dataTask(with: request) { data, response,
error in

    let responseCode = (response as! HTTPURLResponse).statusCode
```

```
    if responseCode == 200 {
        print("SUCCESS")
    } else {
        print("FAILURE")
    }
}

task.resume()
```

Your whole `sendCustomerDetails` function should look like as follows:

```
func sendCustomerDetails() {

    let customer = Customer(name: "Kate Hill",
                            dateOfBirth: "23/05/1995",
                            address: "10600 N Tantau Ave, Cupertino, CA 95014, USA")

    let data = try! JSONEncoder().encode(customer)

    let url = URL(string: "Sample URL here")!

    var request = URLRequest(url: url)
    request.httpMethod = "POST"
    request.httpBody = data
    request.setValue("application/json", forHTTPHeaderField: "Content-Type")

    let task = URLSession.shared.dataTask(with: request) { data, response, error in

        let responseCode = (response as! HTTPURLResponse).statusCode
        if responseCode == 200 {
            print("SUCCESS")
        } else {
            print("FAILURE")
        }
    }

    task.resume()

}
```

***Figure 6.10**: sendCustomerDetails() function*

If you got any API handy to do post request, place the URL, create the codable struct accordingly, and modify the headers accordingly. Upon success or failure, you update the screen accordingly on a real app.

Conclusion

So that is all about networking, where we can make different networking requests for fetching the images, fetching JSON data, and posting the data. This chapter is really important for developing wonderful applications, as most of the applications need to make network requests to fetch and post data. In this chapter, we also learned about codables, where we can convert JSON to Swift data types and vice versa.

In the next chapter, we will learn how to leverage location services and create a sample weather app using location services.

Weather forecast: It may rain.

Points to Remember

- `UrlSession` is a wonderful tool for networking, which allows developers to interact with the web to send and fetch data.
- `URLSession.shared` is a shared singleton object that gives developers the ability to perform default actions such as fetching the contents of your URL.
- Closures are nothing but a block of code; you can see a closure as a function but without a function name.
- The trailing closure is nothing but when the closure is passed as a final argument of the function.
- An escaping is a closure that lives outside the function's life that the closure was passed to.
- A non-escaping closure is, as the name specifies, cannot escape the function; the closure cannot be alive outside the function's life.
- A URL identifies the location of your resource. It can be a web server or the path to your local file.
- `URLRequest` allows developers to make the configuration of the HTTP request.
- Codables helps us to parse through and converse from JSON to Swift data types and vice versa.
- Encodable is the process of converting the Swift data types to JSON or other external representation.
- Decodable is the process of converting the JSON or other external representations to Swift data types.
- `JSONDecoder` allows us to decode the JSON into our instances of data types.
- `JSONEncoder` allows us to encode the instances of our data types to JSON objects.

CHAPTER 7
Leveraging Location Services

Introduction

In this chapter, we are going to learn all about location services and how to use them in the weather app we are going to build. Many apps, such as weather forecasting apps, dating apps, cab ride apps, and maps apps, use location services. Location services play a major role in these apps. Along with learning about leveraging location services, we will also learn how to use weather kits in our app. Let us dig in.

Structure

In this chapter, we will discuss the following topics:

- Weather App
- Core Location
- Extensions
- `WeatherKit`
- `ObservableObject`
- `@Published`
- `Task.detached`
- `CLGeocoder`
- `viewWillAppear(_:)`

Weather App

By now, you know how to create a new project in Xcode. Go ahead and create a new project. Name it **"`Weather Forecast`"** or any name you would want to give to the app.

The main use of this app is to get the weather information of the current location and/

or certain place the user has entered. Let us follow the step-by-step process to reach our main end product. Firstly, in our project, let us get the user's current location, then we can use the WeatherKit to get the weather information of our current location. Let us step right into it.

Core Location

We have to get the device's location. For that, Apple provides a framework called Core Location. Using Core Location, we can obtain the device's location orientation and altitude. The core location framework obtains the device's information using the device's Bluetooth, barometer, cellular hardware, GPS, and Wi-Fi.

To make use of this wonderful framework in our project, we need to use the instances of **`CLLocationManager`**, which will help us deliver the location-related events to our app. Using `CLLocationManager`, we can track any changes to the device's current location, including any small changes with accuracy.

To use the Core Location framework in our project, we need to make a small setup. When you have created your project, your project comes with an `info.plist`. You can find it in your project as follows:

***Figure 7.1**: Project hierarchy*

1. Right-click the `info.plist`, click the **`'Open As'`**, and then click **`'Source Code'`**, as shown in the following screenshot:

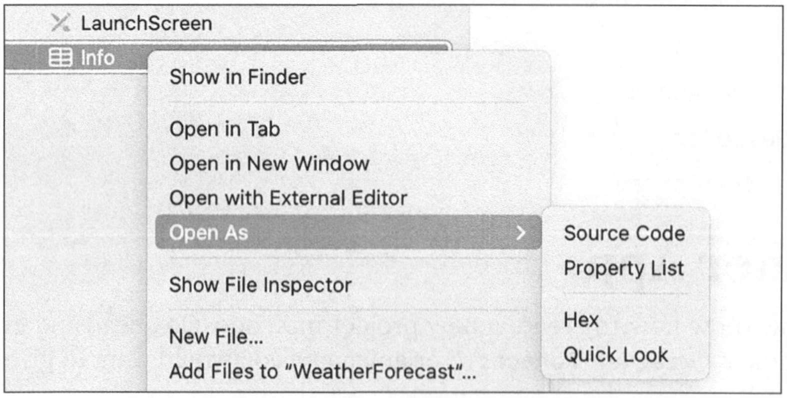

***Figure 7.2**: Opening Info.plist*

2. Now that you opened the `info.plist` as the source code, you should see something as follows:

```
<?xml version="1.0" encoding="UTF-8"?>
<!DOCTYPE plist PUBLIC "-//Apple//DTD PLIST 1.0//EN" "http://www.apple.com/DTDs/PropertyList-1.0.dtd">
<plist version="1.0">
<dict>
    <key>UIApplicationSceneManifest</key>
    <dict>
        <key>UIApplicationSupportsMultipleScenes</key>
        <false/>
        <key>UISceneConfigurations</key>
        <dict>
            <key>UIWindowSceneSessionRoleApplication</key>
            <array>
                <dict>
                    <key>UISceneConfigurationName</key>
                    <string>Default Configuration</string>
                    <key>UISceneDelegateClassName</key>
                    <string>$(PRODUCT_MODULE_NAME).SceneDelegate</string>
                    <key>UISceneStoryboardFile</key>
                    <string>Main</string>
                </dict>
            </array>
        </dict>
    </dict>
</dict>
</plist>
```

***Figure 7.3**: info.plist*

3. Add the following lines after **<plist version="1.0">**

```
<dict>
<key>NSLocationAlwaysAndWhenInUseUsageDescription</key>
<string>This app needs your location to provide accurate weather
information</string>
<key>NSLocationWhenInUseUsageDescription</key>
<string>This app needs your location to provide accurate weather
information</string>
```

The preceding code is nothing but the messages we provide to our app users while requesting permission to get their location. It would look like the following screenshot:

Figure 7.4: *Asking location permission*

Now, it is time to use `CoreLocation` in your `ViewController`, and to do that, we need to import `CoreLocation` first.

Let us have the `CLLocationManager` in our `ViewController` and also assign `CLLocationManagerDelegate` to our `ViewController`.

Now go to your `viewDidLoad()` function, initiate your `CLLocationManager`, and assign `CLLocationManager`'s delegate as our `ViewController` by adding the following lines:

```
locationManager = CLLocationManager()
locationManager?.delegate = self
```

To get the location from the user, we need to request the permission from the user and for that, add the following line of code in your `viewDidLoad()` after the preceding lines.

```
locationManager?.requestWhenInUseAuthorization()
```

This is how your `ViewController` should look like:

```
import UIKit
import CoreLocation

class ViewController: UIViewController, CLLocationManagerDelegate {

    var locationManager: CLLocationManager?

    override func viewDidLoad() {
        super.viewDidLoad()

        locationManager = CLLocationManager()
        locationManager?.delegate = self

        locationManager?.requestWhenInUseAuthorization()

    }

}
```

***Figure 7.5**: ViewController with CLLocationManager*

Let us implement the `CLLocationManagerDelegate` functions to get the current location.

Let us use extensions in our class so that we can keep our `ViewController` and projects moving forward.

Extensions

Extension, as the name implies, is the extension of an existing class, enumeration, structure, or protocol type. This could be really helpful when you do not have access to the source code but you want to add extra functionality to that specific class. This happens mainly when you are using frameworks. Imagine you want to add an extra color to the `UIColor` provided by `UIKit`. You can do it as follows:

```
static var customMadeColor: UIColor {

     return UIColor(red: 66, green: 199.0 / 255.0, blue: 205.0 / 255.0,
     alpha: 1)
}
```

Extensions make our classes look neat. We can implement protocols using extensions. Instead of declaring and implementing all the protocols in one place, we implement different protocols in different extensions as follows:

```
extension ClassName : UITextFieldDelegate {
 // Can implement the delegate functions  here
}
```

```
Extension ClassName: UITableViewDelegate {
// Can implement the delegate functions  here
}
```

Now, let us add the extension for our `ViewController`.

```
extension ViewController {
}
```

`locationManager(_:didUpdateLocations:)` is the required delegate function to fetch the location. So, let us implement this function in our extension as follows:

```
func locationManager(_ manager: CLLocationManager, didUpdateLocations
locations: [CLLocation]) {

    guard let location = locations.last else { return }
    print("The Latitude: \(location.coordinate.latitude), The Longitude:
\(location.coordinate.longitude)")
}
```

This function receives an array of `CLLocations`, and the last item in the array is the current location. If you check `CLLocation`, we got **`'coordinate'`** which is of the type `CLLocationCoordinate2D`, which has latitude and longitude that are of the type of `CLLocationDegrees`.

So the latitude and longitude got our current location's latitude and longitude.

To get the current location, we should also implement '`locationManager(_:didFailWithError:)`' as we need to handle the error in case one arises. Refer to the following for implementation:

```
func locationManager(_ manager: CLLocationManager, didFailWithError
error: Error) {

    if let clErr = error as? CLError {
        switch clErr.code {
        case .locationUnknown, .denied, .network:
            print("Request of Location failed with an error: \(clErr.
localizedDescription)")
        case .headingFailure:
            print("Request of the Heading  failed with error: \(clErr.
localizedDescription)")
        case .rangingUnavailable, .rangingFailure:
            print("Request of the ranging failed with error: \(clErr.
localizedDescription)")
        case .regionMonitoringDenied, .regionMonitoringFailure, .region-
MonitoringSetupDelayed, .regionMonitoringResponseDelayed:
            print("Request of the Region monitoring failed with error: \
(clErr.localizedDescription)")
```

```
        default:
            print("Unknown default error: \(clErr.localizedDescription)")
        }
    } else {
        print("Unknown error occurred while fetching the location: \
(error.localizedDescription)")
    }
}
```

This is what your extension should look like:

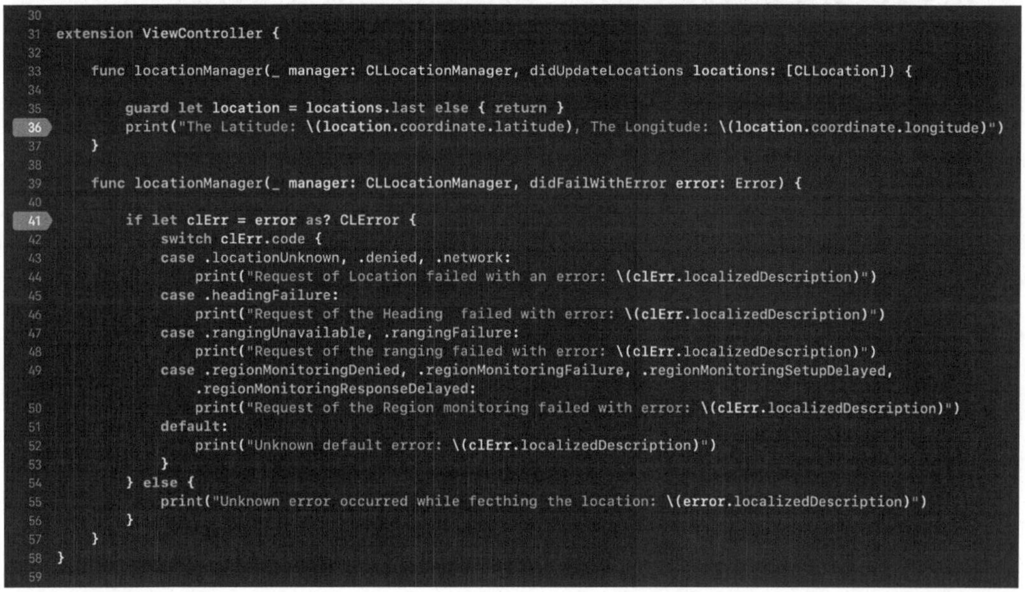

```
extension ViewController {

    func locationManager(_ manager: CLLocationManager, didUpdateLocations locations: [CLLocation]) {

        guard let location = locations.last else { return }
        print("The Latitude: \(location.coordinate.latitude), The Longitude: \(location.coordinate.longitude)")
    }

    func locationManager(_ manager: CLLocationManager, didFailWithError error: Error) {

        if let clErr = error as? CLError {
            switch clErr.code {
            case .locationUnknown, .denied, .network:
                print("Request of Location failed with an error: \(clErr.localizedDescription)")
            case .headingFailure:
                print("Request of the Heading  failed with error: \(clErr.localizedDescription)")
            case .rangingUnavailable, .rangingFailure:
                print("Request of the ranging failed with error: \(clErr.localizedDescription)")
            case .regionMonitoringDenied, .regionMonitoringFailure, .regionMonitoringSetupDelayed,
                .regionMonitoringResponseDelayed:
                print("Request of the Region monitoring failed with error: \(clErr.localizedDescription)")
            default:
                print("Unknown default error: \(clErr.localizedDescription)")
            }
        } else {
            print("Unknown error occurred while fecthing the location: \(error.localizedDescription)")
        }
    }
}
```

Figure 7.6: *ViewController extension with CLLocationManagerDelegate functions*

Place the debug points at the preceding places shown so that we will know that delegate functions are getting called.

Now, it is time to fetch the location. In order to trigger the delegate functions, we need to call the following line in our `viewDidLoad()` function:

```
locationManager?.requestLocation()
```

Just in case you got this app running in the simulator, please go ahead and delete it. This way, when we install the app in the simulator, it will ask for the user's permission.

Go ahead and run it.

When you run it in the simulator, you will see the the screen seeking the user's permission.

But in Xcode, you will see that `locationManager`'s delegate function '**`didFailWithError`**' got triggered.

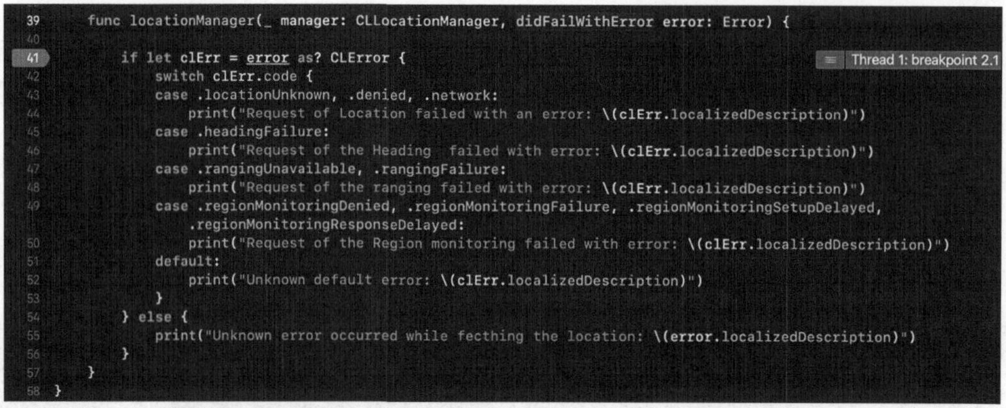

***Figure 7.7**: didFailWithError function triggered*

That is because as an end user, we have not clicked **"`Allow Once`"** or **"`Allow While Using App`,"** which is not allowing our app to fetch the location. Let go of the debug point and click **"`Allow While Using App`."** As you can see, nothing happens. That is because when permission changes, we are not calling `requestLocation()` again.

For that, we need to implement **'`locationManagerDidChangeAuthorization(_:)`'** as follows:

```
func locationManagerDidChangeAuthorization(_ manager: CLLocationManager)
{
    switch manager.authorizationStatus {
    case .notDetermined:
        print("Have not yet determine the location")
    case .restricted:
        print("User's location is restricted")
    case .denied:
        print("User denied to share the location")
    case .authorizedWhenInUse:
        print("User have selected Allow While Using App or Allow Once")

        locationManager?.requestLocation()

    case .authorizedAlways:
        print("When user select option Change to Always Allow")

        locationManager?.requestAlwaysAuthorization()

    default:
        print("default")
    }
}
```

As you can see, when the user selects **"Allow While Using App"** or **"Allow Once,"** we are calling `requestLocation`, which in turn calls **'didUpdateLocations'**.

Also, keep in mind that we only request the user's permission when we first install the app, not every time we are fetching the location or every time we open the app.

So to get the request prompt, let us delete the app in our simulator. Let us go ahead and run it.

As you have seen previously, you will get a prompt for location permission, and **'didFailWithError'** gets triggered as well. Now, let go of the debug point and click **"Allow While Using App"** on the simulator screen. Now, you can see **'didUpdateLocations'** got called,

If you let go of the debug point, you can see your latitude and longitude printed in your console.

```
Have not yet determine the location
Request of Location failed with an error: The operation couldn't
    be completed. (kCLErrorDomain error 1.)
User have selected Allow While Using App or Allow Once
The Latitude: 37.785834, The Longitude: -122.406417
```

***Figure 7.8**: Coordinates printed in the console*

So there you go. We got our current location. Now, go ahead and run the app again without deleting the app in the simulator. This time you will not see a prompt for requesting the user's location and you will see the **'didUpdateLocations'** get triggered without any error, as we gave the permission to fetch the location the first time we installed the app.

So every time we open the app now, we will get our current location.

Now that we got our current location, let us get the weather forecast information for our location. Exciting right!!

WeatherKit

`WeatherKit`, as the name implies, provides the weather information to your app.

`WeatherKit` provides your app with current weather conditions and 10-day weather forecasts.

1. Before we go any further to use the `WeatherKit` in our project, we need to do some setup in our developer account. So open **developer.apple.com/account** in your browser and sign in with your credentials. You should see something as follows:

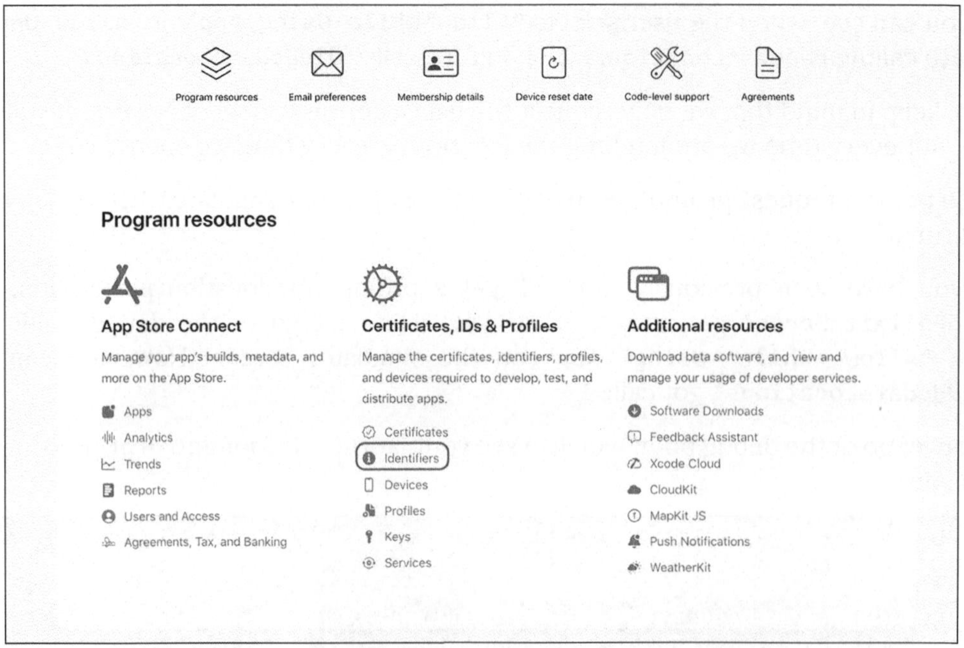

***Figure 7.9**: Developer account*

2. Then you should click the **'Identifiers'**, which was highlighted in the preceding image. Click the **'+'** icon.

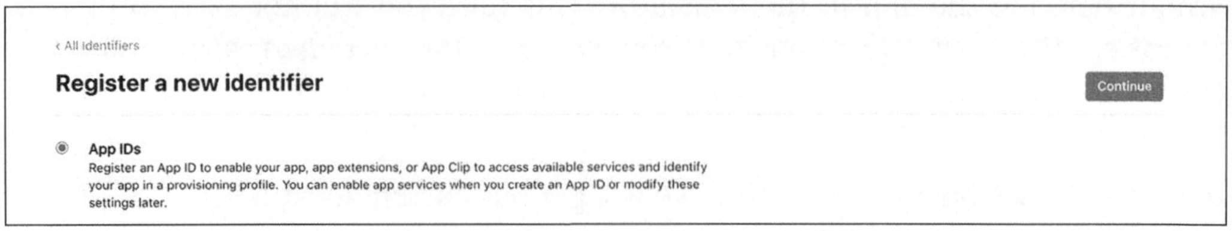

***Figure 7.10**: Developer account*

3. Select **'App IDs'** and click **Continue**. Next, click **'App'** and then click **Continue**. You should see something as follows:

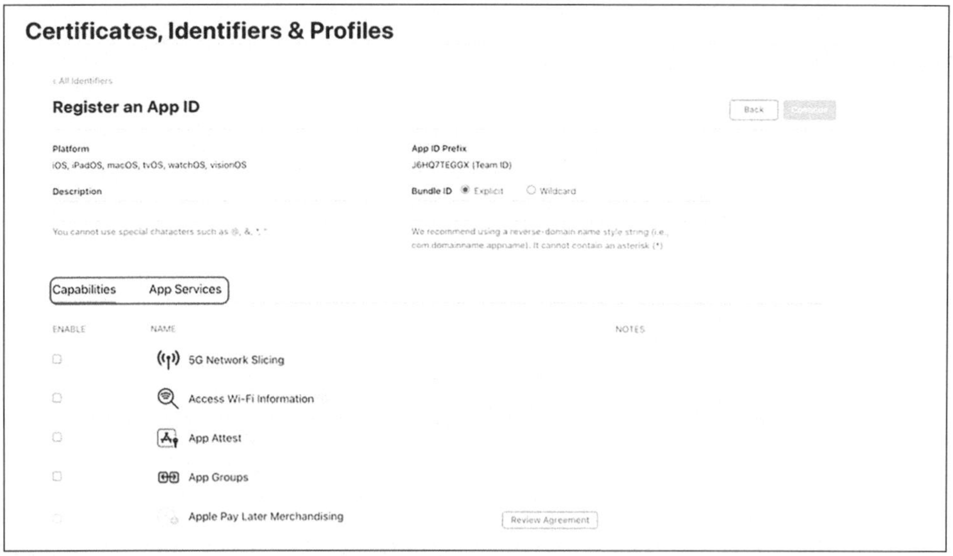

Figure 7.11: Developer account

4. In the **'Capabilities'** list, find **'WeatherKit'**, as shown in *Figure 7.12*.

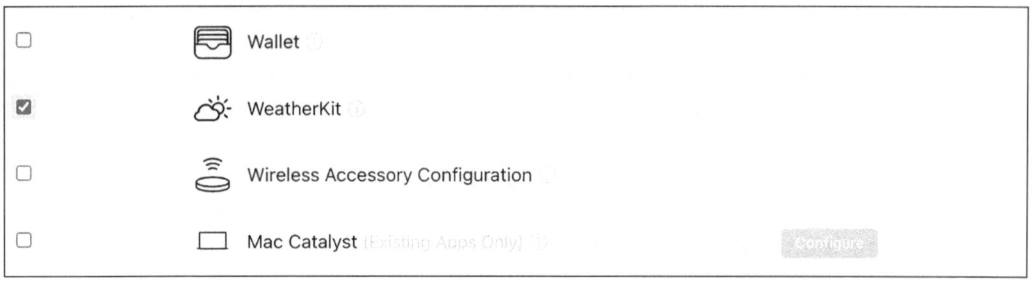

Figure 7.12: Developer account with WeatherKit selected

5. Now, go to **'App Services'** and then select **'WeatherKit'**, as shown in *Figure 7.13*.

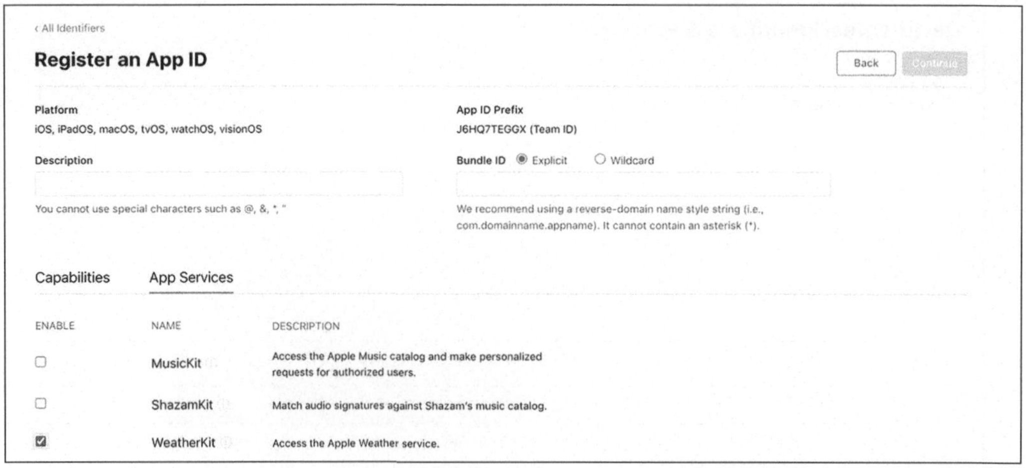

***Figure* 7.13**: *Developer account with App Services selected*

6. Fill in the **'Description'** field with something like **"This app is a weather forecasting app"** and get your **'Bundle ID'** from your project.

7. To get **'Bundle ID'** from your project, open up Xcode with your project. Click the **'WeatherForecast'** in your project navigator and select your project under targets, which are highlighted in the following figure. Open **'Signing & Capabilities'**, and in that you should see **'Bundle Identifier'**, which was also highlighted in following figure. Copy that **'Bundle Identifier'**; in this case, it is **'com.orangeAva.WeatherForecast'** and then paste it into the **'Bundle ID'** field in the browser as follows:

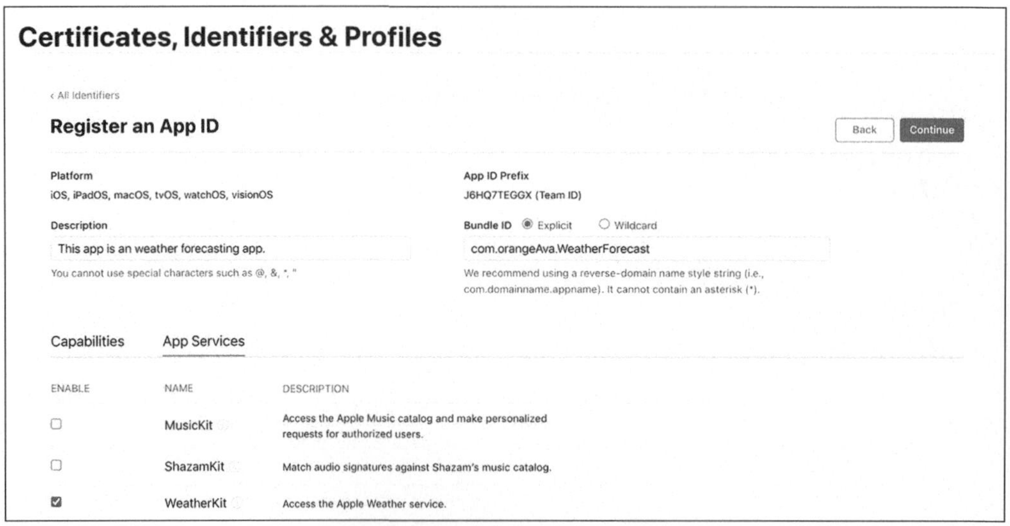

***Figure* 7.14**: *Developer account*

8. Then click **'Continue'** and then click **'Register'**. That is what we have to do in our developer account. Now let us go back to our project in Xcode. Click **'+ Capability'**, as shown in *Figure 7.15*.

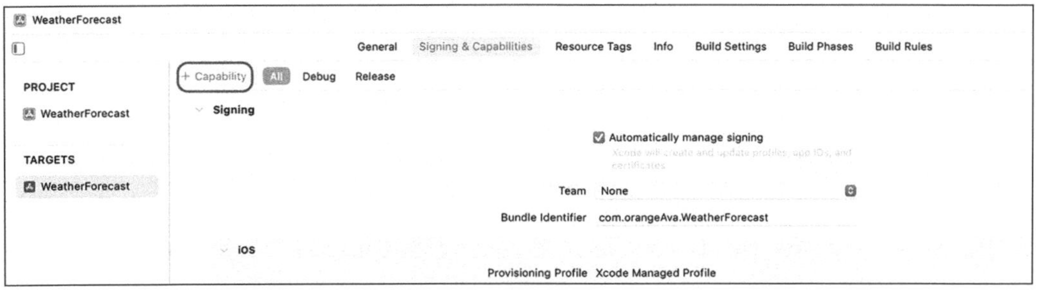

***Figure 7.15**: Xcode project with Signing & Capabilities*

9. It opens a prompt with a search bar and different capabilities. Search for **'Weatherkit'**, as shown in *Figure 7.16*.

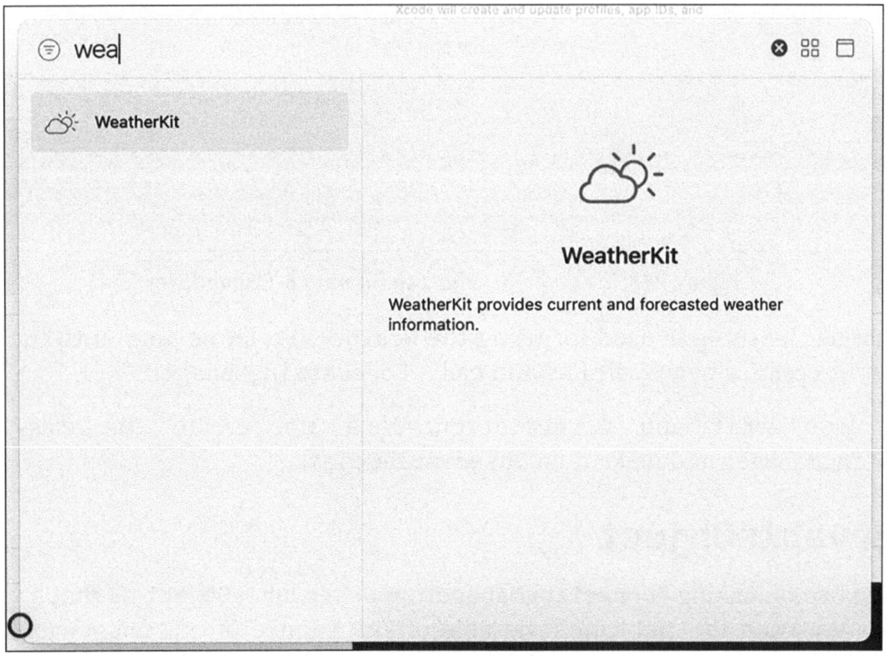

***Figure 7.16**: WeatherKit*

10. Drag the **'WeatherKit'** to the signing and capabilities as follows:

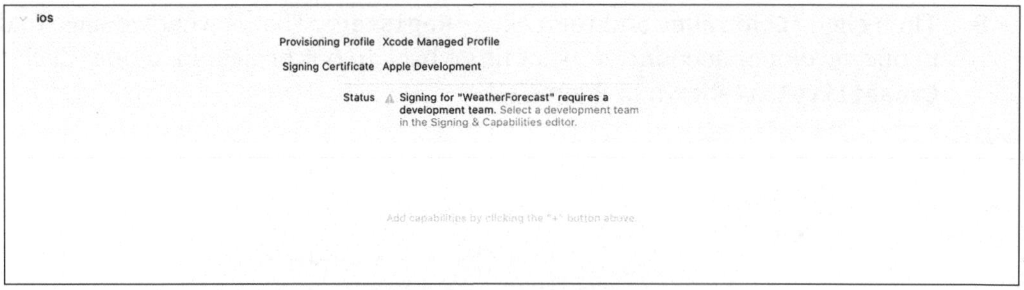

***Figure 7.17**: Xcode project*

11. After dragging, this is how your **`'Signing & capabilities'`** should look like:

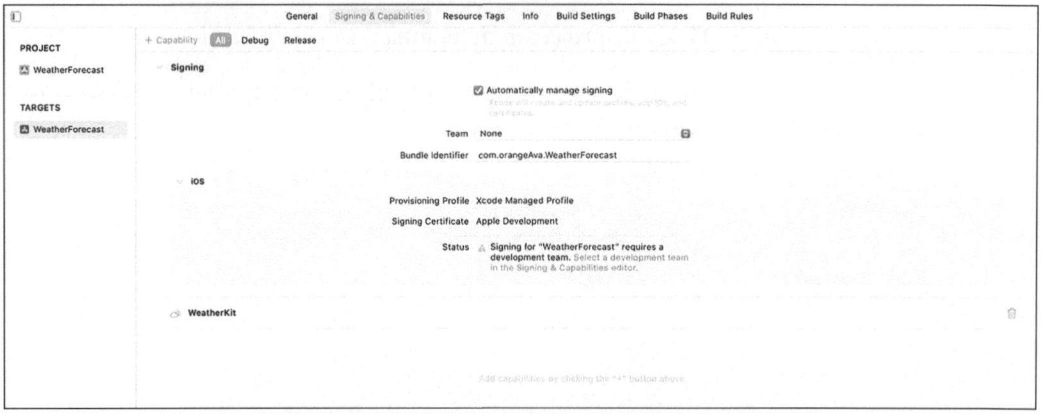

***Figure 7.18**: WeatherKit added to Signing & Capabilities*

Now that all the setup is used for using the `WeatherKit`, let us jump into the coding part. Let us create a new Swift file, and call it `ForecastingManager`.

Import `WeatherKit` and `CoreLocation`. Next up, create the class called `ForcastingManager` and make it an `ObservableObject`.

ObservableObject

The main use of making `ForcastingManager` an `ObservableObject` is that a view will get updated when the 'published' variable of an instance of our `ObservableObject` changes. This happens even when the view does not read the changes.

Create a published var called weather of type **`Weather`** from `WeatherKit` as follows:

```
@Published var weather: Weather?
```

@Published

This will allow us to reload the views whenever there is a change to this object.

This is what your `ForecastingManager` should look like:

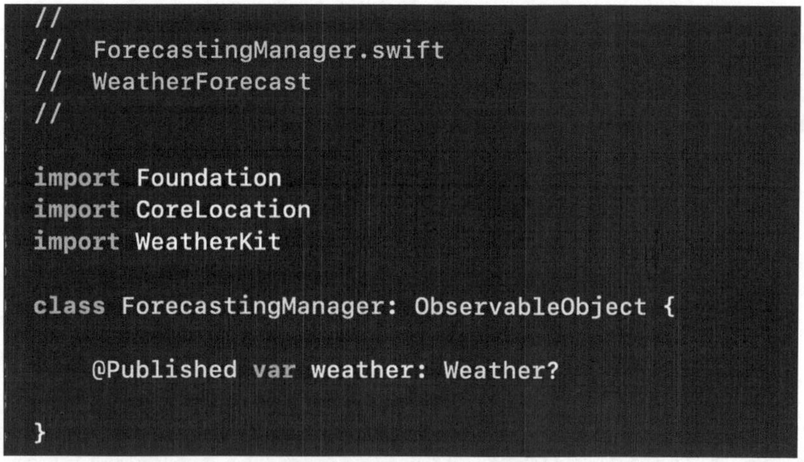

```
//
//  ForecastingManager.swift
//  WeatherForecast
//

import Foundation
import CoreLocation
import WeatherKit

class ForecastingManager: ObservableObject {

    @Published var weather: Weather?

}
```

Figure 7.19: *ForecastingManager*

Next, add a **'temp'** or **'temperature'** variable to your `ForecastingManager` as follows:

```
var temp: String {

        let temp = weather?.currentWeather.temperature

        let convertedTemp = temp?.converted(to: .fahrenheit).description
        return convertedTemp ?? "Loading Weather Data"

    }
```

Instead of returning a static variable, we are having a dynamically changing variable. All we are doing here is getting the **'temperature'** from our **'weather'** variable and converting it into Fahrenheit. As it is optional, we need to provide if the converted value is nil, and that is **"Loading Weather Data."**

Next, we need a function where we can get the **'weather'** based on location, that is, from Latitude and Longitude. The function should look as follows:

```
func getWeather(for latitude: CLLocationDegrees, longitude: CLLocation-
Degrees) async {
    do {
        weather = try await Task.detached(priority: .userInitiated) {
            return try await WeatherService.shared.weather(for:
.init(latitude: latitude, longitude: longitude))
        }.value
    } catch {
        fatalError("\(error)")
    }
}
```

Task.detached

`Task.detached` is used to create a top-level task that is disconnected from the ongoing structured concurrent tasks.

We are doing nothing apart from using `WeatherKit`'s `WeatherService`, which gives us the **'weather'** for `CLLocation`.

```
final public func weather(for location: CLLocation) async throws ->
Weather
```

This is the function from `WeatherService` that we are calling in our `getWeather` function.

This is what your `ForecastingManager` should look like:

```
class ForecastingManager: ObservableObject {

    @Published var weather: Weather?

    var temp: String {

        let temp = weather?.currentWeather.temperature

        let convertedTemp = temp?.converted(to: .fahrenheit).description
        return convertedTemp ?? "Loading Weather Data"

    }

    func getWeather(for latitude: CLLocationDegrees, longitude: CLLocationDegrees) async {
        do {
            weather = try await Task.detached(priority: .userInitiated) {
                return try await WeatherService.shared.weather(for: .init(latitude: latitude, longitude:
                    longitude))
            }.value
        } catch {
            fatalError("\(error)")
        }
    }

}
```

***Figure 7.20**: ForecastingManager with temperature and getWeather*

Let us have var `weatherForecastingManager` of type `ForecastingManager` in our `ViewController` as follows.

```
var weatherKitManager = ForecastingManager()
```

Let us go to your **`Main.storyboard`** and add a label at the center of the screen. This is just for sample purposes.

Add the coding reference for that label. Let us name it as follows:

```
import UIKit
import CoreLocation

class ViewController: UIViewController, CLLocationManagerDelegate {

    var locationManager: CLLocationManager?
    var weatherKitManager = ForecastingManager()

    @IBOutlet var weatherLabel: UILabel!
```

Figure 7.21: *viewController with weatherLabel*

Now let us go to the **'didUpdateLocations'** delegate function and add the following code after the print statement of latitude and longitude.

```
Task {
    await weatherKitManager.getWeather(for: location.coordinate.
latitude, longitude: location.coordinate.longitude)
    weatherLabel.text = weatherKitManager.temp
}
```

This is how your **'didUpdateLocations'** delegate function should look like:

```
func locationManager(_ manager: CLLocationManager, didUpdateLocations locations: [CLLocation]) {

    guard let location = locations.last else { return }
    print("The Latitude: \(location.coordinate.latitude), The Longitude: \(location.coordinate.longitude)")

    Task {
        await weatherKitManager.getWeather(for: location.coordinate.latitude, longitude: location.coordinate.longitude)
        weatherLabel.text = weatherKitManager.temp
    }
}
```

Figure 7.22: *didUpdateLocations delegate function*

What we are doing here is, after we get the Latitude and Longitude of the current location, we are getting the weather for our latitude and longitude, using the function `getWeather(for:)` from our `ForecastingManager`. After getting the weather, we are updating our label in the `ViewController`.

Now go ahead and run it. You need not delete the app. You will see the label at the center will be updated to your current location's weather in Fahrenheit as follows:

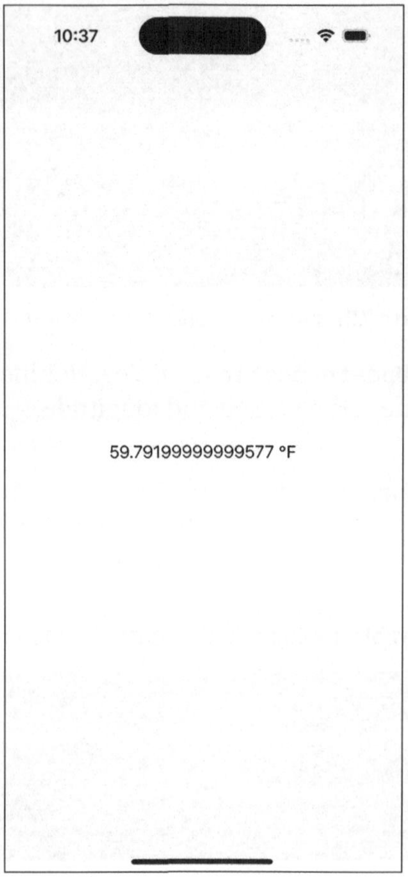

***Figure 7.23**: Simulator with temperature*

We got the weather for our current location and the time to fetch the weather for any location that is given by the user. For that, we need a function that can convert the place name into latitude and longitude, so that we can convert the place entered by the user into latitude and longitude and use the `getWeather(for:)` function of our `ForecastingManager`.

Add the `getCoord(from:)` function as follows:

```
func getCoord(from place: String) {

    let geocoder = CLGeocoder()

    geocoder.geocodeAddressString(place) { placemarks, error in

        guard error == nil else {
                       print("*** Error in \(#function):
\(error!.localizedDescription)")
                       return
```

```
                }

        guard let placemark = placemarks?[0] else {
                      print("*** Error in \(#function): placemark is nil")
                       return
                   }

        let coord = placemark.location?.coordinate ??
CLLocationCoordinate2D(latitude:

CLLocationDegrees(0), longitude: CLLocationDegrees(0))

    print("The Latitude is \(coord.latitude) and Longitude is \(coord.
longitude)")
    }
}
```

CLGeocoder

The `CLGeocoder` is provided by Core Location, which allows us to convert from coordinates to user-friendly location data and from place names to coordinates. The user-friendly information consists of country, state, city, street names, and more information, which consists of even landmarks.

Go ahead and call the preceding function with your city name as a parameter as follows. For example, **'Melbourne'**.

```
getCoord(from: "Melbourne")
```

You can have the debug at the print statement of the Latitude and Longitude to check if our function is working or not. You can run it now.

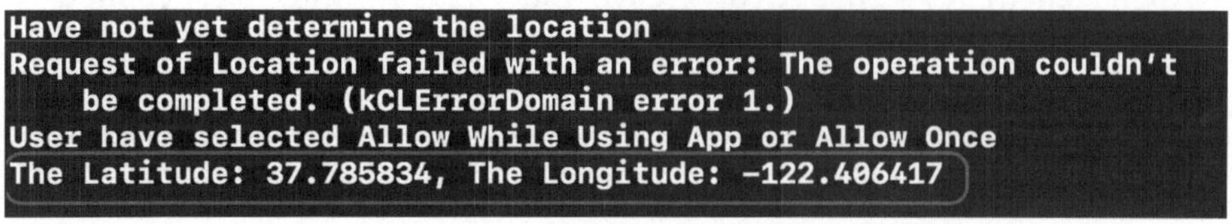

***Figure 7.24**: Coordinates printed in console*

As you can see, the latitude and longitude of the city are printed on the console. So our function worked.

Now, it is time to build the user interface so that the user can enter their city name and get the weather information.

So, firstly, as part of designing:

- When the user opens the app, there should be an `UITableView` with one row showing the weather information for the user's current location.

- The last row (in this case, the second row) should be an 'Add' button.
- When a user clicks the **'Add'** button, it should take the user to the next screen, which has a `UITextfield`, where the user can enter their city name.
- After `UITextfield`, we will have a button, which says 'Get weather'.
- When a user clicks **'Get Weather'**, there is a **'Detailed view'** that shows the weather with the respective image according to the weather.
- Underneath this **'Detailed view'** there is a button, which says **'Add to List'**.
- When a user clicks the **'Add to List'** button, the app should take the user back to our first `TableView` screen, which will have an additional row with this newly added location.

The main thing here is for you to understand the design requirements and build accordingly. The aforementioned points are how the design requirements are given in most of the companies.

Let us go build it.

1. Let us create a new project called **'WeatherForcastingService'**. Go to **Main.storyboard** and add a new `UITableViewController`, which you can embed in the `UINavigationController`, or you can drag the `UINavigatonController`, which comes with `UITableViewController` as its `rootViewController`.
2. Next, we have to create a code reference for our `UITableViewController`, so let us create a new file **'WeatherListTableViewController'**, which is a Cocoa touch class and subclass of `UITableViewController`.
3. Go to your **Main.storyboard**, select your `UITableViewController`, and open **'Identity Inspector'**. Give the **'class'** and **'Storyboard ID'** as **'WeatherListTableViewController'** (the file that we just created). Refer to *Figure 7.25*.

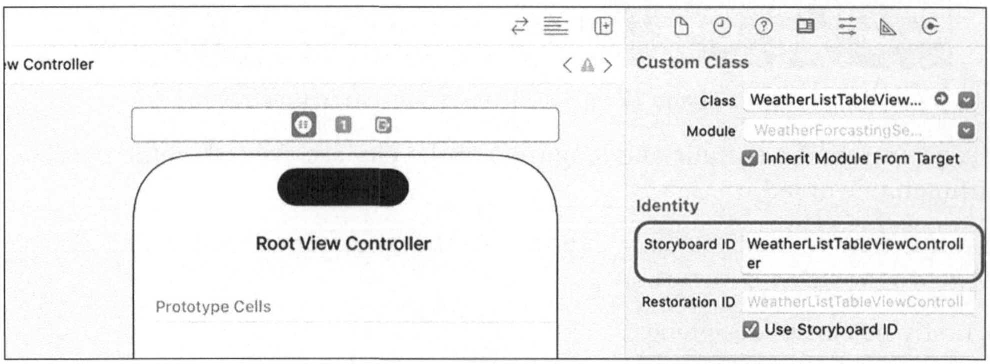

***Figure 7.25**: ViewController with StoryboardID*

Please make sure you check on the **'Use Storyboard ID'** as well.

After assigning your `UITableViewController`, it is time to do your project set, which you can refer to, which includes adding the request location permission message in **info.plist** and adding the background mode capabilities in **'Signing & Capabilities'**.

The next steps are similar to what we did for our `ViewController` for the usage of `CoreLocation` services in our `WeatherListTableViewController`, which include:

4. Importing `CoreLocation` in our `WeatherListTableViewController`.
5. Making our `WeatherListTableViewController` as `CLLocationManager Delegate`.
6. Adding `'var locationManager: CLLocationManager?'` in our `WeatherListTableViewController`.
7. In `viewDidLoad()`, add the following:

    ```
    locationManager = CLLocationManager()
    locationManager?.delegate = self

    locationManager?.requestWhenInUseAuthorization()
    locationManager?.requestLocation() - code
    ```

8. Finally, add the `CLLocationManager` delegate methods as follows, which are the same as we did in the preceding project.

    ```
    func locationManagerDidChangeAuthorization(_ manager:
    CLLocationManager) {
        switch manager.authorizationStatus {
        case .notDetermined:
            print("Have not yet determine the location")
        case .restricted:
            print("User's location is restricted")
        case .denied:
            print("User denied to share the location")
        case .authorizedWhenInUse:
            print("User have selected Allow While Using App or Allow
    Once")

            locationManager?.requestLocation()

        case .authorizedAlways:
            print("When user select option Change to Always Allow")

            locationManager?.requestAlwaysAuthorization()
    ```

```
        default:
            print("default")
        }
    }

    func locationManager(_ manager: CLLocationManager, didUpdate
    Locations locations: [CLLocation]) {
        guard let location = locations.last else { return }
        print("Latitude: \(location.coordinate.latitude), Longitude:
    \(location.coordinate.longitude)")
    }

    func locationManager(_ manager: CLLocationManager, didFailWith
    Error error: Error) {
       locationManager?.stopUpdatingLocation()

        if let clErr = error as? CLError {
            switch clErr.code {
            case .locationUnknown, .denied, .network:
                print("Location request failed with error: \(clErr.
    localizedDescription)")
            case .headingFailure:
                print("Heading request failed with error: \(clErr.
    localizedDescription)")
            case .rangingUnavailable, .rangingFailure:
                print("Ranging request failed with error: \(clErr.
    localizedDescription)")
            case .regionMonitoringDenied, .regionMonitoringFailure,
    .regionMonitoringSetupDelayed, .regionMonitoringResponseDelayed:
                print("Region monitoring request failed with error: \
    (clErr.localizedDescription)")
            default:
                print("Unknown location manager error: \(clErr.local-
    izedDescription)")
            }
        } else {
            print("Unknown error occurred while handling location
    manager error: \(error.localizedDescription)")
        }
    }
```

Now that the app is ready to use `CLLocation` services, let us start setting up our project for the usage of the famous `WeatherKit`.

1. Firstly, we need to do the setup in the Apple developer account, which you can refer to, which includes registering the App ID and adding capabilities and App services.

2. Next, go to your Xcode project and drag the `WeatherKit` capability to your project.

   Your project's **`'signing and capabilities '`** should look as follows:

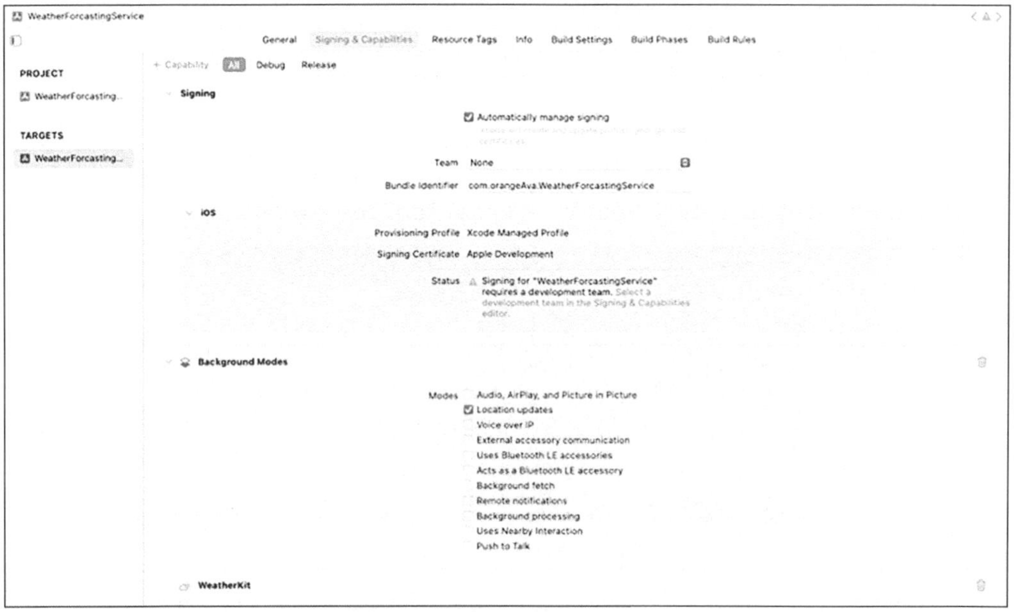

Figure 7.26: *Project's Signing & Capabilities*

3. Go to the preceding project, find the file **`'WeatherForecastingManager'`**, and copy the file to this project.

   Note: *Even if you have added the file in your finder and cannot find it in Xcode, drag it to your project in Xcode from the finder. Click* **`'Finish'`**.

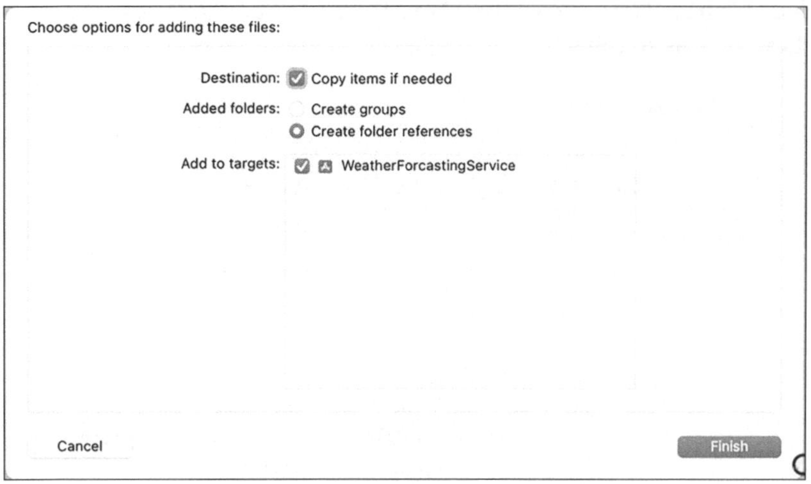

Figure 7.27: *Adding files to your project*

4. Let us utilize the WeatherKit in our **'WeatherListTableViewController'** by importing WeatherKit.

5. Let us add our **'WeatherForecastingManager'** to the **'WeatherListTableViewController'** by adding the following line:

```
var weatherKitManager = WeatherForecastingManager()
```

We need a struct that has a location name and location coordinates so that it is easy to retrieve when needed. Let us go create it. For that, create a new Swift file called LocationItem.swift, and LocationItem is the struct we will be creating in it. This is what your LocationItem.swift file would look like.

```
import Foundation
import CoreLocation

struct LocationItem {

    var locationName: String?
    var coord: CLLocationCoordinate2D?
}
```

***Figure 7.28**: LocationItem*

6. Come back to your **'WeatherListTableViewController'** and add the **'LocationItem'** array as follows:

```
var weatherLocationListArray : [LocationItem] = [] - code
```

This will be used while fetching the locations and loading our tableView.

1. Now, it is time to design our UITableViewCells. Go to your **Main.storyboard** and select your **'WeatherListTableViewController'** in your storyboard. Select **'Table View'**, go to the **'Attribute Inspector'**, and select **'Prototype Cells'** to 2 as follows:

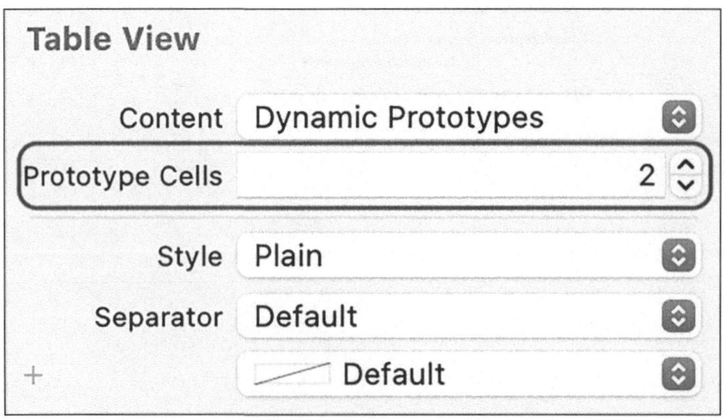

***Figure 7.29**: Prototype Cells in Attribute Inspector*

2. We need two prototype cells as we are designing two cells. Before designing the cells, let us give the table view a background color. In the same Attribute Inspector, go down to find the background color and click it. It will open up the big list; scroll down to custom, as shown in the following figure:

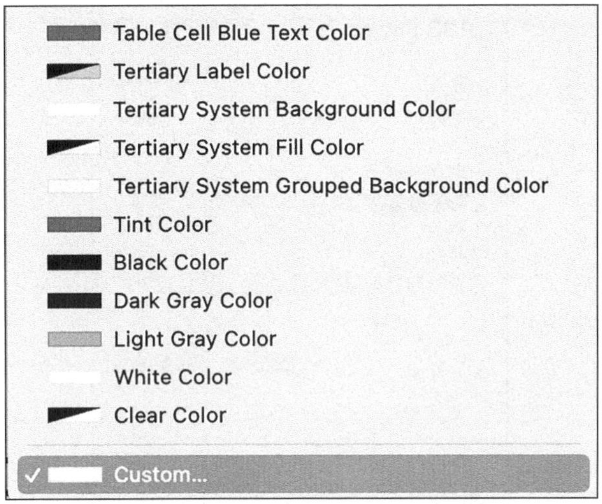

Figure 7.30: *Selecting a custom colour*

3. The following screen appears. Select **`RGB sliders`**.

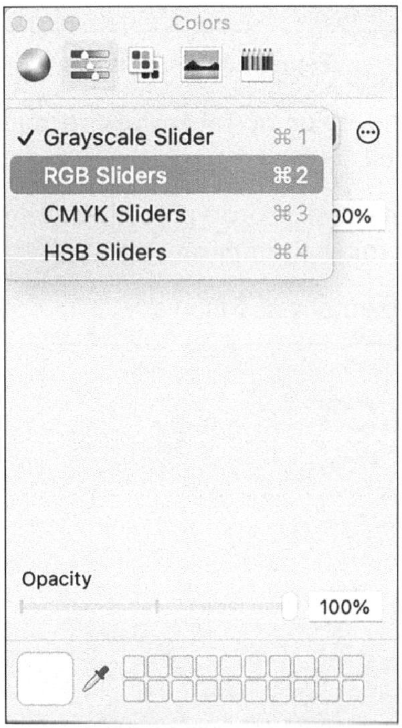

Figure 7.31: *Selecting RGB Sliders*

4. Now change the **Red** to **80**, **Green** to **174**, and **Blue** to **236**, as follows:

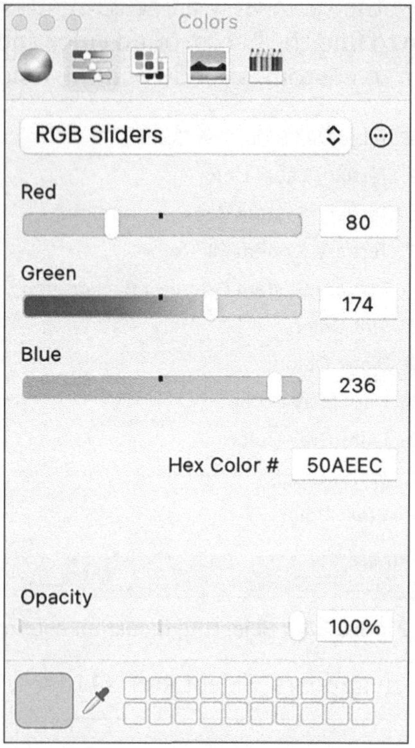

Figure 7.32: *RGB Sliders*

We changed the background color of `TableView` to make it look like a sky. Let us design our first prototype cell.

1. We need three in the first prototype cell. One for location, one for weather conditions, and one for the temperature.

   Place the labels horizontally as follows:

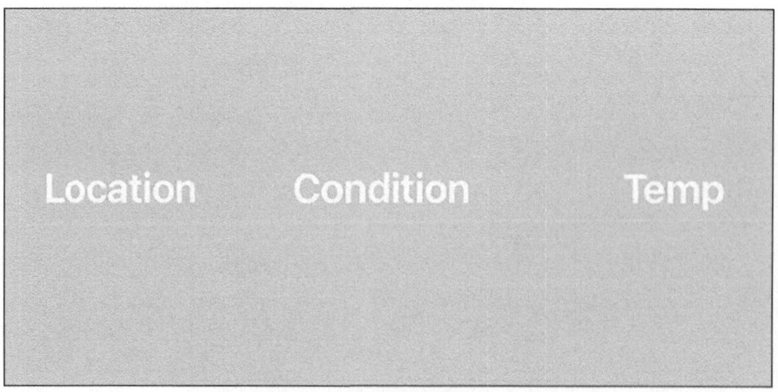

Figure 7.33: *Labels in the prototype cell*

2. Now, it is the constraints time. Align all the labels vertically center to the `tableViewcell`'s `contentView`.

   Select the Location label and add the following constraints:

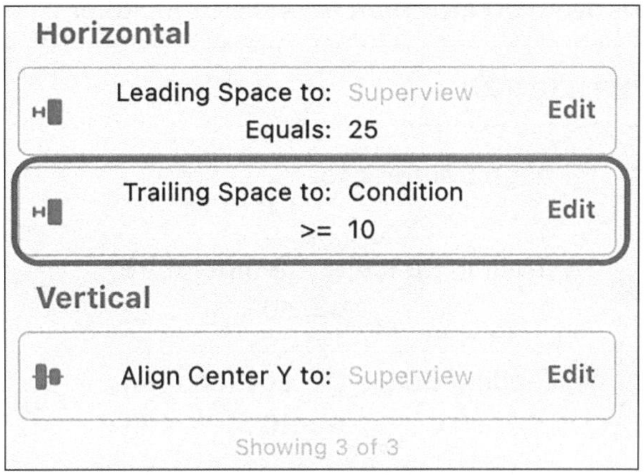

Figure 7.34: *Location label's constraints*

3. You might wonder what is that **`>= 10`** constraint, look at this constraint.

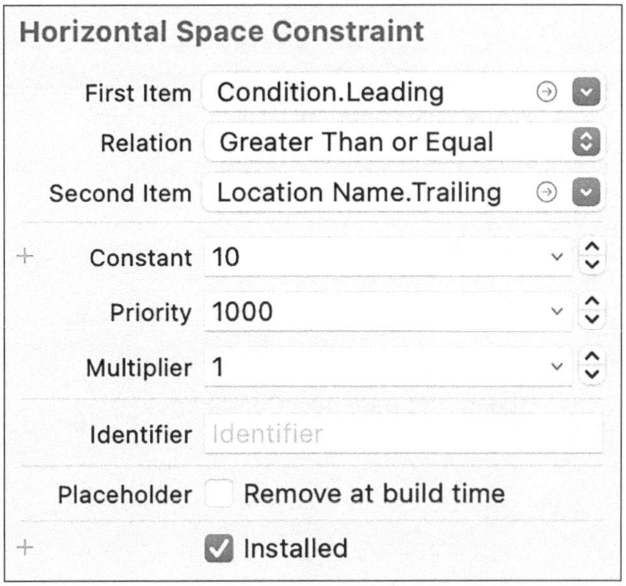

Figure 7.35: *Location label's trailing constraint*

4. All you have to do is select the **`'Condition'`** label, give the leading constraint to the location label, open the constraint, and change the **`'relation'`** from **`'Equal'`** to **`'Greater Than or Equal'`**. What we are doing here is telling that the distance can be anything between the **`'Location'`** label and **`'Condition'`** label, but it should be above 10.

5. Now select the **'Condition'** label, and center it vertically and horizontally to the superview, aka `TableViewCell`'s content view.
6. The final constraint to the **'Condition'** label is the **'trailing'** to the **'Temp'** label, which is again greater than or equal to 10. Refer to the following figure:

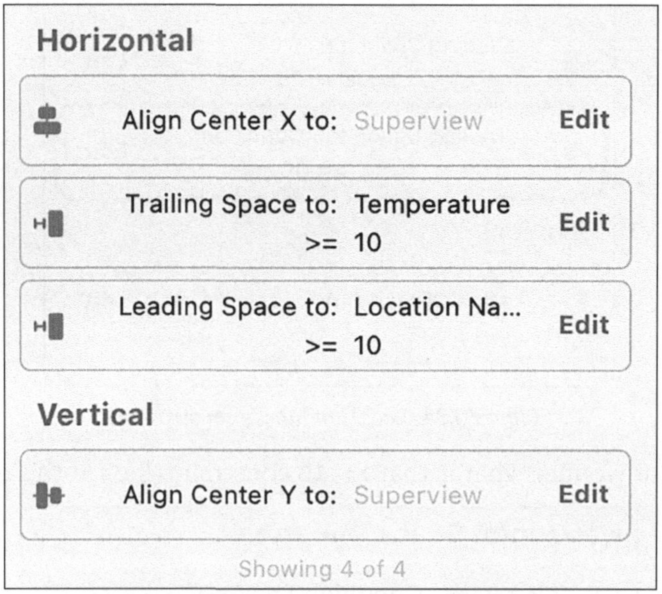

***Figure 7.36**: Condition label's constraints*

7. Add the following constraints to the **'temp'** label:

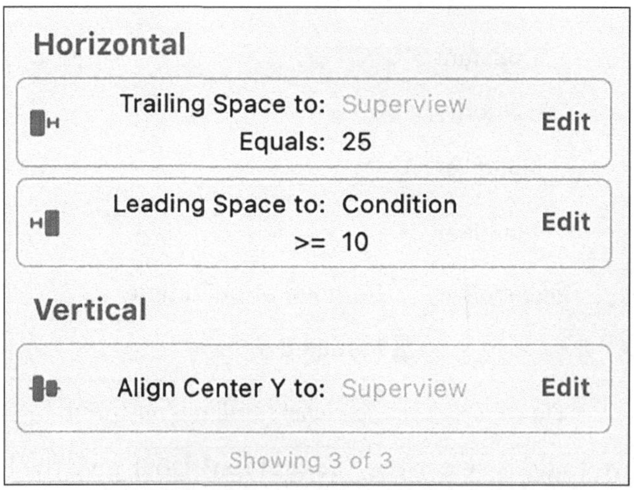

***Figure 7.37**: Temp label's constraints*

8. Lastly, add the `UIActivityIndicatorView` to our cell. Add the following constraints to the Activity Indicator View:

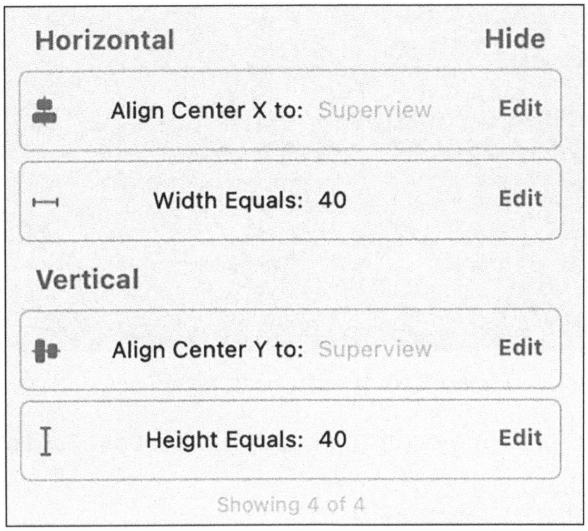

***Figure 7.38**: UIActivityIndicatorView's constraints*

Now that the constraints part is done. Let us create the code reference for this cell. Let us create a class of type `UITableViewCell`. Let us create a new file for that. Name it **'`WeatherListTableViewCell.swift`'** and the class will be `WeatherListTableViewCell`.

1. Go to your storyboard and select your first prototype cell. Go to **`Identity Inspector`** and give the class as follows:

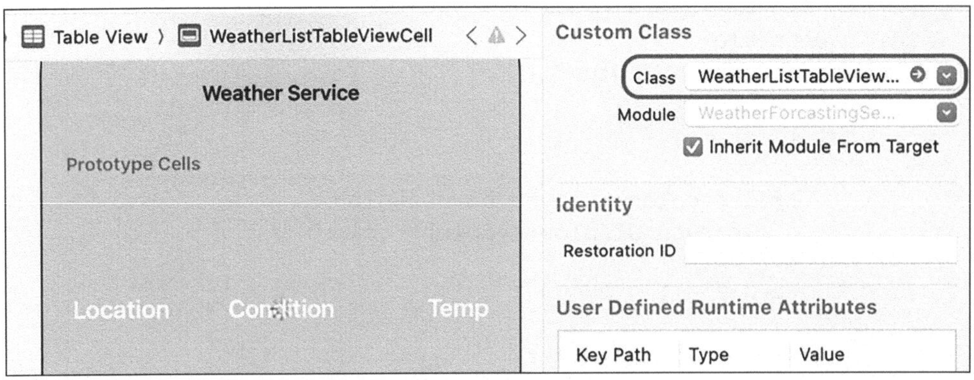

***Figure 7.39**: Defining cell's class*

2. Time to create `IBOutlets` for our labels and spinner. The following figure shows what your `WeatherListTableViewCell` class with `IBOutlets` should look like.

```
import UIKit

class WeatherListTableViewCell: UITableViewCell {

    @IBOutlet weak var locationName: UILabel!
    @IBOutlet weak var weatherCondition: UILabel!
    @IBOutlet weak var temperature: UILabel!
    @IBOutlet weak var spinner: UIActivityIndicatorView!

}
```

***Figure 7.40**: WeatherListTableViewCell*

3. Now, add the following code to your **'WeatherListTableViewCell'**.

```
@IBInspectable
var borderWidth: CGFloat {

    get {
        return layer.borderWidth
    }

    set {
        layer.borderWidth = newValue
    }
}

@IBInspectable
var borderColor: UIColor? {

    get {

        if let color = layer.borderColor {
            return UIColor(cgColor: color)
        }
        return nil
    }

    set {

        if let color = newValue {
            layer.borderColor = color.cgColor

        } else {
            layer.borderColor = nil
        }
    }
}
```

4. After adding the preceding code, go to your **`Main.storyboard`**, select your first prototype cell, which is `WeatherListTableViewCell`, and go to **`'Attributes Inspector'`**. You should see something as follows, which will allow us to change the **`'Border Width'`** and **`'Border color'`** from the storyboard itself.

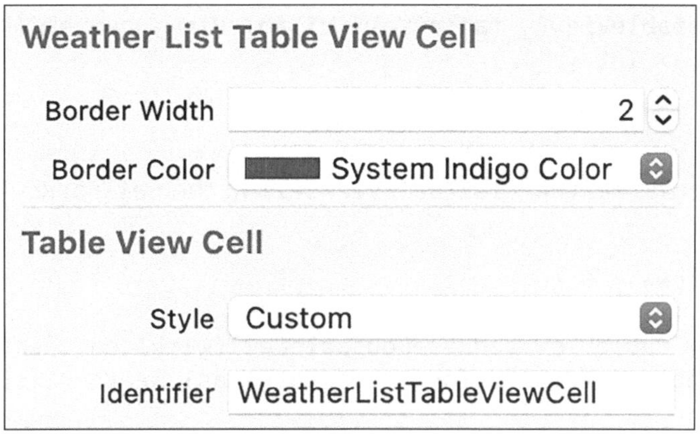

***Figure 7.41**: WeatherListTableViewCell with Border width and Border color*

5. And finally, give the **`'Border Color'`** as System Indigo color or any other color you like.

We will be using this cell, `WeatherListTableViewCell`, to publish the weather data for the current location and different locations that the user wants to know.

Now, it is time to design our second prototype cell. Just add the button at the center of the cell with the following constraints:

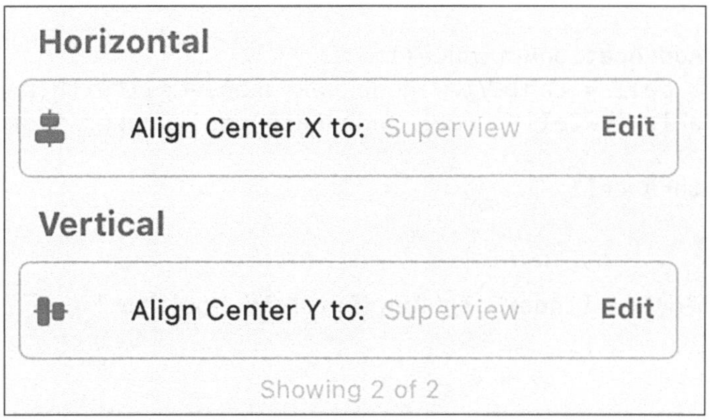

***Figure 7.42**: Button's constraints*

Change the button text to **`'Add Location'`**.

Easy right. Now let us configure our cells in **`'WeatherListTableViewController'`** so that we can see our designed cells in our app.

Later on, we can show cells based upon locations added to our **'weatherLocationListArray'**, but for now, let us show only our two prototype cells. For that, let us return **'2'** for `tableView(_:numberOfRowsInSection:)` that is shown as follows:

```
override func tableView(_ tableView: UITableView, numberOfRowsInSection
section: Int) -> Int {
    2
}
```

Let us configure the `WeatherListTableViewCell` in the `cellForRowAtIndexPath`: as follows:

```
if indexPath.row == 0 {

    let cell = tableView.dequeueReusableCell(withIdentifier:
"WeatherListTableViewCell", for: indexPath) as! WeatherListTableViewCell

    return cell

}
```

The first cell and all the other cells in our `TableView` are **'WeatherListTableView Cells'**; only the last cell is **'AddLocationTableViewCell'**. As of now it is only two cells right, so we are configuring our first cell, which is when the `indexPath.row` is 0 as `WeatherListTableViewCell`. Now let us add the else condition for our **'AddLocationTableViewCell'** configuration as follows:

```
else {

           //AddLocationButtonCell
           let cell = tableView.dequeueReusableCell(withIdentifier:
"AddLocationTableViewCell", for: indexPath) as! AddLocationTableViewCell

           return cell

  }
```

The whole `cellForRowAtIndexPath`: function should look like *Figure* 7.43.

```
override func tableView(_ tableView: UITableView, cellForRowAt indexPath: IndexPath) -> UITableViewCell {

    if indexPath.row == 0 {

        let cell = tableView.dequeueReusableCell(withIdentifier: "WeatherListTableViewCell", for: indexPath) as!
            WeatherListTableViewCell

        return cell

    } else {

        //AddLocationButtonCell
        let cell = tableView.dequeueReusableCell(withIdentifier: "AddLocationTableViewCell", for: indexPath) as!
            AddLocationTableViewCell

        return cell

    }

}
```

***Figure 7.43**: cellForRowAtIndexPath function returning two types of cells*

Let us add one more `TableView` delegate function that will help us improve the look of our `TableViewCells`, and that function is `tableView(_:heightForRowAt:)`, which will allow us to give height to our cells. Enter **`110`** as follows:

```
override func tableView(_ tableView: UITableView, heightForRowAt
indexPath: IndexPath) -> CGFloat {
    110
}
```

1. Now go to your **`Main.storyboard`** and click the **`'WeatherList TableViewController`**'s navigation title, **`'Root View Controller'`**, which is shown in the following figure:

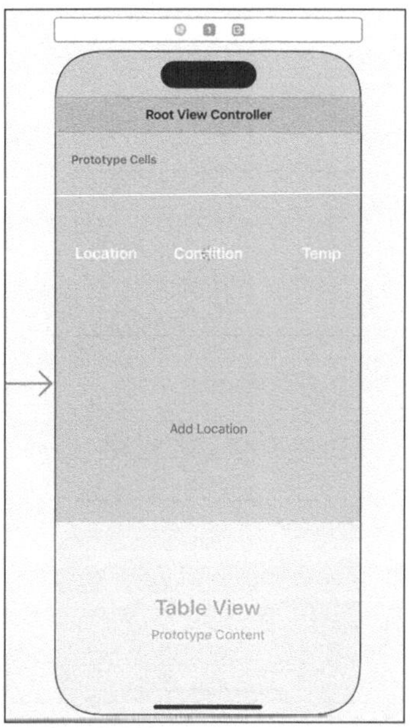

***Figure 7.44**: WeatherListTableViewController*

2. Open up the attributes inspector and change the **`Navigation Item`**'s title to **`'Weather Service'`**. Refer to the following figure:

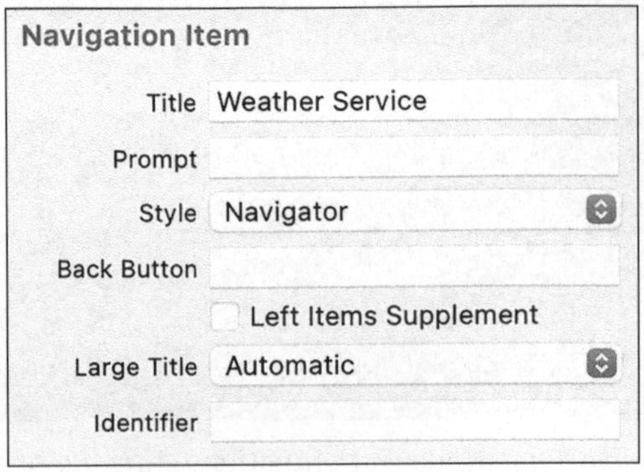

***Figure 7.45**: Navigation Item*

3. Now, it is time to run it. You should be able to see something similar to *Figure* 7.45. If you do not like the colors, change them as per your wish.

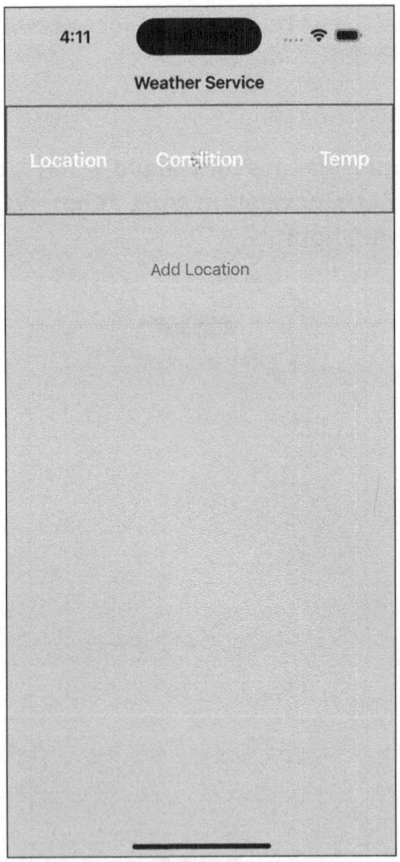

***Figure 7.46**: Simulator with two cells*

As you can see, the cells are beautifully configured. For our first cell, let us get the current location and the weather for our current location. For that, after configuring the **'WeatherListTableViewCell'**, let us request the location as follows:

```
override func tableView(_ tableView: UITableView, cellForRowAt indexPath: IndexPath) ->
    UITableViewCell {

    if indexPath.row == 0 {

        let cell = tableView.dequeueReusableCell(withIdentifier:
            "WeatherListTableViewCell", for: indexPath) as! WeatherListTableViewCell

        self.locationManager?.requestLocation()
```

***Figure 7.47**: cellForRowAtIndexPath: function*

Now go to your `CLLocationManagerDelegate` function **'locationManager(_:didUpdateLocations:)'**, where we are getting our current location and printing the latitude and longitude. After printing the longitude and latitude, let us create the `LocationItem` and assign the current location's coordinates to our `LocationItem` as follows:

```
var currentLocationItem = LocationItem()
currentLocationItem.coord = location.coordinate
```

The other thing we need is the location name as well; for that, we need to convert the coordinates to the place name. For that, let us add the following function in our `WeatherListTableViewController`.

```
func getPlace(from coord: CLLocationCoordinate2D, handler:@escaping(_
cityName: String)-> Void) {

    let lat = coord.latitude
    let long = coord.longitude

    CLGeocoder().reverseGeocodeLocation(CLLocation(latitude: lat,
longitude: long)) { placemarks, error in

        if let placemark = placemarks?.first {
            handler(placemark.locality ?? "No place found")
        }
    }
}
```

So here we are accepting the coordinates as parameters and we get the completion handler, which will be really helpful for us because only after the execution of this function and getting the location name we can move forward.

Inside our function, all we are doing is using the CLGeocoder's `reverseGeocodeLocation(_:completionHandler:)`, which will provide us placemarks. We are taking the first one from our placemarks and taking the locality, which will give us the city name.

Now, let us call this preceding function in **'locationManager(_:didUpdateLocations:)'** as follows:

```
getPlace(from: location.coordinate) { cityName in
    currentLocationItem.locationName = cityName

    if self.weatherLocationListArray.count >= 1 {
        self.weatherLocationListArray[0] = currentLocationItem
    } else {
        self.weatherLocationListArray.append(currentLocationItem)
    }

}
```

We are assigning the `locationName` from the `cityName` we are getting back from our `getPlace` function.

You might wonder about the next part of the logic. Why are we not just adding the `currentLocationItem` to our **'weatherLocationListArray'**? So what are we doing? If the `weatherLocationListArray` is empty, then we are adding it to the array; otherwise, we are replacing the first item in our array. We are doing this because the first cell in our app will always be the current location's weather. Hope that clears any doubt.

Now our work in the 'locationManager(_:didUpdateLocations:)' is done. Let us come back to 'tableView(_:cellForRowAt:)' after requesting the location; we need to add a three-second delay. We are adding this delay because we can implement the next bit of code only after getting the current location, but we do not have a completion handler for 'locationManager(_:didUpdateLocations:)'. For that very reason, we are giving a three-second delay, which is enough time to get the current location. So the three-second delay is added as follows:

```
DispatchQueue.main.asyncAfter(deadline: .now() + 3.0) {

}
```

Inside this, we are fetching the very first `LocationItem` from our `weatherLocationListArray` and assigning the `locationName` to our cell's `locationName` label's text as follows:

```
let currentLocationItem = self.weatherLocationListArray[0]

cell.locationName.text = currentLocationItem.locationName
```

Next, we need to get the weather data, like temperature and weather conditions, from the coordinates we got in `currentLocationItem`. We can do it using the following code:

```
if let lat = currentLocationItem.coord?.latitude, let long =
currentLocationItem.coord?.longitude {

                    Task {
                        await self.weatherKitManager.getWeather(for: lat,
longitude: long)
                       cell.temperature.text = self.weatherKitManager.temp
                        cell.weatherCondition.text =
self.weatherKitManager.condition
                    }
                } else {
                    cell.temperature.text = "Nil"
                    cell.weatherCondition.text = "Nil"
                }
```

This is all inside the `DispatchQueue.main.asyncAfter` block. Refer to *Figure 7.48*.

```
if indexPath.row == 0 {

    let cell = tableView.dequeueReusableCell(withIdentifier: "WeatherListTableViewCell", for: indexPath) as!
        WeatherListTableViewCell

    self.locationManager?.requestLocation()

    DispatchQueue.main.asyncAfter(deadline: .now() + 3.0) {
        let currentLocationItem = self.weatherLocationListArray[0]

        cell.locationName.text = currentLocationItem.locationName

        if let lat = currentLocationItem.coord?.latitude, let long = currentLocationItem.coord?.longitude {

            Task {
                await self.weatherKitManager.getWeather(for: lat, longitude: long)
                cell.temperature.text = self.weatherKitManager.temp
                cell.weatherCondition.text = self.weatherKitManager.condition
            }
        } else {
            cell.temperature.text = "Nil"
            cell.weatherCondition.text = "Nil"
        }
    }

    return cell

}
```

Figure 7.48: *DispatchQueue.main.asyncAfter block in tableView(_:cellForRowAt:)*

Now you can go ahead and run it; you should be able to see something as follows:

***Figure 7.49**: Simulator showing weather data*

You can see there is a spinner in the middle of our cell. Let us get it to work.

We need the spinner to spin while fetching the location and stop spinning after the text is assigned to the labels. Also, the spinner should be hidden after the spinner has stopped spinning. For that, we need to configure our activity indicator with the following lines:

```
cell.spinner.hidesWhenStopped = true
```

When we want our spinner to spin, we can do it by adding the following line, which we are doing before requesting the location.

```
cell.spinner.startAnimating()
```

When we want to stop the spinning, we can do it by adding the following line, which we are doing after assigning the weather data, such as the temperature and condition, to the cell's labels.

```
cell.spinner.stopAnimating()
```

Refer to *Figure* 7.50, which shows where the preceding code has been added.

```
if indexPath.row == 0 {
    let cell = tableView.dequeueReusableCell(withIdentifier: "WeatherListTableViewCell", for: indexPath) as! WeatherListTableViewCell
    cell.spinner.hidesWhenStopped = true
    cell.spinner.startAnimating()
    self.locationManager?.requestLocation()

    DispatchQueue.main.asyncAfter(deadline: .now() + 3.0) {
        let currentLocationItem = self.weatherLocationListArray[0]

        cell.locationName.text = currentLocationItem.locationName

        if let lat = currentLocationItem.coord?.latitude, let long = currentLocationItem.coord?.longitude {

            Task {
                await self.weatherKitManager.getWeather(for: lat, longitude: long)
                cell.temperature.text = self.weatherKitManager.temp
                cell.weatherCondition.text = self.weatherKitManager.condition
                cell.spinner.stopAnimating()

            }
        } else {
            cell.temperature.text = "Nil"
            cell.weatherCondition.text = "Nil"
            cell.spinner.stopAnimating()
        }
    }

    return cell
```

Figure 7.50: *tableView(_:cellForRowAt:) with UIActivityIndicator activation*

Go ahead and run it. You should be able to spin while fetching the data and disappear after the data is assigned to the label.

Now, it is time to get the **'AddLocationTableViewCell'** to work. The functionality we want is that when the user taps on 'Add Location', it should take the user to a new screen, where the user can enter the location name to fetch the weather data. So let us design the new screen first, then configure it to our button tap.

Go to your **Main.storyboard** and add `ViewController`. Firstly, we want a `textfield` where the user can enter the location name and then the submit button. Upon submission, we can convert the user-entered location name to coordinates and then fetch the weather data.

We need to have the `UIActivityIndicator` as well, which starts spinning when submit is clicked and then spots when the weather data is shown.

Finally, we need to have a button to this new location data back to our weather list, back in `WeatherListTableViewController`.

To show the weather data, let us have all the labels inside the view because the weather data labels should be hidden when the user first arrives on this screen. Instead of hiding each and every label, it is simple to hide the view containing the labels. Your newly added `ViewController` should look like *Figure* 7.51. You can design this as per your wish and give constraints accordingly; this way it allows you to be creative. Explore your creativity. But make sure all the following elements are present:

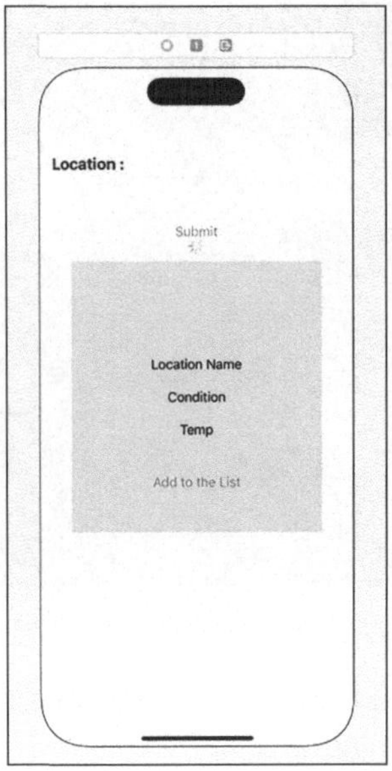

Figure 7.51: *AddNewLocationViewController*

Let us create a code reference for our `ViewController`. Let us call it **'AddNewLocationViewController'**. So we are creating `AddNewLocation ViewController.swift` cocoa touch class of type `UIViewController.`

In this class, import `CoreLocation` and `WeatherKit` because we are fetching the weather data for the user-entered location. Then create the code references/`IBOutlets` for all your UI elements. Here is how your **'AddNewLocationViewController'** should look like:

```
import UIKit
import CoreLocation
import WeatherKit

class AddNewLocationViewController: UIViewController, UITextFieldDelegate {

    @IBOutlet weak var locationTextField: UITextField!

    @IBOutlet weak var submitLocationButton: UIButton!

    @IBOutlet weak var weatherDetailView: UIView!

    @IBOutlet weak var locationName: UILabel!

    @IBOutlet weak var weatherCondition: UILabel!

    @IBOutlet weak var weatherTemp: UILabel!

    @IBOutlet weak var addToTheListButton: UIButton!

    @IBOutlet weak var spinner: UIActivityIndicatorView!

    override func viewDidLoad() {
        super.viewDidLoad()
```

Figure 7.52: *AddNewLocationViewController with @IBOutlets*

Time to add **'WeatherForecastingManager'** to our class as follows:

```
var weatherKitManager = WeatherForecastingManager()
```

Since we have UITextField on our screen, we should think of ways to dismiss the keyboard. One best way is to imagine the keyboard is up as the user is typing the location, and then the user can dismiss the keyboard when they tap anywhere on the screen. This gives the best usability. For that, we need to add the UITapGestureRecognizer to our screen.

UITapGestureRecognizer

As the name implies, the `UITapGestureRecognizer` recognizes the taps made by the user on your app screen.

Add the `UITapGestureRecognizer` to your view in your `viewDidLoad()` function.

```
let tapGesture = UITapGestureRecognizer(target: view, action: #selec-
tor(UIView.endEditing))

view.addGestureRecognizer(tapGesture)
```

Here we gave the selector as `UIView.endEditing`, which actually dismisses the keyboard when `UIView's endEditing(_:)` function is called as it resigns the first responder. So, we do not have to write a new function for that.

Let us think about what we can do in the `viewDidLoad()` function so that when the screen is loaded, we do not want `weatherDetailView` to be visible, and the spinner also should be hidden. Refer to the following figure for what has to be hidden:

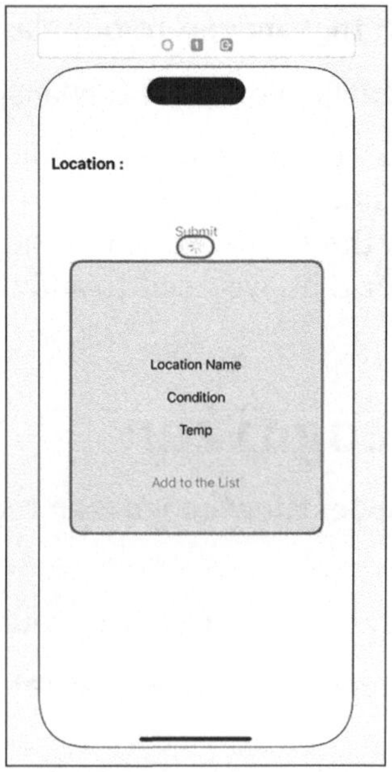

***Figure* 7.53**: *AddNewLocationViewController with weatherDetailView*

1. Now let us go back to the **`Main.storyboard`** and connect our `WeatherListTableViewController` and `AddNewLocationViewController`. For that, click the **'`Add Location`'** button, then click the control and drag to the `AddNewLocationViewController`.

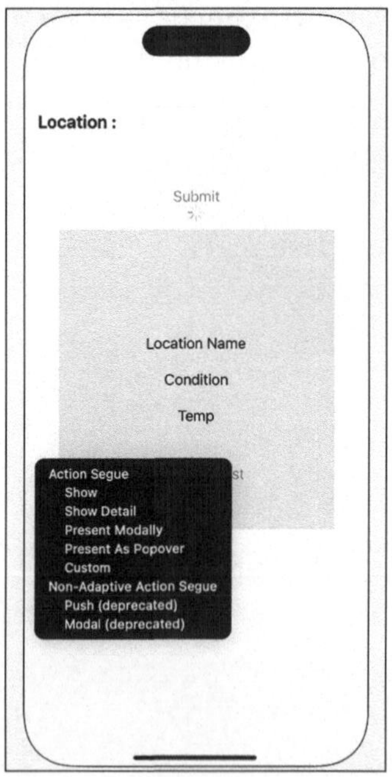

***Figure* 7.54**: *ViewController with different action segues*

2. Click on the **'show'** and you should be able to see the left `navigationItem` appearing on your `ViewController` as follows:

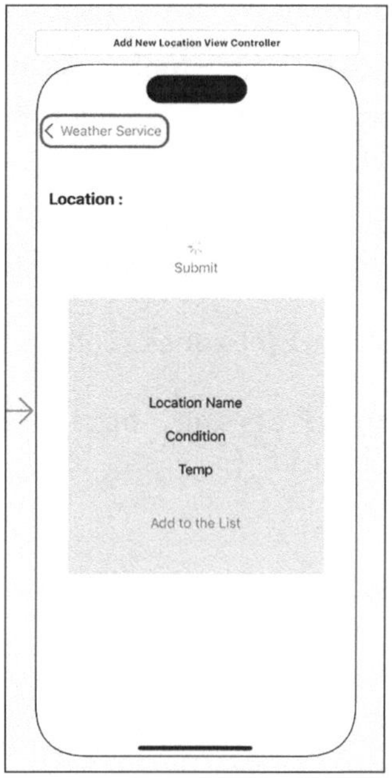

***Figure** 7.55: AddNewLocationViewController with back button*

3. Now go ahead and run it. After the first screen appears, click the **'Add Location'** button. It should take you to the next screen.

4. Go ahead and type something in the `UITextField`. Make sure the keyboard appears on the simulator screen. If not sure how, click '*command* and *k*'.

   Now tap anywhere on the screen, and as you can see, the keyboard disappears!

Time to get our `UITextField` to work. For that, make our `AddNewLocationViewController` as `UITextFieldDelegate` and then assign it as our `locationTextField`'s delegate in `viewWillAppear()` as follows:

```
override func viewWillAppear(_ animated: Bool) {
    super.viewWillAppear(animated)

    self.locationTextField.delegate = self

}
```

`viewWillAppear(_:)`

This function is called before the view of the view controller is about to be added to the view hierarchy system. This is even before the animations are configured.

One more requirement we should think of is that when the user types in the location in the `locationTextField`, we want the user to type in only the characters but not any symbols or numbers as they do not make any sense.

For that, let us use `UITextField`'s delegate function `textField(_:shouldChangeCharactersIn:replacementString:)`, which gets called for every character the user types and adds the following code to it.

```
func textField(_ textField: UITextField, shouldChangeCharactersIn range: NSRange, replacementString string: String) -> Bool {
    do {
        let regex = try NSRegularExpression(pattern: ".*[A-Za-z].*", options: [])
        if regex.firstMatch(in: string, options: [], range: NSMakeRange(0, string.count)) != nil {
            return true
        }
    }
    catch {
        print("ERROR")
    }
    return false
}
```

What we are doing here is that we are returning **'true'** only if the entered character matches the regular expression we gave here, which is just the characters. If anything, we are returning **'false'**, which means the user cannot type that character. If you want to check that magic, go ahead, run it, and test it.

Now that we have our `UITextField` working as per our need, let us get the submit button working. Create the `IBAction` **'submitLocation'** for our submit button in our `AddNewLocationViewController`.

Soon after the user clicks the submit, we want our spinner to show up and start spinning.

Then, to get the weather information for the entered location, we need to convert the location name into coordinates. For that, let us add the function. You can copy that function from the previous controller. For reference, it is the `getCoord(from:)` function.

```
func getCoords(from place:String, completion: @escaping (CLLocationCoordinate2D?) -> ()) {

    let geocoder = CLGeocoder()
    var coord: CLLocationCoordinate2D?

    geocoder.geocodeAddressString(place) { placemarks, error in
```

```
        guard error == nil else {
                      print(“*** Error in \(#function):
\(error!.localizedDescription)”)
                      return
                 }

        guard let placemark = placemarks?[0] else {
                      print(“*** Error in \(#function): placemark is nil”)
                       return
                   }

        coord = placemark.location?.coordinate ?? CLLocationCoordinate2D
(latitude: CLLocationDegrees(0), longitude: CLLocationDegrees(0))
        completion(coord)
    }
}
```

Now back to our **‘submitLocation’** `IBAction`, let us show the spinner and let us get it animating by adding the following code:

```
@IBAction func submitLocation(_ sender: Any) {
    spinner.isHidden = false
    spinner.startAnimating()

}
```

Figure 7.56: *submitLocation function*

After showing the spinner, we need to convert the location name to coordinates; for that, add the following code after the preceding spinner animation code.

```
if let locationEntered = locationTextField.text {

    // converting the name to coords
    getCoords(from: locationEntered) { [self] coords in

    }
}
```

Converting the location name to coordinates gives the facility to get the weather for the given location name. That facility can be achieved by the following code. The following code should be placed inside the preceding closure:

```
Task {
    if let coordinates = coord {
        await self.weatherKitManager.getWeather(for: coordinates.
latitude, longitude: coordinates.longitude)
```

```
        self.spinner.stopAnimating()
        self.weatherDetailView.isHidden = false
        self.spinner.hidesWhenStopped = true
        self.locationName.text = locationEntered
        self.weatherCondition.text = weatherKitManager.condition
        self.weatherTemp.text = weatherKitManager.temp
    } else {
        // Alertview
        let alert = UIAlertController(title: "Error", message: "Some-
thing Went Wrong", preferredStyle: .alert)
        alert.addAction(UIAlertAction(title: "Ok", style: .default))
        self.present(alert, animated: true)
    }
}
```

All we are doing here is quite simple: we are getting the weather and assigning the attained data to the respective UI elements. The alert view is present just in case we do not get the weather. This allows the user to know that there is some error while attaining the weather data.

Time to run it. If you click **'Add Location'**, you will make it to the second screen. Enter any city name and click **'Submit'**; you should be able to see something like the following figure:

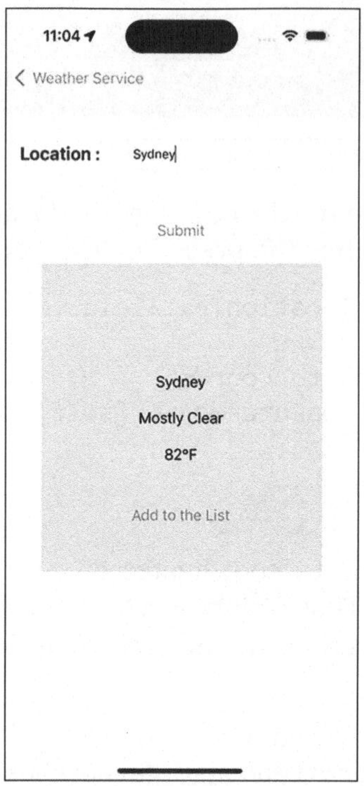

Figure 7.57: *AddNewLocationViewController with location entered*

Now, as you can see, there is an **'Add to the List'** button. The action of this button is to take the user back to the list screen with the newly entered location name. This will allow us to show the newly entered location in our list. To send back the location name, our **'WeatherListTableViewController'** should have the variable; let us add the following code:

```
var newlyAddedLocationName: String?
```

Now get back to the **'AddNewLocationViewController'** and add the **@IBAction** to the **'Add to the List'** button. Inside the **@IBAction**, we need to pop back to our **'WeatherListTableViewController'** and before popping back, assign the **'newlyAddedLocationName'** as follows:

```
@IBAction func addLocationToTheList(_ sender: Any) {

    // popping to list vc with new location data
    let weatherListViewController = self.navigationController?.view
Controllers[0] as? WeatherListTableViewController
    weatherListViewController?.newlyAddedLocationName = locationName.text
    self.navigationController?.popViewController(animated: true)
}
```

The main work is that after coming back to our list screen, we need to load the weather data in our list for the app user.

So, when you are back to the **'WeatherListTableViewController'** the `viewDidAppear()` function gets called. So, what we do here is check if **'newlyAddedLocationName'** is not nil. If it is not nil, we will get coordinates for the location name, create a new `LocationItem`, add it to our **'weatherLocationListArray'**, and finally load our `UITableView`. Let us get that going as follows:

```
override func viewDidAppear(_ animated: Bool) {
    super.viewDidAppear(true)

    if let newLocation = self.newlyAddedLocationName {
        var newLocationItem = LocationItem()
        newLocationItem.locationName = newLocation

        getCoords(from: newLocation) { coords in
            newLocationItem.coord = coords
            self.weatherLocationListArray.append(newLocationItem)
            self.tableView.reloadData()
        }
    }

}
```

Let us change `UITableView` delegate methods accordingly, firstly `tableView (_:numberOfRowsInSection:)`; it was just with the cells with the current location and add button, but now we need to load it from our **'weatherLocationListArray'**. So, the **'tableView(_:numberOfRowsInSection:)'** function is changed as follows:

```
override func tableView(_ tableView: UITableView, numberOfRowsInSection
section: Int) -> Int {
    // #warning Incomplete implementation, return the number of rows
    if weatherLocationListArray.count == 0 {
        return 2
    } else {
        return weatherLocationListArray.count + 1
    }
}
```

Now coming to the **'tableView(_:cellForRowAt:)'** function, let us change the else condition to **'else if'** so that the **'AddLocationTableViewCell'** is added as the final row. Let us go ahead and do it as follows:

```
else if (weatherLocationListArray.count == 0 && indexPath.row == 1) ||
indexPath.row == weatherLocationListArray.count {

            let cell = tableView.dequeueReusableCell(withIdentifier: "Ad-
dLocationTableViewCell", for: indexPath) as! AddLocationTableViewCell


            return cell

        }
```

The **'else if '** condition here is checking if the **'weatherLocationListArray'** count is 0. You might wonder if we have the current location data in that array. But not yet. If you run the simulator, you will see that the two rows are loaded first, and then the data is loaded in the first row later with the spinner. So that gives you a clear explanation of the preceding **'if else'** condition.

Now let us add one more else condition that will help us load the data of the newly added location data in our `UITableView`. It goes as follows:

```
else {
            let cell = tableView.dequeueReusableCell(withIdentifier:
"WeatherListTableViewCell", for: indexPath) as! WeatherListTableViewCell
            cell.spinner.hidesWhenStopped = true
            cell.spinner.startAnimating()
            let locationItem = weatherLocationListArray[indexPath.row]
            cell.locationName.text = locationItem.locationName

            if let lat = locationItem.coord?.latitude, let long = loca-
tionItem.coord?.longitude {
```

```
                Task {
                    await weatherKitManager.getWeather(for: lat,
longitude: long)
                    cell.temperature.text = weatherKitManager.temp
                    cell.weatherCondition.text = weatherKitManager.
condition
                    cell.spinner.stopAnimating()
                }
            }
            return cell
        }
```

The **'else if '** and **'else'** conditions inside the **'tableView(_:cellForRowAt:)'** should be as follows:

```
        return cell

    }  else if (weatherLocationListArray.count == 0 && indexPath.row == 1) || indexPath.row == weatherLocationListArray.count {
        let cell = tableView.dequeueReusableCell(withIdentifier: "AddLocationTableViewCell", for: indexPath) as! AddLocationTableViewCell
        return cell
    } else {
        let cell = tableView.dequeueReusableCell(withIdentifier: "WeatherListTableViewCell", for: indexPath) as! WeatherListTableViewCell
        let locationItem = weatherLocationListArray[indexPath.row]
        cell.locationName.text = locationItem.locationName

        if let lat = locationItem.coord?.latitude, let long = locationItem.coord?.longitude {

            Task {
                await weatherKitManager.getWeather(for: lat, longitude: long)
                cell.temperature.text = weatherKitManager.temp
                cell.weatherCondition.text = weatherKitManager.condition
                cell.spinner.stopAnimating()
            }
        }
        return cell
    }
```

Figure 7.58: *tableView(_:cellForRowAt:) with 'else if' and 'else'*

Time to run it. Run it, click the **'Add Location'** botton, which takes you to the next screen, enter a new location, **'Sydney'**, and click **'Submit'**. You should see the weather data for that location. Click the **'Add to the list'** button, which should take you back to the List screen with the newly added location. The weather data as follows:

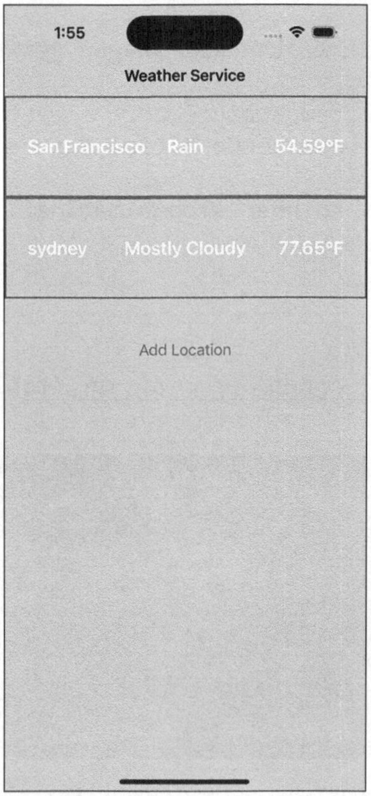

***Figure 7.59**: Simulator with different location data.*

So, there you go. We created one beautiful and useful app. A few things can be improved in this app, which are intentionally kept. A few clues could be that there is a part of the code that is repeated. Find that part of the code and find how you can make it reusable from a single place. Think also about UI improvements; think about how you can improve the user experience even more.

Conclusion

That is it for this chapter. Location services are really useful and used by a lot of apps these days such as dating apps, which show at what distance the person is, and car ride and food delivery apps, which show where your driver is. Leverage the location services and make your app more interesting.

The next chapter is going to be even more interesting, as it is going to be about authentication and involves AWS as well.

Points to Remember

- Using Core Location, we can obtain the device's location orientation and altitude.
- The core location framework obtains the device's information using the device's Bluetooth, barometer, cellular hardware, GPS, and Wi-Fi.
- Extensions are the extensions of existing classes, enumeration, structure, or protocol type.
- `WeatherKit` provides the weather information to your app.
- `WeatherKit` provides your app with the current weather conditions and 10-day weather forecasts.
- The main use of `ObservableObject` is that a view will get updated when the 'published' variable of an instance of our `ObservableObject` changes.
- This will allow us to reload the views whenever there is a change to the `@ published` object.
- `Task.detached` is used to create a top-level task that is disconnected from the ongoing structured concurrent tasks.
- The `CLGeocoder` is provided by Core Location, which allows us to convert from coordinates to user-friendly location data and from place names to coordinates.
- The `viewWillAppear(_:)` function is called before the view of the view controller is about to be added to the view hierarchy system.

CHAPTER 8
Saving Data for iOS Applications

Introduction

This chapter is a fun and important chapter where you will learn about data modeling, which is really important for our app, and if you want to pursue an app developer career, data modeling will be the major milestone to learn about. Next comes the exciting thing, you will be exploring Amazon Web Services (AWS), which is an awesome thing to learn about. Using AWS, we will be saving our app data to AWS and also fetching the data from AWS as well. So, let us dig in.

Structure

In this chapter, we will discuss the following topics:

- Data Modeling
- SQLite
  - Opaque Pointer
  - `sqlite3_prepare_v2`
  - `sqlite3_step`
  - `sqlite3_finalize`
  - `sqlite3_bind_text`
  - `sqlite3_bind_int`
- AWS S3
- Swift Package Manager
- Layer
- `masksToBounds`

- `putObject`
- `putObjectInput`
- `clipsToBounds`

Data Modeling

You might wonder if we are learning about data modeling. This means learning about creating the visualization of the data using diagrams. Actually we are not. The data modeling we are learning here is how to model the data coming from the database to be used in the app. We will also learn how to structure the database as per the data received from the app. We learned in the previous chapters how to create the struct for the data received from the users. For example, in the app if we are collecting the user data such as name, age, and house address. We are creating the struct as follows:

```
struct User {
    var name: String
    var age: Int
    var address: String
}
```

Now we will learn to send the data to the database, and model it as per the data that needs to be stored. This will be really useful in understanding how the app interacts with the database and how you can save and retrieve the data.

In order to save the above data, we need to have a database structure like the following:

`UserID, UserName, UserAge, UserCity.`

Usually in many workplaces, we actually make API calls to send the data to the database, so we just get the endpoints from backend developers. But in order to understand how the backend works, this topic will be really helpful because, in the future, you can actually assist the backend developers in modeling the data as well, which can be efficiently sent to the backend.

Let us get started by creating the sample project with the screen that looks like *Figure 8.1*.

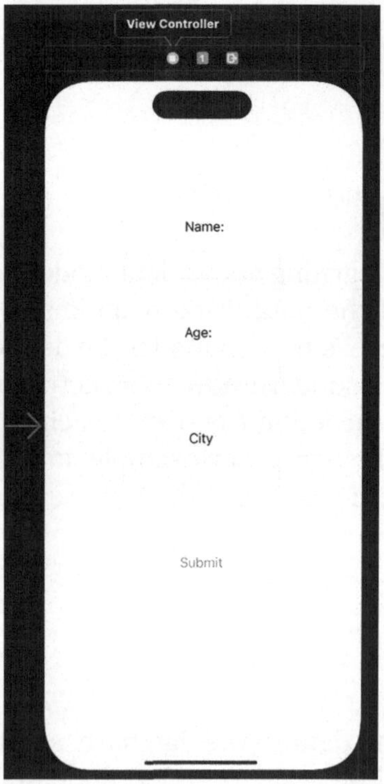

***Figure 8.1**: Storyboard screen with textfields and buttons*

Add the code references for the `textFields` and the **`'Submit'`** button action in your `viewController`.

Now just looking at the screen, you might have got the idea that we will be collecting the user's name, age, and address and saving that to the database.

Coming to the database, we will be using SQLite.

SQLite

SQLite is the most used database engine in the world. SQLite is built into all mobile phones and most computers and comes bundled inside countless other applications that people use every day.

Another advantage is that it is cross-platform, stable, and backwards compatible as well.

Let us add a new `UITableViewController`. The plan here is that when you add the user data, it will insert into our database and then take the user to the next screen, which will fetch the data from our database. In the real world or in a workplace where the data is either saved on the device using SQLite or in an external database, the data is sent using the API calls.

Let us go ahead and create a `UITableViewController` with a prototype cell looking like *Figure* 8.2.

***Figure 8.2**: Storyboard screen with prototype cell*

The next steps include creating a custom class for our prototype cell and assigning it to the prototype cell in the storyboard. For reference for custom class, check *Figure* 8.3.

```
import Foundation
import UIKit

class UserDataCell: UITableViewCell {

    @IBOutlet weak var name: UILabel!
    @IBOutlet weak var age: UILabel!
    @IBOutlet weak var city: UILabel!

}
```

***Figure 8.3**: UITableViewCell class*

In *Chapter 9*, *Authentication*, we will explore a new way to create custom cells. Now, let us create a class reference for our `UITableViewController` as well. Let us call it `UserDataTableViewController`. Please make sure that you provide the class reference in the storyboard for the `UITableViewController` in the Identity Inspector.

Now, it is time to create the '`User`' struct, which will help us to save the user data. For reference, check *Figure 8.4*.

```
class User {

    var userID: Int = 0
    var userName: String = ""
    var age: Int = 0
    var city: String = ""

    init(userID: Int, userName: String, age: Int, city: String) {
        self.userID = userID
        self.userName = userName
        self.age = age
        self.city = city
    }
}
```

***Figure 8.4**: User class*

Now that we have created the necessary struct and `UITableViewController`, let us segue from the `ViewController`'s submit button (where user data will be entered) to the `UITableViewController`.

This will allow the user to move to the next screen when the submit button is clicked. Since this is a sample app, we are not doing the null check on the `UITextfields` to see if the user entered the data or not. But in the real app, we will be doing it. Since we did all the UI things that are needed for this sample app, let us jump into coding for opening the database SQLite3, creating a table, saving it to the table, and retrieving data from the database; in other words, let us jump into the fun stuff.

The first step is, let us create a Swift file called `DataBaseUtility`, which will have all the database-related functions. Firstly, add the following variables, which would be useful in this class.

```
let userDatabase: String = "userDb.sqlite"
var dbOpaquePointer: OpaquePointer?
```

The 'userDatabase' is the name of our database. 'dbOpaquePointer' is the OpaquePointer.

Opaque Pointers

These are really helpful in representing the pointers that cannot be represented in Swift types.

The first function, of course, will be for opening the database.

```
func openUserDatabase()
    {
        let fileURL = try! FileManager.default.url(for: .documentDirectory,
 in: .userDomainMask, appropriateFor: nil, create: false)
            .appendingPathComponent(dataBaseURLPath)
        if sqlite3_open(fileURL.path, &dbOpaquePointer) != SQLITE_OK
        {
            print("Unable to open the database")

        }
        else
        {
            print("Successfully connected to the database")
        }
    }
```

First, you might wonder where this database is being created. It is created inside the user device in Application Support. Second, you might wonder about the use of `'sqlite3_open'`. Are we just creating and opening an existing database? The answer to that is NO. `'sqlite3_open'` opens the existing database, and if the database does not exist, it creates the database.

Here the `sqlite` instance is used as an `opaquePointer` because the `sqlite3` pointer is not a primitive type such as `char` or `string`.

After creating the database, the next step is to create the table inside our database.

```
func createUserTable() {
    let createtabStr = "CREATE TABLE IF NOT EXISTS user(Id INTEGER
PRIMARY KEY,name TEXT,age INTEGER,city TEXT);"
    var createTabStmt: OpaquePointer? = nil
    if sqlite3_prepare_v2(dbOpaquePointer, createtabStr, -1, &create
TabStmt, nil) == SQLITE_OK
    {
        if sqlite3_step(createTabStmt) == SQLITE_DONE
        {
            print("User table created.")
        } else {
            print("Error creating user table.")
        }
    } else {
        print("CREATE statement can't be prepared.")
    }
    sqlite3_finalize(createTabStmt)
}
```

sqlite3_prepare_v2

We need something to execute our SQL statements, so `sqlite3_prepare_v2` does that as the first step of the job. By compiling the SQL statement into byte code, it returns a status code based on the compilation; if it complies, it returns `'SQLITE_OK'` so we can proceed with further steps, or else let us print the error.

sqlite3_step

After compiling our SQL statement, we need to run it, and as it executes the prepared statement, `sqlite3_step` does that important job for us.

sqlite3_finalize

We use the `sqlite3_finalize` to delete the compiled statement, as this will avoid resource leaks, and you should never be using the statement again after being used in `sqlite3_finalize`.

Since we have created the table, let us insert the data into the table using the following function:

```
// func to insert user data into the user table
 func insert(user: User) {
     let insertStatementString = "INSERT INTO user (id, name, age, city)
VALUES (NULL, ?, ?, ?);"
     var insertStatement: OpaquePointer? = nil
     if sqlite3_prepare_v2(dbOpaquePointer, insertStatementString, -1,
&insertStatement, nil) == SQLITE_OK {
         let name: NSString = user.userName as NSString
         let age: Int32 = Int32(user.age)
         let city: NSString = user.city as NSString
         sqlite3_bind_text(insertStatement, 1, name.utf8String, -1, nil)
         sqlite3_bind_int(insertStatement, 2, age)
         sqlite3_bind_text(insertStatement, 3, city.utf8String, -1, nil)
         if sqlite3_step(insertStatement) == SQLITE_DONE {
       print("Successfully inserted row with name \(name), age \(age)
and city \(city).")
 } else {
             print("Could not insert row.")
         }
     } else {
         print("INSERT statement could not be prepared.")
     }
     sqlite3_finalize(insertStatement)
 }
```

sqlite3_bind_text

`sqlite3_bind_XX` usually binds the values provided into statement parameters. `sqlite3_bind_text` here binds the string value into statement parameters.

sqlite3_bind_int

Here it binds the int value into statement parameters.

So, all we are doing is binding the values provided into statement parameters and then executing the prepared statement using `sqlite3_step` and then deleting the compiled statement using `sqlite3_finalize`.

So, we have created a table, and we got the code for inserting user data into the table. The next thing we want to do is show the insert data in our `UITableViewController`. For that, we need a function to read data from our table. Let us do it.

```
func read() -> [User] {
    let queryStatementString = "SELECT * FROM user;"
    var queryStatement: OpaquePointer? = nil
    var users : [User] = []
    if sqlite3_prepare_v2(dbOpaquePointer, queryStatementString, -1,
&queryStatement, nil) == SQLITE_OK {
        while sqlite3_step(queryStatement) == SQLITE_ROW {
             let id = sqlite3_column_int(queryStatement, 0)
            let name = String(describing: String(cString: sqlite3_col-
umn_text(queryStatement, 1)))
            let age = sqlite3_column_int(queryStatement, 2)
            let city = String(describing: String(cString: sqlite3_col-
umn_text(queryStatement, 3)))

            users.append(User(userID: Int(id), userName: name, age: In-
t(age), city: city))
            print("Query Result:")
            print("\(name)) | \(age) | \(city)")
        }
    } else {
        print("SELECT statement could not be prepared")
    }
    sqlite3_finalize(queryStatement)
    return users
}
```

You can figure out what the aforementioned function is doing with the definitions provided. The different thing we are doing here is retrieving the data instead of inserting the data; the SQL query is different.

Finally, one remaining function is to delete the data. So, when the end user chooses to delete the user data from the app, it needs to be deleted in the database as well, as we need to read the data from the table in the database the next time we load the data to the `UITableViewController`. Add the following code to your `databaseUtility`.

```
func deleteByID(id: Int) {
    let deleteStatementStirng = "DELETE FROM user WHERE id = ?;"
    var deleteStatement: OpaquePointer? = nil
    if sqlite3_prepare_v2(dbOpaquePointer, deleteStatementStirng, -1,
&deleteStatement, nil) == SQLITE_OK {
        sqlite3_bind_int(deleteStatement, 1, Int32(id))
        if sqlite3_step(deleteStatement) == SQLITE_DONE {
            print("Successfully deleted user .")
        } else {
            print("Could not delete user.")
        }
    } else {
        print("Can't prepare DELETE statement.")
    }
    sqlite3_finalize(deleteStatement)
}
```

Here we are deleting the user using the id.

Now, it is time to utilize our `DatabaseUtility` functions on our app screens.

The first thing is to go to your `ViewController`. In order to use `DatabaseUtility` functions in your `ViewController`, you need to initialize it in your class. Add the following code in your class:

```
    var dbUtility: DatabaseUtility = DatabaseUtility()
```

Then go to your `@IBAction` of your submit button, let us say `'submitUserDetails'`. Go ahead and add the following code to your `IBAction`:

```
@IBAction func submitUserDetails(_ sender: Any) {
      if userName.isEmpty || userAge == 0 || userCity.isEmpty {
          return
      }

      let user = User(userID: 0, userName: userName, age: userAge,
city: userCity)
      dbUtility.insert(user: user)
      nameTextField.text = ""
      ageTextField.text = ""
      addressTextField.text = ""
  }
```

In the aforementioned function, we are checking if the `userName`, `userAge`, and `userCity` are empty. If they are not empty, then we are creating a `'User'` and then inserting it into the database using `'dbUtility.insert(user: user)'`. If you want, you can have the debug pointer in your insert function, or we already have the print statement for our confirmation.

Before going ahead and running, we have one more task remaining, which is to add `UITextFieldDelegate` functions to capture the data from the `textFields` and assign it to the respective variables. Let us make our class confirm to `'UITextFieldDelegate'`, as shown in *Figure* 8.5.

```
class ViewController: UIViewController, UITextFieldDelegate {
```

***Figure* 8.5**: *ViewController confirming to the UITextFieldDelegate*

In `viewDidLoad()` function, let us assign the `UITextField`'s delegates.

```
    self.nameTextField.delegate = self
    self.ageTextField.delegate = self
    self.addressTextField.delegate = self
```

The next step is to add the `UITextFieldDelagate`'s function as follows:

```
func textField(_ textField: UITextField, shouldChangeCharactersIn range: NSRange, replacementString string: String) -> Bool {

    let textFieldText: NSString = (textField.text ?? "") as NSString
    let updatedString = textFieldText.replacingCharacters(in: range, with: string)

    if textField == nameTextField {
        userName = updatedString
    } else if textField == ageTextField {
        userAge = Int(updatedString) ?? 0
    } else if textField == addressTextField {
        userCity = updatedString
    }

    return true
}
```

As mentioned before, all we are doing is capturing the text from the `UITextField` and assigning it to the respective variables.

Add the following code delegate function as well:

```
func textFieldShouldReturn(_ textField: UITextField) -> Bool {
    textField.resignFirstResponder()
    return true
}
```

Now it is our favorite time–time to run. Go ahead and run it.

Go ahead, fill the `UITextFields` and click **`Submit`**.

Since we got segue for our `Submit` button, after clicking the button it takes you to the next screen, but before that our code in `IBAction` gets executed. If you want to check, please have debug points and give it a go. Before forwarding to the next, the data will be inserted into database. You can check the console logs for confirmation, which will say, **"`Successfully inserted row with name Kate, age 32, and city Sydney.`"**

Now that we have successfully inserted the data into the database, it is time to read the data from the database so that we can show the data in our `UITableViewController`.

Let us go to our **'`UserDataTableViewController`'** or whatever you called your `UITableViewController` and add the array of **'`User`'** as follows:

```
var users: [User] = []
```

Now, it is time for `UITableView` data source methods. The number of sections will be 1, and the number of rows will be the aforementioned `users.count`.

Coming to the '`cellForRowAtIndexPath:`' function, we should use our preceding custom cell that we have created.

```
let cell = tableView.dequeueReusableCell(withIdentifier: "UserDataT-
ableViewCell", for: indexPath) as! UserDataTableViewCell
```

Please make sure that you have assigned the cell's '`Identifier`' in `Main.storyboard`; otherwise, the aforementioned code will not work. For reference, check *Figure* 8.6.

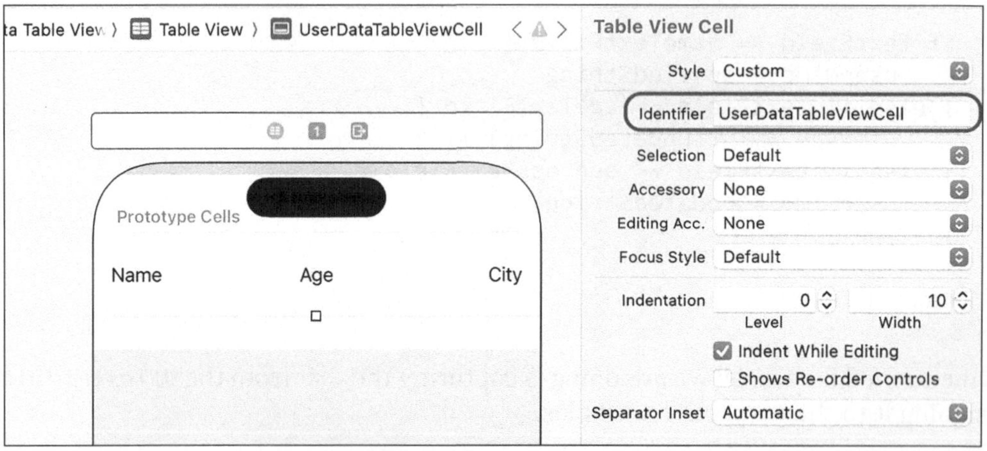

***Figure 8.6**: UITableViewCell Identifier*

Coming back to **'`cellForRowAtIndexPath:`'**, add the code as follows:

```
override func tableView(_ tableView: UITableView, cellForRowAt indexPath: IndexPath) -> UITableViewCell {

    let cell = tableView.dequeueReusableCell(withIdentifier: "UserDataTableViewCell", for: indexPath) as!
        UserDataTableViewCell

    let user = users[indexPath.row]

    cell.name.text = user.userName
    cell.age.text = String(user.age)
    cell.city.text = user.city

    return cell
}
```

Figure 8.7: *Configuring the cell*

All we are doing here is getting the **'User'** from our **'users'** array and assigning the attributes of User to the respective labels.

So in *Figure* 8.7, our `UITableView` is fetching the users from the '`Users`' array, but we have not filled the **'Users'** array; for that, we need to fetch the data from the database and assign it to our array. Add the following code to the `viewDidAppear() func`; you need to add `viewDidAppear()` in your `UITableViewController`.

```
let userDataBase = DatabaseUtility()
let usersFromDatabase = userDataBase.read()
users = usersFromDatabase
self.tableView.reloadData()
```

All we are doing here is utilizing the `DatabaseUtility`'s `read()` function to read the data from the database and assign it a **'users'** array. For reference, check *Figure* 8.8.

```
override func viewDidAppear(_ animated: Bool) {
    super.viewDidAppear(animated)

    let userDataBase = DatabaseUtility()
    let usersFromDatabase = userDataBase.read()
    users = usersFromDatabase
    print("users count \(users.count)")

    sleep(4)
    tableView.reloadData()

}
```

Figure 8.8: *Using DatabaseUtility*

The reason we are doing in `viewDidAppear` is that we got a segue from our **'Submit'** button to the `UITableViewController` and we got **'submitUserDetails'** `IBAction` for our button. Because we got the segue, when the **'Submit'** button is clicked, the `viewDidLoad()` function of our `UITableViewController` gets called; it gets called even before the `IBAction` of our **'submit'** button gets executed. Which means `viewDidLoad()` of our `UITableViewController` gets called even before inserting the data, so there will be nothing to read from the database or only data will be available. If you want to give it a try, have debug points in `viewDidLoad()` and `viewDidAppear()`, and check it for yourself.

Now, it is time to run the app. Go ahead and run it. Enter any data in the `UITextfields`.

Click the **'Submit'** button; you should see something like *Figure* 8.9.

Figure 8.9: *Simulator screen with new row showing up*

Our `UITableViewController` looks weird because we do not have `UINavigationController`. So, let us go add it by going to `Main.storyboard` and clicking `UITableViewController` on **'Editor'** in the Menu above, and then clicking **'Embed In'** and selecting **'Navigation Controller'**. For reference, check *Figure* 8.10.

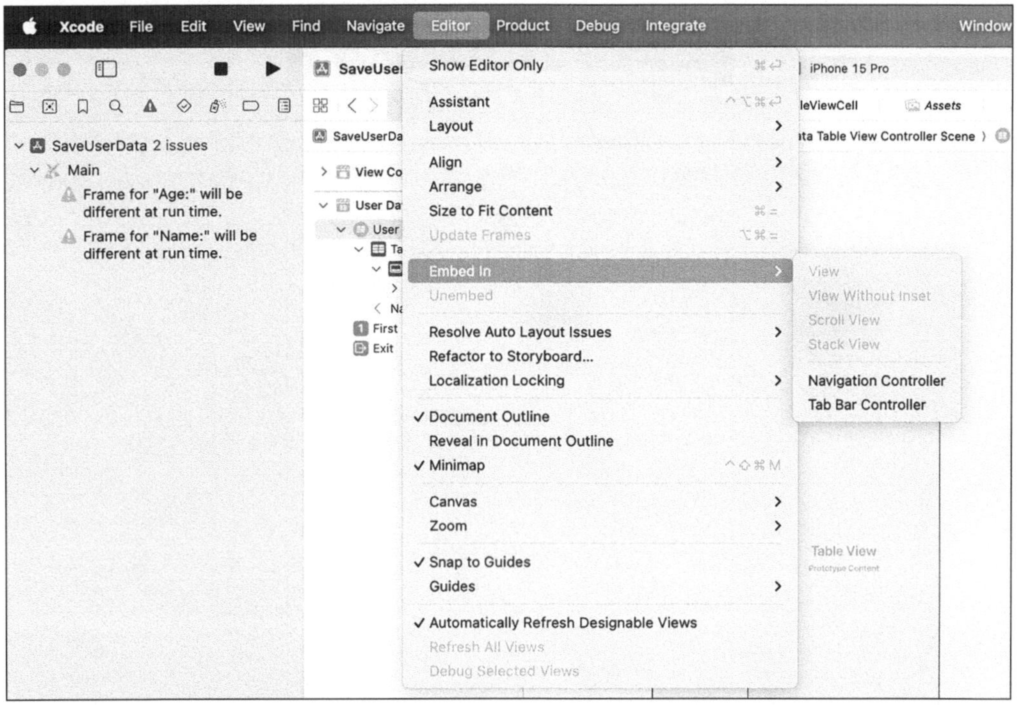

Figure 8.10: *Embedding the UIViewController in Navigation controller in storyboard*

Your storyboard should look like *Figure* 8.11.

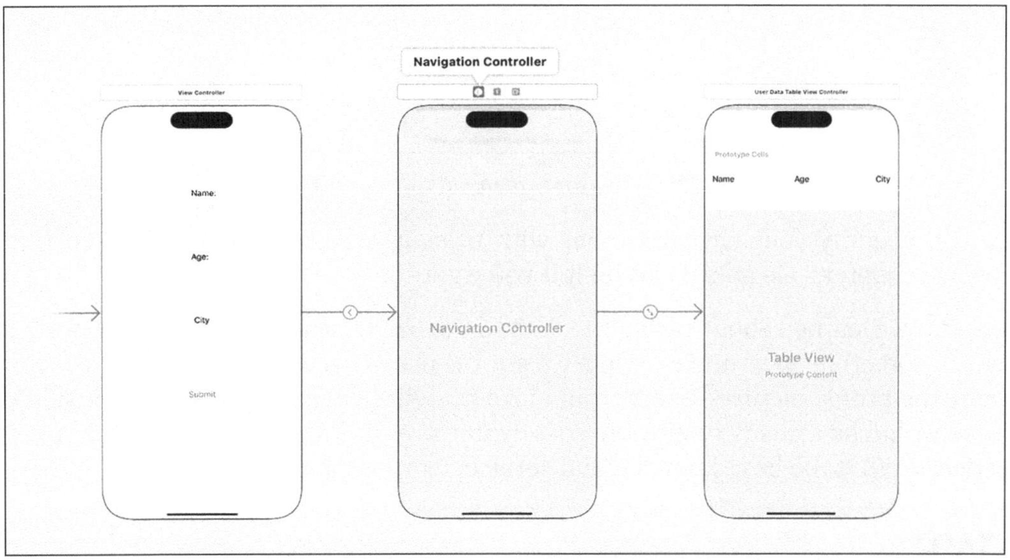

Figure 8.11: *Storyboard with ViewControllers*

Now go ahead and run it, add the data in the first screen, and click **'Submit'**. You should see something like *Figure* 8.12.

Figure 8.12: *Simulator screen with new rows inserted*

You can beautify your navigation bar with titles as well, which we explored in the previous chapters. Go ahead and do it if you want to.

Now that we learned about saving the data to the database and retrieved it as well. Let us learn something new and exciting; we got the user's name, age, and city. How about having the profile picture? Users would love it, right? But saving the image inside the device would be a costly operation, so why not save it in the cloud and fetch it when needed? AWS is the best-known cloud service; let us explore that.

AWS

If you are a developer already, you should know what cloud computing is; if not, then cloud computing consists of computing services such as databases, storage, servers, networking, and many other services over the internet (in the cloud). We can say that all services, like databases, are up in the virtual cloud, and many applications will access them and fetch the data or pull in the required services. The major benefit of cloud computing is, imagine, the amount of servers and databases that a company has to maintain in order to launch and run an application. If the number of users for an application increases, the company has to make major changes to the data storage and maintain the data center. But if you are using cloud computing, everything is easily maintained and scalable too. Netflix is one major application that uses cloud computing to run the video-streaming service.

AWS, which means 'Amazon web services', is one that provides such wonderful cloud-based services and is cost-effective too.

AWS S3

AWS S3 or Amazon S3 means Amazon Simple Storage Service, which is a famous cloud storage service with features such as scalability, security, performance, and data availability.

Amazon S3 can be used to save huge amounts of structured and unstructured data. In S3, the data is saved in key-based object storage fashion.

The famous companies that use S3 for their web content storage are Pinterest, Reddit, Netflix, and Airbnb. Interestingly, Amazon itself uses the S3 service to store project data.

In order to use the amazing AWS services in our project, we need to integrate the AWS SDK. As we are using the Swift language, we need a Swift language SDK, which you can get from here at: 'https://github.com/swift-aws/aws-sdk-swift.git'

There are ways to integrate the SDKs into iOS projects using pods, Carthage, and the recently used package manager. So, let us take the recent way (using package manager) to stay updated.

Swift Package Manager

Swift Package Manager (SPM) is used to automate the process of linking dependencies, compiling, and downloading. You can create your project as Swift package to give it to other projects to consume your project. In a similar fashion, we can use SPM to integrate other projects into our project. This whole SPM is integrated into the Swift build system; we do not need CocoaPods or Carthage if you use SPM. The only condition is that the other third-party project should be SPM compatible in order for us to consume it using SPM.

1. To add our SDK to the project, Go to the `Xcode` menu -> click `File` -> Click **`'Add Package Dependencies'`**, as shown in *Figure* 8.13.

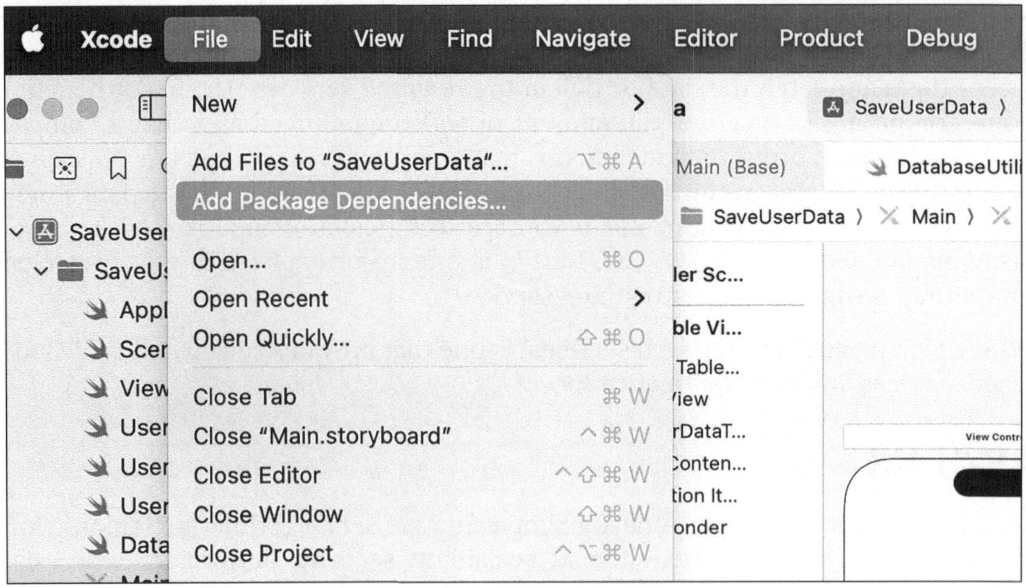

Figure 8.13: *Adding packages*

You will see something as *Figure* 8.14.

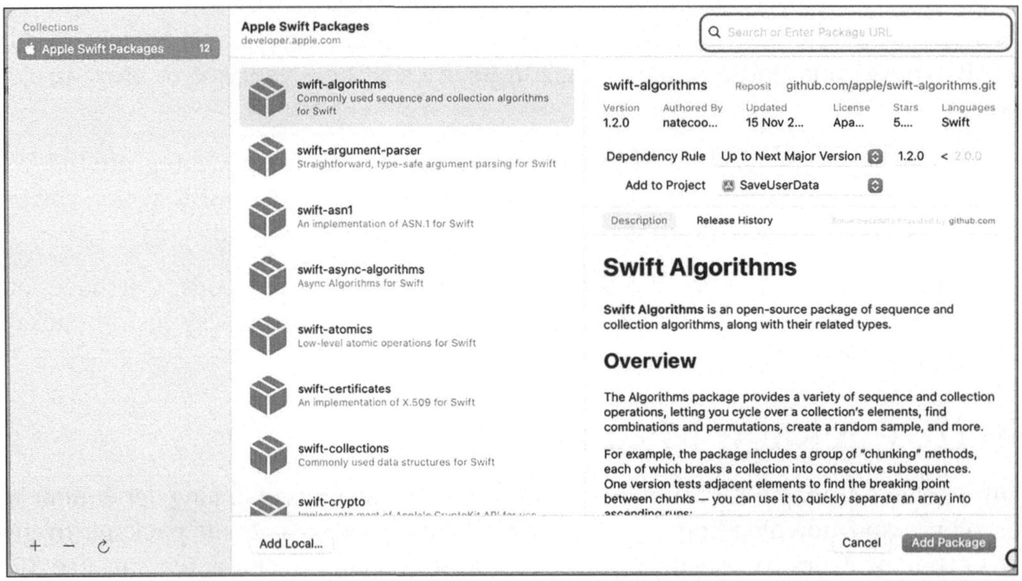

Figure 8.14: *Searching packages*

2. In the search bar, place the URL, '`https://github.com/awslabs/aws-sdk-swift.git`'. You will see something as follows:

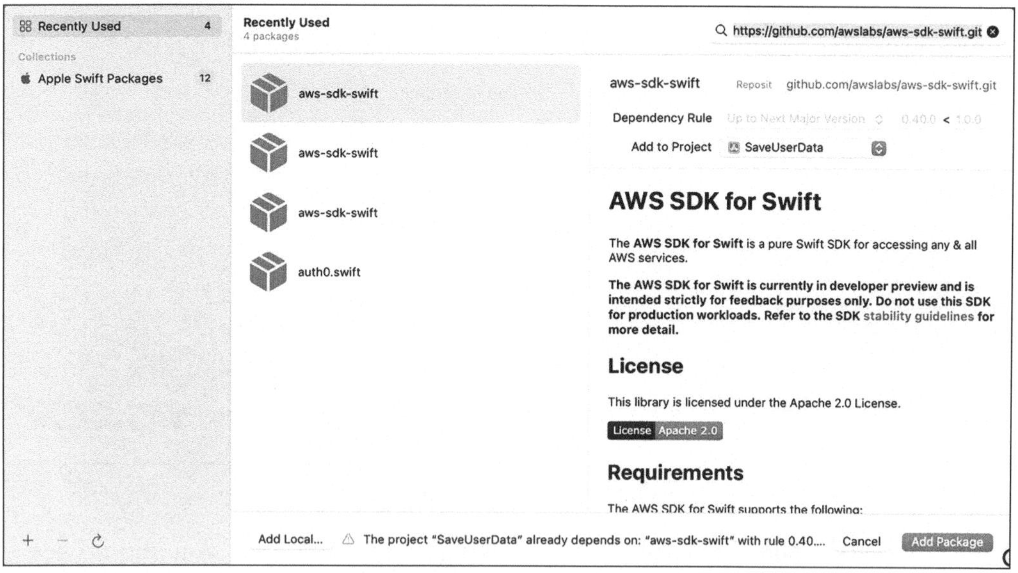

Figure 8.15: *Adding AWS package*

3. Click the **`'Add Package'`**. You will see that package manager is fetching the SDK, as shown in *Figure* 8.16.

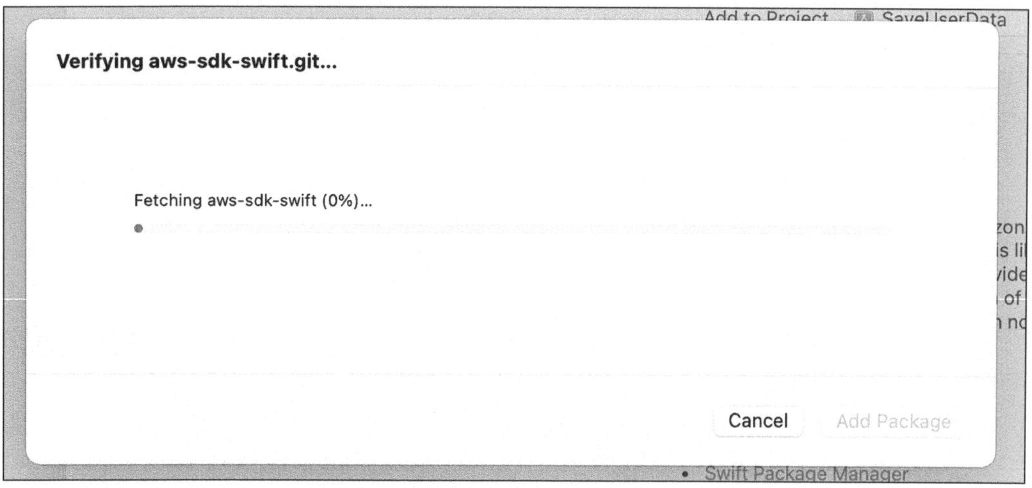

Figure 8.16: *Fetching AWS package*

4. You will see something as *Figure* 8.17, asking to choose the package products.

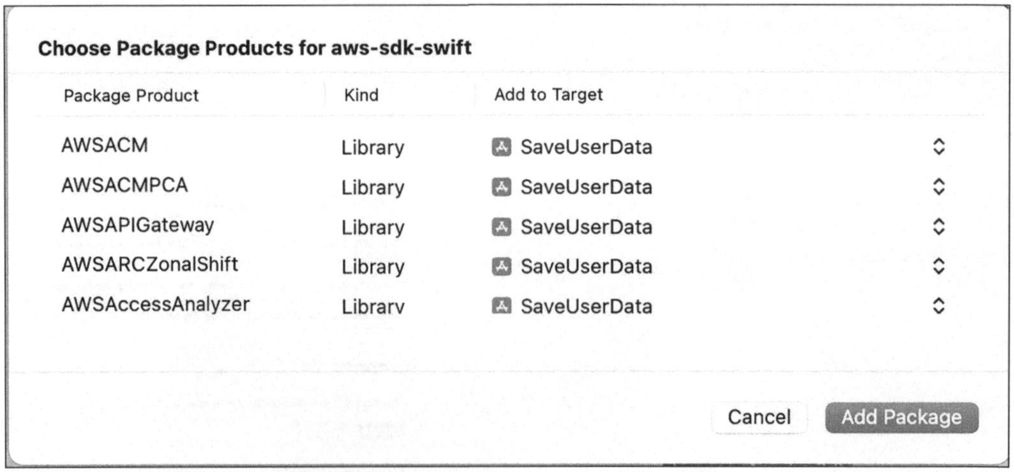

Figure 8.17: *Choosing package products*

5. Click the **'Add Package'**. After clicking **'Add Package'**, you should see the SDK added to your project in your project navigator.
6. Apart from seeing in the project navigator, you can click your project in the project navigator and click **'Package Dependencies'**, as shown in *Figure* 8.18.

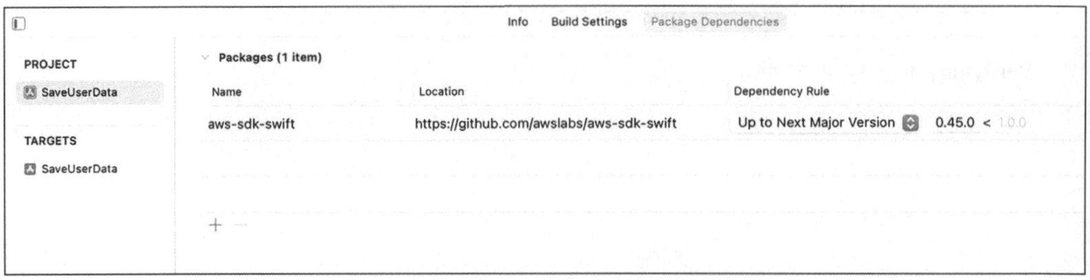

Figure 8.18: *Package dependencies*

So before going any further, let us modify our screens so that the user can upload the image.

1. First, let us add an `UIImageView` to our `ViewController`. Something like the following figure, adjust the other view's and `textField`'s constraints accordingly.

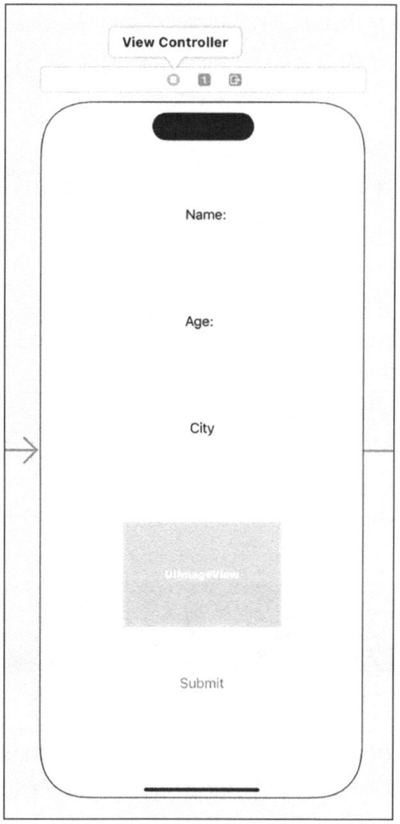

Figure 8.19: *UIImageview added to the UIViewController*

2. Add the `UIImage` code reference in our `ViewController` as follows:

```
@IBOutlet weak var userImageView: UIImageView!
```

Figure 8.20: *UIImageview code reference*

3. The next step is that when the user clicks the `UIImageView` we have added, it should open the gallery on the user's phone. So for that first, we need to add `UITapGestureRecognizer` on top of `UIImageView`. This allows the user to tap on the `UIImageview`, and we can add functionality to open up the gallery. Write the following code in `viewDidLoad()` function:

```
let tapGuestureRecognizer = UITapGestureRecognizer(target: self,
action: #selector(self.imageViewTapped(_:)))
self.userImageView.isUserInteractionEnabled = true
self.userImageView.addGestureRecognizer(tapGuestureRecognizer)
```

We need to set the isUserInteractionEnabled of UIImageView to true; otherwise, the gesture recognizer would not work.

4. And add the following function in your ViewController.

```
func imageViewTapped(_ sender: UITapGestureRecognizer) {

}
```

5. The aforementioned function gets called when the user taps on the added `UIImageView`. So let us add the code for opening up the gallery inside the preceding function.

```
func imageViewTapped(_ sender: UITapGestureRecognizer) {
    let imagePicker = UIImagePickerController()
    imagePicker.delegate = self
    imagePicker.sourceType = .photoLibrary
    self.present(imagePicker, animated: true, completion: nil)
}
```

As you have added the aforementioned code, you might notice the warning as follows:

Figure 8.21: *imageViewTapped function with a warning*

6. For that, all you need to do is assign the `ViewController` `UIImagePickerControllerDelegate` and `UINavigationControllerDelegate`, as shown in *Figure 8.22*.

Figure 8.22: *ViewController with delegates*

7. Now, you will notice that the warning is gone. Add the following `UIImagePickerControllerDelegate` function; this will help us assign the image selected by the user to our `UIImageView`.

```
func imagePickerController(_ picker: UIImagePickerController,
didFinishPickingMediaWithInfo info: [UIImagePickerController.
InfoKey : Any]) {

        if let image = info[UIImagePickerController.InfoKey.orig-
inalImage] as? UIImage {
            userImageView.image = image
        }

        picker.dismiss(animated: true, completion: nil)
}
```

Before running the project and adding the image to the `UIImageView`, let us do one more thing, which is to add the border and rounded corners to the `UIImageView`. This is because without the border, we would not recognize the `UIImageView` on the screen. If you want, you can give it a try.

```
To add the border to the UIImageView, add the below code in viewDid-
Load() function.
userImageView.layer.masksToBounds = true
userImageView.layer.borderWidth = 0.7
userImageView.layer.borderColor = UIColor(red: 227/255, green: 227/255,
blue: 227/255, alpha: 1.0).cgColor
userImageView.layer.cornerRadius = 10
```

Layer

The View has a layer that is of type `CALayer`, so any View always has an underlying layer; the view is dependent on its layer for most of the data; the view gets the data from its layer directly.

masksToBounds

What `masksToBounds` does is it makes the sublayers clip to the layer's bounds. So, all the sublayers of the layer that are extended outside its boundaries will be clipped to the layer's boundaries. Keep in mind that the `subview`'s layers, sublayers of the current layer, and the shadows count as sublayers too.

So, in this case, we are providing the corner radius, so any sublayer's going out of the corner radius provided will be clipped to the layer's corner radius.

Next, we are giving border color. For this, we are creating the color by giving the combinations of RGB. As the `borderColor` is of type `cgcolor`, we are getting the `cgcolor` from the `UIColor` we have created.

`CGcolor` is used by Core Graphics to represent colors, the `CGcolor` objects, and its functions help us in providing the convenient and fastest way of setting and managing colors.

You can also add a label underneath the `UIImageView` saying Tap to add the image, and hide it after the image is added to the `UIImageView`. Since this is the sample app and we are the only users and we know to tap the `UIImageView` to add the image, we are not doing it. But if you want to do it to improve your skills, go ahead and do it.

Once you have added the border, go ahead and run it. You should be seeing something like *Figure* 8.23.

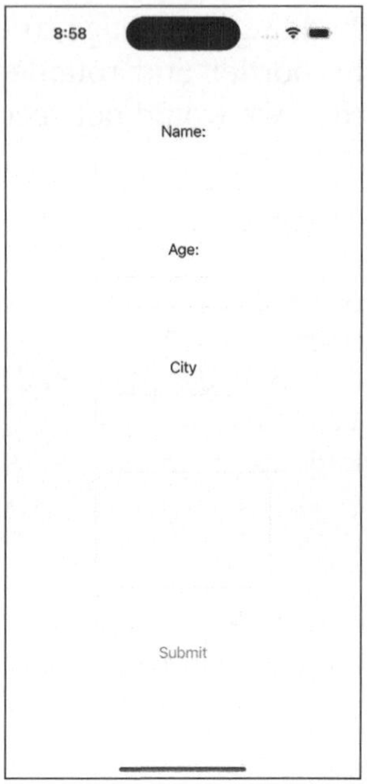

Figure 8.23: *UIViewController with UITextFields and Button*

And you can go ahead and tap on the `UIImageView`; it should open the gallery, as shown in *Figure* 8.24.

Figure 8.24: *Simulator screen opening up camera roll*

After selecting the image in the gallery, it gets assigned to the `UIImageView`, as shown in *Figure* 8.25.

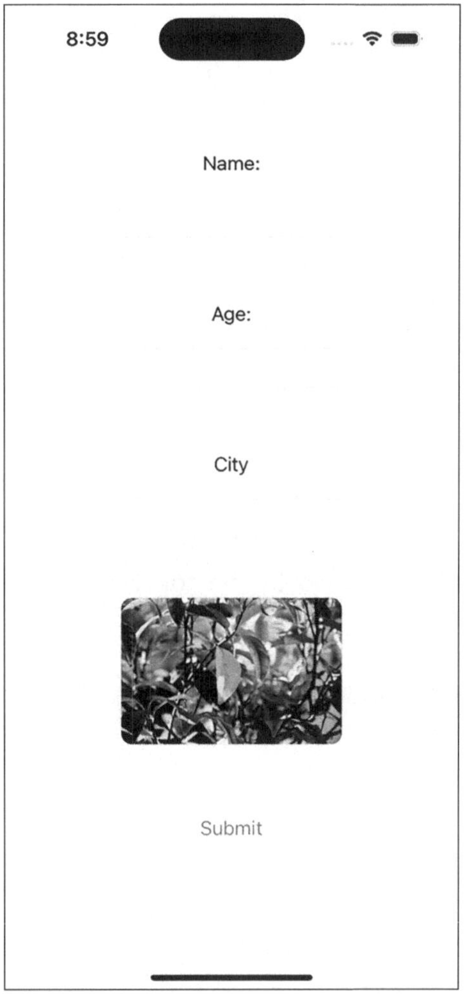

Figure 8.25: *Simulator screen with chosen image*

Now let us get back to AWS. To move forward, we need to get the access key and secret key, so let us do it.

1. To get the access key and secret key, go to the AWS console. By searching on Google **`'AWS Console'`**, click the first link as shown in *Figure* 8.26; this is the easiest way to go into the console rather than typing the link that is provided here, as the link is lengthy.

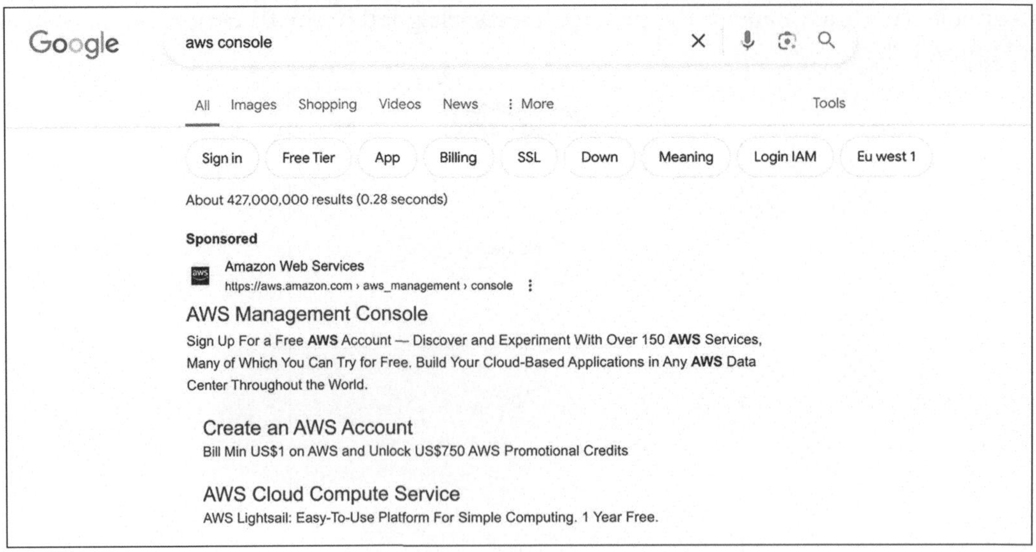

Figure 8.26: *Searching AWS Console*

2. Create an account if you do not have one. After creating the account, it takes you to the console page. Go to the top-right corner of the page and click your name. There will be a drop-down where you can find the **'Security credentials'**, as shown in *Figure 8.27*.

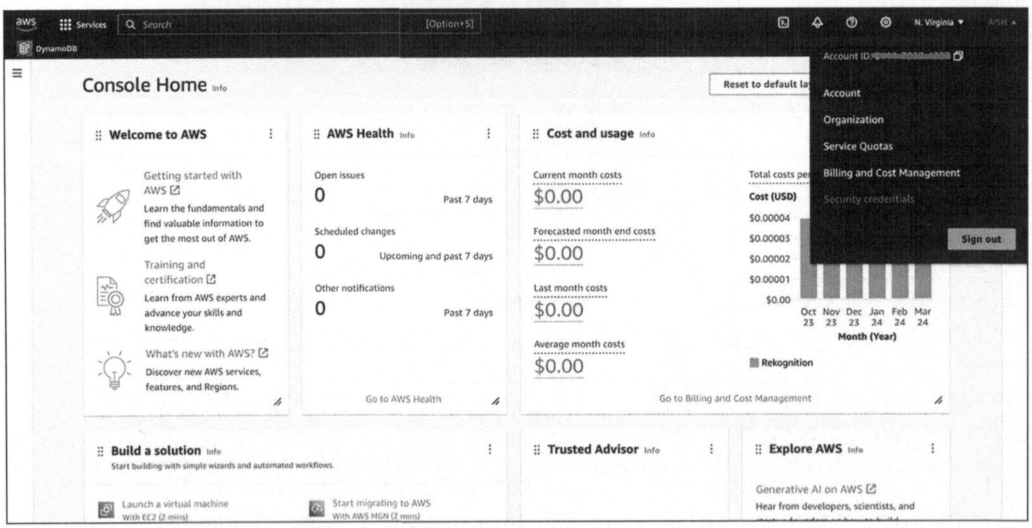

Figure 8.27: AWS Console

3. Click the **'Security credentials'**; it takes you to the **'My security credentials'** page. If you scroll down, you will find the **'Access keys'** column, as shown in the succeeding figure.

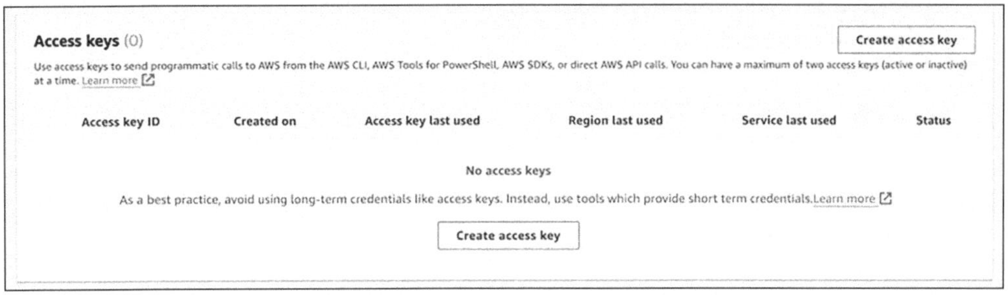

Figure 8.28: *Access keys*

4. Here we need to click the **`'Create access key'`**. You might get a screen as *Figure* 8.29; click **`'I understand creating a root access key is not a best practice, but I still want to create one.'`** It may not be the best practice, but this is a sample app; it is totally ok. This app will allow you to understand the usage of cloud services. If the company you are working for is using any cloud service or AWS, they will take care of the permission policies, root users, and the permissions to the root users. So do not worry, and let us create the access key.

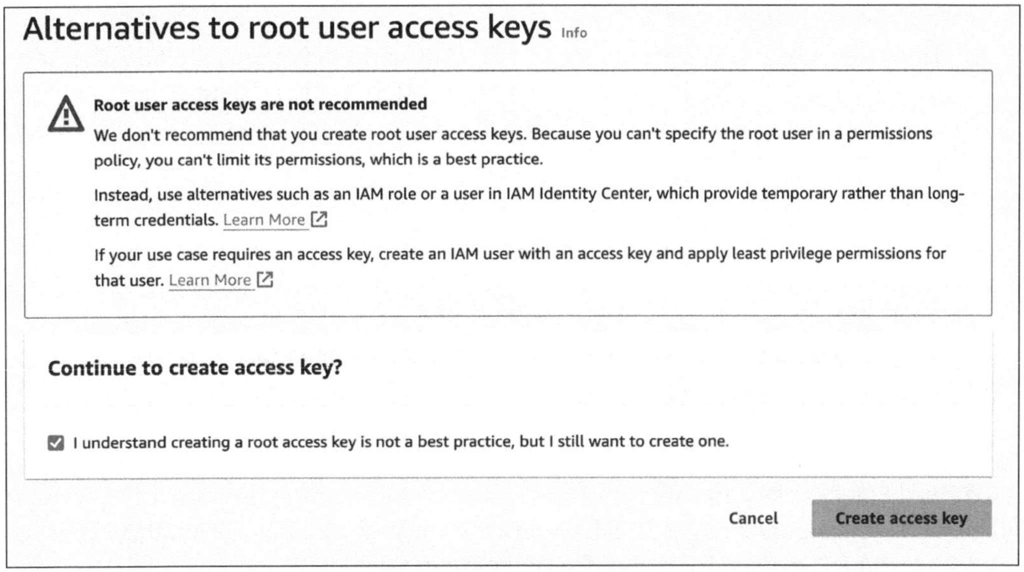

Figure 8.29: *Creating access keys*

5. Click the **`'Create access key'`**. You will see the Access key and Secret Access key as follows:

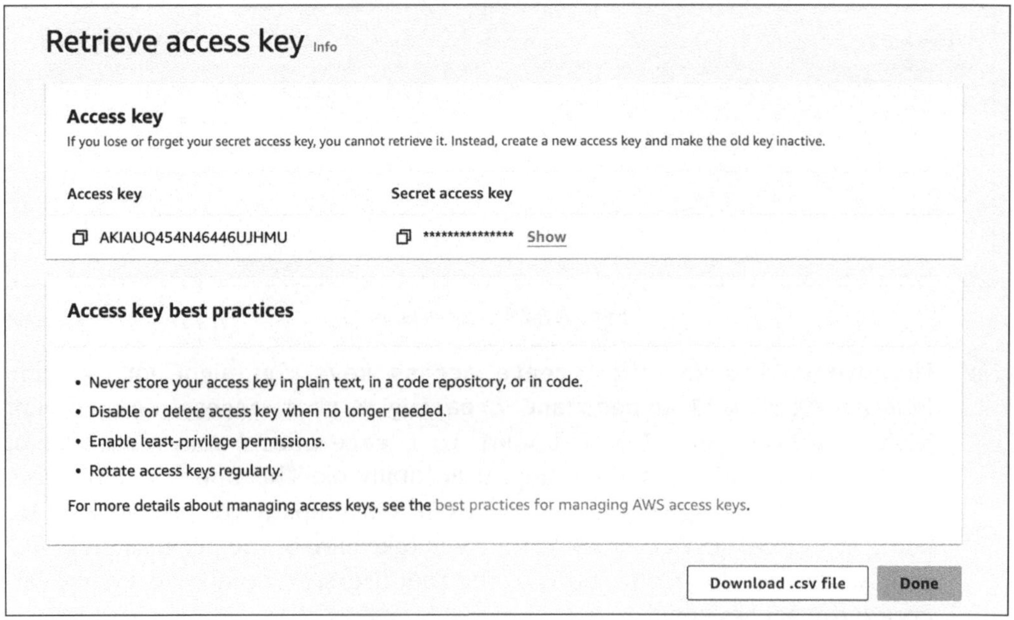

Figure 8.30: *Retrieving access key*

6. Here you have two options, option 1–you can click **`show,`** beside the secret access key, and save it somewhere safe. Option 2–click **`'Download .csv file'`** and open it in **`'Numbers'`** app. You will find the **`'Access key ID'`** and **`'Secret access key'`** as follows:

Figure 8.31: *Access Key ID and Secret access key*

As we got the access key and secret key, let us jump into coding the `AWSUtility`, which will allow us to save the images in S3. Create a class with the name **`'AWSUtility'`**, and make sure you import the following frameworks in your class.

```
import UIKit
import Foundation
import AWSS3
import ClientRuntime
import AWSClientRuntime
import Network
```

In our class let's add the succeeding code,

```
let bucket = "UserImages"
let client = AWSClient(
    credentialProvider: .static(accessKeyId: "Your-Access-Key",
secretAccessKey: "Your-Secret-Key"),
    httpClientProvider: .createNew
)
```

Where we are just specifying the bucket name and creating an AWS client, in place of `"Your-Access-Key"` and `"Your-Secret-Key,"` paste the `'Access key'` and `'Secret key'` that we have created.

Or another efficient way is to specify the access key and secret key as environment variables. This way it is preferred, as in many workplaces the environments are provided to mobile teams; trying this will be a wonderful practice for that.

1. For that, all you need to do is click the project, and the options shown as in *Figure* 8.32.

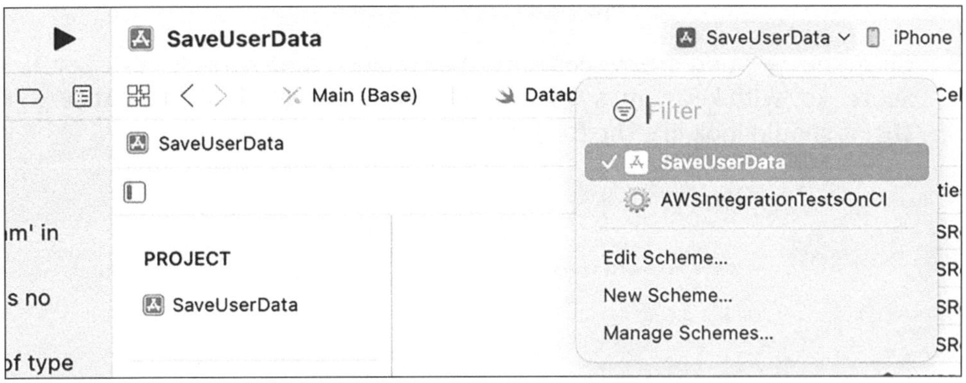

Figure 8.32: *Editing Scheme*

2. Click the **`'Edit Scheme'`**; you should be able to see something as follows:

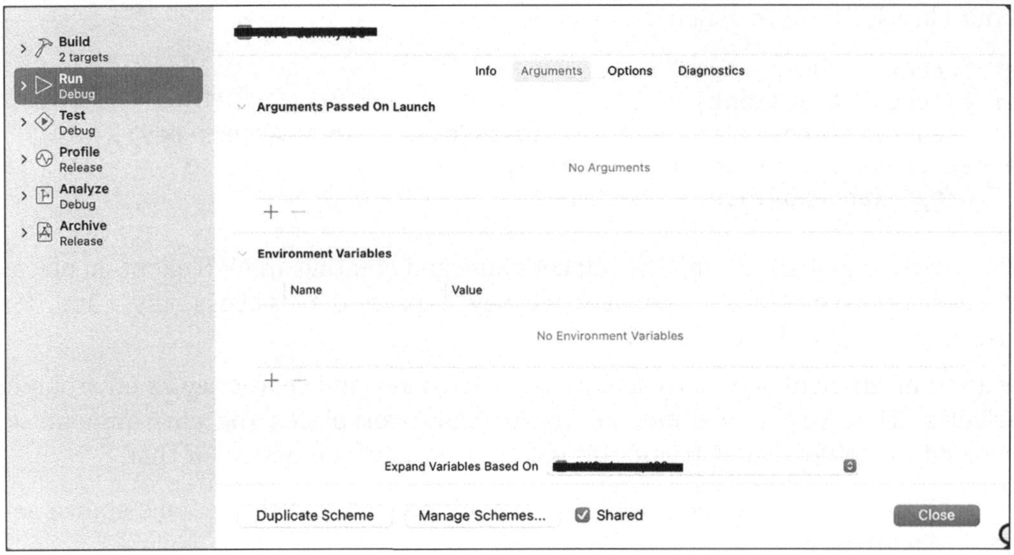

***Figure 8.33:** Editing Scheme*

3. Click the **'+'** under `Environment Variables`, add your Access key ID and Secret key with key names **`'AWS_SECRET_ACCESS_KEY'`** and **`'AWS_ACCESS_KEY_ID'`**; it should look like the following figure:

***Figure 8.34:** Adding Environment variables*

Note: *If you are using the aforementioned way (specifying in code), make sure you are using the same client that we have created above for all other operations we will be doing, such as getting S3 buckets, getting images, or uploading images.*

Before jumping into the code, let us create a bucket in the AWS S3 bucket.

1. Go to your AWS console, and you will see the search bar on the top, as shown in *Figure* 8.35.

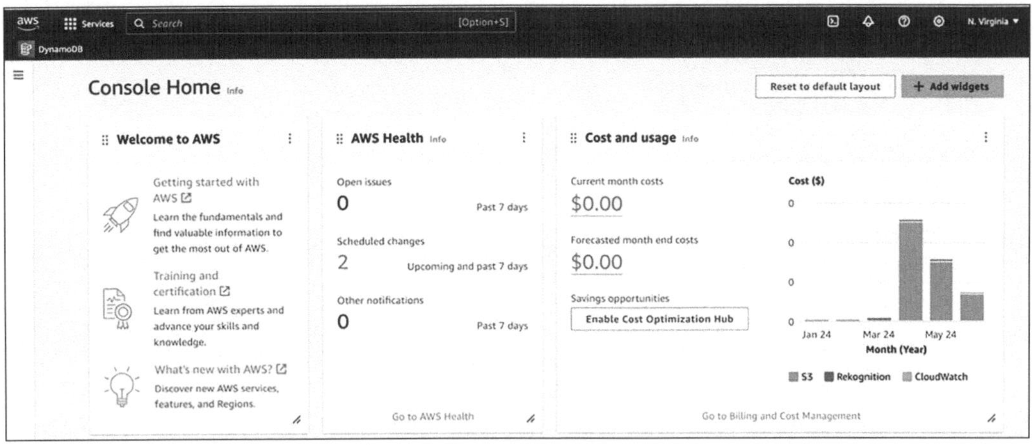

Figure 8.35: *Amazon console*

2. Search s3 in the search bar and click the first option, as shown in *Figure* 8.36.

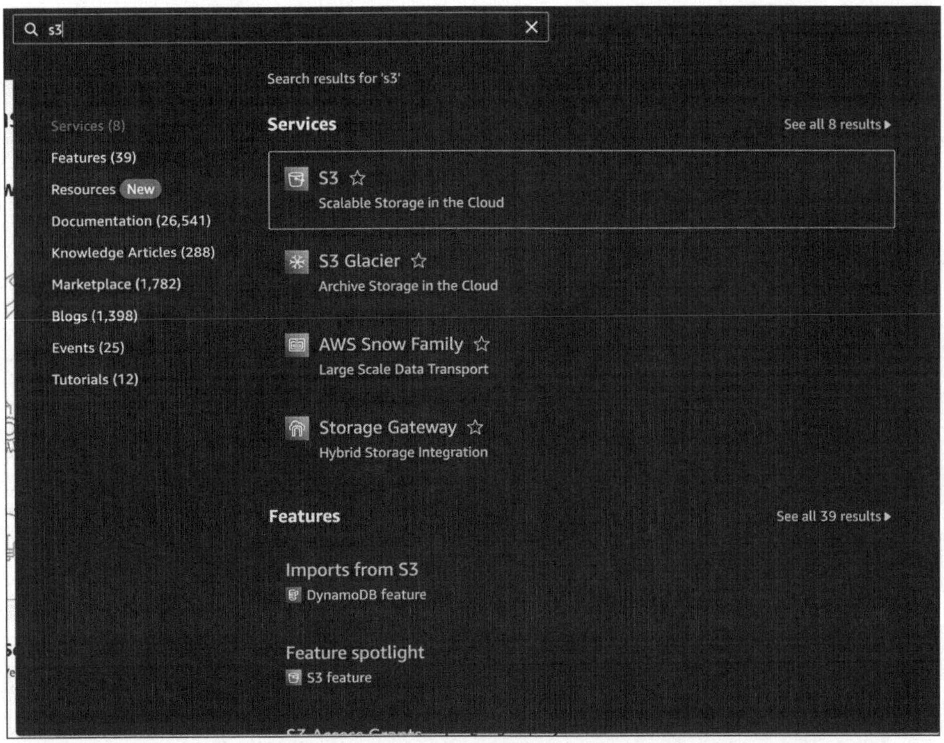

Figure 8.36: *Amazon console with S3*

3. You will see general purpose buckets; click the **'Create bucket'**; the page loads as shown in *Figure 8.37*.

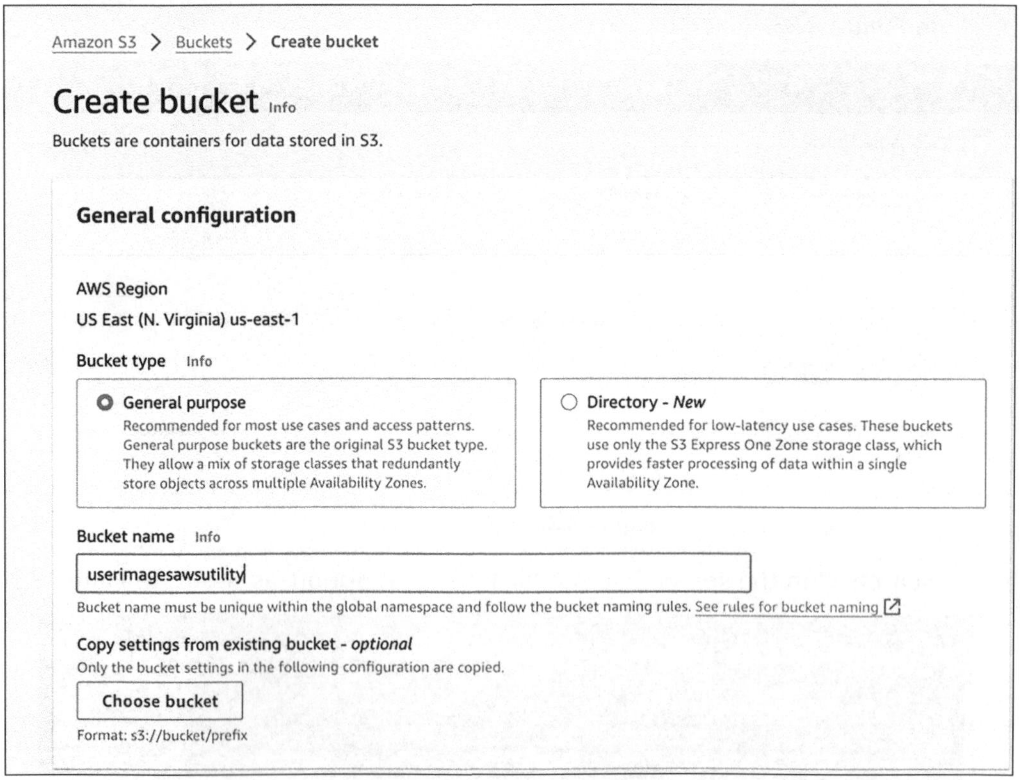

Figure 8.37: *Creating S3 bucket*

4. Give the bucket name and scroll down to find the **'Create bucket'** button. Click the **'Create bucket'** button. Just make sure we are creating a **'General purpose'** bucket, as shown in *Figure 8.38*.

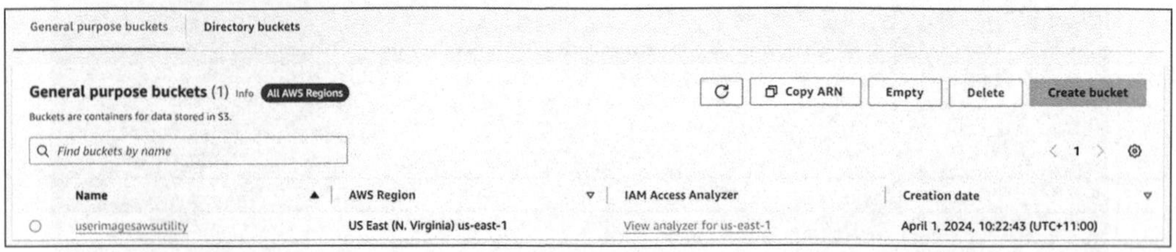

Figure 8.38: *S3 bucket in the console*

Have the bucket name handy inside your class using the following code:

```
let bucket = "userimagesawsutility"
```

Just to check if you are connected to the S3, let us get all the buckets in your S3 service with the following code. Going forward, we are getting Client using **'try**

S3Client(region: "us-east-1")' in all the succeeding functions; this is when we got the secretKey as the environment variables in the scheme; otherwise, we should use the same preceding client we got.

```
func getS3BucketNames() async throws -> [String] {

        // Get an S3Client to the access Amazon S3.
        let s3Client = try S3Client(region: "us-east-1")

        let s3Output = try await s3Client.listBuckets(
            input: ListBucketsInput()
        )

        // Getting the bucket names.
        var bucketNames: [String] = []
        guard let buckets = s3Output.buckets else {
            return bucketNames
        }
        for bucket in buckets {
            if let bucketName = bucket.name {
                print("Bucket Name: \(bucketName)")
                bucketNames.append(bucketName)
            }
        }

        return bucketNames
    }
```

All we are doing here is connecting to the AWS S3 client using region, access ID, and secret key (specified in the file). Please make sure you specified the region correctly. Call this function in your `viewController`; you should be able to see the bucket names in the logs.

Now let us write code to upload the image to the S3. Check the following code:

```
/// Upload an image to an S3 bucket.
/// - Parameters:
///   - bucket: bucket name
///   - key: unique key for the image
///   - data: Image data
func uploadImage(key: String, withData data: Data) async throws {
    let client = try S3Client(region: "us-east-1")
    let dataStream = ByteStream.data(data)

    let input = PutObjectInput(
        body: dataStream,
        bucket: bucket,
        key: key
```

```
    )
    _ = try await client.putObject(input: input)
}
```

putObject

`PutObject`, to put it in simple terms, it adds/inserts an object into the S3 bucket. S3 never takes up the partial object, and keep in mind that you cannot update the single strand of metadata of an existing object using `PutObject`. So in order to update the metadata, you need to add the entire object with updated metadata.

To use `putObject`, to upload an image to S3, we need to use `PutObjectInput`.

putObjectInput

Think of this as a datatype, such as String or Int, that can be used for `putObject`.

We need a key, which is the unique key for our image. This key will be helpful while our image is uploaded.

Now, it is time to call this function (`uploadImage`) in our `ViewController` after the image is selected, so that it will be uploaded to S3. Let us call this function in `imagePickerController(_:didFinishPickingMediaWithInfo:)`.

Before calling this preceding function, we need to create the key for our image, which we did in `imagePickerController(_:didFinishPickingMediaWithInfo:)`; check *Figure* 8.39 for reference.

```
func imagePickerController(_ picker: UIImagePickerController, didFinishPickingMediaWithInfo info:
    [UIImagePickerController.InfoKey : Any]) {

    if let image = info[UIImagePickerController.InfoKey.originalImage] as? UIImage {
        userImageView.image = image

        let userDataBase = DatabaseUtility()
        let usersFromDatabase = userDataBase.read()
        let usersCount = usersFromDatabase.count

        let userIDKey = userName + String(usersCount + 1)

        Task {
            do {
                let util = AWSUtility()
                //convert the image to the Data
                if  let data = image.pngData() {

                    try await util.uploadImage(key: userIDKey, withData: data )
                }

            } catch  {
                print("An AWS S3 service error ")
            }
        }
    }

    picker.dismiss(animated: true, completion: nil)
}
```

Figure 8.39: *imagePickerController delegate function with DatabaseUtility and AWSUtility*

So, for key creation, we are getting the number of items in our database and adding 1 to it, and we will be merging this with the user's name. For example, if the user's name is `'Kate'` and we have 7 items in the database already, Kate's image's key will be `Kate8`. The last step before calling this function is converting the `UIImage` to the data. Now, go ahead and run it. After running it, add the user's data in the required fields and select the image, as shown in *Figure* 8.40.

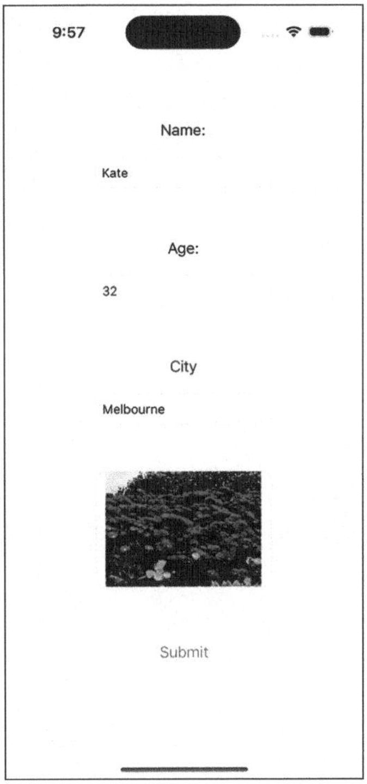

Figure 8.40: *Simulator screen with image attached*

As we are uploading the image to S3, while selecting the image from the gallery, it should already be uploaded to the S3. Let us go to S3 console and check it (sometimes it takes longer to upload to S3, it could be internet speed or any other reason, but it uploads; be patient). Following is the S3 console with the image uploaded.

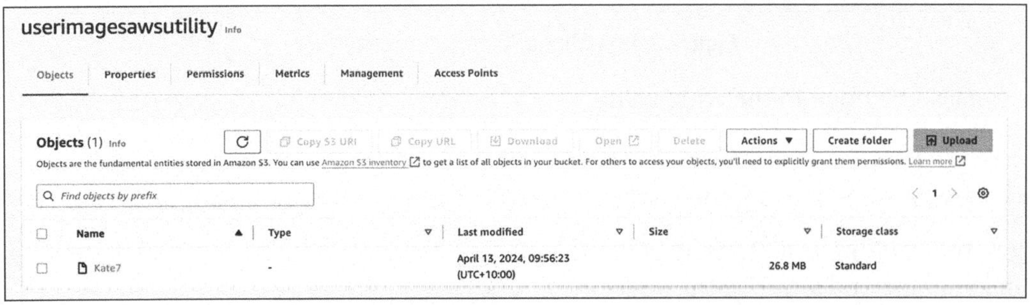

Figure 8.41: *S3 bucket with user data inserted*

You might wonder why S3 got the Kate7 as the key because previously we got items in our database, which is causing this to start the keys with 1 or to have sync between S3 and data, delete the app in simulator, and delete the items in S3 in console. Install the app in the simulator and try the preceding task again. You will see the keys coming with 1 as a prefix.

Before going forward, let us do something beautifying. If you look at the image in the simulator, you might see that our image fills up our `imageView` and looks weird. To fix that, all you need to do is select the `UIImageView` in your `ViewController` in your storyboard, go to the Attributes Inspector, select the Content Mode, and change it to **`'Scale To Fill'`**. For reference, check *Figure* 8.42.

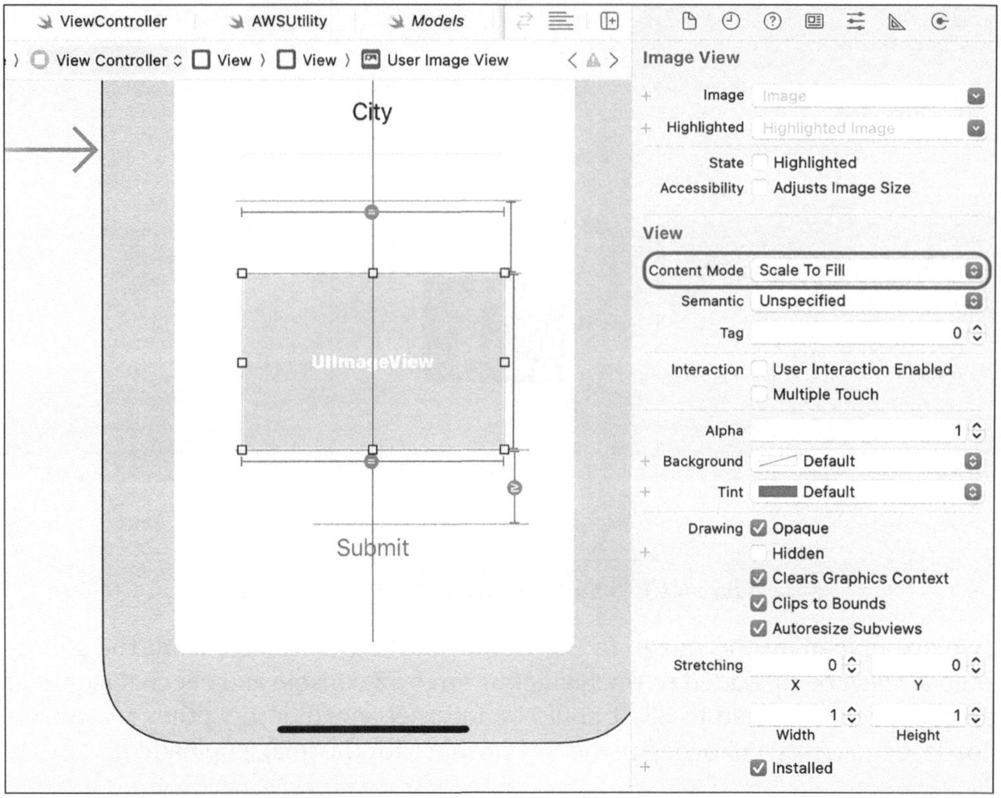

Figure 8.42: *UIImageView's content mode*

It can also be done in the code using:

```
userImageView.contentMode = .scaleToFill
```

If you want to do it using the code, add the preceding code in `viewDidLoad()`.

Now the exciting time to read the image from S3 is simple and easy. All we need is a bucket name and key. Use the succeeding code:

```
func readFile(key: String) async throws -> Data {
    let s3Client = try S3Client(region: "us-east-1")
    let s3Input = GetObjectInput(
        bucket: bucket,
        key: key
    )
    let output = try await s3Client.getObject(input: s3Input)

    guard let body = output.body,
          let data = try await body.readData() else {
        return "".data(using: .utf8)!
    }

    return data
}
```

The returning object is of type Data; now we need to convert it to `UIImage` type so that we can show it in our `UITableViewController`. Check the following code for converting Data to `UIImage`:

```
func getImage(with key: String) async throws -> UIImage? {

let data = try await readFile(key: key)
let image = UIImage(data: data)
return image
}
```

In this we can just call the `getImage(with:)` function, which gets the data from S3 and converts it to `UIImage`.

1. To make use of the aforementioned function, we need to add the `UIImage` to our `UITableViewController`'s cell as follows:

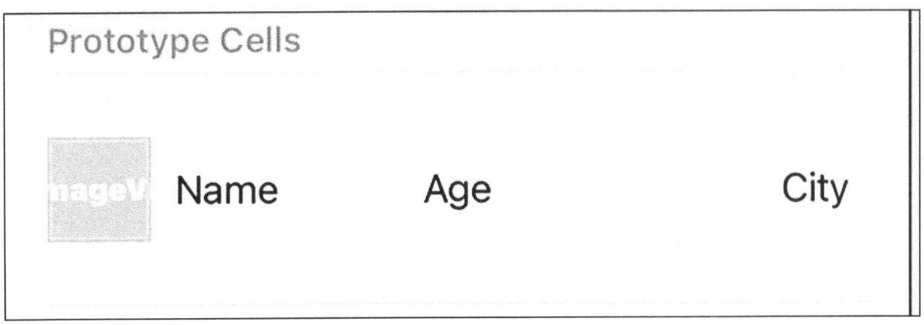

Figure 8.43: *Prototype cell*

2. Add the coding reference of the `UIImageView` to the `UserDataTableViewCell` as follows:

```
class UserDataTableViewCell: UITableViewCell {

    @IBOutlet weak var name: UILabel!
    @IBOutlet weak var age: UILabel!
    @IBOutlet weak var city: UILabel!
    @IBOutlet weak var userImageView: UIImageView!
}
```

Figure 8.44: *UITableViewCell class*

3. Now, modify the `cellForRowAtIndexPath:` as follows:

```
override func tableView(_ tableView: UITableView, cellForRowAt
indexPath: IndexPath) -> UITableViewCell {

        let cell = tableView.dequeueReusableCell(withIdentifier:
"UserDataTableViewCell", for: indexPath) as! UserDataTableViewCell

        let user = users[indexPath.row]

        cell.userImageView.layer.borderWidth = 0.5
        cell.userImageView.layer.borderColor =  UIColor.black.
        cgColor
        cell.userImageView.contentMode = .scaleToFill
        cell.userImageView.layer.cornerRadius = 5.0
        cell.userImageView.clipsToBounds = true

        Task {
            do {
                let awsUtil = AWSUtility()
                let key = user.userName + String(indexPath.row + 1)
                if let userImage = try await awsUtil.getImage
                (with: key) {
                    cell.userImageView.image = userImage

                }
            } catch {
                print("An Amazon S3 error")
            }
        }

        cell.name.text = user.userName
        cell.age.text = String(user.age)
        cell.city.text = user.city

        return cell
    }
```

For clarity, check the following image for extra code relating to `UserImageView`.

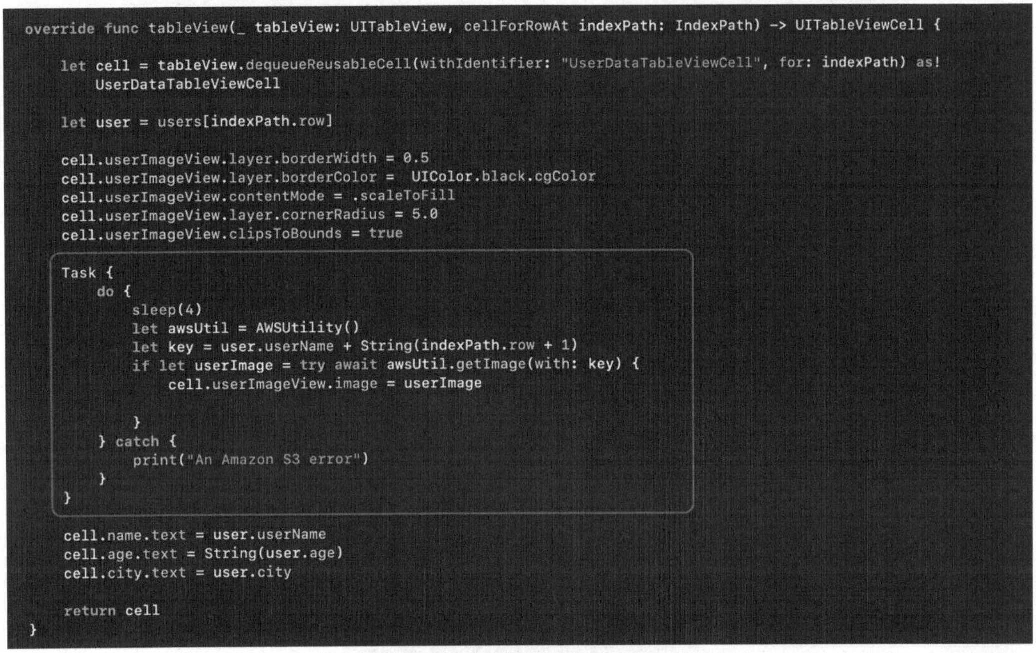

```
override func tableView(_ tableView: UITableView, cellForRowAt indexPath: IndexPath) -> UITableViewCell {

    let cell = tableView.dequeueReusableCell(withIdentifier: "UserDataTableViewCell", for: indexPath) as!
        UserDataTableViewCell

    let user = users[indexPath.row]

    cell.userImageView.layer.borderWidth = 0.5
    cell.userImageView.layer.borderColor =  UIColor.black.cgColor
    cell.userImageView.contentMode = .scaleToFill
    cell.userImageView.layer.cornerRadius = 5.0
    cell.userImageView.clipsToBounds = true

    Task {
        do {
            sleep(4)
            let awsUtil = AWSUtility()
            let key = user.userName + String(indexPath.row + 1)
            if let userImage = try await awsUtil.getImage(with: key) {
                cell.userImageView.image = userImage

            }
        } catch {
            print("An Amazon S3 error")
        }
    }

    cell.name.text = user.userName
    cell.age.text = String(user.age)
    cell.city.text = user.city

    return cell
}
```

Figure 8.45: *Getting an image from S3 and inserting it into the cell*

All we are doing here is adding rounded corners and borders to UserImageView.

clipsToBounds

When you set the `clipsToBounds` to true, it makes sure that `subviews` of the view are clipped to the boundaries of the view. In the aforementioned scenario, we are setting `clipsToBounds` to true for the `userImageView` after adding the rounded corners, so it does not allow anything to go outside of the rounded corners' boundaries that we have added.

Then we are getting the key using username and `indexpath`; finally, we are getting the image from S3 and displaying it in the cell.

Before running it, if you want to increase the row height for your cell, add the following code:

```
override func tableView(_ tableView: UITableView, heightForRowAt index-
Path: IndexPath) -> CGFloat {
    100.0
}
```

One more thing to do, add sleep(4) before reloading the `tableView` in `viewDidAppear(_:)`; your `viewDidAppear` should look like the following:

```
override func viewDidAppear(_ animated: Bool) {
    super.viewDidAppear(animated)

    let userDataBase = DatabaseUtility()
    let usersFromDatabase = userDataBase.read()
    users = usersFromDatabase

    self.tableView.reloadData()

}
```

Figure 8.46: *Getting users from Database*

We are adding the `sleep(4)` before reloading the `tableView`, just to have extra time to upload the image.

Now comes the exciting part! To test it, simply delete the app in the simulator and remove the data from the S3 console. Then go ahead and run it. Add the required data and add the image as well. Before clicking **`submit`**, which takes us to the next screen, let us check s3 if the image is uploaded to s3 or not. Once you make sure it is uploaded, click the **`submit`** button. You should see something like *Figure* 8.47.

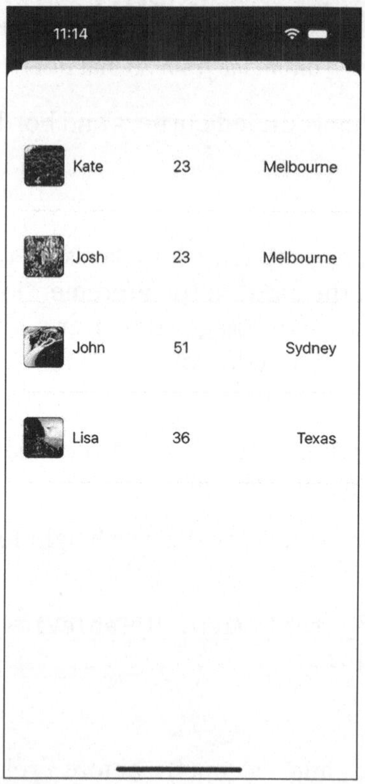

Figure 8.47: *User's data getting displayed in UITableview*

Sometimes it takes time to load the images to `UIImageView`; please wait until images are loaded; if any image is not loaded, just check if it exists in AWS s3 or not.

So, this is how we use AWS to store and retrieve the data. AWS is an amazing way to learn and use the cloud services. The sample app helps you get a better understanding of how the cloud services work. In the real world, many companies rely on different cloud services, but the baseline stays the same, so work with the sample app, experiment with it, try to update a particular object, and try to retrieve it. Have fun learning.

Conclusion

That is it for this chapter. We learned the important topics in this chapter. Saving the data and using the cloud services are super important for any app. The digital world is moving towards leveraging cloud services because of the wonderful benefits they get.

In the next chapter, we will learn about the most important topic for any app, that is, Authentication. Keep learning and enjoy coding !

Points to Remember

- SQLite is built into all mobile phones and most computers and comes bundled inside countless other applications that people use every day.
- AWS, which means `'Amazon Web Services'`, is provides wonderful cloud-based services and is cost-effective too.
- AWS S3 or Amazon S3 means Amazon Simple Storage Service, which is a famous cloud storage service with features such as scalability, security, performance, and data availability.
- Swift Package Manager (SPM) is used to automate the process of linking dependencies, compiling, and downloading.
- When you set the `clipsToBounds` to true, it makes sure that `subviews` of the view are clipped to the boundaries of the view.

CHAPTER 9
Authentication

Introduction

In this chapter, you will learn the basic and important features of any app. You will be learning about Authentication using Auth0 in this chapter. If the authentication is not good enough and secure, you will lose the app's users' trust. So, let us learn this important feature, personalize our apps for the users, and gain their trust. Before learning about Authentication, as promised, we will be learning to create `UITableViewCell` in a different way to the way we learned previously. Let us dig in.

Structure

In this chapter, we will discuss the following topics:

- Creating `UITableViewCell` in a Different Way
- XIB
- Auth0
    - The Big Why
    - OAuth 2.0
    - How
- `plist`
- Adding Associated Domains
- JWT

Creating `UITableViewCell` in a Different Way

We already know how to create a customized cell and use it in our `TableViews`, but it is always better to know other ways to create the cells, because when you go and work for different companies, they might have already got the projects with cells built this way, then you will know how to modify them and also create more cells in a similar way.

Firstly, create a new project and remove the `ViewController` from your **`Main.storyboard`**. You can also delete the `ViewController.swift` as well. The next step is to add `UITableViewController` to the storyboard. Create the `TableViewController.swift` of type UITableViewController.

Next, we do not need to create the prototype cells in our `UITableViewController`; rather, we will be creating an XIB file for our cells.

XIB

In simple terms, these are the custom views, which can be used or reused throughout our entire project; it is not just the cells, but you can create any custom views or customized UI components. The full form of XIB is XML Interface Builder; in the background, the XIBs are converted to NIBs (machine-readable) during compile time; the full form of NIB is **`'NextStep interface builder'`**.

1. To create an XIB file, right-click your project in the project navigator, click **`'New file'`**. In the next-pop up, select **`Empty`**, as shown in *Figure 9.1*, and click **`Next`**.

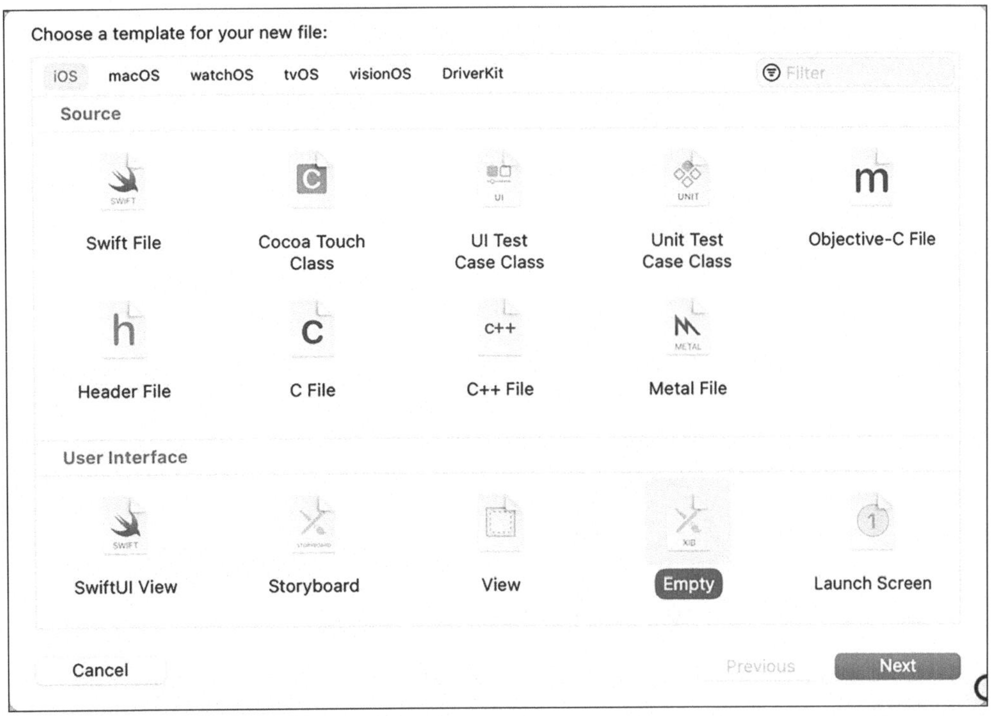

Figure 9.1: *Creating new .xib*

2. Specify **`'CustomTableViewCell'`** for the **`'save as'`** field and click **`Create`**.

3. You should be able to see the empty storyboard; click **'+'** on the top and search for `UITableViewCell`, as shown in *Figure* 9.2.

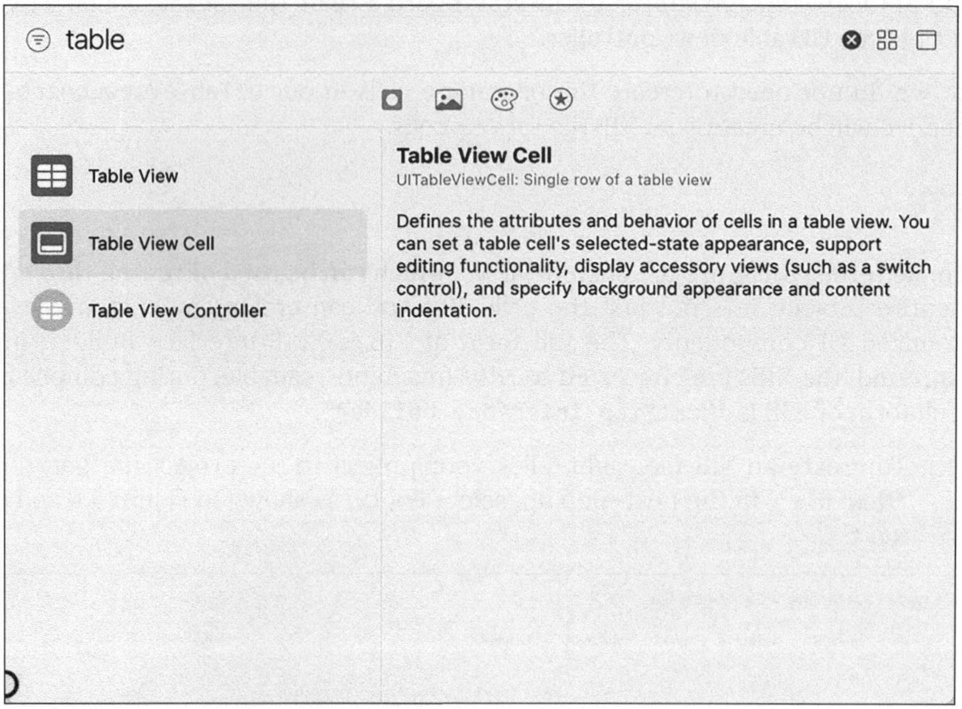

***Figure* 9.2:** *Choosing UIcomponent*

4. Drag that **'`Table View Cell`'** to your XIB storyboard, and you should see something like *Figure* 9.3.

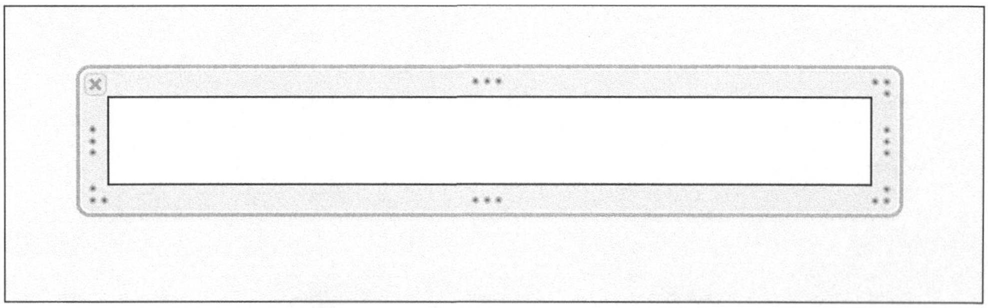

***Figure* 9.3:** *UITableVIewCell in xib*

5. Now add the label to the cell at the center and add the respective constraints.

6. Next, let us create the code reference for our cell. For that, create a new file `CustomTableViewCell.swift` of type `UITableViewCell`. Add a `UILabel` reference to your `CustomTableViewCell.swift`, as shown in *Figure* 9.4.

```swift
import UIKit

class CustomTableViewCell: UITableViewCell {

    @IBOutlet weak var label: UILabel!

    override func awakeFromNib() {
        super.awakeFromNib()
        // Initialization code
    }

    override func setSelected(_ selected: Bool, animated: Bool) {
        super.setSelected(selected, animated: animated)

        // Configure the view for the selected state
    }

}
```

Figure 9.4: *CustomTableVIewCell with UILabel reference*

7. Before using our `CustomTableViewCell`, let us go to our XIB file and give our cell the reuse identifier in attributes inspector, as shown in *Figure* 9.5.

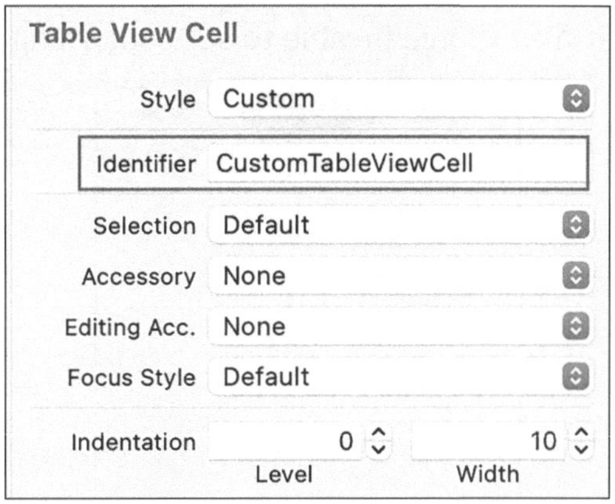

Figure 9.5: *CustomTableVIewCell's identifier*

8. Let us use our custom cell in our `TableViewController`. Go to `TableViewController.swift`, register our `CustomTableViewCell` by placing the following code in `viewDidLoad()`.

```
let nib = UINib(nibName: "CustomTableViewCell", bundle: nil)
tableView.register(nib, forCellReuseIdentifier: "CustomTableView-
Cell")
```

Here we are creating UINib using our XIB file. We use `UITableView`'s register function to register the `UITableViewCell` class to use in creating table view cells. Without registering, you cannot use `CustomTableViewCell` in your `UITableView`.

9. The next steps include specifying `numberOfSections` to `1` and `numberOfRowsInSection` to `5`.

   Now coming to `tableView(_:cellForRowAt:)`, we can use our cell as usual as the following after registering.

   ```
   let cell = tableView.dequeueReusableCell(withIdentifier: "Custom-TableViewCell", for: indexPath) as! CustomTableViewCell
   cell.label.text = "Cell \(indexPath.row + 1)"
   ```

   It is important to typecast the cell; otherwise, we will not be providing the text to the label in our `CustomTableViewCell`. For reference, check the succeeding figure:

```
override func tableView(_ tableView: UITableView, cellForRowAt indexPath: IndexPath) -> UITableViewCell {
    let cell = tableView.dequeueReusableCell(withIdentifier: "CustomTableViewCell", for: indexPath) as! CustomTableViewCell
    cell.label.text = "Cell \(indexPath.row + 1)"

    return cell
}
```

***Figure 9.6**: tableView(_:cellForRowAt:) function with CustomTableViewCell*

Now go ahead and run it. You should be able to see something like *Figure* 9.7.

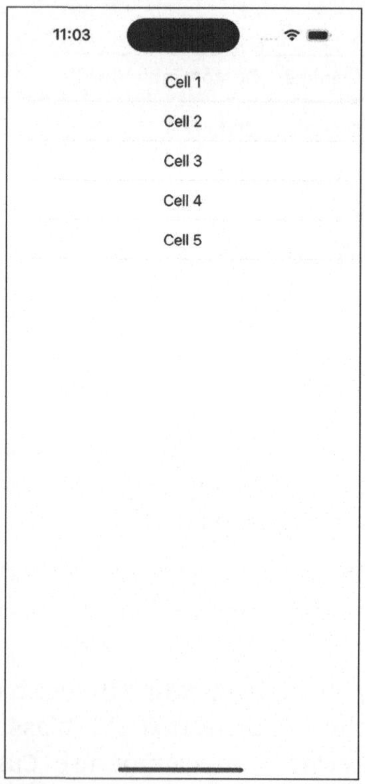

***Figure 9.7**: Simulator with CustomTableViewCells*

So that is it. The new way to create and use customized `UITableViewCell`.

Auth0

Time for learning new important and awesome topics. This will allow you to learn how the authentication of any app works. It is not that every app uses Auth0, but the authentication is done in a similar fashion; some apps might use Auth0, and some other apps use different SDKs, such as ForgeRock SDK, which does similar things with some extra or less features than Auth0.

The Big Why

Auth0 gives us the enterprise-level feature such as SSO (Single Sign-On) super quick. This can help us save money and time; by not needing countless months of development, it gives setup of Google-level authentication. Money and time will be hugely saved using Auth0.

OAuth 2.0

OAuth 2.0 is a framework that that gives end users access and the protocols necessary for authorization.

We can create our own protocols for authorization, but the one we create may not be up to standard; OAuth 2.0 is the best and can be implemented on mobile or web.

Coming to Auth0, it is a company that provides OAuth 2.0 authorization; it can be thought of as a wrapper around OAuth2.0. Using Auth0, we do not have to write the code for user management; everything is done via auth0.

Working of Auth0

From the following diagram, you will be able to understand how Auth0 works:

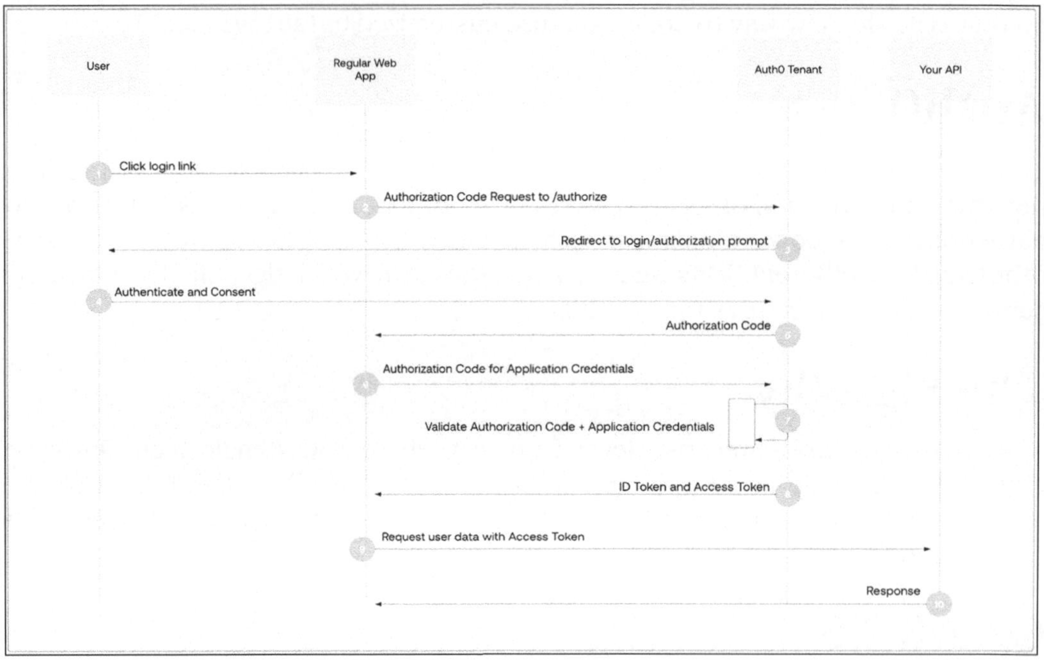

Figure 9.8: *Workings of Auth0*

Working Flow of Auth0

1. User clicks **`Login`** button in our app.
2. Auth0's SDK redirects our user to Auth0 Authorization Server using (/ authorizeendpoint).
3. Auth0 Authorization Server prompts the user to login with an authorization prompt.
4. User authenticates with one of the Auth0 configured login options and will see a consent prompt listing the permissions Auth0 will give to the application.
5. Auth0 Authorization Server sends user back to our App with single-use authorization code.
6. Auth0's SDK sends authorization code, application's client ID, and application's credentials, such as client secret and Private Key JWT, to Auth0 Authorization Server (**/oauth/tokenendpoint**).
7. Auth0 Authorization Server verifies authorization code, application's client ID, and our app's credentials.
8. Auth0 Authorization Server sends back ID token and access token.

9. Our app can use the access token to call the Auth0 API to get information about the user.
10. API responds with requested data, such as user information.

Without any wait, let us create the sample project to get our Login working using Auth0 and see all the aforementioned steps in live action. After creating the project, go to your main storyboard and add the following to the buttons and label to your `ViewController`.

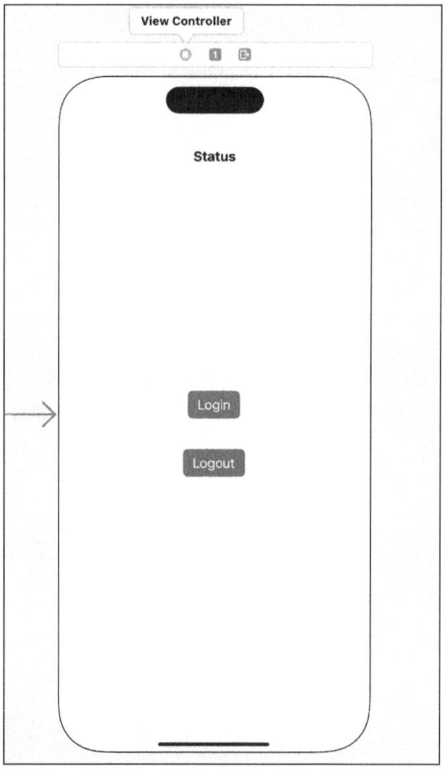

Figure 9.9: *UIViewController with buttons*

Now, it is time to add the Auth0 SDK to our project; let us add it in the most recent way, using packages.

1. Go to your Xcode file menu and click **"`Add Package Dependencies.`"** For reference, check *Figure* 9.10.

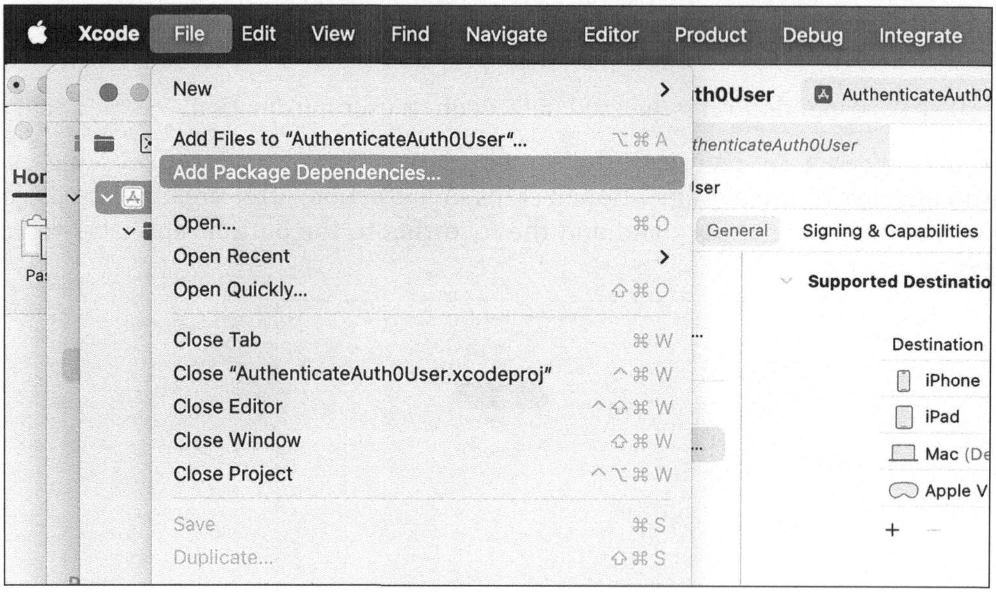

Figure 9.10: *Adding package dependencies*

2. It shows a prompt to add the package. In the search, place this URL: **'https://github.com/auth0/Auth0.swift'**; it shows up Auth0.swift; just click the **'Add Package'** button, and that is it, the SDK is added to your project. For reference, check *Figure 9.11*.

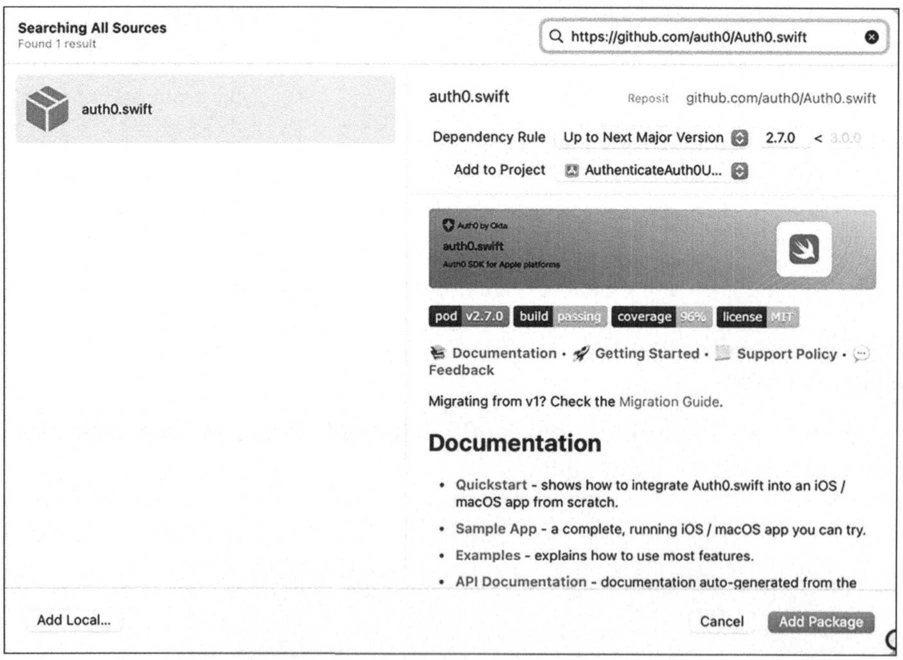

Figure 9.11: *Adding package dependencies of auth0*

Now that we have added the SDK, let us do the setup in Auth0 so that we can access Auth0.

1. Head on to **'https://auth0.com/'** and sign up. After signing up, you will see the page similar to *Figure* 9.12.

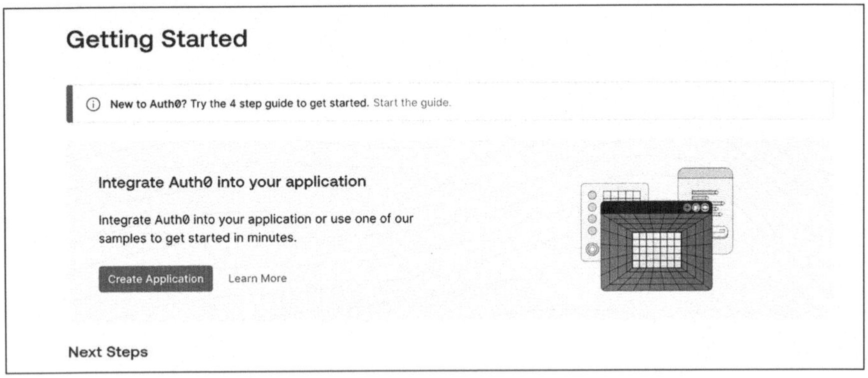

***Figure* 9.12:** *Getting started Auth0*

2. You can explore the page, which gives you a little knowledge about what you can do with Auth0. Click **'Create Application'**, as we are creating the native app. Click the **'native'** and give your app a name, as shown in *Figure* 9.13. The app name could be anything; you could even leave it as **My App**, but give the name where you can identify it. Click **Create**.

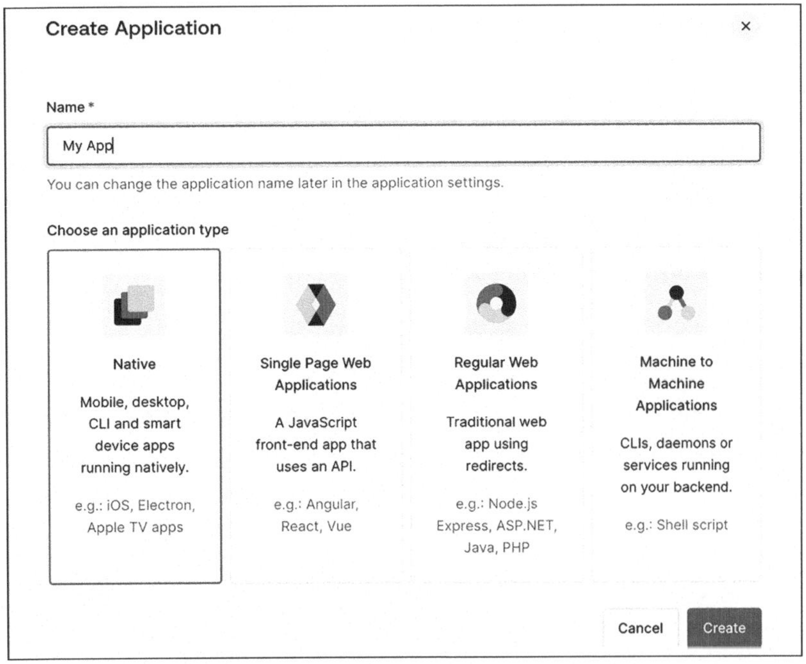

***Figure* 9.13:** *Creating Application in Auth0*

3. It lands you on the **'Get Started'** page. You can explore getting started by clicking iOS/macOS, or you can directly go to the **'Settings'** page.

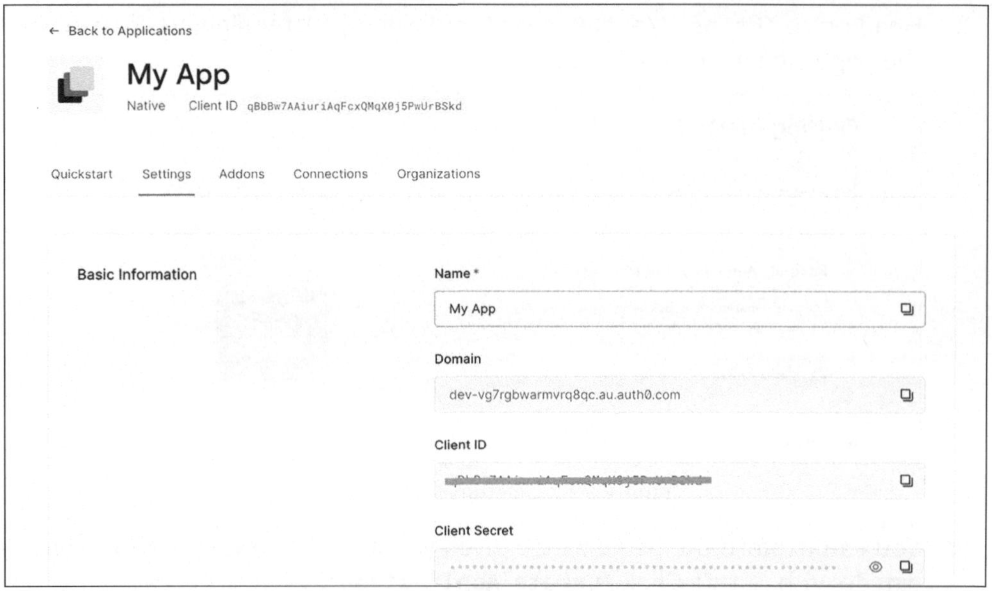

Figure 9.14: *Application settings in Auth0*

So, when you have landed in the settings page, Domain and Client ID are given; we need these in order for our app to access the Auth0, and to do that, we need to create a plist in our app.

`plist`

`plist` are known as property list files, mainly used for setting the configurations. If you check your project, there will be an `info.plist` already; you can modify that `plist` in order to have customized settings for your app. In some workplaces, they modify it to access special domain-based URLs.

In the following code, we are creating a `plist` for Auth0 so that Auth0 gets configurations from our app.

1. To create the plist, go to your Xcode -> **File Menu** -> **New** -> **File**, and search for **Property List**, as shown in the succeeding figure:

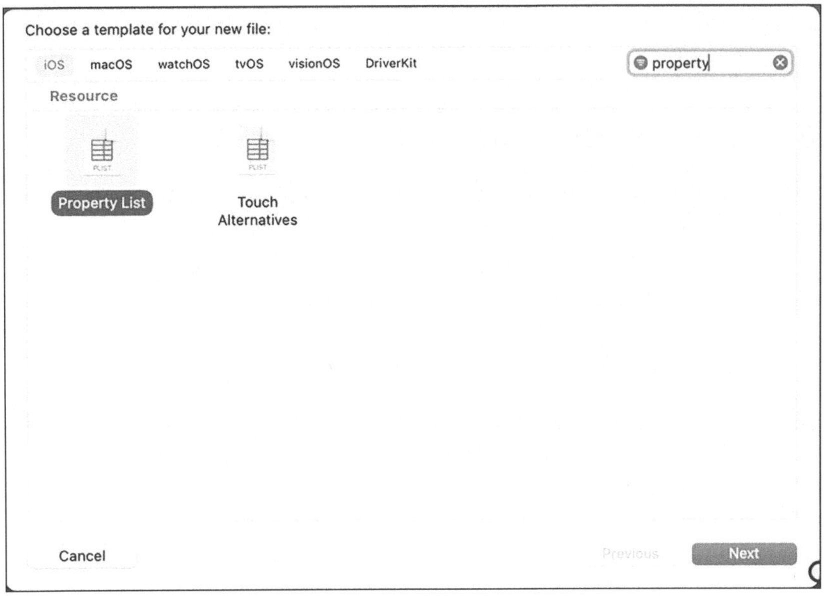

Figure 9.15: *Creating plist*

2. Click **`Next`** and name it **`Auth0`** (it is number zero, not the letter o) and click **`'Create'`**.
3. In Project Navigator, find your `Auth0.plist`, right-click **`'Open As'`**, and click **`'Source code'`**. Place the following code inside your `plist` tags.

```
<dict>
        <key>ClientId</key>
        <string>Your Client Id</string>
        <key>Domain</key>
        <string>Your Domain</string>
</dict>
```

Your `plist` should look like the following figure:

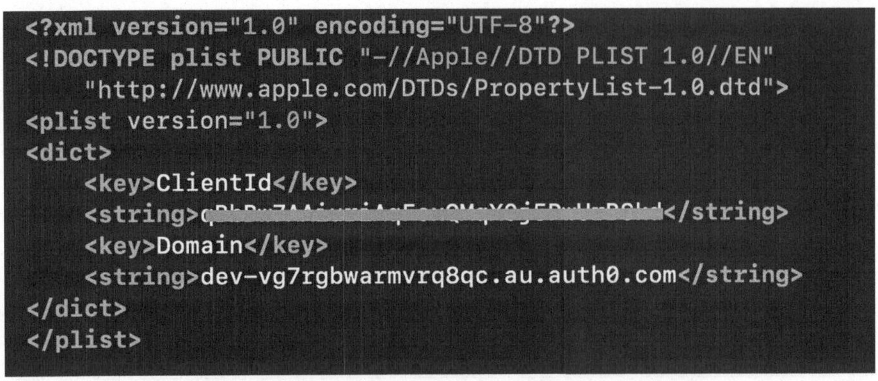

```
<?xml version="1.0" encoding="UTF-8"?>
<!DOCTYPE plist PUBLIC "-//Apple//DTD PLIST 1.0//EN"
    "http://www.apple.com/DTDs/PropertyList-1.0.dtd">
<plist version="1.0">
<dict>
    <key>ClientId</key>
    <string>[illegible]</string>
    <key>Domain</key>
    <string>dev-vg7rgbwarmvrq8qc.au.auth0.com</string>
</dict>
</plist>
```

Figure 9.16: *Adding ClientID and Domain in plist*

Please make sure you paste your Client ID and Domain from your settings of the Auth0 website in your `plist`.

Adding Associated Domains

The next step is to add your **`'Associate Domains'`** capability. There are two mandatory requirements to do this. Number 1 requirement is that you need to have Xcode 15.3, as mentioned by Auth0, for this capability. The second requirement to add this capability is that you need to have a provisioning profile, and before creating the provisioning profile, you need to create the App Identifier with Associated Domains capability in your Apple developer account. So, let us jump into the Apple Developer account.

1. Sign in to your Apple Developer account; you should see something like *Figure 9.17*.

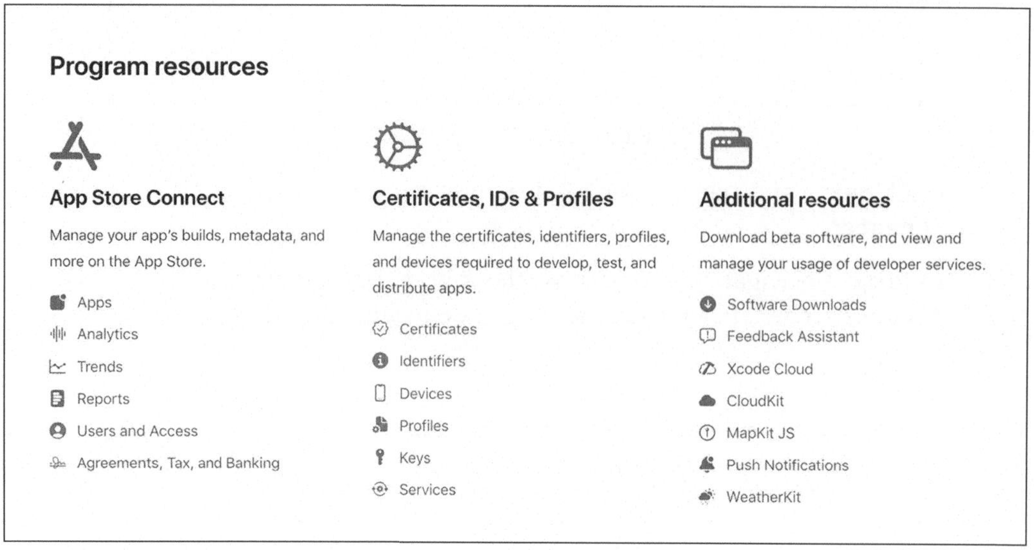

Figure 9.17: *Program resources*

2. Click **`'Identifiers'`**, and in the Identifiers page, click the **`'+'`** button, as shown in *Figure 9.18*.

Figure 9.18: *Certificates, Identifiers, and profiles in developer profile*

3. Click **`'App IDs'`** and click **`'Continue'`**. Select **`'App'`** when you must select the type and click **`'Continue'`**.

4. Specify the **`'Bundle ID'`** of your app in the Bundle ID section. To get the Bundle ID, go to your Xcode project. In the Project Navigator, select your project and click the Target, as shown in *Figure* 9.19.

Figure 9.19: *Project's signing & capabilities*

5. There you can find the Bundle Identifier; paste this in the Bundle ID section in the Apple developer account, as shown in the following figure:

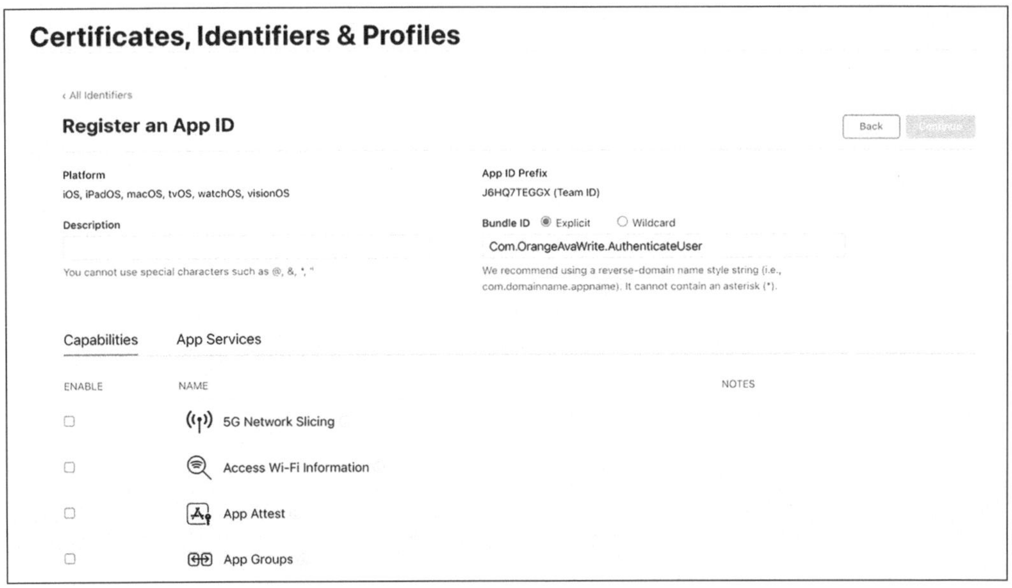

Figure 9.20: *Registering App ID in Developer account*

6. Then you can add the description in the Description field of what our app does; in this case, it could be **`'Authenticates the user.'`**

7. Next, as you can see capabilities in *Figure* 9.20, go to that capabilities section in the Apple developer account and select **`'Associate Domains'`** as follows:

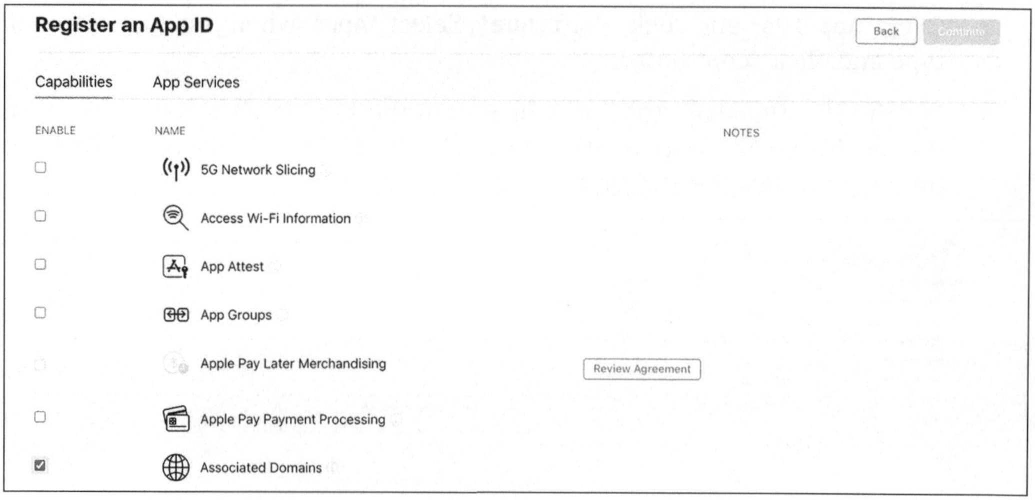

Figure 9.21: *Selecting Associated Domains while creating App ID*

8. Then click **'Continue'**; it takes you to the confirmation page, check all the details for confirmation, and then click **'Register'**. Then it takes you back to the Identifiers page, where you will see your App ID.

Now. It is time to create the provisioning profile.

1. Click **'Profiles'** in the menu on the left, as shown in *Figure* 9.22.

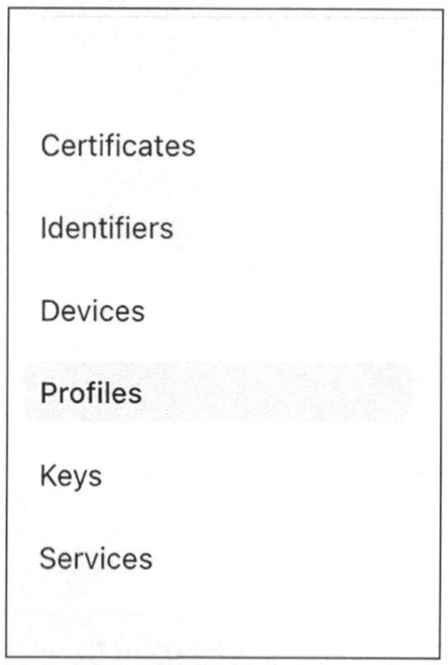

Figure 9.22: *Selecting profiles*

2. Click the **'+'** beside the Profiles heading; you will head to the **'Register a New Provisioning Profile'** page, click **'iOS App Development'**, and click **'Continue'**. In the next page, it will ask you for the App ID. Select the App ID we just created, as shown in *Figure* 9.23.

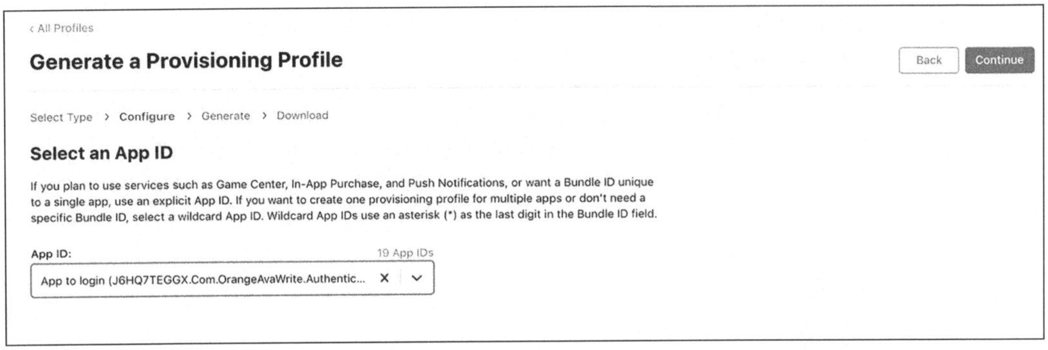

Figure 9.23: *Generating provision profile*

3. In the **'Select Certificates'**, select your developer certificate; if you do not have one, go to **'Certificates'** and create one.
4. Once you have selected your Certificate, click **Continue**. In the next section, it asks you to select the **'Devices'** you want your app to be run on. If you want to run your app on your iPhone, this is where you select your iPhone. Your devices will be listed as per the Apple ID you use.
5. Now, click **'Continue'**. In the next section, it asks you for the **'Provisioning Profile Name'**, give it a name, and click **'Generate'**.
6. Now come back to your Xcode, click your project's target, and click **'Signing & Capabilities'**. Now you can find **'Team'**. Select the drop-down and choose the Team (if you are using your Apple developer account, it will show your name). If you are not signed in into your Xcode, click **'Add an Account'** and add your account details, and choose your account for **'Team'**.

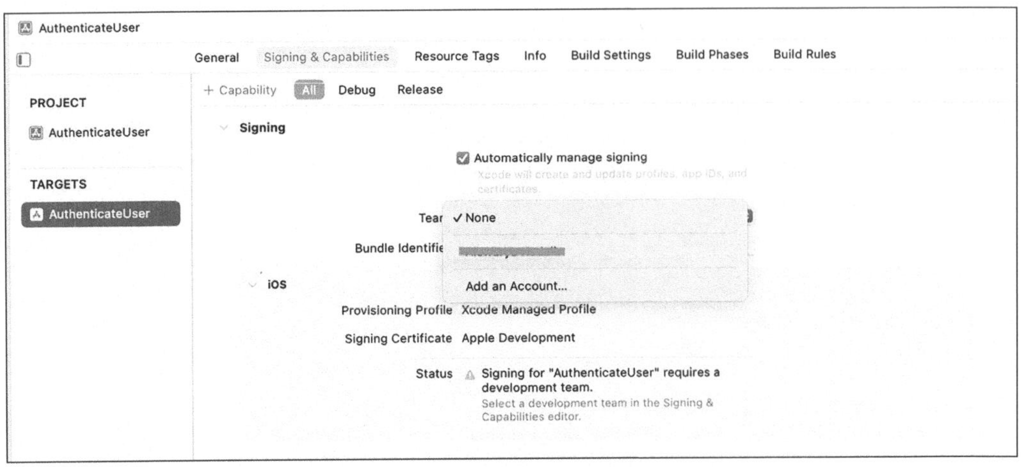

Figure 9.24: *Selecting team for your project*

7. Make sure **'Automatically manage signing'** is selected, as it will automatically

select the Provisioning profile associated with your app; otherwise, you will have to specify manually.

8. Now in the same **'Signing & Capabilities'**, we need to add the Capability. To add the Capability, click the **'+'** button, as shown in *Figure 9.25*.

Figure 9.25: *Adding Signing & Capabilities*

9. Search for **'Associated Domains'** and drag it to your '**Signing & Capabilities'**. After adding, click **'+'** underneath it and add **'webcredentials:your domain'**. Here, your domain means the domain given by Auth0. You can check the Auth0.plist and get the domain from there, or you can get it from the Auth0 portal by going to your Application and then its settings page. The Associated Domain capability should look like *Figure 9.26*.

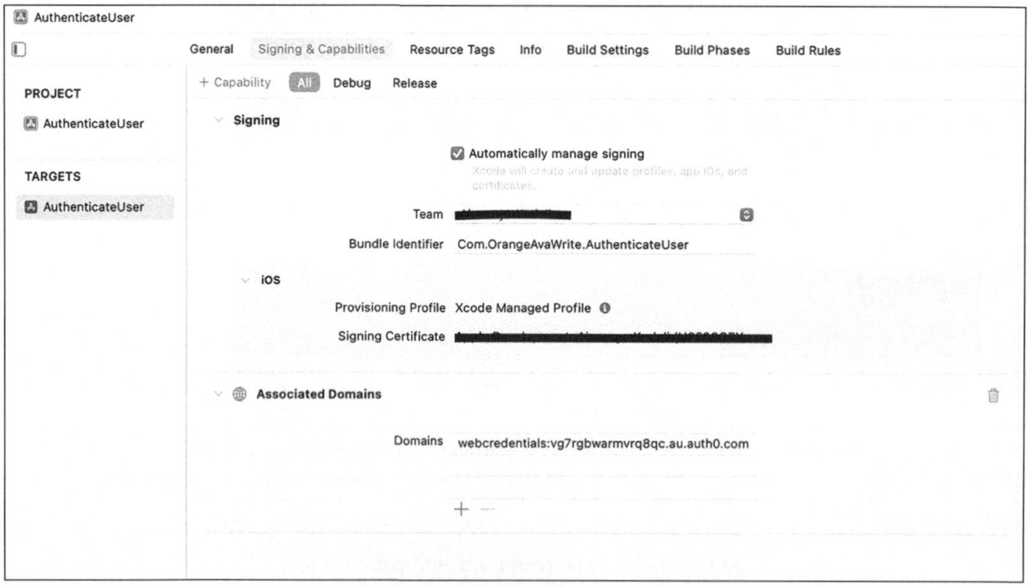

Figure 9.26: *Adding Associated Domains*

10. Now the final step of the setup, we need to add the callback URLs so that our app can call the Auth0 URLs while logging in and logging out. For that, let us prepare the callback URL first. Replace `YOUR-DOMAIN` and `YOUR-BUNDLE-ID` with your Auth0 Domain and the bundle ID of your app from Xcode.

    ```
    https://YOUR-DOMAIN/ios/YOUR-BUNDLE-ID/callback, YOUR-BUNDLE-ID://YOUR-DOMAIN/ios/YOUR-BUNDLE-ID/callback
    ```

11. Now go to your Auth0 portal and select your Application in Applications. Then go to the **'Settings'** page and scroll down. You will find Application URIs as follows:

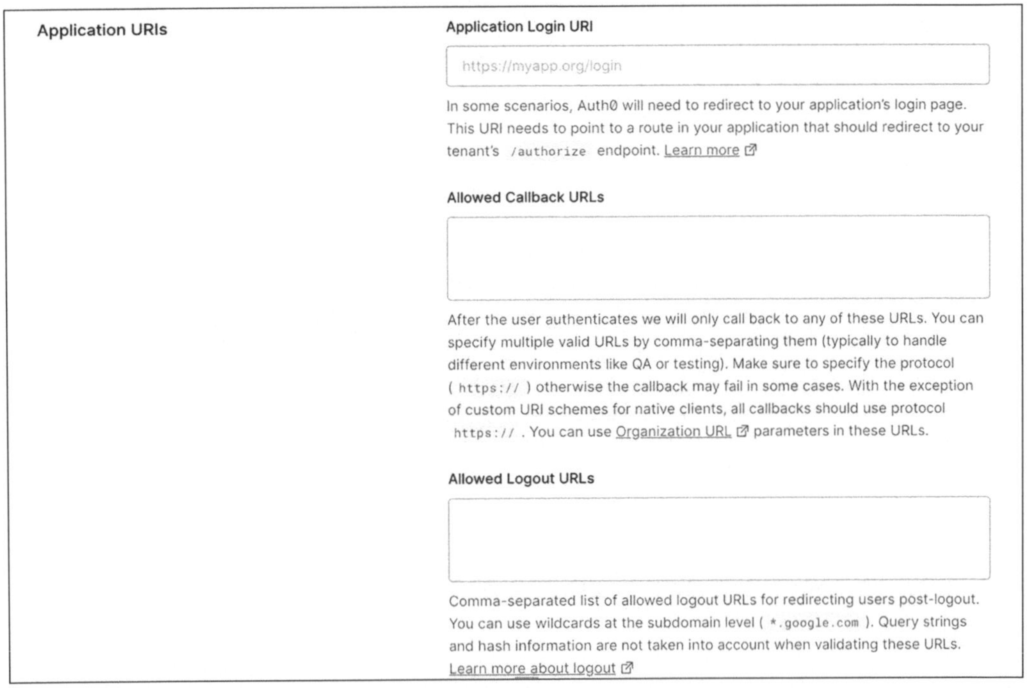

Figure 9.27: *Adding Application URIs*

12. Place the URL we have created in the **'Allowed Callback URLs'** and **'Allowed Logout URLs'** sections and click **'Save Changes'**.

We can also configure a custom domain in Auth0. For callback URLs, we just replace the custom domain instead of the domain that we got from Auth0.

Since we did all the setup, let us go back to Xcode and do some coding. Go to your **Main.storyboard**, add the code reference for your label; let us say **'statusLabel'** as this is updated as Login and Logout status. And can also give the code reference of the actions @IBAction to the buttons as **'loginTapped'** and **'logoutTapped'**.

Open up your `ViewController.swift` file and import **'Auth0'** and **'JWTDecode'**.

In your `viewDidLoad()`, hide the `statusLabel` by using **`'statusLabel.isHidden = true'`**`-code`, as we do not need to see statusLabel after launching the screen.

In `loginTapped @IBAction`, place the following code:

```
Auth0
            .webAuth()
            .useHTTPS()
            .start { result in
                switch result {
                case .success(let credentials):
                    print("Obtained credentials: \(credentials)")

                    self.statusLabel.isHidden = false
                    self.statusLabel.text = "Logged in"

                    //Access the user info
                    print("The jwt", credentials.idToken)
                    guard let jwt = try? decode(jwt: credentials.idToken),
                          let name = jwt["name"].string
                    else { return }
                    print("Name: \(name)")

                case .failure(let error):
         self.statusLabel.isHidden = false
         self.statusLabel.text = "Failed with error"
                    print("Failed with: \(error)")
                }
            }
```

Your **`'loginTapped()'`** should look like *Figure* 9.28.

```
@IBAction func loginTapped(_ sender: Any)  {
    Auth0
        .webAuth()
        .useHTTPS()
        .start { result in
            switch result {
            case .success(let credentials):
                print("Obtained credentials: \(credentials)")

                self.statusLabel.isHidden = false
                self.statusLabel.text = "Logged in"

                //Access the user info
                print("The jwt", credentials.idToken)
                guard let jwt = try? decode(jwt: credentials.idToken),
                      let name = jwt["name"].string
                else { return }
                print("Name: \(name)")

            case .failure(let error):
                print("Failed with: \(error)")
            }
        }
}
```

Figure 9.28: *loginTapped @IBAction*

What we are doing here is communicating with Auth0 after pressing the Login. This starts web authentication, which uses the callback URLs we have specified in Auth0 settings, and after providing the credentials and logging in. From the credentials obtained, we get a JWT token from **'idToken'**.

JWT

If you are a developer already, you might know what JWT is. It is a JSON Web Token, which allows us to securely transmit the data between different parties in the form of a JSON object. The data we are transmitting is digitally signed using a public/private key pair, which is an awesome way to verify the data.

We can actually check what JWT is; by pasting this token in JWT.io, it decodes it for you. Later on, while we are running the app, we check on `idToken` by pasting it in JWT.io.

We are updating the status label as **'Logged in'** on successful login. Now coming to **'logoutTapped'** `IBAction`, place the following code in **'logoutTapped()'**:

```
Auth0
    .webAuth()
    .clearSession(federated: true) { result in
        switch result {
        case .success:
```

```
            self.statusLabel.isHidden = false
            self.statusLabel.text = "Logged out"
            print("Logged out")
        case .failure(let error):
            print("Failed with: \(error)")
        }
    }
```

All we are doing here is clearing up sessions in Auth0.

So before going ahead and running the app, we need to actually have users in the database; in order to login, we need to have registered users. No, we are not creating registration screens and registering users; instead, we are going to take the shortcut. The shortcut is to add the Users in the Auth0 database directly.

1. For that, all we have to do is go to your Auth0 portal and click **'User Management'** from the menu; for reference, check *Figure* 9.29.

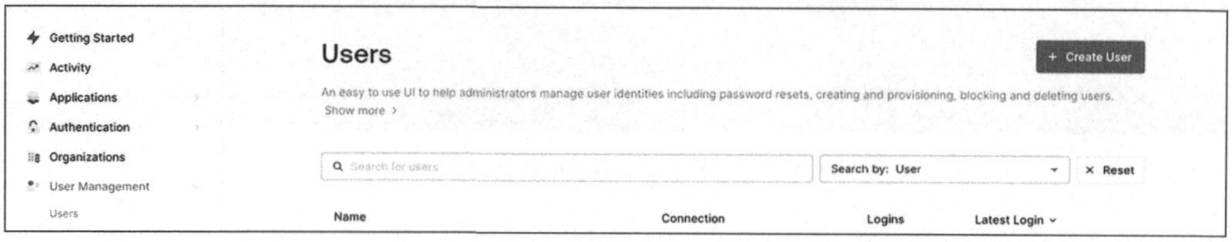

Figure 9.29: *Creating users in Auth0 portal*

2. Click the **'Create User'**, as shown in *Figure* 9.30.

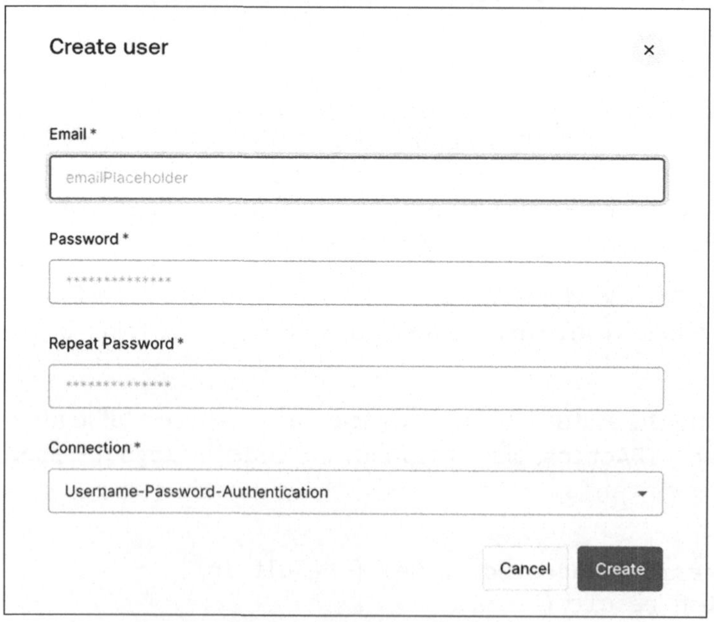

Figure 9.30: *Creating user in Auth0 portal*

3. Enter your email address or any other email address you can use, enter the password, and repeat the password. Make sure the **`'Connection'`** is **`'Username-Password-Authentication'`**. Click **`'Create'`**. You should see your User appearing in the list, as follows:

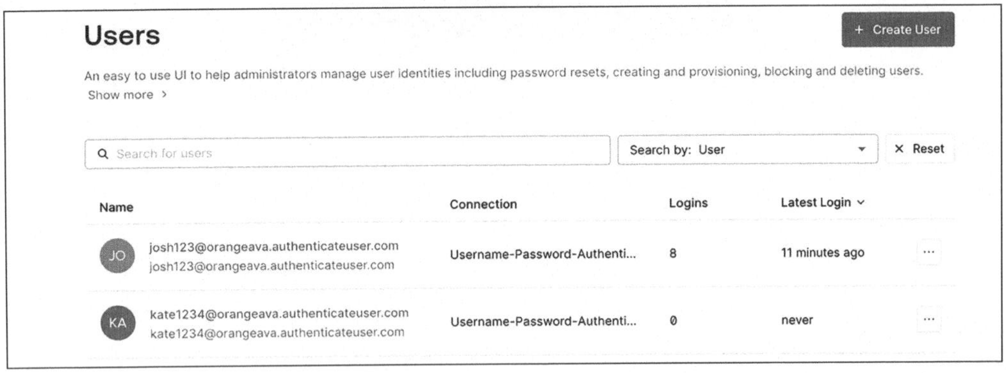

Figure 9.31: *Created users in Auth0 portal*

4. You can create as many users as you wish. After you are done with User creation, it is time to go ahead and run our app.

   Go ahead and run it.
   You should see your screen something like *Figure* 9.32.

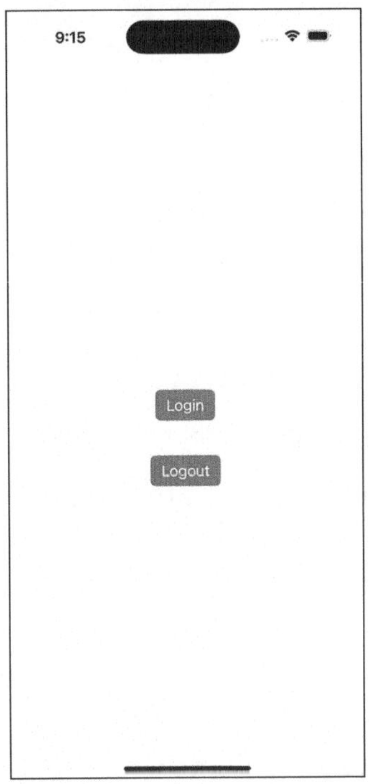

Figure 9.32: *Simulator screen with buttons*

5. Now click the **'Login'** button. It gives you an alert that your app wants to use Auth0 to sign in; click **'Continue'**. It should open up the Auth0 webpage for login as shown in *Figure* 9.33.

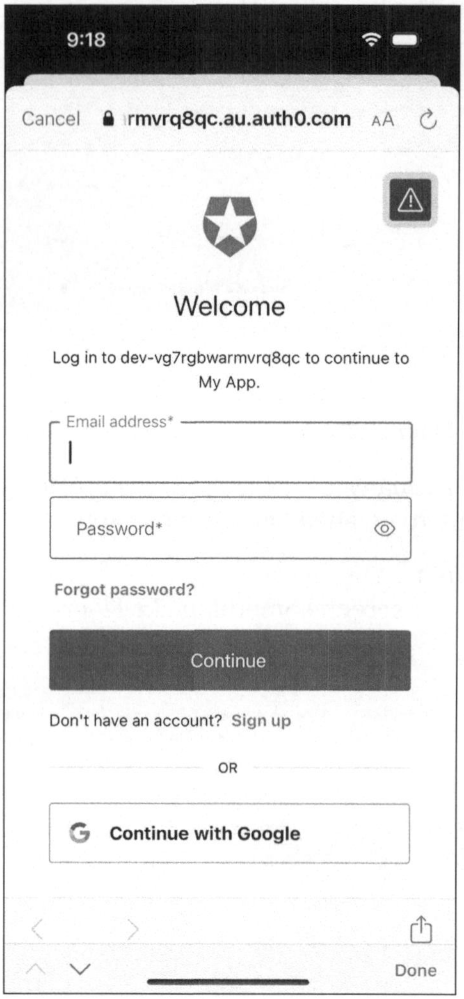

Figure 9.33: *Auth0 page*

6. Enter the user email and password that were given when you had created the User in the Auth0 portal and click **'Continue'**. You should have our status label updated to **'Logged In'**, as shown in *Figure* 9.34.

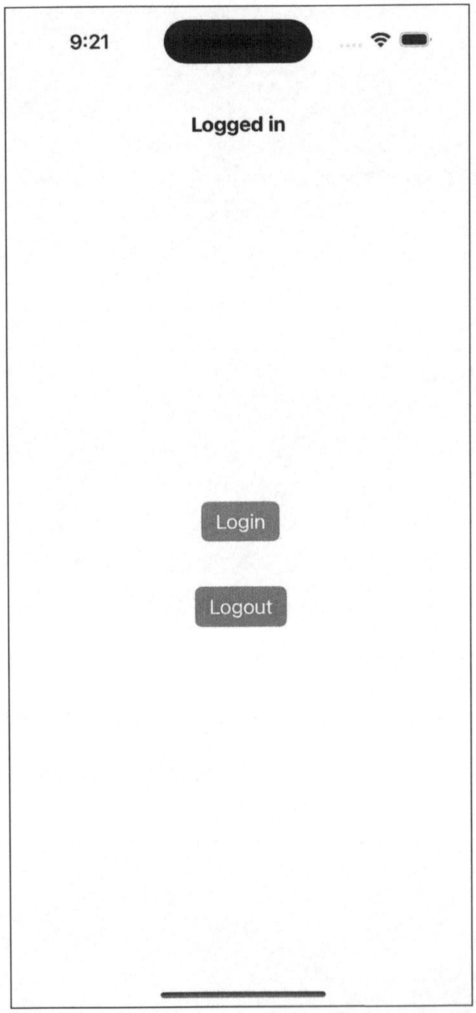

Figure 9.34: *Logged in status updated in simulator screen*

7. Now go ahead and click **`'Logout'`**. You can see that our status label is updated accordingly.

Before wrapping up, let us decode the JWT token from the credentials after logging in to the https://jwt.io/ website.

1. For that, all you need to do is have a debug point in the following line, as shown in the following image in your @IBAction `loginTapped`.

```
@IBAction func loginTapped(_ sender: Any)  {
    Auth0
        .webAuth()
        .useHTTPS()
        .start { result in
            switch result {
            case .success(let credentials):
                print("Obtained credentials: \(credentials)")

                self.statusLabel.isHidden = false
                self.statusLabel.text = "Logged in"

                //Access the user info
                print("The jwt", credentials.idToken)
                guard let jwt = try? decode(jwt: credentials.idToken),
                      let name = jwt["name"].string
                else { return }
                print("Name: \(name)")

            case .failure(let error):
                self.statusLabel.isHidden = false
                self.statusLabel.text = "Failed with error"
                print("Failed with: \(error)")
            }
        }
}
```

Figure 9.35: *Getting user credentials in loginTapped @IBAction*

2. Now run the app, enter your credentials in the webpage, and click **'Continue'**.
3. On successful login, you should see the debug pointer reached the line we had our debug pointer, as shown in *Figure* 9.36.

```
                self.statusLabel.text = "Logged in"

                //Access the user info
                print("The jwt", credentials.idToken)                Thread 1: breakpoint 1.1 (1)
                guard let jwt = try? decode(jwt: credentials.idToken),
                      let name = jwt["name"].string
                else { return }
                print("Name: \(name)")

            case .failure(let error):
                self.statusLabel.isHidden = false
                self.statusLabel.text = "Failed with error"
AuthenticateUser 〉 Thread 1 〉 0 closure #1 in ViewController.loginTapped(_:)      Line: 39  Col: 50
```

Figure 9.36: *Printing* JWT

4. Click **'step over'**, which is highlighted in the preceding image, and then you should see the JWT printed in the console, as follows:

```
The jwt
eyJhbGciOiJSUzI1NiIsInR5cCI6IkpXVCIsImtpZCI6IlRYNUdRZGhTR2VkX2lmanV3OUtQTiJ9
.eyJuaWNrbmFtZSI6Impvc2gxMjMiLCJuYW1lIjoiam9zaDEyM0BvcmFuZ2VhdmEuYXV0aGVudGljYXR
ldXNlci5jb20iLCJwaWN0dXJlIjoiaHR0cHM6Ly9zLmdyYXZhdGFyLmNvbS9hdmF0YXIvMmZkY2U5OWY
5MTkxM2Y0ZTYxZjFmMTU4MGJjOTUyNjg_cz00ODAmcj1wZyZkPWh0dHBzJTNBJTJGJTJGY2RuLmF1dGg
wLmNvbSUyRmF2YXRhcnMlMkZqby5wbmciLCJ1cGRhdGVkX2F0IjoiMjAyNC0wNC0yMVQyMzozMTo0NS4
1MDBaIiwiZW1haWwiOiJqb3NoMTIzQG9yYW5nZWF2YS5hdXRoZW50aWNhdGV1c2VyLmNvbSIsImVtYWl
sX3ZlcmlmaWVkIjpmYWxzZSwiaXNzIjoiaHR0cHM6Ly9kZXYtdmc3cmdid2FybXZycThxYy5hdS5hdXR
oMC5jb20vIiwiYXVkIjoicUJiQnc3QUFpdXJpQXFGY3hRTXFYMGo1UHdVckJTa2QiLCJpYXQiOjE3MTM
3NDIzMDUsImV4cCI6MTcxMzc3ODMwNSwic3ViIjoiYXV0aDB8NjYxZjU5Mjk2ODU0OTRmZmM2YjhkODV
mIiwic2lkIjoiUjZaTGVTYUQ2Nkh2aG9tdGU1WHUtVzNaYThGaG9BTzIifQ
.HvJ-DEJtlgOxe-ggE-qYAJYDQYkGkTqT-pmY2URUA0OtOGWaVUWtWnexW6SGewnCFimcoQn12OWhcVe
UO0olTLMspTDf8hG7HBmNJza6xB0qW-N2IwT0OkkLtMbKSvF1dxEMW-xNcpne0VPozlehR_1X4iDAPiT
M6J2FPzcWSzh6YcRxqpMGUiJB-2EG6FwUkNX_MqMe15vL57cqbu1mnPBMUkUR6drB2VM51RsvXN2nxvU
```


Figure 9.37: *Printed JWT in console*

5. Copy that JWT token and open the https://jwt.io/. If you scroll down, you will see something like *Figure 9.38*.

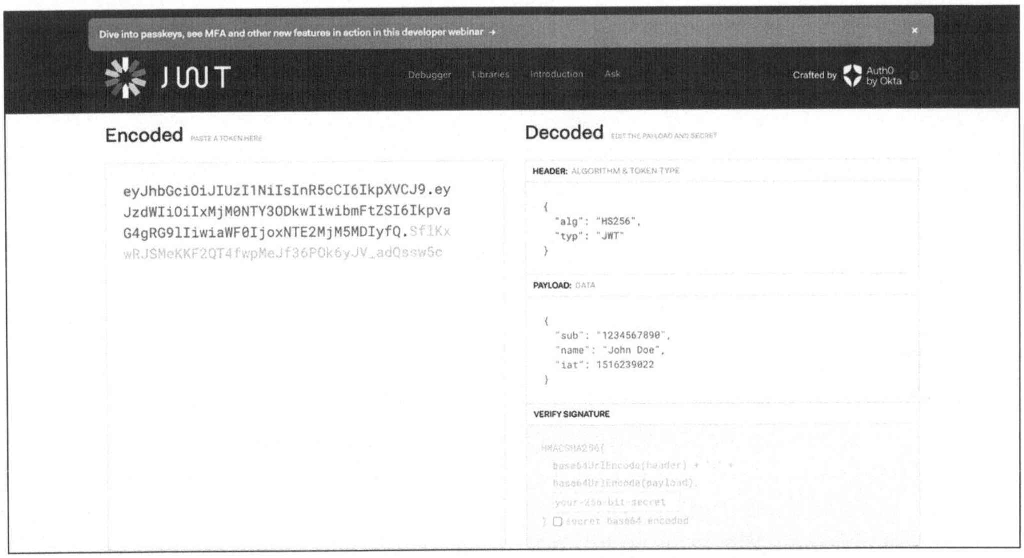

Figure 9.38: *JWT.io website*

6. Replace the token in the **Encoded** section with your token that you copied from Xcode. After pasting your token, you should see all your user data.

Figure 9.39: *Decoding the JWT*

Can you imagine how much data we are sending JWT, isn't it amazing.

Conclusion

Authentication, any developer or company who is developing an app or web should put their user secure authentication as a top red priority. Some digital companies got special teams just to work on user authentication, so now you know how important it is to use standardized frameworks in order to avoid the major malfunctions in user management. Use all the knowledge acquired in all the chapters and try building awesome apps. Maybe you will build the next Facebook; who knows, keep coding and create a stunning world.

Points to Remember

- OAuth 2.0 is a framework that provides the protocols to provide authorization and provides the access to the end user.
- Auth0 is a company that provides OAuth 2.0 authorization; it can be thought of as a wrapper around OAuth2.0. Using Auth0, we do not have to write the code for user management; everything is done via auth0.

- `plist` are known as property list files, mainly used for setting the configurations.
- JWT is JSON Web Token, which allows us to securely transmit the data between different parties in the form of a JSON object. The data we are transmitting is digitally signed using a public/private key pair, which is an awesome way to verify the data.

Index

A

Action Segues 132
Action Segues, aspects
  custom 132
  popover 132
  present modally 132
  show 132
  update, details 132
App Development 35
App Development, concepts
  designing 35
  development 36
  Idea 35
  release 36
  test 36
app slicing 22
app slicing, cases 22-25
app slicing code, adding 26, 27
Associate Domains 318
Associate Domains, provisioning 320-323
Associate Domains, steps 318-320
Auth0 311
Auth0, setup 315, 316
Auth0, steps 313, 314
Auth0, uses 311
Auth0, workflow 312, 313
Auto Layout 10
AWS 280
AWS, aspects
  AWS S3 281
  Swift Package Manager (SPM) 281-285
AWS, layer
  clipsToBounds 303-305
  masksToBounds 287-293
  putObject 298
  putObjectInput 298-300

C

CGRect 53-55
CGRect, key points
  Footer 56
  Section 57-59
CLGeocoder 233
Closures 198
Closures Return, types
  Implicit Returns 199
  Shorthand Arguments 200
Closures, types
  Escaping 200
  Non-Escaping 201
  Trailing 200
  URL 201
Codables 204
Codables, types
  Decodable 205-208
  Encodable 204
Constraints 10

D

Data Modeling 267, 268
Decodable, types
  JSONDecoder 209-211
  JSONEncoder 212, 213
Dictionary 61-64
DispatchQueue 166-169

DispatchQueue, fundamentals
beginUpdates() 169
endUpdates() 170-174
DispatchQueue, steps 177-182

E

else 263
else if 262, 263

G

Guard Let 187-190
Guard Let, features 192
Guard Let, steps 192-195

I

idToken 325
IF Let Function 186
ImageView,
optimizing 20, 21
IndexPath 46
IndexPath, aspects
array 49-52
CGRect 53
Deprecation 47-49

J

JWT 325
JWT, steps 326-332

N

NavigationController 121
NavigationController,
steps 125, 126
NavigationController,
ways 122

O

OAuth 2.0 311
Opaque Pointers 270, 271
Opaque Pointers, fundamentals
sqlite3_bind_int 273-277
sqlite3_bind_text 273
sqlite3_finalize 272
sqlite3_prepare_v2 272
sqlite3_step 272

P

plist 316-318

R

RootViewController 123
RootViewController,
steps 123, 124

S

SQLite 268-270
Structs 164, 165
Structs, requirements 165, 166

T

TableViews 37
TODO Development, process
designing 147, 148
developing 148-157
idea 147

U

UIAlertAction 64, 65
UIAlertController 60, 61
UIBarButtonItem 182
UIBarButtonItem, steps 183, 184
UIButton 6, 75
UIButton, implementing 76
UIButton, performance 76-79
UIDatePicker 184-186
UIImageView 13, 14
UIImageView Constraints,
adding 15-20
UIImageView, ways 14, 15
UIKit 6
UILabel 6
UINavigationBar 132-134
UINavigationBar,
configuring 134-136
UINavigationBar,
performance 137-144
UINavigationController,
case 127-130
UINavigationController,
steps 131
UIPageControl 67, 106, 107

UIPageControl,
implementing 110-112
UIPageControl,
ways 107-109
UIPickerView 112
UIPickerView,
implementing 114-119
UIPickerViews 67
UIPickerView, steps 113, 114
UIScrollView 67
UIScrollView Constraints,
optimizing 69-75
UIScrollView,
implementing 68
UIScrollView, parts 69
UIScrollViews 67
UIStackView 94
UIStackView,
implementing 96-105
UIStackViews 67
UIStackView, steps 94
UITableView 37
UITableView, aspects
delegate 43
function 43
protocol 43
UITableViewCell 46, 306
UITableViewDataSource 43
UITableViewDelegate 43-45
UITableView, ways 38-42
UITapGestureRecognizer 255
UITapGestureRecognizer,
steps 256, 257
UITextField 80
UITextField,
implementing 82-89
UITextFields 67
UITextField, steps 81, 82
UITextView 90
UITextViews 67
UITextView, steps 91-93
UIView 6
URL, resources
URLRequest 201
URLSessionDataTask 201
URLSessionDownloadTask 202-204
URLSessionUploadTask 202
URLSession 198
URLSession.shared 198

V

ViewController 6-9
ViewController, aspects
area, visualizing 11-13
Auto Layout 10
Constraints 10
Hierarchy View 10
ViewController, ways 8
ViewDidLoad 28
viewWillAppear(_:) 257-260

W

Weather App 215
Weather App, aspects
core location 216-218
Extensions 219-222
WeatherKit 223
WeatherKit, key points
CLGeocoder 233-237
ObservableObject 228
@Published 228, 229
Task.detached 230-232
WeatherKit, process 240-247
WeatherKit, steps 223-228

X

Xcode 2
Xcode, debugging 29-32
Xcode Screens, building 5
Xcode, steps 2-4
XIB 307
XIB, steps 307-310